ARCHITECTURAL
MATERIALS
FOR
CONSTRUCTION

Architectural Materials for

CONSTRUCTION

HAROLD J. ROSEN, P.E., FCSI
TOM HEINEMAN, FCSI

Illustrations Drawn by
PETER M. ROSEN, RA

McGraw-Hill

New York   San Francisco   Washington, D.C.   Auckland   Bogotá
Caracas   Lisbon   London   Madrid   Mexico City   Milan
Montreal   New Delhi   San Juan   Singapore
Sydney   Tokyo   Toronto

Library of Congress Cataloging-in-Publication Data

Rosen, Harold J.
    Architectural materials for construction / Harold J. Rosen
and Tom Heineman.
        p.   cm.
    Includes bibliographical references and index.
    ISBN 0-07-053741-0 (hardcover)
    1. Building materials.   2. Architecture.   I. Title.
TA403.6.R66   1996
691—dc20   95-45663
                                                    CIP

Sections of this book appeared in Harold J. Rosen's *Construction Materials for Architecture* © 1985 by John Wiley and Sons, Inc.

McGraw-Hill

A Division of The McGraw·Hill Companies

1 2 3 4 5 6 7 8 9 0   KGP/KGP   9 0 0 9 8 7 6 5

ISBN 0-07-053741-0

The sponsoring editor for this book was Wendy K. Lochner, and the production supervisor was Pamela A. Pelton. It was set in Optima by North Market Street Graphics.

Printed and bound by Quebecor/Kingsport Press.

This book is printed on acid-free paper.

The detailed information, drawings, tables, and other data in this book have been accumulated over the years by the author from governmental sources, trade organizations, building materials manufacturers, and other professional specification writers. The author has made a reasonable attempt to ascertain the validity of the data presented herein, but does not warrant, and assumes no responsibility for the accuracy or the completeness of the text material, drawings, and other data. The user as in any other investigation must consult all sources of information and make a professional judgment based on all the relevant data.

McGraw-Hill books are available at special quantity discounts to use as premiums and sales promotions, or for use in corporate training programs. For more information, please write to the Director of Special Sales, McGraw-Hill, 11 West 19th Street, New York, NY 10011. Or contact your local bookstore.

CONTENTS

PREFACE

As the author of several books on specification writing, I have constantly reiterated the admonition that a knowledge of specification writing is not in and of itself sufficient for one to be a good specifier. The truly competent specifier requires a broad knowledge of construction materials. However, for the most part, this knowledge has not yet been acquired in our colleges and universities.

In addition, the specifier, architect, and selector of construction materials must be able to assess, evaluate, and utilize these materials in a design so that the product performs as intended with the least amount of deterioration, degradation, or failure.

Materials are manufactured that have a wide range of characteristics, and one must select a product having those criteria that will perform, given the economics and the longevity that are essential for the specific project. For products that are manufactured on the job site (i.e., concrete, masonry, roofing, waterproofing, etc.), the basic ingredients comprising the finished product and quality of work involved in the on-site operations must be mastered so that the finished product achieves a high degree of durability.

Paralleling the need for a comprehensive understanding of materials is the requirement for a rational method of evaluating and selecting products for a specific use in a project. The absence of such an investigative tool invites possible construction failure, since some pertinent performance characteristic may have been overlooked during the course of the usual review, unrelated to a programmed evaluation.

Chapter 1, Performance Considerations, sets forth such a rational method of evaluation and selection. This approach had its genesis in a course entitled, "A Systematic Approach to Building Material Evaluation and Selection," which I began directing at the University of Wisconsin, Extension, in 1975, under the supervision of Philip M. Bennett, Program Director. In addition to the systematic approach outlined in Chapter 1, several materials are subjected to the same analysis throughout this book so that the reader may understand the process more productively and will be encouraged to utilize the approach in the quest for better solutions.

The materials dealt with in this book, while encompassing the basic materials generally encountered in a project, are primarily those that are produced or assembled on the site, such as architectural concrete, masonry, ornamental metal, architectural woodwork, roofing, waterproofing, curtain walls, and so forth. They all require a knowledge of on-site manufacture to produce the desired end results. In addition, the book presents in detail the utilization of older materials for new, innovative uses, such as concrete for architectural purposes and building stone for thin exterior panels. Newer products and techniques such as single ply roofing, inverted roofing, sealants, curtain walls, modern day paints, and seamless flooring are likewise discussed along with the means to evaluate and assess their specific characteristics.

Having spent some 40 years as a specifier, commencing during World War II, and as the author of *Specifications Clinic for Progressive Architecture* for some 20 years, I have accumulated a wealth of information that should be transmitted to those involved in the business of material selection, evaluation, and specifying.

This undertaking has been lightened by the generous cooperation of a number of individuals. My son Peter, an architect who prepared the illustrations; Gordon Wildermuth, a partner in the firm of Skidmore Owings & Merrill, who permitted me to select photographs from work in which I was involved; Werner Wandelmaier, a partner in the firm of I.M. Pei & Partners, who permitted me to utilize photographs of some of that firm's work; and Maurice Lehv, who photographed a number of pictures from various publications, which appear throughout this book.

HAROLD J. ROSEN

Tamarac, Florida

I heartily agree with the purpose of this book as Harold Rosen has put it forth: the need for designers and preparers of contract documents to augment their detailing and writing skills. Deeper appreciation of materials, how they fit in the building fabric and how they age—gracefully or otherwise—adds much to the accomplished work.

And another cheer for Rosen's hint that it is good for the head of the design team to have an awareness of the technical limitations—and more important, the possibilities—that exist within our palette of materials.

Although there are many technical details buried among this book's topics, I hope that we have consistently touched on some of the basic, broad, unquantifiable properties of our materials. These fundamental properties can stub the toe of the designer who ignores them. They are also properties that can take wing in the designer's imagination.

From time to time we have tried to drop practical hints or overlooked facts that are not readily found in glossaries or systematic compendia of building product information. We hope to transmit a little judgment—and even some wisdom—along with the dry facts.

Many of this book's truths and none of its errors have come from colleagues who are known for their pursuit of good design and good building. Among these I particularly want to thank Everett G. Spurling, Jr., FAIA, FCSI, CCS of Bethesda, Maryland; James Owen Power, FASCE, FCSI, CCS structural engineer and Paul Reiner, AIA, CSI, CCS specifications consultant (both of Miami); and William Early, CSI, CCS, RCI of Illinois Roof Consulting Associates, McHenry, Illinois.

Tom Heineman

Miami, Florida

ARCHITECTURAL
MATERIALS
FOR
CONSTRUCTION

One Liberty Plaza, New York, NY: typical example of a window wall using steel windows and a painted steel facade. Skidmore, Owings & Merrill, Architects. *(Photographer, Bo Parker, New York, NY.)*

PERFORMANCE CONSIDERATIONS

The performance of building materials, products, components, and assemblies can be comprehended more fully if certain basic information regarding these characteristics is understood.

Building materials and their composites must serve an intended function over a certain life span of the structure. Some materials, such as concrete, masonry, stone, metals, and plaster, will usually last the lifetime of the building. Other materials, such as roofing (built-up bituminous and elastomeric sheets), sealants, and paints, have more limited life expectancies and will require replacement after some period of time. The useful life expectancy of materials is related to the environmental conditions for which they were first selected; their durability or service life is a function of that environment.

Predictions as to the behavior and performance of traditional building materials under given geographical and environmental conditions can be made quite accurately. However, since there has been less use experience with more recently developed building materials, primarily those which are the products of modern-day chemistry, metallurgy, and technology, the same long-term performance behavior lessons cannot be applied to them.

Indeed, even traditional materials fare differently when used and exposed in new climes such as the harsh environs of the Middle East. Witness also the unusual behavior of stone and copper, which survived centuries of use in Venice and Athens but are now succumbing to the effects of environmental industrial fumes and acid rain.

The performance, or service life, or durability of a material is a function not only of environment (weather, temperature, rain, humidity, ozone, bacterial attack, solar radiation, etc.) but also of physical interaction, both natural (wind loads, seismic forces) and human-made (pollution, physical abuse). The influence of environmental and physical interaction results in failure as a result of chemical degradation, excessive expansion and contraction, unusual wear, and a host of other types of failure.

PERFORMANCE CHARACTERISTICS

The performance level of both traditional and new materials may be assessed more accurately by evaluating certain characteristics when selecting products that must serve their intended function over a period of time, taking into consideration the natural environment and the human-made elements that must be endured.

The performance characteristics to be investigated on a rational basis include the following:

Structural serviceability
Fire safety
Habitability
Durability
Compatibility

Some test procedures may be empirical and others may subject the material to environmental conditions approximating the situation to which the material will be exposed, but testing alone will not necessarily predict the final outcome. Knowledge and analytical evaluation are additional ingredients to be used along with testing in predicting performance.

The evaluation process is enhanced by creating a comprehensive listing of subcategories of the five major performance categories to reduce the likelihood of overlooking certain important performance characteristics when making an evaluation.

STRUCTURAL SERVICEABILITY

The performance characteristic of structural serviceability includes resistance to natural forces such as wind and earthquake; structural adequacy; and physical properties such as strength—including compression, tension, shear, and behavior against impact and indentation.

A more expanded listing, although not necessarily complete, includes the following:

Natural Forces
Wind
Seismic

Strength
Compression
Tension
Shear
Torsion
Modulus of rupture
Indentation
Hardness

Architects generally rely on structural engineers to solve such problems as building live and dead loads, seismic forces, wind pressures, earth and water pressures, compression, tension, torque, and so forth. There are times when the architect must recognize that, in evaluating an architectural product or a component, appropriate structural performance characteristics must be reviewed to ascertain whether the proposed products and their installation details also will withstand certain of these forces.

Curtain walls are subjected to wind loads and the selection of glass sizes and thicknesses, and metal retaining members must be carefully analyzed to ensure structural integrity. When new glass products are introduced, consideration must be given to double glazing, triple glazing, combinations of clear and/or coated glass, and annealing and tempering processes to ensure that the configuration selected will withstand the wind loads.

Roofing materials are oftentimes subjected to wind uplift. Architects must review roofing systems and the working drawing details to verify the structural serviceability of the installation.

FIRE SAFETY

An investigation of fire safety includes the resistance of building materials against the effects of fire. A more comprehensive list of these performance characteristics would include the following:

Fire resistance
Flame spread
Smoke development
Toxicity

While fire safety should include design of structures to reduce and isolate fires, such as compartmentation, smoke shafts, areas of refuge, and so forth, this volume is concerned with an evaluation process of building products so that the required fire safety is evaluated and products selected to withstand and reduce the fire hazard.

Fire Resistance

Fire resistance is the capacity of a material or an assembly of materials to withstand fire or provide protection from it; this is characterized by the ability to confine fire, to continue to perform a structural function, or both.

While a steel beam or a steel column will not burn, its ability to perform a structural function is limited because the temperature rise in the steel to about 1000 to 1200°F will produce structural failure. By enveloping the steel in concrete, masonry, drywall, or spray-on fireproofing, its fire resistance is enhanced as a composite.

Fire endurance is a measure of the elapsed time during which a material or assembly provides fire resistance. ASTM E119 is a test method for determining fire endurance (elapsed time), which is a measure of fire resistance.

When evaluating materials or assemblies for fire endurance performance characteristics, there are several standard test methods as follows:

ASTM E119   Fire Tests of Building Construction and Materials
ASTM E152   Fire Tests of Door Assemblies
ASTM E163   Fire Tests of Window Assemblies
UL 263   Standard Fire Test

Flame Spread

Once a fire has developed, the rate and extent of flame spread are influenced by a number of factors that may vary from one fire situation to another. However, experience and evidence illustrate that the flame spread can be greatly influenced by the flammability of the surface materials or linings.

Since the rate of flame spread is a measure of how quickly fire will spread and develop, there are cogent reasons to select surface or lining materials that have a low flame spread index, or rating. Flame spread index is a numerical designation or classification applied to a building material or composite which is a comparative measure of its ability to resist the spread of flame over its surface. To evaluate the flame spread index, there are several ASTM test methods available, as follows:

ASTM E84   Surface Burning Characteristics of Building Materials
ASTM E162   Surface Flammability of Materials using a Radiant Heat Energy Source
ASTM E286   Surface Flammability of Building Materials using an 8 Foot Tunnel Furnace

ASTM makes this caveat regarding the test methods:

This standard should be used to measure and describe the properties of materials, products or systems in response to heat and flame under controlled laboratory conditions and should not be used for the description or appraisal of the fire hazard of materials, products, or systems under actual fire conditions.

However, numerous building codes have adopted these test procedures and will accept the flame spread index or classification of a material based on these test methods. Figure 1-1 illustrates the ASTM E84 Test Tunnel.

Smoke Development

The products of combustion include smoke, toxic gases, and vapors along with the flame. Smoke is particulate matter consisting of very fine solid particles and condensed vapor and constitutes most of the vis-

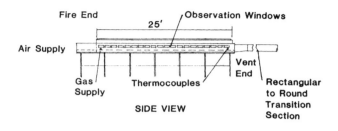

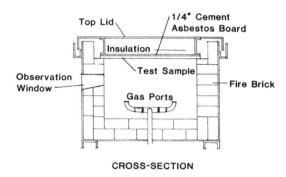

FIGURE 1-1 ASTM E84 Test Tunnel. *(Reprinted, with modifications, with permission from ASTM, 1916 Race Street, Phila., PA 19103.)*

ible part of the products of combustion. The main danger from smoke is reduced visibility, which may impede escape from a fire situation and prolong the exposure of occupants to toxic fumes.

The smoke development index or density is a numerical classification based on test method ASTM E84. Some codes may require that surface materials or linings for public exit corridors and stair halls use products with a Class A or low smoke density number.

Toxicity

Gas is one of the products of combustion. Toxic gases such as carbon monoxide, hydrogen cyanide, hydrogen chloride, and nitrogen dioxide are lethal. The Uniform Building Code and the BOCA Basic Building Code have toxicity requirements. These codes require that the products of combustion for interior finishes on walls and ceilings be no more toxic than those of untreated wood under similar conditions. However, a standard test method that can verify these requirements is lacking.

A test method in use in some areas to determine toxicity includes the heating of the test specimen in a furnace with the decomposition products wafted over to a chamber containing mice. The mice are then examined for lesions, weight loss, and other toxic reactions. The combustion products generated by a specific material under observation must be less toxic than those generated by wood, which is the referenced standard. A recent review entitled *A Critical Review of the State-of-the-Art of Combustion Toxicology,* dated June 1982 by the Southwest Research Institute, examines the various test methods and other studies concerning combustion produced toxic gases.

HABITABILITY

The performance characteristics of habitability include livability as characterized by thermal efficiency, acoustic properties, water permeability, hygiene, comfort, and safety. An expanded version would include the following:

Thermal Properties
Thermal expansion
Thermal transmittance and resistance
Thermal shock

Acoustic Properties
Sound transmission
Sound absorption
Noise reduction coefficient

Water Permeability
Water absorption
Permeability—water vapor transmission
Moisture expansion and drying shrinkage

Hygiene, Comfort, Safety
Toxicity
Vermin infestation
Slip resistance
Mildew resistance
Air infiltration

Thermal Properties

Thermal Expansion

Some buildings exhibit failures relating to thermal expansion and contraction soon after completion or after a significant time frame. These failures include cracking of glass and masonry, failure of sealant joints, heaving of pavement slabs, and so forth. In addition to being unsightly, cracks in exterior surfaces may permit water infiltration, which may result in more serious structural impairment as deterioration proceeds.

Most materials expand with rising temperatures and contract upon cooling. For inorganic solid materials such as masonry, metals, and concrete, the increase in length per unit length for one degree rise in temperature is known as the linear coefficient of thermal expansion. Values for these coefficients of expansion are known and are available in handbooks for design purposes. Organic materials such as sealants and built-up roofing are elastic and move with temperature changes but do not have a memory and do not necessarily revert to their original position or configuration after temperature cycling.

Thermal Transmittance and Resistance

Heat transfer through a material or an assembly of various materials occurs as a result of heat flow from the warmer side to the cooler side. Such heat transfer is proportional to the temperature difference between the two surfaces and further depends upon the specific material or materials and their thickness.

Heat resistance is a measure of the impedance to the flow of heat that a material or an assembly of materials offers.

The American Society of Heating, Refrigerating and Air Conditioning Engineers has defined a series of various coefficients of heat transfer, and ASTM likewise defines under its various standards certain heat transfer terms that are pertinent to their standards. Some of the terms that are frequently associated with building materials are rephrased here. To that extent they may not be as precise, but perhaps they are less obscure.

Thermal conductance—C or C-factor. The time rate at which heat flows through 1 square foot of a material of known thickness in 1 hour when the temperature difference between the surfaces is 1°F. Thermal conductance is expressed as Btu per (hour) (square foot) (°F).

Thermal conductivity—K or K-factor. The time rate at which heat flows through a homogeneous material, 1 inch thick, 1 square foot in area, in 1 hour when the temperature difference between the surfaces is 1°F. Thermal conductivity is expressed as Btu per (hour) (square foot) (°F per inch).

Thermal resistance—R or R-value. The reciprocal of a heat transfer coefficient (R = 1/C or 1/U). Thermal resistance is expressed in Btu per hour per square foot per °F.

Thermal transmittance—U or U-value. The time rate of heat flowing through 1 square foot of material, in 1 hour, when the temperature difference between the surfaces is 1°F. Sometimes called the "Overall Coefficient of Heat Transfer." Thermal transmittance is expressed as Btu per (hour) (square foot) (°F).

The most useful coefficient or factor in thermal design calculations is the R-factor, because resistances are additive whereas conductances and conductivities are not additive. R-values are particularly useful for estimating the effects of components of various materials of a system because they can be directly added.

The U-value of a component assembly can be determined by ASTM C236, Test for Thermal Conductance and Transmittance of Built-Up Sections by Means of the Guarded Hot Box. However, the rational method of estimating the U-value by calculation may be determined by adding the resistances R and dividing into 1, thus

$$U = \frac{1}{R_1 + R_2 + R_3 + \cdots}$$

Thermal Shock

The phenomenon of thermal shock is exhibited when a sudden stress is produced in a material as a result of a sudden temperature change. As an example, in some climates or geographical areas, materials (especially dark surfaces) may be exposed to high temperatures of the sun. A sudden rain storm may cause a marked decrease in temperature in a short time interval, producing a thermal shock in the material. Colored glass, brick, and ceramic glazes may exhibit thermal shock under these circumstances.

Acoustic Properties

Acoustics is the science of heard sound, including the propagation, transmission, and effects of sound. Sounds are an integral and necessary or unnecessary part of our daily lives. Those that are necessary (speech communication, music, etc.) are desirable and wanted. Those that are unnecessary (traffic, machinery, jet engines) or which audibly interfere with what we are trying to hear are unwanted sounds, which are generally referred to as noise regardless of their character.

Sound Transmission

Sound transmission is the passage of sound from one space to another as between rooms (through walls, floors, ceilings, doors, partitions, etc.) or from an exterior source to an inside space (through walls, windows, roofs, etc.).

To reduce sound transmission one must consider the sound-isolating properties of the intervening construction, whether it is a wall, partition, floor, or ceiling. This sound-isolating property is the ability of the intervening medium to dissipate significant amounts of sound energy. The sound-reducing capability of the intervening construction is determined by its sound transmission loss (TL), which is the reduction in the sound pressure level usually expressed in decibels.

A construction that transmits only a small amount of noise will have a high sound transmission loss. Conversely, a construction that is paper thin will transmit most of the noise generated and will have a negligible sound transmission loss.

A standard test method and laboratory procedure for the measurement of airborne sound transmission losses is ASTM E90. The transmission loss value measured by this test method results in a single number rating or value called the sound transmission class (STC). Table 1-1 lists some common construction STC values for walls and partitions.

TABLE 1-1
AIRBORNE STC VALUES FOR CERTAIN WALLS AND PARTITIONS

Partition or wall construction	STC value
3-in. concrete	47
12-in. brick	56
3-in. cinder block with ⅝-in. plaster, both sides	45
6-in. hollow concrete masonry unit	43
12-in. hollow concrete masonry unit	48
2 × 4 in. wood studs, 16-in. O.C., ½-in. gypsum board, both faces	32
Stud wall as above with 2-in. insulation	35
2 × 4 in. wood studs, 16-in. O.C. with ⅜-in. gypsum lath and ½-in. plaster, both faces	46
3⅝-in. metal studs, 24-in. O.C. with ⅝-in. gypsum board, both faces	41
3⅝-in. metal studs, 24-in. O.C. with double layer ⅝-in. gypsum board, both faces	47

Sound Absorption

Sound absorption is a measure of the property of a material or a construction to absorb sound energy. Sound-absorbing materials have the ability to absorb sound to one degree or another and reflect back a percentage of that sound. They serve as a medium to absorb appreciable amounts of sound energy.

Typical sound-absorbing materials are carpets, acoustical tile, and sound-absorbent products fabricated of porous materials such as fibrous or cellular plastic.

The sound-absorptive quality of a material or a construction (fibrous materials with cloth or perforated facings) is a function of the incident sound to the reflected sound expressed as a ratio varying from 0 (no absorption) to 1.0 (perfect absorption). Test Method ASTM C423, Sound Absorption and Sound Absorption Coefficients, describes a method of testing and reporting the average sound absorption characteristics of a room, an object such as a screen, and the absorption coefficient of a specimen of sound-absorptive material such as acoustical ceiling tile.

Noise Reduction Coefficient

For a sound-absorptive material and similarly for a hard surface (e.g., plaster, concrete block), a single number rating called the noise reduction coefficient (NRC) is reported. The NRC is the average of the sound absorption coefficients of a material tested at 250, 500, 1000, and 2000 Hz, rounded to the nearest multiple of 0.05. Generally, materials with an NRC of 0.50 provide 50 percent sound absorption and 50 percent sound reflection. As the percentage increases to 1.0, the material becomes more efficient as a sound absorber. As the NRC approaches 0, the material tested becomes a reflector of sound. Table 1-2 illustrates some typical materials and their NRC values.

Water Permeability

Some building materials and constructions are affected by water, which exists in three phases: solid—*ice;* liquid—*water;* gaseous—*water vapor.* Many buildings develop material failures as a result of water entering into their systems.

For example, when water enters exterior concrete, masonry, or similar construction and subsequently freezes to ice, cracking may occur because of the volume increase of water changing from the liquid to the solid state. When gaseous water vapor is trapped below built-up bituminous roofing, blistering of the membrane may result. When water vapor enters a building from the ground and subsequently condenses, condensation may manifest itself as peeling paint or rotting roof timbers. Figure 1-2 illustrates loss of adhesion from moisture.

The harmful effects of water on building materials cannot be emphasized enough. The number of harm-

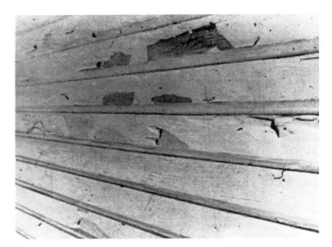

FIGURE 1-2 Loss of paint adhesion due to moisture vapor buildup within building.

ful effects is endless and includes corrosion, efflorescence, decay, blistering, and dimensional change. If the entrance of water can be controlled through proper detailing, a building can be made more durable, with considerable reduction in maintenance and repair.

Water Absorption

The absorption of water into a building material or system may result in a number of deleterious effects. The following examples should alert the designer and specifier when making materials selections, design decisions and field inspections.

1. *Dimensional changes.* An increase in moisture content may cause a corresponding dimensional or volume expansion. This phenomenon may occur in brick, mortar, and concrete subjected to rain. As the moisture content decreases, a corresponding reduction in dimension occurs. Thus, changes in moisture content may cause stresses resulting in shrinkage cracks or breaking away from adjacent materials.

2. *Chemical attack.* The absorption of water into a building material or system may induce a chemical reaction such as corrosion of metals; acid rain attack on metals, stone, and concrete; and sulfate reaction with concrete. This chemical reaction does not take place in the absence of water. Therefore, careful detailing or selective choice of materials will inhibit or negate this chemical attack.

TABLE 1-2
NRC COEFFICIENTS FOR CERTAIN BUILDING MATERIALS

Material	NRC
Brick	0.05
Carpet (no underlayment)	0.45
Carpet (40 oz underlayment)	0.55
Concrete masonry units painted	0.05
Resilient flooring on concrete	0.05
Glass	0.05
Plaster on lath	0.05
Plywood paneling	0.15
Acoustical tile	0.55 to 0.85, depending on type and mounting

3. *Efflorescence and leaching.* Liquid water entering into masonry, concrete, or mortar may dissolve certain soluble salts and cause leaching of these salts to the surface as the water migrates outward. This may result in efflorescence on the exterior face of the material or crystallization behind the surface, which may cause surface rupturing. See Figure 1-3 for effects of efflorescence.

4. *Blistering.* Occasionally when built-up roofing is installed there is a danger of entrapping water in the system as the work progresses. In that event, there is the possibility that the sun's heat will result in a blister formation within the built-up roof system.

5. *Freeze–thaw.* Temperature alone generally has no serious effect on materials. However, when there is absorption of water into a material the effect of freezing can be destructive, depending on the pore structure of the material. Witness the scaling of concrete from pavement slabs as a result of freeze–thaw in the absence of air entraining admixtures in concrete. See Figure 1-4 for effect of frost action on brickwork.

FIGURE 1-4　Effect of freeze–thaw reaction on brickwork. Note spalled rubble at base.

FIGURE 1-3　Efflorescence due to leaching of soluble salts from masonry.

Permeability–Water Vapor Transmission

Vapor diffusion (water in a gaseous state) is another example whereby water enters into a structure through assemblies and is responsible for deterioration of building materials and assemblies. The maximum amount of water that can exist in the gaseous state is dependent upon the temperature of the air. As the air temperature rises, its ability to hold more moisture increases. When air at a given temperature has absorbed all the vapor it can, the air is saturated or has 100 percent relative humidity (RH). If the air contains only half as much water vapor at the same temperature, it is said to have 50 percent RH.

The movement of water vapor is generally independent of air movement. Vapor actually moves by diffusion from areas of high vapor pressure to areas of lower pressures; air with more vapor has a higher vapor pressure.

Condensation is the process in which water vapor changes into a liquid. When warm air laden with moisture is cooled, or touches a cool surface, it reaches its "saturation" temperature and condenses and changes back to water. The temperature at which it occurs is called the *dew point.*

The control of moisture movement in the form of water vapor is essential. A certain amount is necessary for life and comfort. In some industrial buildings low relative humidities in the 15 to 25 percent range are required. In other situations relative humidities in the 40 percent range are required. The permissible relative humidity of a given area is the calculated RH which that construction can tolerate for a given outside temperature and relative humidity without developing condensation on any critical surfaces.

The selection of building materials to reduce the flow of vapor in order to control condensation is therefore critical. The vapor flow resistance of a material is the inverse of the ability of the material to permit vapor to flow, or its *permeance.* The unit of permeance is called the *perm,* which is defined as one grain of water passing through 1 square foot in 1 hour under the action of a vapor pressure differential of 1 inch of mercury, or $P = 1$ grain/h-ft^2 in. Hg.

Vapor barriers are materials or systems which retard the flow of vapor under specified conditions. In residential construction a vapor barrier having a perm rating not exceeding 1 is considered adequate. In cold storage buildings a perm rating of 0.01 is considered a high limit. The term *vapor barrier* therefore is not to be construed as a material which offers complete resistance to the flow of vapor. *Vapor stop* would be a more appropriate term in that context.

Table 1-3 illustrates the water vapor permeance of some building materials.

Moisture Expansion and Drying Shrinkage

Some building products that have the capacity to absorb water will expand upon the introduction of water and contract again on drying. Certain porous materials such as masonry, concrete block, concrete, and mortar will behave in this manner, as will wood and fibrous material such as carpets.

Moisture deformation is generally reversible for some materials, such as wood doors which swell with

TABLE 1-3
WATER VAPOR PERMEANCE OF BUILDING MATERIALS

Material	Perm
4-inch brick	0.8
¼-inch plywood	0.72
¾-inch plaster on metal lath	15.0
1 mil aluminum foil	0.0
Polyethylene, 4 mil	0.08
Polyethylene, 6 mil	0.06
Roofing felt, 15-pound asphalt, saturated	5.6
Two coats asphaltic paint on plywood	0.4
Two coats enamel on gypsum plaster	0.5–1.5

high humidity in summers and shrink again in winter. For other materials such as concrete, mortar, and plaster, the initial shrinkage that occurs during drying and curing may be irreversible.

To offset the effects of expansion and contraction due to moisture gain or loss, some building elements are assembled with a provision for movement. Failure may occur when clearances are insufficient, slotted connections freeze and do not allow movement, or the degree of movement is larger than sealant joints can tolerate.

The specifier and the designer must select materials that will make allowance for movement and detail the assembly to avoid deformation and cracking failure. In addition, the control of humidity and water during the construction period must be observed and certain operations performed under controlled conditions to avoid prolonged exposure of certain materials to high humidity.

Hygiene, Comfort, Safety

Occupants of buildings may be affected by the selection of products which may have an adverse reaction on them due to a variety of problems associated with health, safety, and/or comfort. With some products, one would have to be a clairvoyant to forecast the dangers inherent in a product on an individual many years later. For example, the problems associated with the use of asbestos were not recognized immediately, since it took 15 to 20 years for the diseases attributable to asbestos exposure to manifest themselves in individuals.

Toxicity

Aside from toxic fumes resulting from combustion, there are building products which may create toxic and noxious fumes as a result of degradation of the chemicals inherent in the product or the release of volatile solvents contained therein.

Recent studies seem to suggest that certain formaldehyde insulation formulations may be emitting gases that cannot be tolerated by some individuals.

Tar products have been known to produce skin irritations and rashes. Roofers tending tar kettles or applying built-up tar roofs have had minor skin cancers that have been traced to tars. Some paint materials using highly volatile solvents must be mixed and applied under controlled conditions, with the applicators wearing respirator devices to safeguard themselves against exposure.

Vermin Infestation

Organic building products are subject to attack by the lower forms of plant life, including fungi, bacteria, and algae. The building products affected are primarily wood and oils contained in some paint products.

The conditions under which the organisms responsible for this type of degradation grow and multiply best are warm temperatures, water, oxygen, and sometimes light. By introducing mildewcides, bactericides, and other types of inhibitors, manufacturers can reduce the occurrence and degree of vermin infestation in those materials subject to attack under the ideal prevailing conditions.

Slip Resistivity (Safety)

A safety factor related to the selection of flooring or paving is slip resistivity. In addition one must consider whether the areas within which the flooring materials will be used will be wetted by water spillage, wet cleaning, rain, or some other source of water.

A measure of the comparative slip resistivity of a flooring material under dry or wet conditions can be determined by using several test methods as follows:

ASTM F489   Test for Static Coefficient of Friction of Shoe Sole and Heel Materials as Measured by the James Machine

ASTM F609   Test for Static Slip Resistance of Footwear Sole, Heel, or Related Materials by Horizontal Pull Slipmeter (HPS)

Military Spec. MIL-D-3134J Deck Covering Material Par. 4.7.6 Non-Slip Properties

The ASTM test procedures noted above can be evaluated by ASTM F695, Standard Practice for Evaluation of Test Data Obtained by Using the HPS Machine or the James Machine. There is also ASTM D2047, which measures the static coefficient of friction on polish-coated floor surfaces, as measured by the James Machine. See further discussion of slip resistivity as it affects flooring in Chapter 9 under Performance Characteristics, Safety.

Mildew Resistance

Under the heading of Durability in this chapter, reference is made to the bactericidal attack of fungi on some building products, causing a degree of deterioration. Not only do fungi, bacteria, and algae effect the durability of building products, but their ability to feed on organic building products may have an effect on the health of the building occupants. It would therefore be prudent to investigate the materials to be selected and provide measures to inhibit growth and propagation of the fungal or bactericidal attack.

Air Infiltration

Comfort for the occupants of a building can be affected by air infiltration, which may produce whistling noises, admit dust, and cause condensation. The extent of air leakage depends upon the design of the building enclosure, the quality of the materials and work, and the action of air pressure differences across openings.

The amount of air infiltration through exterior windows, doors, and curtain walls can be determined by ASTM test method E283. The use of weatherstripping will reduce the amount of air leakage, including the infiltration of dirt and moist air.

DURABILITY

Durability includes the dimensional stability of a material as well as its ability to withstand the rigors of wear, weathering, and other disintegrative influences. An investigation of durability would include the following:

Resistance to Wear
Abrasion
Scratching
Scrubbing
Scuffing

Weathering
Freeze–thaw
Ozone
Fading
Chemical fumes

Bactericidal
Ultraviolet (UV) radiation

Adhesion of Coatings
Delamination
Blistering

Dimensional Stability
Shrinkage
Expansion
Volume change

Mechanical Properties
Resistance to splitting
Resistance to bursting
Resistance to tearing
Resistance to fatigue

The property *durability* assessed in its broadest concept, includes stability against human-made hazards (i.e., wear, abrasion, and chemical attack as in industrial plants) as well as the ability to endure the exterior environment (i.e., rain, frost, sunlight, and heat). This property is often difficult to assess, especially for new products, since short-term test results do not lend themselves to long-term extrapolations. Oftentimes the considered judgment of experts is required, based on knowledge and experience rather than on simple pass-fail tests. However, the user must be made aware of the concept of durability so that certain precautions are exercised in material selections considering the "hazard" to which the material will be exposed.

Resistance to Wear

Fitness for purpose should be the prime consideration. For example, acoustical and insulating products perform such functions based on their cellular, fibrous structure; as a result they are generally fragile. When these products are installed on ceilings as acoustical tile or within assemblies as insulation, their exposure to wear is practically eliminated. However, if they are installed where they are subject to human-made hazards their life span becomes considerably reduced.

Abrasion Resistance

The abrasion resistance of a material is its ability to resist being worn away or to maintain its original appearance when rubbed.

Flooring materials are prime examples of materials in place which are most affected by the hazard of abrasion. Selections of flooring materials will be governed by the type of occupancy. An executive office with negligible traffic can be covered with the most delicate of carpeting, whereas entrance corridors to public school buildings will require rugged, wear-resistant materials to withstand volume traffic of a harsh nature.

An early ASTM test for abrasion resistance of a flooring material was and still is C501, Relative Resistance to Wear of Unglazed Ceramic Tile by the Taber Abraser, designed to determine the abrasion resistance of ceramic tile. In the absence of other standard abrasion tests, ASTM C501 was used for materials other than ceramic tile, such as resilient tile and cementitious and resin matrix terrazzo.

At present there are a number of tests to measure the abrasion resistance of several building materials, as follows:

ASTM C779	Abrasion Resistance of Horizontal Concrete Surfaces
ASTM C944	Abrasion Resistance of Concrete or Mortar Surfaces
ASTM D2394	Simulated Service Testing of Wood Base Finish Flooring
ASTM F510	Resistance to Abrasion of Resilient Floor Coverings
ASTM C241	Abrasion Resistance of Stone Subjected to Foot Traffic

In addition to wear variation of floors one can also measure the wear resistance of paints and coatings by a standard test procedure ASTM D968, Abrasion Resistance of Coatings of Paint by the Falling Sand Method.

Scratching, Scrubbing, Scuffing

Materials that may be subjected to scratching should be investigated to determine whether the manufacturer offers suitable touch-up products that can cosmetically hide the scratches or whether other satisfactory procedures can be utilized to eliminate or minimize them.

Materials that will be subjected to scrubbing and/or scuffing require test data to indicate the expected number of scrubbings and/or scuffings before replacement is required. For example, certain scrub tests exist to ascertain the longevity of paints and textiles exposed to repeated scrubbings, and similar test methods exist for floor polishes exposed to markings, scratching, and scuffing.

Weathering

Materials exposed on the exterior of a structure will be subjected to the rigors of the particular environment where the structure is located. Temperature, rainfall, UV, ozone, chemical industrial fumes, and fungal attack will each have a deleterious effect on some materials. Some materials will withstand these elements better than others. Materials indigenous to a specific climate will exhibit minimum deterioration in that locale but will disintegrate over a period of time when used in other climes. Witness the use of brownstone for buildings in New York City. Quarried in the Midwest, the material eroded after years of exposure in the New York environment. The marbles and granites used on the Acropolis in Athens weathered successfully for thousands of years until the exhaust fumes of modern-day industry and automobiles intermixed with water produced an acid rain that weathered the stone appreciably in a matter of years—so much so that the Caryatids of the Erechtheum have been removed to a museum to safeguard them against further deterioration (see Figure 1-5).

FIGURE 1-5 Caryatids at Acropolis temporarily protected prior to removal to a museum.

It is essential to understand that few materials are in and of themselves durable. Interaction of the environment with the material will determine its durability. Oftentime coatings (organic or metallic) will prolong the life expectancy of a material. Occasionally the detailing of certain features will have an effect on the life span of the materials or assemblies.

Freeze–Thaw

A reference to freeze–thaw was made under the heading of Habitability, Water Permeability. Materials having the capacity to absorb water—especially masonry, cementitious materials, and soils—may experience a freeze–thaw phenomenon which induces stress leading to either minor or major failures, such as cracks or disengagement from the structure depending on the severity of the condition. Air entrainment in concrete has reduced the effects of freeze–thaw. Similarly, frost susceptibility is reduced in soils when fines below sieve size 200 are less than 10 percent.

Ozone

Ozone is oxygen containing three rather than the normal two atoms of oxygen. Ozone is prevalent in the upper atmosphere and also is produced at ground level by electrical discharges. Since it is unstable, it is extremely reactive. Building materials that oxidize, primarily rubber and certain plastics unless properly compounded, will react with ozone and become brittle or crack. An ASTM test method to determine the degree of deterioration of rubber by ozone is D1149.

Fading (Colorfastness)

Some materials exposed to sunlight can undergo a fading of color. The degree to which material colors are fast or tend to fade can be determined by certain test procedures as follows:

ASTM C798	Color Permanency of Glazed Ceramic Tile
ASTM C538	Color Retention of Red, Orange and Yellow Porcelain Enamel
ASTM D1543	Color Permanence of White Architectural Enamels
ASTM G45	Fading and Discoloration of Non Metallic Materials

Chemical Fumes

Gases that can enter into the weathering process are certain pollutants such as ozone, sulfur dioxide, oxides of nitrogen, and chemical fumes that are the by-products of industrial plants. These gases in combination with rain, sand, dust, and wind can impinge upon exposed surfaces and cause degradation of coatings, organic building materials, metals, and masonry materials.

The chemistry of the building material selected for a given exposure and the nature of the environment may cause a chemical reaction. Thus, it is essential to select a material that will better maintain its stability and durability in a known industrial environment.

Copper gutters and flashings can survive in most environments. However, when these structures are located near coal burning plants, sulfurous fumes will attack and pinhole the metal.

The simple solution of providing a coating that can resist the chemical fumes is all that is required to overcome the problem. Sometimes minor changes in the chemical makeup of a manufactured material can have a profound influence on its ability to resist chemical attack.

Bactericidal

The most prevalent forms of attack on building materials are fungal decay of wood and mildew of certain paints.

Fungi feed on and therefore decompose a wide variety of organic building products, particularly wood and oil-based paints. Paints based on synthetic resins do not support mildew growth. However, mildew can grow on latex paints which have thickeners or emulsifiers that contain cellulose or protein derivatives.

For fungi to grow and prosper, certain conditions must be met. These include moderately warm temperatures, water, and a source of food such as cellulosic products or proteins and fats.

In an environment which is ideal (temperature, water, and food) fungi will thrive. As the environment becomes less ideal, the growth becomes slower.

For wood near soils or water, wood-preservative treatments are usually sufficient to discourage fungi attack.

For paints and coatings, the addition of a mildewcide to the paint will be sufficient to deter mildewing.

Mildew resistance tests for paints are covered in Federal Test Standard No. 141, method 6271.1, and in ASTM D3274, Evaluating Degree of Surface Disfigurement of Paint Films by Fungal Growth.

Ultraviolet (UV) Radiation

Electromagnetic radiation is energy propagated by an electromagnetic field. The electromagnetic spectrum runs the gamut from gamma rays with the shortest wavelengths to AM radio waves with the longest wavelengths (see Table 1-4).

Ultraviolet radiation lies in the wavelength range of 10 to 380 nm, just below the visible light spectrum.

Radiation, particularly UV, has an effect on the durability of certain building products. It acts by changing the chemical structure of polymers used in organic building products and thereby affecting their physical characteristics. Fortunately the intensity of destructive UV is a small part of the total solar radiation and is reduced as the angle of the sun decreases and by clouds and smoke. However, sufficient UV is received in southern climes to cause degradation of building materials, particularly in the presence of oxygen, water, and heat.

Natural rubber, neoprene, butyl, EPDM, and some sealants will experience UV degradation unless properly compounded with antioxidants and UV absorbers.

Artificial weathering tests, carbon arc, and mercury lamps have been used to determine durability when exposed to UV. More recently xenon light weatherometers, ASTM G26, which duplicate natural UV more closely, have been used to test the effect of exposure of building materials to UV.

TABLE 1-4
ELECTROMAGNETIC SPECTRUM

Type of radiation	Approximate wavelength limit (mm)	
Gamma rays	from	0.0000000005
	to	0.0000005
X-rays	to	0.00005
Ultraviolet radiation:		
Extreme UV	to	0.00001
Far UV	to	0.00020
Middle UV	to	0.00032
Near UV	to	0.00038
Visible light	to	0.0007
Infrared radiation:		
Near IR	to	0.003
Middle IR	to	0.03
Far IR	to	0.3
Hertzian waves:		
Microwave	to	100.0
FM, TV	to	2000.0
Shortwave	to	100,000.0
AM radio	to	800,000.0

Adhesion of Coatings

To some extent, under the heading Habitability, Water Permeability, the subject of water infiltration has been discussed with its attendant problems. While paints and coatings are to some degree water repellants and retard the flow of water inward, the vapor-permeable type will permit water vapor to move outward as well under favorable conditions. However, when water enters through failures in the paint film of an impervious coating, blistering may occur as the result of water vapor buildup. This is induced by the effect of the sun causing a heat buildup with subsequent evaporation of the water in the substrate.

Dimensional Stability

As a result of both daily and seasonal changes in air temperature, solar heating, and radiative cooling, temperature variations occur that cause building materials to undergo dimensional changes including expansion, contraction, and volume changes.

In the design of a building, when one selects materials to be used on the exterior, the properties of the material or of those used in combination must be completely understood, since the exterior environment will have an effect on dimensional stability. It may be necessary to locate the materials where mechanisms that would cause dimensional instability are least active.

For example, built-up roofing will expand and contract when exposed to the elements. There will also be volume changes in the asphalt or tar used as the flood coat. By changing the location of the built-up roofing so that the insulation is installed above the roofing, the dimensional change in the built-up roofing is minimized. Figure 1-6 illustrates this improvement in roofing.

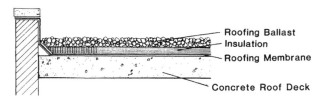

FIGURE 1-6 Inverted insulated protected roof system.

Mechanical Properties

Materials and components that exhibit movement may be subjected to splitting, bursting, tearing, and fatigue. Movement may be induced by temperature change, moisture content changes, and application of loads such as wind, snow, and occupancy. Hence, the durability of materials and components is a function of the stresses developed as a result of temperature and moisture changes and application of loads.

Deformation Due to Loading

Stress in a building material may be induced by wind loads, snow loads, or occupancy loads. The amount of stress depends on the magnitude of the load. With loading, an unrestrained material deforms, although the order of magnitude may be small. Many materials have elastic properties and up to certain load limits will resist permanent deformation. The ratio of stress to strain is known as the modulus of elasticity (E) where

$$E = \frac{stress}{strain} \ or \ \frac{load \ per \ unit \ area}{deformation \ per \ unit \ dimension}$$

This constant of proportionality, the ratio of stress to strain, represents the inherent ability of the material to resist elastic deformation. The elastic limit is the greatest stress which a material is capable of sustaining without permanent deformation upon complete release of the stress. When the elastic limit is exceeded, a permanent set may be induced in the material. Materials that observe this stress-strain ratio are metals, wood, concrete, and masonry. Organic materials such as built-up roofing, elastomeric roofing, and sealants, and materials such as glass do not observe this elastic ratio because they are plastic materials and also because their mechanical properties change with aging and weathering.

However, even the materials that fall within the parameters of the stress-strain range of deformation will experience another type of degradation when subjected to sustained or long-term loading, which will not fully disappear when the loading is removed. This deformation is called creep or plastic flow.

Temperature Changes

Mechanical properties of materials will change with temperature. Physically, a change in temperature, in addition to change in length, will alter the hardness and strength of a material. Thermoplastics, such as neoprenes, PVCs, EPDMs, whose temperatures may rise with exposure to the sun, will soften and result in a diminution of the tensile strength. In extreme cases this may lead to bursting, tearing, or splitting. Sealants that are properly formulated will resist forces imposed by elevated temperatures. Low temperatures will cause sealant joint widths to expand as the panel sections between them contract. Since the sealants are expanding while they are simultaneously getting colder and stiffer, an added burden is imposed on their ability to perform. The rate of temperature change is an important factor with these materials, since organic compounds can generally tolerate slow rates of strain more readily than fast rates of strain.

Moisture Content Changes

The freezing of water in porous materials such as concrete, stone, brick, and concrete block is in some measure the cause of cracking, splitting, or bursting. Frost failure occurs in materials that are both wet and cold. Materials having high porosity and small pores are generally more susceptable to this phenomenon, and alternating freeze–thaw cycles contribute to splitting and scaling of these materials.

COMPATIBILITY

In the design of buildings there are very many situations where differing materials are joined together as the result of detailing specific configurations. When differing materials are in contact with one another on the exterior of a building, they are subjected to moisture, temperature changes, radiation, and oxygen. These external weathering events can aggravate the incompatibility of the materials, leading to corrosion, degradation, and material failure.

Less frequently, incompatibility of materials may occur as a result of a chemical process or the emanation of fumes within a structure that may have a corrosive or other deteriorating effect.

Compatibility includes the ability of materials and systems to withstand reaction with adjacent materials in terms of chemical interaction, galvanic action, and degradation of physical properties.

Galvanic Action

The most common experience with incompatibility of exterior materials is that of bringing dissimilar metals in contact with one another. In the presence of moisture a galvanic cell is created, causing a flow of current from one metal (the anode) to another metal (the cathode), resulting in the corrosion of the metal serving as the anode at the expense of the metal serving as the cathode. For example, steel nails used in conjunction with copper flashing or roofing will act as anodes and corrode.

This phenomenon of galvanic action is referred to as the electromotive force (*emf*), which is an electrical potential difference that causes the movement of electricity or tends to produce an electric current. The electromotive force series (EMF Series) is a listing of chemical elements arranged according to their standard electrode potentials. The "noble" metals such as gold are positive, the "active" metals such as zinc are negative. The "noble" metals at the bottom of the EMF Series are the least susceptible to corrosion; the "active" metals at the top of the Series are the most susceptible. The EMF Series for metals used in building construction is shown in Table 1-5.

TABLE 1-5
ELECTROMOTIVE FORCE (EMF) SERIES

Magnesium
Aluminum
Zinc
Chromium
Iron or steel
Stainless steel
Cadmium
Tin
Lead
Copper
Brasses
Monel
Silver
Platinum
Gold

To eliminate the possibility of galvanic action, felts, paint coatings, or bitumen have been employed to separate dissimilar roofing metals. Conversely, this principle of EMF has been used advantageously to prevent corrosion by creating a slight positive charge at structures such as water towers and underground pipe lines, to reduce galvanic electrical conductance and thereby eliminate corrosion.

Chemical Incompatibility

The problems of incompatibility were dramatically increased with the advent of new human-made chemical building materials after World War II. A case in point was the introduction of modern-day sealants. An early sealant was utilized for the sealing of joints in marble on the United Nations Building in New York. Within a short period of time, a pinking discoloration was noticed on the white marble that was ultimately attributed to the sealant. By reformulating the sealant, the discoloration of the marble was overcome.

When paints or coatings are resurfaced with different coatings, tests should be performed to ascertain the compatibility of the new coating systems to prevent lifting, softening, emulsification, and degradation that may result from chemical incompatibility of the new and the old systems.

Endless tales of similar mishaps have occurred when dissimilar materials brought together for the first time exhibited either chemical or galvanic reactions. To reduce the possibility of incompatibility, it is essential to require that manufacturers of materials be apprised of the proposed use of specific materials within a certain detail and configuration and perform necessary tests to determine possible incompatibility prior to use.

Differential Movement

Incompatibility also includes the differential thermal movement. Again, when diverse materials are used within the same configuration, their rates of thermal expansion should be checked to make certain that they are not so disparate as to cause buckling or separation because of uneven thermal expansion or contraction.

Differential movement also occurs when components of different absorption rates are placed in the same assembly, causing fractures, crumbling, or crushing to occur along meeting planes and within the weaker component. An example of this is careless patching of architectural concrete, mortar in exposed stone masonry, or plaster. More than a test patch and a brief period of observation is needed here: the properties of the host and imported materials must be researched to ascertain their laboratory-curing shrinkage, absorption, and thermal properties. Where appropriate, accelerated testing under cycles of wetness/dryness, high and low temperature should be undertaken.

ENVIRONMENTAL CONSIDERATIONS

To the traditional broad performance categories of structural serviceability, fire safety, habitability, durability, and compatibility, one must add concern for the environment in the selection of materials: the effect of a designer's choice of material on human life, nature, resources, and the future of our planet. Individual conscience and our society's concerns have placed environmental matters high in evaluating the total and ultimate performance of materials in our palette. More and more frequently, private sector and government clients require that attention be given to environmental criteria.

SAFETY

A material is expected to be non-hazardous in more ways than just an immediate hazard to life, health and safety—a threat such as flammability or toxicity. A material must not have injurious edges and it must not naturally degrade to a dangerous condition. A floor material should be selected to help people not to slip or trip. Cooking surfaces must not endanger the elderly. A roof and its rooftop equipment must not contribute dangerous flying missiles to the damage done by hurricane winds.

The health of the public ranks foremost. A material and the assembly in which it is placed must not poison the population as lead paint, formaldehyde vapors, and asbestos fibers do.

Other living things must also be considered. Plant-killing chemicals, fish-killing effluents, leachings from waste, seaside lighting that deceives egg-laying sea turtles, structures that confuse birds—all of these aspects of design and material selection pass through the environmental calculus.

NATURAL RESOURCES

Some materials that architects and engineers have long taken for granted are known to be in short supply. Our supply of easily mined gypsum is exhaustible. Many designers avoid selecting black walnut, teak and redwood when they plan hardwood furniture, trim and veneers. None of these materials is scarce, strictly speaking; the consumer knows however that their renewal rate cannot compare to past (and present) levels of use.

Thus, the decision to use or not use certain materials is tempered by their renewability—whether they are being replenished by recycling as is the case of aluminum, cellulose fiber, and copper—or whether they are easily replaced by nature, as is the case with southern pine.

ENERGY

The energy content of each material can not only be calculated but also is being published more and more. The energy required to extract (or recycle), to form or fabricate, and to install—each can be weighed against the energy budget of alternative choices. Thus the energy contained in an EIF wall assembly may be compared with the energy consumed in the manufacture of a glass and aluminum curtain wall.

The energy that is consumed in service—or which may be conserved—by the choice of this or that material can be researched or calculated. In the case of an EIF assembly and a glass-aluminum curtain wall, the energy conservation that is represented by the overall R-value, reflection coefficients, as well as by cleaning and other maintenance expenditures, can all be factored in.

SERVICE AND BEYOND

The length of service of materials and assemblies can be computed and compared, taking into account aesthetics, recoating, repairs and need or likelihood of replacement. By such analysis a brick wall may out-serve a wood wall, or a slate roof out-serve an asphalt shingled one, even though the initial cost of the former is higher.

Some materials age gracefully and never appear to require replacement if just routine maintenance is observed. On the other hand, some technically advanced materials can look disreputable after only a few years of service and will require expensive rehabilitation just to keep them minimally acceptable. Centuries-old Italian brick structures, with plaster missing in random places all over the exterior, are not only thought to be charming, but also are sometimes replicated—crumbling plaster and all—in new historically evocative designs. We also have a name for a technologically sophisticated plastic that fades and chalks after a few years: *tacky* we call it.

When the day comes to demolish or replace, can the material be salvaged and reused? Can it be salvaged for recycling? Does its disposal create a problem?

All of these considerations are part of the flourishing and expanding art of taking the environmental impact of every major material selection into account—along with other more traditional performance criteria.

LBJ Library, Austin, TX: travertine paving. Skidmore, Owings & Merrill, Architects. *(Photographer, Ezra Stoller © ESTO.)*

SITEWORK

Architectural materials utilized for sitework are associated with designs for the paving and surfacing of such areas as walks, plazas, platforms, steps, roads, and promenades.

Engineering materials usually employed for streets, roads, and walks are asphaltic concrete and portland cement concrete. These are generally designed by engineering specialists, except that color, texture, and patterns are generally controlled by architects. Even the so-called blacktop (asphaltic concrete) can assume a grayish rather than a black appearance by the introduction of broken stone of a grayish hue seeded into the surface. The architect will also lay out patterns in concrete paving and make decisions on texturing the concrete to likewise control the architectural aesthetic qualities of walks and paved surfaces.

Architectural materials used for paved surfaces are myriad and include brick, clay tile, terrazzo, stone, precast concrete blocks, and quarry tile. In many instances information on these materials will be found under separate chapter headings. This chapter discusses similar materials unique to sitework and methods of setting.

PAVING

CAST-IN-PLACE CONCRETE

The basic technology in using concrete both for interior slabs and as a site paving material is discussed toward the end of Chapter 3. Further techniques germane to exterior paving follow.

Inserts

In exterior slabs, decorative inserts are often used in place of control and isolation joints. Redwood or pressure preservative treated lumber is the most common linear divider material. For longevity and freedom from splintering, the lumber should be held a fraction of an inch below the surface of the concrete, and the pieces should be positively held down by anchors or by beveling each divider to a slight dovetail profile.

Feature-tile inserts in exterior concrete slabs can be executed only with much labor. The measuring of the tile insert locations and the removal of concrete must be performed while the concrete is still plastic. Judiciously used, the effect of inserted features can change an ordinary-looking expanse of concrete into something with human scale and warm associations.

Tile Over Concrete

Sometimes large panels of quarry or other decorative tile are desired, with strips of flush concrete between and surrounding. As with feature tiles, the execution can be difficult. Consider casting the tile-supporting concrete areas separately from the raised concrete strips, complete with isolation joints filler material. Then the sealant joints that are recommended by the Tile Council of America (TCA) for isolating exterior panels of tile will be true movement-accommodating joints since they will, in effect, run through the entire slab thickness.

The requirements of TCA are stringent and require early planning. Sealant-filled joints, on suitable backer rod material, must be planned at least every 16 ft in both directions, preferably 12 ft both ways. If the difference between summer high and winter low temperature is less than 100°F (56°C), the joint width can be as little as ½ in. when 12 ft on centers (13 mm, 3.6 m oc) or ⅜ in. when 16 ft on centers (20 mm, 5 m oc). For exterior decks exposed to the sky in northern latitudes, TCA says that ¾-in. joints 12 ft apart (20 mm, 3.5 m oc) are usually needed.

Each control, isolation or construction joint in the slab below should have a corresponding sealant-filled tile joint directly above it. It is wise to design both grouted and sealed joints in the tile at least ½ in. (13 mm) wide, preferably ¾ in. (20 mm), and to see that the concrete joints below are at least the same width. If tile is installed over unjointed concrete, provision should be made to have the deepest practicable saw-cut joints made in the surface of the concrete and to fill them with sealant.

Scoring and Crack Control

Control, isolation and construction joints in concrete are discussed in Chapter 3.

In addition to control and isolation joints, exterior concrete slabs are usually scored after floating or troweling to divide them into panels of 10 to 21 ft² (1–2 m²). Scoring, if impressed deeply in the concrete, further helps to concentrate cracking along these induced lines of weakness. Water runoff from the traffic surface is also helped slightly.

Steel fabric secondary reinforcing is not ordinarily effective or needed in exterior concrete walks and slabs. Primary steel reinforcing—fabric or bars—for anticipated heavy vehicular loads is sometimes needed.

Much of the random cracking that is observed in exterior concrete is from shrinkage. Aside from controlling the water content of such concrete at placement and moist-curing it, the most effective way of reducing cracks is to add organic fibers to the mix as the secondary reinforcing. The fibers should be naturally alkali-resistant products such as polypropylene (an olefin) or nylon (polyamide). They must be adequately sized for strength and properly mixed for uniform dispersion. Propylene fibers can impart a hairy finish to the concrete which is soon worn away in traffic. Nylon rarely does this.

Since secondary reinforcing controls only shrinkage and temperature cracking and serves no load-resisting purpose, the thickness of the concrete should not be reduced because of the presence of fibers or steel.

Exterior Surface Treatments

Frequently an exposed aggregate finish is desired on exterior concrete to give a better appearance than broomed or nonslip concrete. Exposed aggregate finish is specified in general fashion in ACI 301, Chapter 11. The designer specifies the type, size, and color of the aggregate, which is usually ⅜ to ⅝ in. (10–16 mm) hard, durable stone. Angular stone has better slip resistance.

Surface textures can be floated or troweled directly into concrete slabs. Textures that imitate travertine, pitted limestone, and other natural materials can be had by the right choice of tool and such aids as stones, broken ice, and rock salt. A mock-up that can be inspected in the designer's office, or successive site-built mock-ups for approval by the designer, is the surest guide to satisfactory execution.

Adding pigments to concrete to reduce reflection can be a major factor in pedestrian comfort, especially in shopping areas, schools, and public squares. This is of great importance in Sun Belt areas where solar radiation is intense and many of the regionally produced portland cements are almost white. Have you noticed that the concrete at the largest theme parks in Orlando is pigmented gray? Color is most effectively imparted to concrete by alkali-resistant pigments that are mixed and cast with the concrete. If uniformity and long-term appearance are not important, there are dry pigments and pigmented stains that can be applied to the surface during finishing.

Pigments vary in their resistance to fading and color change over years of use; it is good to get specific advice on colors of proven durability from pigment producers. The final color can be determined only by casting trial samples with actual aggregate, cement, and pigment and then adjusting.

BRICK PAVING

Material

Paving brick is a vitrified, dense, hard brick made from fire clay or shale designed for use where abrasion and wear are important factors. ASTM C902, Specification for Pedestrian and Light Traffic Paving Brick, is a standard for paving brick. Paving brick is available in thicknesses as thin as ½ inch and up to 2½ inches in thickness and in various face dimensions. In addition to paving brick, both building brick and facing brick are utilized for brick paving where certain colors and textures are unique to specific projects.

Setting Brick Paving

Brick intended for walks, pavements, plazas, and so forth may be set in mortar, on a properly prepared sand bed, or on bituminous asphalt setting beds. The latter utilizes a mixture containing 7 percent asphalt and 93 percent fine aggregate. Patterns may include herringbone, running bond, and so forth.

PRECAST CONCRETE PAVING

Concrete paver units are relatively new products that are used both for pedestrian and vehicular traffic. The pavers are produced in countless shapes, sizes, and colors, with many configurations and designs. Interlocking shapes are available as well. These pavers are made to meet material standard ASTM C936 and have a compressive strength of approximately 8500 psi.

The interlocking pavers are generally laid on a dry sand bed with tight joints filled with sand. For pedestrian use the pavers are nominally 2⅜ in. thick, with

3⅛ in. thick units used for vehicular traffic. Soil sub-grades and base courses should be compacted as per recommendations of the Interlocking Concrete Pavement Institute.

STONE PAVING

In Chapter 4, under heading of Building Stones, a number of stone materials are described. All of them may be used for paving in limited degrees. In addition to those building stones, several others such as bluestone and quartzite are also used. Paving stones may consist of large slabs laid in an ashlar pattern, or small, irregularly shaped stones laid out in a random pattern.

Flagstones are thin slabs of stone used for flagging or paving. They are generally fine-grained sandstone, bluestone, quartzite, or slate, but thin slabs of other stone may be used for this purpose.

Generally, paving stone may be as thin as ⅞ inch. However, the thickness should be a function of the face size to prevent breaking during transportation and handling. Stone producers should be consulted to ascertain minimum thickness requirements relative to face size selections.

Abrasion Resistance

Since wearing by abrasion is an important physical characteristic, a test method to determine abrasion resistance is an important guide to the selection of stone. ASTM C241, Test for Abrasion Resistance of Stone Subjected to Foot Traffic, is such a useful tool. Generally, the granites have the highest degree of resistance to abrasion. A ranking of abrasion resistance as conducted by the National Institute of Standards and Technology is as follows:

Material	Abrasion resistance
Granite	37 to 88
Limestone	1 to 24
Sandstone	2 to 26
Slate	6 to 12
Travertine	1 to 16

Slip Resistance

When selecting stone surfaces that may be wetted from time to time due to exposure to the weather, consideration must be given to the type of finish. Obviously, a polished finish would be ruled out immediately and perhaps honed finishes for some stone species.

The rough-sawn or shot finishes and the natural cleft finishes are ideal where antislip qualities are desirable as is the thermal finish.

To determine antislip resistance, laboratory tests using the James Machine or the horizontal pull slipmeter (HPS) described in Chapter 1 under Durability-Hygiene, Comfort, and Safety, may be utilized.

See Chapter 4 for finishes of granite, marble, travertine, sandstone, slate, and limestone.

Setting Beds

Stone paving is generally set in mortar, although some may be set in sand beds. Modified latex mortars that can reduce the thickness of setting beds are also used frequently for stone setting. When granite, marble, limestone, and travertine are set in mortar, they should be set in nonstaining waterproof cement mortar.

Mortar is generally composed of one part portland cement to three parts sand. Nonstaining cement should comply with ASTM C91. Stones should be placed on setting bed mortar and tamped with a rubber mallet until firmly bedded and then removed. The back of the stone should then be parged with a grout of wet cement and returned to its initial position and tamped into place.

When set on sand, the beds should be firmly tamped to preclude settlement.

Materials

Bluestone

Bluestone is a dense, hard, fine-grained sandstone of bluish gray color that splits easily along original bedding planes to form thin slabs. It is also available in buff, lilac, and rust colors.

Finishes for bluestone include:

Natural cleft   Having the natural seam split

Rubbed   Rubbed with coarse industrial diamonds after wire sawing

Thermal   A flame-textured finish obtained by heating

Exposed edges of bluestone may be diamond sawed, rubbed, snapped, rocked, or thermal. Bluestone has a wear and abrasion resistance of $H_a = 49$ when tested in accordance with ASTM C241.

Granite

Granite* paving may consist of large panels of stone for pedestrian use or small blocks intended for vehicular use or pedestrian malls or walks (see Figure 2-1).

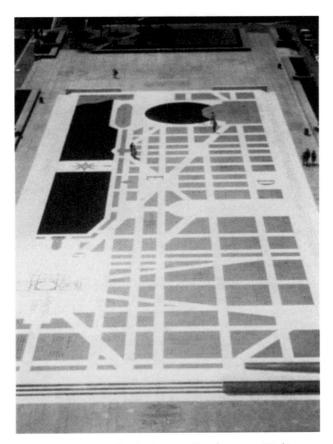

FIGURE 2-1 Pennsylvania Avenue. Development, Washington, DC: granite—Sunset Red, Academy, Carnelian, and Bright Red; thermal finish. George E. Patton/Venturi & Rausch, Architects. *(Courtesy of Cold Spring Granite Company.)*

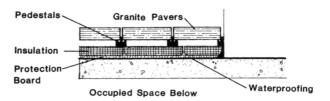

FIGURE 2-2 Granite pavers mounted on pedestals.

Granite is particularly suitable as a paving material when mounted on pedestals for plaza areas, over occupied areas, as shown in Figure 2-2.

Limestone

Limestone* for use as paving in commercial and public areas should have a minimum abrasive hardness of 10 as per ASTM C241. It is also essential to provide proper slope to drain the surface to avoid moisture collection or ponding. If limestone is contemplated for exterior paving or steps, it would be prudent to consult with the supplier or producer to obtain information on details and limitations of the material.

Marble

Only Grade A marble* should be considered for exterior paving. Thickness is a function of face size with respect to handling, transportation, and setting. The marble supplier and quarry should be consulted for optimum thickness requirements. See Figure 2-3 for typical marble installation.

Sandstone

The sandstones* exhibit excellent wear and abrasion-resistant characteristics and make good exterior paving materials. They are more typical of installations known as flagging where utilitarian rather than aesthetic qualities are paramount.

* See Chapter 4 for physical characteristics, colors, and finishes.

FIGURE 2-3 American Republic Building, Des Moines, IA: gray marble flooring on interior carried into outdoor courts. Skidmore, Owings & Merrill, Architects. *(Photographer, Ezra Stoller © ESTO.)*

FIGURE 2-4 LBJ Library, Austin, TX: travertine paving. Skidmore, Owings & Merrill, Architects. *(Photographer, Ezra Stoller © ESTO.)*

Slate

When slate* is used, edges for joints in the field of paving are generally sawn. Where edges are exposed at platform ends or stair treads, they may be rubbed or honed. A minimum abrasive hardness of 8 as per ASTM C241 should be specified.

Travertine

Crevices, craters, and holes in travertine* used for paving may be filled with travertine chips, and mortar rubbed finish is best used for exterior surfacing. See Figure 2-4 for exterior travertine paving.

TERRAZZO

For exterior terrazzo paving see Chapter 9, rustic terrazzo. Figure 2-5 illustrates a structural rustic terrazzo installation.

FIGURE 2-5 U.S. Steel—One Liberty Plaza, New York, NY: rustic terrazzo paving. Skidmore, Owings & Merrill, Architects. *(Photographer, Ezra Stoller © ESTO.)*

LANDSCAPE WALLS, PLANTERS, AND SCREENS

MASONRY GARDEN WALLS

For low walls, unreinforced mortar-set brick and stone walls can often be designed to sitting height, depending on the cohesiveness of the soil behind the wall and surcharges that may be put upon it. With proper batter and plenty of contact surface between stones,

low stone walls can sometimes be designed without any mortar at all.

Low garden walls are often used as tree wells where it is desired to save mature trees when the finish grade is elevated a few feet. A landscape architect must be consulted to determine if proper drainage is being provided for the trees, and to ensure that the root system will not be damaged by the fill.

Low walls and tree wells must be designed with safety in mind. The wall or well should generally extend at least knee-high above the high-side ground level to protect unwary walkers, unless railings or dense, permanent plantings are in place for protection.

The top course of any low wall that may be sat or walked upon should not only be firmly mortared in, but also an acrylic additive should be added to the mortar to increase bond strength. This is particularly important in climates where there are many annual freeze–thaw cycles; high-bond mortar will be less likely to permit bricks or stones to loosen due to weather or traffic.

MASONRY AND CONCRETE RETAINING WALLS

Unless the wall is very low and the overturning forces very slight, landscape walls should be designed as retaining walls of reinforced concrete or masonry. When the wall is circular or arched in plan, it is often possible to do without reinforcing.

The face of the wall may be architectural concrete, brick, stone, or some other applied facing. The Brick Institute of America (BIA) in its Technical Note 17n, guides the design of both gravity (unreinforced) and simple reinforced masonry walls.

For greater heights or greater loads, BIA's Technical Notes 17e, 17f, and 17g offer guidance. Similar guides, but based on concrete masonry construction, are to be found in the National Concrete Masonry Association's (NCMA) Tek 4, Tek 13, and Tek 50.

TIMBER LANDSCAPE WALLS

Heavy timber, doweled or spiked in place, can be used in garden walls, low planters, steps, and curbs.

Creosoted railroad ties, both used and new, became popular in landscape design a few decades ago. However, since creosoted timber is not attractive and is irritating to the skin, heavy metal- and borate-treated timber dominates the market today. Clear preservatives such as pentachlorophenol that were formerly employed to give a cleaner appearance are toxic to human beings.

HEAVY METAL PRESERVATIVES

Today's commercial preservative of choice for pressure treatment of heavy timber in contact with earth is often the nonirritating CCA (chromated copper arsenate), pressure applied following American Wood Preserving Bureau (AWPB) standard LP22. CCA does not significantly leach out of the wood in exterior service since the pressure treatment forces it into the cells of the wood. Although CCA makes wood darker, imparting a greenish cast, it weathers to a more natural color, and will take stains to bring it in harmony with the rest of the landscape design.

Because many chemicals formerly used to poison the soil against termite infestation have been banned, and because termite treatment of soil is rarely performed away from the building itself, it is important to properly protect landscape timber that is in contact with untreated soil.

Heavy-metal preservative treatment for landscape timber and boards is almost always done in large pressure vessels, following the American Wood Preservers Association AWPA C2 standard. The most commonly used preservatives—ACC, ACA, and CCA are described under Preservative Treatment, Standards, in Chapter 6.

Acid copper chromate (ACC) and the arsenic-bearing ACA and CCA preservatives lose only a small quantity of their toxins to the soil and watercourses over the years due to leaching. However, even the small quantity of arsenic and chromium thus released to the environment may be considered unacceptable by designers, owners, and public agencies.

One alternative chemical that may be used in pressure treatment is alkaline copper quat (ACQ), which lacks both arsenic and chromium in its makeup. Quat, which is short for a quaternary compound, serves as a low-toxicity, biodegradable, co-biocide in conjunction with copper oxide (CuO). Thus, only a small quantity of copper compounds, considered more benign than arsenic and chromium compounds, will permanently enter the soil over the service life of an ACQ preservative.

Wood that will be in contact with soil must be treated to retain from 0.40 to 1.00 lb/ft^3 of ACQ, depending on the use. For most landscape uses the lower figure is sufficient, except buried poles, which must be treated to retain 0.60 lb/ft^3 of ACQ. Only hot-dipped galvanized and stainless steel fastenings—never aluminum—should be used with ACQ-treated timber.

BORATE PRESERVATIVES

An emerging technology in exterior wood protection is the use of borates. Ideally, these waterborne or glycol-borne preservatives are not impregnated under pressure; rather, they work best self-diffusing themselves through moist timber. Treatment is done by concentrating the boron compound on the surfaces of unseasoned wood and then storing the treated wood for sufficient time for it to dry slowly as the diffusion from areas of high concentration to low concentration proceeds. However, if the green wood has not been borate-treated, an alternative method of application is to spray, brush, or inject the seasoned wood. For large seasoned timbers, pressure borate treatment may be the most effective method.

Borate preservatives do not affect the color of the green wood or the wood when it has seasoned. Borates are nontoxic until large concentrations are reached. They leach from the wood into the soil so little as to be almost unmeasurable. Since a small quantity of boron in soils is necessary for proper growing of plants there should be no problem in even limited leaching.

American Republic Building, Des Moines, IA: sandblasted, gap-graded, gray granite aggregate. Skidmore, Owings & Merrill, Architects. *(Photographer, Ezra Stoller © ESTO.)*

3

ARCHITECTURAL CONCRETE

With the invention of portland cement in 1824 by Aspdin, an Englishman, and its subsequent manufacture in the United States in 1871, concrete became a basic building material for use as a structural element in foundations, framing, and floor systems.

Since concrete is a plastic, moldable material, architectural designers have long attempted to experiment with concrete as an exposed architectural expression. An early example of architectural concrete is Frank Lloyd Wright's First Unity Temple in Oak Park, Illinois, built in 1906 (see Figure 3-1).

It was not until after World War II that sufficient technical know-how was accumulated by architects and engineers and painstaking reeducation of concrete contractors was undertaken to achieve and construct credible designs in both cast-in-place architectural concrete and architectural precast concrete.

FIGURE 3-1 Architectural concrete as utilized by Frank Lloyd Wright, First Unity Temple, Oak Park, IL. *(Photographer, Marvin Tetenbaum.)*

CONCRETE USAGES

The use of concrete may be channeled into a number of areas as follows:

Structural
Pile foundations
Footings
Foundation walls
Structural members—Floors, walls, roofs

Special Techniques
Slip form
Lift slab
Tilt-up
Prepacked concrete

Architectural Forms
Ribbed slab
Waffle slab
Flat slab
Thin shell
Folded plate

Paving
Highways
Airfields
Roads
Walks
Ramps and steps

CONCRETE INGREDIENTS

Concrete is a mixture of portland cement, aggregates, and water. In addition, admixtures are often incorporated to impart certain characteristics, and reinforcement is used to increase tensile strength.

CEMENT

Portland Cement

ASTM C150, the standard specification for cement used in the United States, lists five types of portland cement, as shown in Table 3-1.

Many soils in the western and southwestern parts of the United States, as well as Florida, have high sulfate content. In these areas Type II cement is commonly provided by ready-mix producers. There are areas of highly alkaline soil in which Type V cement is advisable to resist severe sulfate attack.

TABLE 3-1
TYPES OF PORTLAND CEMENT

Type	Use
I	Standard portland cement for general use when special properties are not required.
II	For use where moderate sulfate resistance or moderate heat of hydration is desired.
III	For high early strength, developing almost twice the strength of Type I at three days. Used especially for cold weather concreting.
IV	For use when a low heat of hydration is desired, as in mass concrete for dams to diminish cracking or in other massive members. It is also slow setting and attains its strength over a longer period.
V	A sulfate-resisting cement for use where severe sulfate conditions are encountered and where alkaline waters or soils are present.

Standard portland cement, domestic or imported, is usually a grayish color, although some cements routinely produced in Florida and Texas are almost white in color. White cements and buff cements of consistent color are produced in Texas to ASTM C150 standards. White cement—along with near-white aggregates—is often used for above-grade architectural concrete where the designer wants a dramatic look. White cement also makes a suitable base for obtaining true colors by the addition of pigments.

In sunny climates the darkest obtainable portland cements produce the most comfortable outdoor terraces and walks. Small quantities of black, brown, or clay-red pigments can be added to light-colored cements to ease eyestrain for pedestrians.

Formerly, portland cement was usually the sole cementitious material used in concrete mixes. Since the 1970s there has been an increase in the employment of materials other than portland cement to impart special properties to concrete.

Pozzolan and Slag Cements

ASTM C595, the standard for blended hydraulic cements, lists six types:

IS	Portland blast furnace slag cement
IP	Portland-pozzolan cement (3500 psi cube strength)
P	Portland-pozzolan cement (3000 psi cube strength)
S	Slag cement for use with portland cement
I(PM)	Pozzolan-modified portland cement
I(SM)	Slag-modified portland cement

Pozzolan materials are siliceous or siliceous-aluminous in composition, and are often derived from naturally occurring minerals. In themselves they have almost no cementing value, but they react with the wet calcium hydroxide that is formed as concrete sets. The resulting pozzolan-$Ca(OH)_2$ compound is a cement. Pozzolan-containing concrete is rarely employed in building construction, but it can be found in some dams and civil engineering structures, especially in western states of the United States.

Portland blast furnace slag cement (Type IS) is normally made by blending, at the mixing plant, portland cement with 30 to 50% (25–70% limit) fine granulated blast furnace slag (ASTM C989, Grade 120). The resulting concrete will have, as compared to a straight portland cement mix:

- Slightly better workability, particularly when placing low slump concrete
- Easier slab finishing due to workability and retarded initial set
- A slower release of heat and therefore less tendency to develop cracks while setting
- Better resistance to sulfate attack (when the slag content is greater than 50 percent) and reduced chance of alkali-silica reactions
- Slightly lower permeability
- Increased resistance to chloride attack
- Faster strength gain after curing starts and slightly higher compressive strength when cured

Fly Ash

ASTM C618 classifies fly ash and natural pozzolans as:

Type C   Fly ash from very soft coals and lignite

Type F   Fly ash from anthracite and most bituminous coals

Type N   Natural pozzolans from certain diatomites, shales, cherts, and volcanic ash, as well as pozzolans calcined from some clays and shales

Type F fly ash is widely used in concrete mixes, in part because it can often be purchased from nearby power plants at a fifth the cost of portland cement. This solves a waste disposal problem and recycles a material in which there is already a large investment of energy. Type C tends to be darker in color than Type F, may be less consistent in its chemical analysis, and produces a higher heat of hydration than Type F.

Type F or C is used to replace a fraction of the portland cement in the concrete mix. The fly ash combines with the free $Ca(OH)_2$ produced by the cement–water reaction to form a hydraulic cement gel. Type F is sometimes lighter in color, sometimes darker, than the portland cement—a lot depends on the efficiency of the coal-burning plant. The addition of fly ash to concrete makes for a more workable mix.

Microsilica

Like fly ash and other pozzolans, microsilica is inert until it reacts with the alkali released by portland cement when wet. Microsilica—or silica fume, a waste product of certain electric furnace processes—is about 100 times finer than portland cement. Along with its cement gel-producing function it fills voids surrounding even the finest aggregate particles, thus densifying the concrete, reducing its permeability, and making it more plastic during placement. Microsilica is so fine in its powdered state that it is difficult to handle when blending into a mix; it is usually added as an aqueous slurry.

Microsilica, along with water-reducing plasticizers, has been the most important factor in the high-strength revolution in concrete design. Concrete strengths above f'_c = 8000 lb/in^2 (55 200 kPa) are no longer uncommon, and for demanding uses it is possible to obtain ready-mix concrete of f'_c = 17,000 lb/in^2 (117 200 kPa).

The addition of microsilica to a concrete mix makes for a more cohesive (sticky) concrete, but one that is workable at low water-cement ratios. The densifying effect of microsilica decreases water absorption by the concrete. Pilings and bridge decks are often better protected from salt intrusion and its effects by silica fume than by surface coatings, rust inhibitors, and epoxy-clad rebars. Microsilica concrete improves the freeze–thaw cycle performance of concrete and makes it more abrasion resistant.

AGGREGATES

Aggregates are inert materials that do not react with cement and water. They generally consist of gravel, crushed gravel, broken stone, and sand. Aggregates are defined by size as coarse and fine, with coarse aggregate being that fraction which is retained on a ¼-inch sieve and fine aggregate being that which passes a ¼-inch sieve. Both coarse and fine aggregate are specified by ASTM C33, which sets standards for grading, deleterious substances, and soundness. In special cases where desired by the architect, fine aggregate may be produced by crushing the specific coarse aggregate chosen.

Gap-Graded Aggregates

Aggregates are graded so that the finer particles fill the voids between the larger aggregates. This reduces the amount of cement paste (cement and water) required and results in a more economical mix. However, for some architectural applications, gap-graded aggregate produces a very pleasing appearance. In a normal gradation of coarse and fine aggregates, the end result of an exposed aggregate finish is a somewhat nonuniform distribution of the aggregates. In a gap-graded mix there is a large percentage of coarse aggregate and a small percentage of fine aggregate, with no aggregate in the intermediate size range. As a result, gap-graded mixes show a uniform size distribution of the exposed aggregate. See Figure 3-2 for an example of a gap-graded, cast-in-place concrete.

Most normally graded concretes have matrix volumes (air, water, cement, and sand) of 55 percent or more. Gap-graded concrete reduces this matrix to 45–50 percent, which accounts for the larger proportion of visible coarse aggregates.

A laboratory test program initiated by the Portland Cement Association and described in their *Development Department Bulletin D90* establishes criteria for design mixes, slump, and air content. These criteria, along with the special care involved in taping form joints and vibration control, provide the technical requirements needed by architects, engineers, and contractors to obtain architectually exposed gap-graded concrete.

Special Aggregates

While gravel and stone are the principal coarse aggregates used in concrete, architects are increasingly searching for decorative aggregates to enhance their architectural concrete designs. Such decorative aggregates include granite, quartz, quartzite, crystalline aggregates, onyx, pebbles, marble, glass, ceramic, alundum, and emery. They can be obtained from numerous aggregate suppliers nationwide. See Figure 3-3 for photographs of panels of special aggregates. Also see Figure 3-4 for a structure utilizing a granite aggregate.

When using an aggregate for which there is very little technical information as to its reaction with the cement paste, it is essential to perform a petrographic analysis in accordance with ASTM C295. This analysis will determine the physical and chemical properties of the aggregate and its prospective performance as a concrete ingredient.

Lightweight Aggregate

An aggregate for use in lightweight structural concrete is produced by heating such materials as clay, shale, or slate. During the calcining or sintering process, the gases formed inside the material expand it to a lightweight, porous form. The concrete resulting from the use of lightweight aggregates weighs approximately 75 to 110 pounds per cubic foot. Lightweight aggregate is specified to comply with ASTM C330.

FIGURE 3-2 American Republic Building, Des Moines, IA: sandblasted, gap-graded, gray granite aggregate. Skidmore, Owings & Merrill, Architects. *(Photographer, Ezra Stoller © ESTO.)*

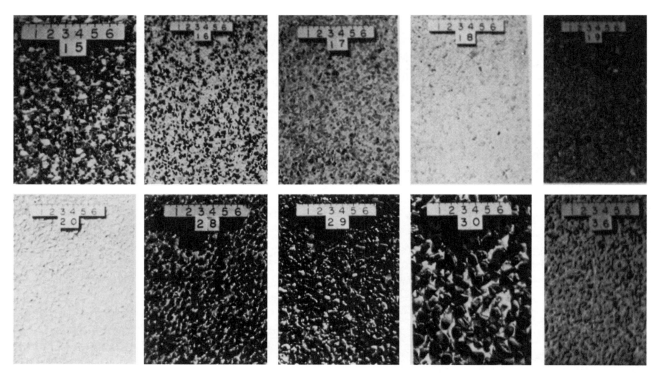

Panel No. 15. Use of three aggregates—verde antique, white marble, and pink granite, on a white background produces a colorful surface.

Panel No. 16. The combination of black obsidian and milky quartz results in a striking contrast.

Panel No. 17. Rose quartz presents a pleasing variety of pink shades against a white matrix.

Panel No. 18. The green of the exposed cordierite aggregate produces a lighter hued surface when viewed from a distance.

Panel No. 19. Pink feldspar is a platy rock that orients itself in the horizontal position during consolidation. The resulting exposed-aggregate surface is very dense and uniform. The large flat crystals reflect light from myriad surfaces.

Panel No. 20. The exposure of very white silica stone on an integrally colored light blue background is most interesting. The distant viewer sees a moderate blue surface with the exposed aggregate barely visible. A closer view shows the mild contrast caused by exposure of the aggregate.

Panel No. 28. Reddish brown Eau Claire gravel contrasts with uniform white background.

Panel No. 29. Use of expanded slag fines results in a coarse-textured white background for the reddish brown Eau Claire aggregate.

Panel No. 30. A chemical surface retarder produced the correct degree of exposure of the 3/4-in. (19-mm) to 1-in. (25-mm) Eau Claire aggregate.

Panel No. 36. Exposure of pink marble on white background provides a subtle coloration.

FIGURE 3-3 Panels of various exposed aggregates. *(Used with permission of Portland Cement Association.)*

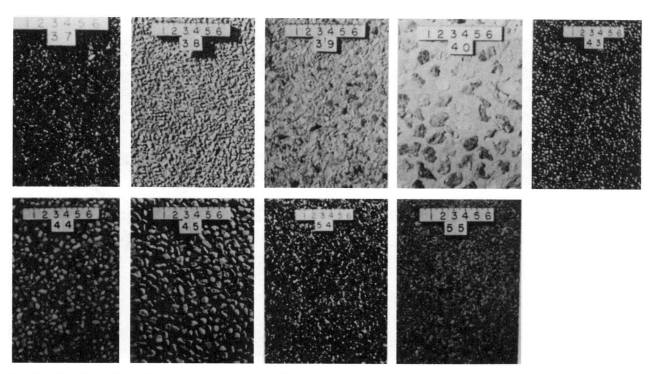

Panel No. 37. Black labradorite rock fractures along crystal faces, and exposed portions sparkle in the sunlight. Aggregate of the size shown here results in a very black surface.

Panel No. 38. White marble in a matrix of silica sand and white cement produces an all-white panel.

Panel No. 39. The brown-yellow-white quartz fractures into flat pieces that orient themselves against the bottom surface of the form. The result is excellent exposure of the quartz.

Panel No. 40. The form was covered with a surface retarder and pink marble was handplaced uniformly on it. White cement-sand mortar was placed over the marble and consolidated. Backup concrete was then placed and consolidated.

Panel No. 43. Dark expanded shale fines produce a dark background that contrasts with the buff-colored Elgin pea gravel.

Panels No. 43, 44, and 45 demonstrate the effect of increasing the size of coarse aggregate. A range of surface retarders produced the correct reveal for the aggregates.

Panel No. 54. A single-colored green glass was used for the exposed aggregate, yet a two-color effect was obtained due to the difference in size of the translucent aggregates. A special glass that was nonreactive with portland cement was used.

Panel No. 55. Combination of a reflective orange glass with a nonreflective brown natural aggregate makes a very interesting panel.

FIGURE 3-3 (continued) Panels of various exposed aggregates. *(Used with permission of Portland Cement Association.)*

FIGURE 3-4 Hirshhorn Museum, Washington, DC: sandblasted Swenson Pink granite aggregate. Skidmore, Owings & Merrill, Architects.

WATER

Generally, potable water is satisfactory for making concrete or the cement paste that binds the aggregates together. If the source of water is suspect, it should be analyzed to ensure its use as one of the ingredients of concrete.

When water and portland cement are mixed, a chemical reaction, hydration, takes place, producing a cementitious product (cement paste) that binds the aggregates together and forms concrete.

ADMIXTURES

A concrete admixture is defined in ASTM C125 as "a material other than water, aggregates, and portland cement used as an ingredient of concrete and added to the batch immediately before or during its mixing."

If properly designed, proportioned, and handled, concrete should not require the use of an admixture. The proper design mix and the selection of suitable materials should result in workable, durable, watertight, and finishable concrete. However, there are instances when an admixture is desirable—for example, when special properties are required that cannot be obtained by normal methods or as economically. Certain special properties that are primarily of interest to the architect include the following: (1) retarding or accelerating the time of set, (2) accelerating of early strength, (3) increase in durability to exposure to elements, (4) reduction in permeability to liquids, (5) improvement of workability, (6) bonding of gypsum and portland cement plaster, (7) antibacterial properties of cement, and (9) coloring of concrete.

Certain special properties that can be controlled or achieved through the use of admixtures, and which are of interest to the structural engineer, include the following: (1) control of alkali-aggregate expansion, (2) reduction of heat of hydration, (3) modification in rate of bleeding, (4) decrease in capillary flow of water, and (5) reduction of segregation in grout mixtures.

It should be stated unequivocally that admixtures are not a substitute for good concreting practices. Admixtures affect more than one property of concrete, sometimes affecting desirable properties adversely.

Therefore, trial mixes should be made that reproduce job conditions, using the admixtures with the design mix. The compatibility of the admixture with the other concrete ingredients should then be observed, taking into account its effect on the properties of the fresh and hardened concrete. When special properties are required, and the use of an admixture is decided on, then those admixtures being considered for use should conform with applicable ASTM Specifications.

The classification of admixtures can be established rather broadly—insofar as architectural specifications are concerned—as follows: (1) air-entraining admixtures; (2) set-controlling (retarding) admixtures; (3) accelerating admixtures; (4) workability agents; (5) dampproofing and permeability-reducing admixtures; (6) bonding agents; (7) fungicidal, germicidal, and insecticidal admixtures; (8) coloring agents; and (9) superplasticizers.

Air-Entraining Admixtures

The admixture that has obtained the widest recognition and use to improve durability of concrete exposed to a combination of moisture and cycles of freezing and thawing is an air-entrainment agent. The mechanism through which air-entrained concrete resists the disruptive effects of frost action is in the large number of minute air bubbles that are distributed uniformly throughout the cement paste.

Entrainment of the air may be produced by means of air-entraining admixtures added to the concrete ingredients before or during the mixing of concrete, or through the use of an air-entraining portland cement. The materials used for air entrainment include natural wood resins, fats, and oils that have been chemically processed. Air entrainment admixtures should meet the requirements of ASTM C260. Conformance with these specifications will ensure that the admixture functions as an air-entraining agent, that it can effect a substantial improvement in the resistance of concrete to freezing and thawing, and that no essential property of the concrete is seriously impaired.

The use of air-entrained concrete has become so widely accepted that cements containing air-entraining admixtures are included in ASTM and Federal Specifications. The admixture is interground with portland cement during the manufacture of air-entraining additions; air-entraining cements should

conform to the requirements of ASTM Specifications C226 and C175, respectively.

Set-Controlling Admixtures

Admixtures that delay the setting time of concrete are termed retarders. They are used principally to overcome the accelerating effect of high temperatures during the summer and to delay the initial set of concrete when difficult or unusual conditions of placement are required.

In exposed architectural concrete, set retarders can be used to keep concrete plastic for a sufficiently long period of time so that succeeding lifts can be placed without developing cold joints. Retarders are also used to expose the aggregate in the surface of concrete. This can be achieved by applying a retarder to the forms or to the surface of horizontal planes, thereby inhibiting the setting of the surface layer of the mortar. Upon removal of the forms, the surface mortar is removed by wire brushing or sand blasting, thus exposing the aggregate to produce unusual surface texture effects.

Retarders generally used as admixtures are ligno-sulfonic acid and its salts, and hydroxylated carboxylic acids and their salts. These should meet the applicable requirements of ASTM C494, Type B.

Accelerating Admixtures

Accelerating admixtures are used to achieve high early strength and to shorten the time of set. High early strength results in earlier removal of forms, reduction of required time for curing and protection, earlier use of a structure, and partial compensation for the retarding effect of cold weather.

Chemicals used as accelerators are organic compounds of triethanolamine and calcium chloride. Accelerators should conform to ASTM C494, Type C, and calcium chloride should conform to ASTM D98. However, calcium chloride may cause discoloration and its use should be avoided for architectural concrete.

Calcium chloride should not be used in the following situations: (1) in prestressed concrete, because it may cause corrosion of the steel; (2) where aluminum and steel are embedded in concrete because electrolytic corrosion will take place in a humid environment; and (3) in lightweight insulating concrete on metal decks.

Plasticizers

Plasticizers do more for concrete than make it more workable under shovel, vibrator, float, and trowel. By making concrete fully plastic with less water, the water-cement ratio can be kept low and the concrete's compressive strength kept high.

Several of the ingredients discussed to this point serve to plasticize a concrete mix: Slag cement, fly ash, microsilica, and air-entraining agents all make the concrete workable and allow the water content to be low.

Lignosulfonate-based water-reducing admixtures were once the only water reducers available. They can reduce water content by as much as 15 percent. Lignosulfonates are produced following the ASTM C494, Type A standard. They are widely used.

High-Range Water Reducers

High-range water reducers (HRWR) have been in use in Japan since 1965 and later in North America. They can reduce water content by 30 percent or more.

These superplasticizers have contributed to the recent revolution in concrete design by coming along just when they were needed to make the extensive

pumping of concrete practical. More than half of the trucks that go to building sites today are delivering concrete to pumps, which must maintain a constant flow of concrete to placement points that are often 200 m away—or 100 m higher than—the pump.

Early HRWRs operated by placing negative charges on cement particles, causing them to repel each other, thus reducing friction. They had to be added to the mix at the worksite.

Today's HRWRs coat the cement particles. This controls the hydration process and reduces friction, making for plasticity. ASTM C494, Type F, is the standard for high-range water-reducing admixtures; Type G contains a retardant as well. HRWRs can now be added at the batching plant.

Most superplasticizers are sulfonated melamine-formaldehydes (SMF) or sulfonated naphthalene-formaldehydes (SNF), and are available as solids or as liquids. Slumps of as much as 10 in. (250 mm) are obtained within a few minutes of dosing with the admixture. The resulting mix is practically self-leveling yet remains cohesive without bleeding, segregation, or loss of strength. See Figure 3-5 for the effect of plasticizers on the flowability of cement paste.

By controlling the hydration, concrete can now often be placed in hot weather and farther from the batching plant without the need for ice or retarders in the mix. HRWRs enable better bond to be had with reinforcing, higher lifts to be placed in walls, and for concrete strength to develop faster. Slabs on grade tend to have less bleed water, less shrinkage cracking, and are less permeable.

Since HRWR admixtures make possible a high degree of workability, the creation of architectural

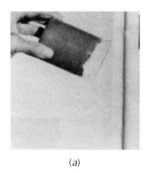

(a)   (b)   (c)   (d)

FIGURE 3-5   Effect of plasticizers on the flowability of cement paste. *(Reproduced from Canadian Building Digest No. CBD 203.)* (a) No plasticizer, (b) with 0.3 percent HRWR superplasticizer, (c) with 0.3 percent lignosulfonate, (d) with 0.4 percent lignosulfonate.

shapes becomes less restrictive. Architects are allowed the latitude to experiment and develop new forms.

Corrosion Inhibitors

Nitrites have been added to concrete mixes to reduce the electrolytic corrosion of inserts and reinforcing bars. Their effectiveness is still being assessed. Rather than jump to this form of protection the designer should carefully consider these alternative strategies:

- Densify the concrete with HRWR admixture or by adding fly ash or slag cement to the mix. This will inhibit the entry of water into the concrete—with water's potential for creating an electrolyte solution.
- Coat the bars with epoxy. Sometimes plain or galvanized reinforcing sets up a battery with differing metals also embedded in the concrete, such as cast iron inserts or nonferrous items.

Dampproofing and Permeability-Reducing Admixtures

The terms *dampproofing* and *waterproofing* imply prevention of water penetration of dry concrete or stoppage of transmission of water through unsaturated concrete. However, admixtures have not been found to produce such results. The terms, therefore, have come to mean a reduction in the rate of penetration of water into dry concrete or in the rate of transmission of water through unsaturated concrete from the damp side to the dry side.

Admixtures claimed to have dampproofing properties include soaps, butyl stearate, and certain petroleum products.

Experts put little credence in the effect of admixtures on the reduction of permeability. The watertightness of concrete depends primarily upon obtaining a well-cured paste having a water-cement ratio not over 0.6 by weight (6¾ gallons of water per bag). Concrete made with less than 5½ gallons of water per bag and well cured, produces a good, watertight concrete.

Fungicidal, Germicidal, and Insecticidal Agents

Antibacterial cements are usually those having an admixture ground into the cement to impart fungicidal, germicidal, or insecticidal properties to the cement. These materials include phenols and copper compounds, which are useful in tile joints in such areas as locker rooms, food plants, and dairy plants.

Coloring Agents

Pigments added to concrete to produce color are termed coloring admixtures. They should be colorfast, chemically stable, and have no adverse effect on the concrete. These pigments are generally inorganic oxides of the synthetic type.

BONDING AGENTS

Bonding agents are coatings that are used to increase the bond strength between green concrete and a new pour, between old and new concrete, and for bonding gypsum plaster or cement plaster to concrete.

One class of prepared agents includes polyvinyl chloride (PVC), polyvinyl acetate (PVA), styrene-butadiene (SBS), or acrylic latex mixed with portland cement (and sometimes sand). Prepared epoxy bonding agents are also used. In place of prepared agents, the user can make a slurry coat of neat portland cement and water, possibly adding an acrylic admixture to the mixing water.

A bonding agent that is nonreemulsifiable should be used at exterior locations and wherever moisture is prevalent.

One study in 1994 by the Canadian National Research Council's Institute for Research in Construction has concluded that a neat cement slurry over wetted concrete performed better than several latex bonding agents. However, there were advantages to latex materials in low temperature placements, as well as in work over porous or friable concrete. The study tested for compressive strength, modulus of rupture, bond strength, shear strength, and freeze–thaw resistance.

ARCHITECTURAL CAST-IN-PLACE CONCRETE

Since concrete is a free-forming plastic material, architects have long had a fascination with the architectural possibilities that a plastic yet structural material like concrete has to offer. The initial drawback to exploring these possibilities stemmed from the fact that concrete was associated with its long-time role as a structural material hidden in foundations, and covered when used in columns and supports. Additionally, since concrete was not construed as an architectural element, concrete contractors made no effort to develop techniques to safeguard finished work during the construction process. It was not until many years later that enterprising architects working with cooperating contractors developed the necessary criteria to extricate concrete from its use in the foundations of buildings and use it in various forms and finishes as a structural finish material featuring the aesthetic qualities inherent in most finish materials.

Architectural cast-in-place concrete can be achieved quite readily today with very little additional premium as a result of the pioneering effort of a number of architects and contractors. To ensure a more complete success, it is essential that drawings define the scope of architectural cast-in-place concrete to differentiate it from the normal structural concrete; likewise, there should be a separate specification section identified as "Architectural Cast-in-Place Concrete" so that contractors are forewarned regarding what is expected of them when performing this work. This strategy will alert the contractor to the fact that there are significant differences between this phase of the concrete work and that shown and specified for foundations, slabs, and concealed concrete.

DESIGNING

The decision to use architectural cast-in-place concrete requires an assessment of a number of factors that have an influence on its successful achievement. Proper configuration and size of a member must be considered since form sizes, reinforcing, placing, joint location, and form stripping will affect the member configuration.

The design will include location of vertical and horizontal expansion joints, construction and contraction joints, so that these occur at inconspicuous places or are highlighted to accent certain features.

Architects should avoid the use of large, flat, smooth, uninterrupted expanses of concrete surfaces, since these are the most difficult finishes to achieve uniformly. The use of textured form surfaces, induced textured finishes, and other relief features will minimize minor blemishes, whereas such blemishes will be exaggerated on wide, uninterrupted, smooth surfaces.

Since the structural aspects will have a significant influence on the ultimate outcome, it is essential that the structural engineer be involved at the outset. The engineer's input will be necessary to guide the architect so that the architectural appearance will not be marred by loading and stresses that may induce excessive cracking, spalling, or defects and thus detract from the aesthetic qualities.

PRELIMINARY INVESTIGATIONS

The sources of the major components of concrete—that is, portland cement and aggregates—should be investigated to determine whether satisfactory materials are available locally or whether, in the case of specific unusual aggregates, they must be obtained from distant sources, which will affect the cost.

Samples representing the desired surface, color, texture, and aggregate configuration should be cast, and the selected final architect's sample should be available for inspection and examination by prospective bidders. A minimum size of 18 or 24 inches square by 2 inches thick should suffice to display visual surface characteristics and depth to allow for mechanical texturing.

PRECONSTRUCTION CONFERENCES AND MOCK-UPS

A preconstruction conference should be held at which the architect, engineer, general contractor, and concrete subcontractor are present. At this conference the special requirements of the specifications and drawings can be explained by the architect and engineer, and the contractors can raise any questions regarding aspects of these documents that might impose impediments. Such a conference usually provides the basis for continuing dialogue, cooperation, and coordination throughout the concreting process.

A preconstruction mock-up is a valuable tool in the overall achievement of a successful concreting operation. A full-scale mock-up should be representative of the typical building module and should incorporate all of the elements that would normally be encountered during the course of construction. The building team that will be responsible for its execution should witness the construction of the forms, the placing of reinforcement, the taping of form joints, the placement of concrete accessories, the placement and vibration of concrete, the curing process, the removal of forms, the finishing techniques, and the patching and repairing of surface defects. The mock-up becomes in effect the proving ground for the efficacy of the design, the materials selections, and the construction procedures.

CONCRETE INGREDIENTS

Cement

To minimize color variation, cement of the same type and brand, from the same mill and raw material, should be used for all the architectural concrete on the same project. For large projects, there should be assurance from the manufacturer that ample supplies are available to satisfy the requirements of the project.

White cement can vary slightly in color between brands or mill sources and the same caveats apply to its use as for the normal gray cement. The use of mineral pigments to provide good color intensity and uniformity with white cement should be carefully selected and controlled.

Aggregates

As with cement, aggregates should be specified to come from one source for the duration of the project, and the supply should be adequate to fulfill the project requirements.

Where the surface will not be exposed to reveal the aggregate, the selection of the coarse aggregate will not affect or influence the appearance of the architectural concrete. The fine aggregate in an as-cast finish will, however, influence the appearance, especially if a darker fine aggregate is used with light-colored or white cement.

In cases where the aggregate is exposed, special attention must be paid to its selection and use. Aggregates with proven service records or those subjected to satisfactory laboratory testing and in some cases to petrographic analysis (ASTM C295) will serve admirably. Soft, nondurable aggregates including some marbles, limestones, and high-calcium materials are not suitable for exterior use. Aggregates containing iron-based minerals, which react with moisture and cause staining should be avoided for exterior use.

Where the surface of the concrete will be treated after hardening, consideration should be given to the choice of aggregate and the method of treatment (e.g., abrasive blasting, bushhammering, tooling, chemical retardation). For some aggregates the treatment selected may cause the aggregate to become dull or hazy and for others the appearance may be heightened due to the treatment. An early research program and investigation is essential to establish ultimate choices.

Admixtures

Air-entraining admixtures are useful both in increasing durability and improving workability, especially for harsh mixes.

The new superplasticizers offer a multitude of new advantages, that is, higher strength, lower water-cement ratios, and improved workability. The use of superplasticizers in exposed aggregate surfaces must be reviewed, since their fluidity may affect uniform appearance.

The use of calcium chloride as an accelerating admixture is not recommended, since it contributes to the corrosion of metal reinforcement and accessories and may mottle or darken architectural concrete.

It would be prudent to restrict the use of fly ash and admixtures and to obtain preliminary mix design information on those mixes containing admixtures, especially to verify color variation.

DESIGN MIXES

For as-cast finishes, design mixes do not differ materially from those used in good structural concrete practice. Improved workability, however, is essential in order that the concrete be brought into intimate contact with the forms, especially where textured forms are used so that the face pattern of the concrete will be a reproduction of the form face.

Where exposed aggregate finishes are required, the mix design is a factor of the aggregate sizes, depth of exposure, the cement factor, aggregate shapes, slump, and workability. Engineers and concrete testing laboratories qualified in this type of work should be sought out for their expertise.

REINFORCING AND ACCESSORIES

Reinforcing and metal accessories should be located at least 2 inches from an exposed exterior surface to ensure proper coverage and avoid surface staining due to rust. Where metal is closer than 2 inches from the surface, galvanizing should be considered.

Epoxy-coated steel reinforcing, as described in ASTM A775, can be considered in place of galvanized steel. It is still wise to keep the bars a full 2 in. (50 mm) from the face. It is even wiser to reduce the water permeability of the concrete by means of an HRWR admixture, fly ash, or slag cement. The extra protection is needed because epoxy-coated bars cannot be produced without some pinholes or holidays: ASTM A775 allows up to six per meter or one each foot. (Damaged galvanized bars are still protected by zinc metal that lies within a few millimeters of any small break in the coating.) Also, damage to epoxy-coated bars during shipping and placing is frequent.

Stainless steel tie wire should be used for tying reinforcement, to avoid staining exposed surfaces. The wire should be bent back, away from forms.

Supporting chairs, spacers, or bolsters should be stainless steel or high-density plastic of a color that matches the concrete, or galvanized steel with mushroom plastic-tipped legs of a color that matches the concrete. See Figure 3-6 for concrete accessories.

FORM MATERIALS

Architectural concrete can be textured by one of two basic methods: (1) molding it in the plastic state (off-the-form concrete), or (2) treating the hardened surface. These two methods offer a number of variations that give the architect a wide range of choices. In making decisions concerning selection of forming materials and the economics involved with varying types, it is essential to understand that lumber and plywood (except those with plastic overlays) are absorbent. Absorbent forms can affect the color of the concrete through variations in absorptivity. Increased absorption will reduce the water-cement ratio, resulting in a darkening of the concrete surface. There can be variations in this effect as a result of the different absorbencies of adjacent forms. In addition, as the forms are reused, the absorbency decreases and the darkening effect on the concrete surface becomes less. As a result of varying absorption rates and reuse of forms, considerable variation in concrete surface color will ensue.

Lumber

For off-the-form finishes, lumber is used with either a smooth finish such as flooring, or No. 1 grade, T&G surfaced boards, or a textured finish derived from lumber that has been rough sawn, sandblasted, or otherwise distressed to impart a textured finish to the concrete. See Figure 3-7 for lumber used as forms for varying surface results in concrete.

Finished Hardwood Lumber

Form surfaces made of flooring often utilize T&G, random length, end-matched $^{25}/_{32}$-inch-thick hardwood boards in either 2¼-inch or 3¼-inch width. Either a medium grade or the lowest grade recognized by

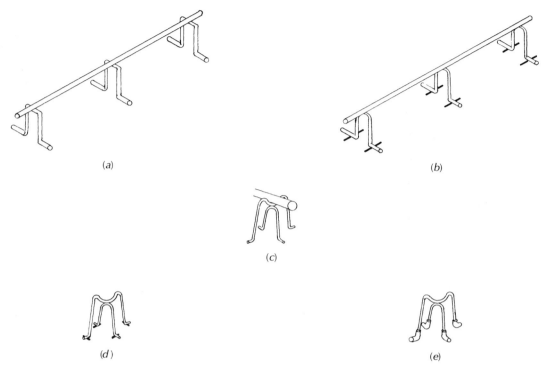

FIGURE 3-6   Concrete accessories. (*a*) Slab bolster, (*b*) stainless dowles on chairs, (*c*) individual high chair, (*d*) stainless dowels on chairs, (*e*) plastic protected legs.

National Oak Flooring Manufacturers Association can be used, as shown in Table 3-2, which is based on NOFMA hardwood grades.

It is best not to try to use hardwood flooring in curved forms. The flooring must be blind nailed to prevent staining of the concrete.

Rustic Lumber Formwork

A rustic forming surface is often achieved by laying up either smooth surfaced or rough sawn lumber in random thicknesses, widths, and lengths. Usually square edge lumber—hardwood or softwood—in a utility grade is employed, knots and all. As in all rustic work, the boards lend themselves to curves perpendicular to the board lengths, as long as the radius is kept larger than 10 feet: the larger the radius, the smaller the fins at the board joints that remain after stripping. Typically nominal 4-, 6-, and 8-inch-wide lumber may be used, sawn to ¾-, 1-, and 1¼-inch thicknesses, or planed to these same thicknesses less ⅛ inch. The ends of the random lengths should be staggered so as not to line up.

TABLE 3-2
HARDWOOD FLOORING GRADES
FOR CONCRETE FORMS

	Contains no knots or holes	Contains some knots, worm holes, or checks
Red oak and white oak	Select plain	No. 2 common
Maple, beech, birch, and pecan	Second grade	Third grade

Plywood

For architectural concrete, plywood with plastic overlays (medium or high density) produces a smooth, pleasing concrete surface. Using plywood without this overlay will result in concrete surfaces which reflect graining and boat patches—a telegraphing of the plywood onto the concrete.

(a)

(c)

(b)

FIGURE 3-7   Off-the-form concrete finishes. (a) No. 1 Grade T&G surfaced boards, (b) No. 1 Grade square edged boards. Note leakage at joints, (c) slash grain lumber, with surfaced edges drawn together to prevent leakage. *(Figure used with permission of Portland Cement Association.)*

Steel

Since steel is impervious, a uniform color usually results from its use. Since steel can be made to special sizes, the number of joints can be reduced. The thickness of the steel form is important to ensure against deflections between support members. To prevent rusting and staining, epoxy coatings or parting agents with rust inhibitors should be applied. Steel forms can provide between 50 and 100 reuses.

A plywood product developed in Finland made of a plastic-coated birch plywood, sometimes called Finn-Fir, is gaining increased popularity. This is due to its availability in larger special sizes, thereby reducing the number of joints, and its better-than-average reuse factor.

Fiberglass-Reinforced Plastic

Plastic forms usually are a product of cloth fiberglass or random glass fibers and polyester resin formulations. Since the form can be molded to almost any shape and size, jointing can be practically eliminated. Although this form may be the most expensive, the final cost is low because of its almost unlimited reuse, its light weight for erection, and its reduced number of joints.

FORMING

Since placing and consolidation of architectural concrete are more severe, there is a need to ensure that the formwork be more securely braced to avoid bulging, offsets, and similar distortions. This may include the addition of extra backup members beyond that required for usual structural needs. The requirements of ACI 347, "Recommended Practice for Concrete Formwork," require modification in order to assure more rigid formwork.

Form Liners

When off-the-form finishes are desired, form liners applied to the structural forms may be utilized. The form liner will impart its inherent texture to the finished concrete surface. Form liners may be plastic, such as rigid PVC, acrylonitrile-butadiene-styrene (ABS); fiberglass-reinforced polyester; urethane; or rubber mattings.

Form Joints

Leakage at form joints results in the formation of surface blemishes that cannot be eradicated, even with abrasive blasting. See Figure 3-8 for disfigurement resulting from leakage at joints.

The resulting blemish is characterized by visible aggregate adjacent to normal dense concrete, and a significant color change. The use of liners with joints offset from the joint of the structural forms will reduce leakage. A rustication strip at joints, securely fastened and sealed at the joint, will also minimize leakage. Silicone or other rubber-base sealants used at butt joints will help prevent leakage. Where exposure of

Circular Fiber Column Forms

These treated cardboard tubes are very strong due to their circular shape and are commonly available in lengths up to 20 feet, although lengths up to 50 feet have been fabricated on special order. Diameters range from 6 to 48 inches, in 2-inch increments.

A seamless grade circular fiber form is made by some producers. Specify this seamless grade for exposed, painted, or lightly textured work. Standard grade (or no mention of grade) should be used only if the columns or bollards will be covered with at least ¼ inch of cement plaster (stucco) or if the work will be fully concealed from view.

A mistake that is sometimes made is to detail annular recesses in columns or bollards that are to be cast using cylindrical fiber or plastic forms. It is almost impossible for the contractor to insert and secure rustication strips for reveals inside the form in such a way that they will stay in position during concrete placement and vibrating.

FIGURE 3-8 Leakage at joints is not eradicated even with sandblasting.

the aggregate is desired by blasting, bushhammering, or tooling, a thin, pressure-sensitive tape may be used to prevent leakage at joints. Taped joints should be inspected prior to placing concrete to make certain that the tape has not moved.

Form Ties

When designing for architectural concrete, consideration must be given to the type of tie system to be employed, since the selection of a specific type will have an influence on the aesthetics of the finished concrete.

Since each tie system leaves a characteristic hole, the architect must be familiar with the different systems and the profiles of the holes they create.

Ties used in architectural concrete should leave no metal closer than 1½ inches from the surface, and generally fall within the following types:

Snap tie. A stainless steel single member with a positive break-back feature and an optional plastic cone. Without the cone, the snap tie leaves the smallest hole.

Coil tie. An assembly utilizing reusable coil bolts, washers, and cones. Coil ties can be used for re-attachment of formwork or false work and are available in stainless or galvanized steel.

She-bolt tie. A type of tie and spreader bolt where the end fastenings are threaded into the end of the bolt, thereby eliminating cones and the size of the hole. The outer fastening devices are reusable.

He-bolt tie. A type of tie where the outer fastening devices are reusable, with an expendable female threaded unit left in the wall.

All of these ties leave round and relatively clean holes that may be patched flush, recessed, or plugged with cement cones to match surrounding concrete. Where the holes are to be exposed, a representative pattern of the tie layout should be drawn on the architectural drawings and be checked on shop drawings to ensure a consistent arrangement. See Figure 3-9 for concrete form ties.

PLACING AND CONSOLIDATING

The concrete contractor's crew and supervisor are the most important aspect of this phase of the concrete operation. They must be advised as to the special care and attention to be given to the material, which is to be construed as an architectural finish and as such must be handled judiciously from start to finish. A description of the methods and sequence of operations should be submitted by the contractor for approval by the architect and engineer. The preconstruction mock-up and conference should include the concrete contractor's key personnel so that they are impressed with the importance of their involvement.

The scheduling of ready-mix trucks to the site should be coordinated to avoid excessive mixing while waiting or delays in placing. Nonuniform mixing can contribute to nonuniformity of appearance, and delays result in the formation of cold joints.

Trucks used for conveying of architectural concrete should be cleaned after every delivery and should not be used for transporting other mixes to avoid contamination of the specified architectural mix.

Concrete should be placed or deposited (never poured) in uniform layers to prevent segregation and so that vibrators are not used to move concrete into final position. By placing concrete in final position rather than pouring, splatter is avoided on forms that may result in blemishes as it hardens on the form face.

Consolidation of concrete by vibrators is particularly important in architectural concrete to minimize surface voids and to blend lifts of concrete in successive layers to ensure uniformity of appearance. ACI 309, Consolidation of Concrete, provides a detailed recommendation on selection of vibrators and procedures.

SURFACE TREATMENT

Off-the-form finishes are those imparted to the concrete surface on the basis of the form or liner face and are indelibly etched into the surface during the casting and molding stage. Surface treatment implies exposing the fine or coarse aggregate of the hardened concrete after the forms are removed. This can be

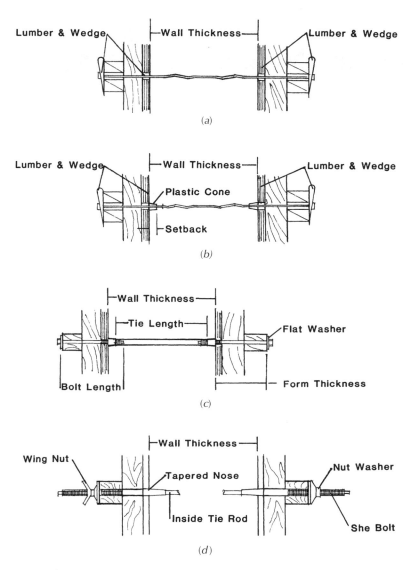

FIGURE 3-9 Representative form ties. (*a*) Snap ties, (*b*) Snap tie with plastic cone, (*c*) Coil tie with plastic cone, (*d*) She bolt.

accomplished by methods such as abrasive blasting (sandblasting), bushhammering, or mechanical tooling. Other means of exposure used less frequently are brushing and washing before the concrete reaches full strength, high-pressure water jet, surface retardation, and acid wash. As noted earlier, surface treatment will affect the appearance of the coarse aggregate and the selection of aggregate to enhance its appearance is paramount. See Table 3-3 for terminology and brief description of formed finishes recognized by ACI 301.

Abrasive Blasting (Sandblasting)

Sand or abrasive materials are used in blasting to reveal the mix ingredients of the concrete to specific depths to achieve certain architectural effects. These effects are illustrated in Figure 3-10 and are classified as follows:

1. *Brush blast.* A light scouring of the concrete surface is achieved that removes some surface blemishes and slightly exposes the fine aggregate.

      (a)   (b)   (c)   (d)

FIGURE 3-10 Degrees of abrasive blasting finish. (a) brush, (b) medium, (c) light, (d) heavy. *(From* Guide to Cast-In-Place Architectural Concrete *Practice (ACI 303R-74) (Rev. 1982) ACI Committee 303 American Concrete Institute.)*

2. *Light blast.* Approximately ¹⁄₁₆-inch depth of reveal, removing the surface skin sufficiently to expose fine aggregate with occasional exposure of coarse aggregate. A uniform color results from the primary influence of the fine aggregate.
3. *Medium blast.* Approximately ⅛- to ³⁄₁₆-inch depth of reveal, sufficient to expose coarse aggregate.
4. *Heavy blast.* Approximately ¼- to ½-inch depth of reveal, exposing the coarse aggregate to a maximum projection. A gap-graded aggregate is desirable for heavy blast texturing.

Blasting may be performed with abrasive materials such as silica sand (or wet sand, where air pollution standards prevail), aluminum carbide, or black slag particles. Blasting is performed at a time which is dictated by a number of factors, including scheduling, economics, strength of concrete, and hardness of aggregate. Prior trial tests on the mock-up will provide useful information, as will trial tests on basement walls, to establish criteria and techniques.

Generally, the time at which blasting is performed is related to the depth of reveal. The deeper the reveal, the sooner the blasting should be performed after removal of forms.

Bushhammering

Bushhammering is a process in which mechanically or hand-operated hammers remove the skin of hardened cement paste from the surface of the concrete

TABLE 3-3
CONCRETE FINISHES DESCRIBED IN ACI 301

		Term	Paragraph	
Formed finishes	**As-cast finishes**	Rough form finish	10.2.1	Default finish: Surfaces not exposed to view
		Smooth form finish	10.2.2	Default finish: Surfaces exposed to view
	Rubbed finishes	Smooth rubbed finish	10.3.1	Carborundum brick
		Grout cleaned finish	10.3.2	Apply grout/cork float or stone/burlap/damp cure
		Cork floated finish	10.3.3	Apply mortar/rubber float/stone/fog/cork float
	Architectural finishes	Textured finish	13.5.1	Usually from rough wood, metal, or rubber form liner
		Exposed aggregate finish	13.5.3	Provided by retarder, blast, or hammering
		Aggregate transfer finish	13.5.2	
		Scrubbed finish	13.5.3.1	Brush scrubbing of partially set concrete
		Sand blast finish	13.5.3.2	Specify degree of blasting
		Tooled finish	13.5.3.3	Specify chipping, brush hammering, etc.
		Applied finish preparation	13.5.4	For surfaces receiving plaster, tile, etc.

and fracture the coarse aggregate at the face of the concrete to reveal an attractive, varicolored, and textured surface.

Power hammers can be driven electrically or by compressed air. (See Figure 3-11 for pneumatic bushhammer.) Hand hammers are used for small as well as for restricted locations. By using this technique, the normal thickness of material removed from the face of the concrete is about ⅛ inch; however, by going over the surface more than once, a greater thickness of material can be removed.

Concrete should not be bushhammered until it has attained a strength of at least 3500 psi. Since it is economically unfeasible to do bushhammering until all forms have been removed, it generally cannot be started until three weeks or longer after casting, by which time the desired strength has been achieved.

Since bushhammering reveals the aggregate, the selection of the coarse and fine aggregate is of great importance. As a general rule, crushed-stone coarse aggregate is more suitable for bushhammering than uncrushed gravel. The use of uncrushed gravel can lead to bond failure between the aggregate and the matrix, which may cause some of the aggregate particles to become loose and fall out. The aggregates that behave best under bushhammering are those that can be cut or bruised without fracturing. Most of the igneous rocks, including granites, are well suited for this purpose. So are the hard limestones.

The treatment of arrises also requires careful design. Although one can use hand bushhammers right up to the arris, one should recognize the possibility of inadvertently damaging the sharp corner, thereby requiring repair which will be visible in the completed work. This problem can be dealt with in two ways: (1) by providing chamfered or rounded corners of at least 1½ inches radius; (2) by attaching a ¼-inch wood fillet at least 2 inches wide to form a plain margin up to which the tooling can be carried.

Mechanical Tooling

Fracturing of the surface of concrete other than bushhammering is produced by scaling, chipping, jackhammering, and tooling, using tools appropriate to the texture and configuration desired of the exposed aggregate surface.

Scaling is done with a pneumatic device that rotates and fractures the concrete close to the surface without imparting deep reveals.

Jackhammering is performed with a chiseled or pointed tool at a time when the concrete has attained a high strength so that coarse aggregates are not dislodged during the process.

Tooling produces reeded, striated, and corrugated patterns, depending upon the type of tool used and its orientation as the concrete is worked. Tooling should be kept uniform throughout the work to obtain the desired effect.

When concrete surfaces are fractured by bushhammering or tooling, the hammers, chisels, and tools must be inspected periodically to ensure that they are not worn to the point where the appearance of the fractured surface is no longer uniform.

PATCHING AND REPAIRING

For off-the-form concrete, patching and repairing obviously follow form removal. For exposed aggregate finishes, patching and repairing are best done after the abrasive blasting or mechanical tooling has exposed the aggregate, since the patch or repair can be damaged through the action of aggregate exposure.

Patching requires matching of the adjacent concrete surfaces in color and texture. Trial mixes of the cement used (gray, buff, or tan) should include some percentage of white cement as well as the original fine and coarse aggregate. The amount of white cement to be used will depend on dried samples that have cured a minimum of 7 days and preferably 28

FIGURE 3-11 Pneumatic bushhammer. *(Used with permission of Portland Cement Association.)*

days. Depending on the size of the patch, the coarse aggregate may either be part of the mix or hand placed after patching. The patching and repair are usually an artisan's task and require diligence and careful quality of work.

Where off-the-form concrete is to be patched, the patch should be compressed into place with the same form or liner used initially to obtain the same imprint to match adjoining surfaces.

Where necessary, areas to be patched should be cut back to sound material so that the patch will adhere to a sound surface.

ARCHITECTURAL PRECAST CONCRETE

Architectural precast concrete has been utilized since the 1920s, but it was not until the 1950s that its use became more widespread. This has come about through the introduction of more efficient, controlled, and coordinated manufacturing facilities. Such plants usually include organized production, quality control, more reliable quality of work through year-round employment, and the advantages of production in a controlled environment.

Architectural precast concrete has a number of functional advantages. These include incorporation of structure along with aesthetics as in the design of load-bearing elements, the inclusion of sound isolation, thermal insulation, and the ability to erect the elements at the site during all types of weather. Where structural requirements dictate, elements may be prestressed.

Since precast units are a manufactured product, it is essential to work with precasters during the early design development stages in order to get input from the precaster as to the design limitations with respect to manufacturing capabilities, transportation, and erection. The characteristics that precasters can provide information about include draft (the ability to strip the unit from the mold), sizes (limitations on transportation from plant to site), reinforcement (for handling and erection), connections, tolerances, (as-cast and erection), finishes, joint treatment, and the

use of master molds to keep costs in line. See Figure 3-12 for typical Precast Concrete Institute guidance on draft requirements.

MATERIALS

The materials used for precast units (i.e., cement, aggregate, coloring pigments, admixtures, etc.) are in general similar to those used in cast-in-place concrete, and with the similar admonition that all materials come from the same source for quality control.

SAMPLES AND MOCK-UPS

It is advisable to visit precasters' facilities and view the various samples, finishes, textures, and aggregates that are available. For major projects, the owner's expenditure of funds for the development of preconstruction samples and mock-ups would be advisable. The mock-up would serve as a jumping-off point to

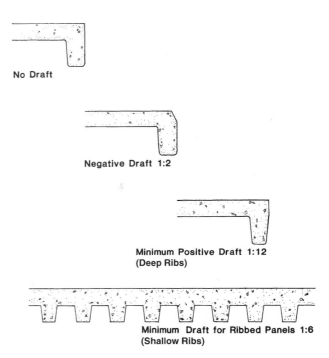

No Draft

Negative Draft 1:2

Minimum Positive Draft 1:12
(Deep Ribs)

Minimum Draft for Ribbed Panels 1:6
(Shallow Ribs)

FIGURE 3-12 Draft concepts for precast concrete. *(Courtesy of Precast/Prestressed Concrete Institute.)*

improve the appearance or make modifications to reduce cost without sacrificing the design intent.

Project samples should be at least 18 inches square by 1½ inches thick. For major projects, 4-foot-square samples should be requested after approval of the 18-inch-square samples, especially if exposed aggregate is involved. Mock-ups should be representative of a full-size, typical module.

FINISHES

There is an abundance of finishes for architectural precast concrete, giving the designer a wide choice. Essentially, finishes can be achieved during any one of three distinct phases in the manufacturing process: prior to casting, before hardening, and after hardening.

Prior to Casting

These finishes can be predetermined and obtained using forms and special materials within the forms:

1. *Smooth finishes.* Obtained simply by using nonporous forms such as fiberglass, steel, sealed plywood, overlaid plywood, or sealed concrete. The smooth-form surfaces impart a similar surface on the faces of precast architectural concrete.

2. *Textured finishes.* Result from using patterned or textured form liners such as rubber matting, textured fiberglass forms, rough sawn wood, or any variety of form which has been textured or patterned. See Figure 3-13 for special textured form liners.

3. *Special finishes.* Acquired by placing selected materials other than concreting materials at the bottom of the form. These materials may be ceramic tile, marble, granite, brick, or cobbles. They may be placed so as to obtain a complete facing, or they may be spaced so that a mortar joint is formed between them by the concrete matrix.

Before Hardening

These finishes are induced upon the faces in contact with the forms before hardening during the precasting process:

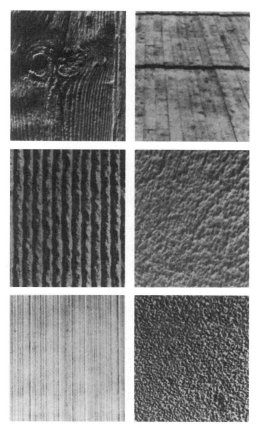

FIGURE 3-13 Various patterned and textured form liners attached to forms to produce precast textured surfaces. *(Courtesy of Precast/Prestressed Concrete Institute.)*

1. *Chemical retardation.* Retarders are applied to those surfaces of the forms which correspond to the panel faces selected for aggregate exposure. Upon placing the concrete in the forms, the retarders inhibit and slow down the chemical process involved in concrete hardening. The retarded cement paste is then removed by jetting with water and/or brushing. The degree of etching can result in any one of three textured surfaces:

a. *Light etch.* The outer surface of the cement paste and sand is removed, resulting in only a minute exposure of coarse aggregate, approximately ¹⁄₁₆ inch reveal.

b. *Medium etch.* A greater amount of the cement paste and sand is removed, resulting in a partial exposure of the coarse aggregate, approximately ⅛- to ⅜-inch reveal.

c. *Heavy etch.* A significant amount of cement and aggregate is removed, resulting in a uniform appearance of coarse aggregate, approximately ¼- to ¾-inch reveal.

2. *Treatment of exposed face.* These finishes are applied to the surfaces of the exposed face of the precast unit while it is still in the plastic state. Such a technique may consist of brooming, stippling, or using a roller with a textured surface to impart the desired texture on the exposed face.

After Hardening

These finishes are obtained after the precast units have been cast and have attained their required strength.

1. *Acid etching.* Light and medium etching, described previously for chemical retardation, may be achieved by brushing the units with acid or dipping in an acid bath.

2. *Abrasive blasting.* Light, medium, and heavy exposure of aggregates may be obtained by blasting the units with sand or an abrasive aggregate. The best possible appearance of the final surface will be achieved by using a gap-graded concrete mix of low slump and adequate cement content. Gap grading, or skip grading as it is sometimes called, omits some of the intermediate sizes of coarse aggregates normally included in standard concrete mix. Gap-graded mixes result in a uniform size distribution of the exposed coarse aggregate. Abrasive blasting may sometimes result in a dulling of the aggregate, including the loss of sharp edges.

3. *Bushhammering.* This is a process in which mechanically or hand-operated hammers remove the skin or hardened cement paste from the surface of the concrete, fracturing the coarse aggregate at the face of the concrete to reveal an attractive varicolored and textured surface. Power hammers are faced with a number of points and are driven by electricity or compressed air. Hand hammers are used for small areas as well as in restricted locations. The precast members should not be bushhammered until they have obtained a strength of about 3750 psi. The aggregates that behave best under bushhammering are those that can be cut or bruised without fracturing. Most of the igneous rocks, including granite, are well suited for this purpose, as are the

hard limestones. Since corners can be damaged during bushhammering, it is essential to use either a rounded corner or stay about 1 or 2 inches away from corners.

4. *Honing or polishing.* In this process the faces of exposed units are ground to the desired appearance by mechanical abraders, starting with a coarse grit and ultimately finishing with a fine grit.

Appropriate aggregates to use in exposed aggregate finishes are granite, quartz, quartzite, crystalline aggregates, onyx, pebbles, marble, glass, ceramics, silica sand, and special abrasives such as carborundum and alundum. In using aggregates in concrete it is recommended that a petrographic analysis be made to determine their suitability as a concrete aggregate.

Other textures and finishes are possible. However, it is recommended that procedures can be reviewed with precasting plants to determine feasibility and economics. See Figures 3-14 and 3-15 for illustrative examples of precast concrete buildings.

FIGURE 3-14 Typical precast panel being hoisted for placement on precast facade. *(Courtesy of Precast/Prestressed Concrete Institute.)*

FIGURE 3-15 Typical precast structure and an insert showing light aggregate exposure using a retarder. *(Courtesy of Precast/Pre-stressed Concrete Institute.)*

SPECIAL CONCRETING TECHNIQUES

PREPACKED CONCRETE

Prepacked concrete, also known as intrusion or grouted concrete, was developed essentially for placement under water, for mass concrete bridge piers, and for heavy concrete work such as the construction of steam hammer foundations and the restoration of dams. The same principle can be applied to architectural concrete finishes where specially selected aggregate is desired for exposure to obtain aesthetic effects.

With ordinary concrete, cement, fine and coarse aggregates, and water are mixed together before being placed within the formwork. In the prepacked method, the forms are filled with coarse aggregate only; subsequently, the interstices are grouted with a specially prepared mortar. The final stage in the process for architectural concrete is to expose the aggregate by removing the skin of cement by wire brushing, sandblasting, bushhammering, or grinding.

Structural concrete placed in normal construction contains approximately 1950 pounds of coarse aggregate per cubic yard. In prepacked concrete, about 2700 pounds of coarse aggregate per cubic yard can be obtained. This provides approximately 23 percent more aggregate available for exposure at the surface. In addition, with ordinary concrete, there can be segregation of aggregate so that some aggregate may not be near the surface upon exposure by sandblasting or wire brushing.

The materials for prepacked concrete should all be obtained from the same source in order to be of consistent quality and color; otherwise, variations in material will be reflected in the finished product.

The formwork for prepacked concrete must be of a high standard to prevent deformation and the loss of grout at joints, due to the internal pressure of the expanding mortar. To prevent loss of grout, joints in the formwork should be sealed.

The operation of placing the coarse aggregate can be assisted by the use of form vibrators. Generally, the coarse aggregate is placed in horizontal layers in a minimum void content. The selection of coarse aggregate is the choice of the architect; it may range in size from ⅜ inch to 3 inches. The aggregate should be washed thoroughly and well drained of water before use; care should be taken to prevent it from becoming contaminated while on the site. Generally, the coarse aggregate should not be dropped into the forms from heights greater than 5 feet.

The mortar used for prepacked concrete is usually an activated cement mortar having an intrusion aid. The intrusion aid contains a dispersing agent and a chemical that reacts with the alkalis of the cement to form a gas. Its action improves the workability of the grout, reduces bleeding, and causes a slight expansion before final setting.

The mortar is placed during the grouting process through 1-inch-diameter steel pipes, placed vertically and spaced about 2 feet O.C. or as necessary to insure uniform placement of grout. Initially, the outlet end of the pipe is about 2 inches above the bottom of the formwork. The pipes are raised as the grout rises. After grouting has progressed sufficiently, the pipes should extend to a depth of 12 inches in the grout. In order to check the level of the grout in the forms, holes are sometimes bored in the forms that can be plugged later. Another means of checking grout levels is to install small lights of acrylic plastic in the forms so that the grout may be seen. Forms are generally vibrated during the grout intrusion process to help distribute the grout uniformly.

The sandblasting of the surface to expose the aggregate should be carried out as soon as possible after the forms have been stripped.

CYCLOPEAN CONCRETE

Cyclopean concrete is an example in which pre-packed concrete is used to obtain a unique architectural effect with boulder-size aggregate.

Concrete walls using exposed granite aggregate from 4 to 8 inches in size have been erected for dormitories at Yale University. The following sequence was used in the construction of 12-inch-thick bearing walls:

The back form was erected to a full 8 feet height, and the front form was erected in 2-foot increments to facilitate placing the stone. The granite was tipped into the forms from wheelbarrows, but was hand-placed where necessary.

The forms were coated with a retarder to delay the set of the grout surface. Two-inch-diameter grout pipes, placed 4 feet on centers, extended to the bottom of the forms.

A 1:2 grout of soupy consistency was pumped into the forms to fill the voids in the stone, and the grout pipes were slowly raised as the grout rose in the forms. The lower ends of the pipes were kept below the surface of the grout, and the grout elevation was determined by tapping the forms. The forms were stripped the following day, and the grout was scraped off the surface of the stone. See Figure 3-16 for typical cyclopean concrete test panel.

SLIP FORMING

Slip forming is a technique using sliding forms that move continuously and shape the concrete as they slide over the freshly placed mix. Vertical slip forms have been used to shape silos, storage bins, and chimneys for industrial uses, but have been adapted architecturally to shape elevator towers, stair towers, and vertical enclosing elements of buildings.

Steel forms are used and move at a rate of about 6 to 12 inches per hour, with the process continuing

FIGURE 3-16 Test panel of cyclopean granite placed by prepacked method.

around the clock, and with the forms moving so that they leave the formed concrete only after concrete is strong enough to retain its shape and support its own weight. The procedure is akin to an extrusion process.

A jacking system raises the forms and the working deck assembly, which in turn are supported on steel rods embedded in the concrete. Since it is a 24-hour operation, the logistics for supplying the concrete and manpower require careful planning.

Although a smooth finish is cast, the hardened surface can be treated by abrasive blasting or bush-hammering to obtain the required exposed aggregate texture. Design mixes incorporating special aggregates to be exposed may be used as in any architectural concrete work.

TILT-UP CONSTRUCTION

In the tilt-up system, panels of concrete are cast in a horizontal position, on a flat, smooth, and level bed with a parting agent between the bed and the panel. Both load-bearing and non-load-bearing wall panels may be cast in this manner with required reinforcement, and if needed with prestressing strands.

The panels are then rotated about their bottom edges into a vertical position and secured to the structure through connections embedded in the panels.

For architectural purposes, exposed aggregate surfaces can be obtained by using the sand embedment method. In this method, a layer of fine sand is spread over the bottom of the form to a depth of about one-third the diameter of the aggregate. Pieces of aggregate are pushed into the sand to obtain the densest possible coverage.

After the aggregate is in place, water is sprayed to settle the sand around the aggregate so that each piece is embedded securely to a depth of about one-half to one-third the diameter.

Steel reinforcement is placed on plastic or galvanized chairs, and the concrete is carefully placed over the embedded aggregate.

As an alternate method, the aggregate can be placed on the form and then sprinkled with fine, white, dry sand to a depth of one-half to one-third the aggregate.

After proper curing, the panels are raised, and any sand clinging to the exposed aggregate is removed by brushing, airblasting, or washing with water. See Figure 3-17 for typical tilt-up construction.

FIGURE 3-17 Precast panel being tilted up into position. *(Used with permission of Portland Cement Association.)*

FORMS FOR ARCHITECTURAL CONCRETE

Structural concrete using normal or lightweight aggregates with off-the-form finishes is used to obtain unusual shapes due to the plasticity of concrete. These shapes are achieved through cast-in-place procedures or precast and prestressed techniques to develop unusual architectural forms.

CONCRETE SLABS

The simpler shapes are those used for floor–ceiling concrete slabs as follows: flat slab, flat plate, and ribbed slab.

Flat Slab

A concrete slab reinforced in two or more directions, generally without beams or girders. The supports are columns with dropped panels which pick up the floor loads. Generally this construction is used for bays that are almost square and require heavy loading, as in warehouses, garages, and so forth. See Figure 3-18 for flat slab construction.

Flat Plate

Where lighter floor loads are encountered, as in apartment buildings, office structures, dormitories, and so forth, a modified flat slab is used without drop panels. This type of construction provides a flat continuous ceiling without breaks, making for easier subdivision of like spaces. See Figure 3-19 for flat plate construction.

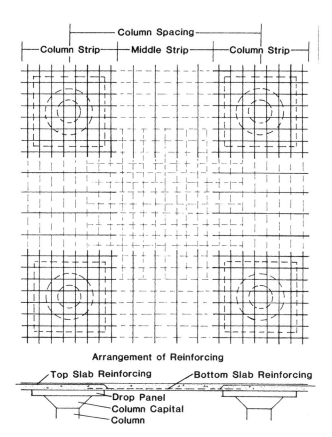

Arrangement of Reinforcing

FIGURE 3-18 Two-way flat slab. *(Reprinted from Huntington and Mickadeit,* Building Construction, *5th Ed., New York: John Wiley & Sons, Inc., 1981.)*

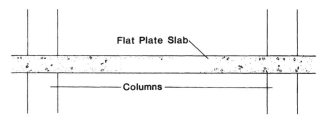

FIGURE 3-19 Flat-plate floor construction.

Folded Plate

This construction consists of thin, flat elements of concrete, connected together to form a series of triangles when viewed from the end (similar to accordion folds), and capable of carrying a load over a long span. See Figure 3-21 for folded plate construction.

Ribbed Slab

A ribbed slab is a reinforced concrete panel consisting of a thin slab reinforced with a series of ribs. When the ribs are in two directions it produces a waffle pattern. See Figure 3-20 for ribbed slab construction.

SHELLS, ARCHES, AND DOMES

Unusual shapes are obtained through casting or precasting and require competent structural engineers to work with the architectural designer to achieve a wide multitude of thin shell constructions. Thin shell construction is characterized by relatively thin slabs and web sections as follows: folded plate, arches, and domes.

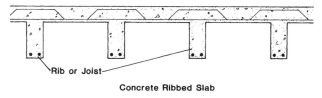

Concrete Ribbed Slab

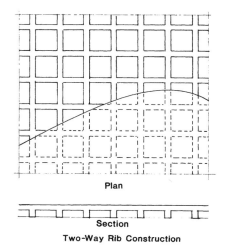

Plan

Section

Two-Way Rib Construction

FIGURE 3-20 Ribbed slabs. *(Reprinted from Huntington and Mickadeit,* Building Construction, *5th Ed., New York: John Wiley and Sons, Inc., 1981.)*

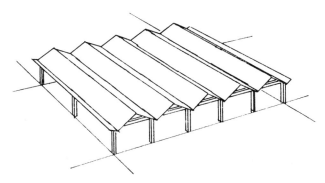

FIGURE 3-21 Folded plate roof. *(Reprinted from Huntington and Mickadeit, Building Construction, 5th Ed., New York: John Wiley & Sons, Inc., 1981.)*

Arches

The curved arch or barrel arch forms an opening width (span) and a height (rise) resembling a barrel with a constant cross section. Barrel arches are used extensively for long spans as roofs over armories, gymnasiums, field houses, and so forth. See Figure 3-22 for barrel shell roof.

Domes

Where circular structures are designed, such as gymnasia, field houses, and auditoria, the accompanying roof is usually a dome-shaped structure. The dome acts as a membrane and has a tension ring at its major

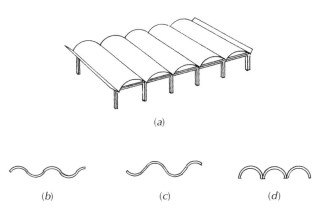

FIGURE 3-22 Barrel shell roof. *(Reprinted from Huntington and Mickadeit, Building Construction, 5th Ed., New York: John Wiley & Sons, Inc., 1981.)*

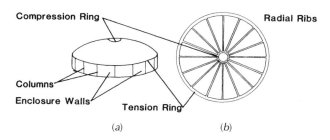

FIGURE 3-23 Circular dome roof. *(a)* Dome. *(b)* Pattern with radial ribs. *(Reprinted from Huntington and Mickadeit, Building Construction, 5th Ed., New York: John Wiley & Sons, Inc., 1981.)*

circumference and a compression ring at the top of the dome. Some domes are often constructed using a mound of earth as the form, then lifted into final position after the concrete has set. See Figure 3-23 for circular dome roof.

PROTECTION OF ARCHITECTURAL CONCRETE

Architectural concrete, either precast or cast-in-place, often requires a clear protective sealer to overcome a number of concerns as follows: (1) temporary mottling and darkening of the surface after a rainstorm, (2) accretion of dirt and soot on exposed aggregate surfaces, (3) change in color of the matrix due to attack by atmospheric pollutants, and (4) the etching of gray and bronze glass below when alkalis leach from the concrete onto the glass.

To overcome these problems, one may use an application of clear coating to preserve the initial appearance of exposed concrete. Generally, the preferred coating should be clear, water repellent, and a breathing type. These coatings function primarily as follows: (1) by reducing water penetration, they minimize mottling and darkening due to rainstorms; (2) by reducing water penetration, free alkali in concrete is not leached out onto the concrete; (3) they tend to make the surface self-cleaning, reducing the accumulation of dirt; (4) they tend to reduce atmospheric attack on the cement matrix; and (5) the breathing qualities of the coatings provide for uniform weathering.

Many coating types have been marketed by manufacturers as a panacea for the problems outlined above. However, they are not without their own contributory problems. Some have a relatively short life span. Some actually attract soot. Some develop a glossy appearance that changes the architectural effect. Some darken the exposed aggregate and the cement matrix considerably, thereby altering the architectural appearance.

The ideal coating should be clear, nondiscoloring, long lasting, and should not make any discernible change in the color of the aggregate or in that of the matrix.

The Portland Cement Association investigated a wide variety of clear coatings and published its findings in Bulletin D137, 1968, "Clear Coatings for Exposed Architectural Concrete." Sixty products were investigated to determine their effectiveness in protecting exposed aggregate concrete and smooth concrete surfaces against the elements. These coatings consisted of acrylics, polyurethanes, polyesters, silicones, waxes, epoxies, styrenes, and in some products, mixtures of these chemical formulations.

In the accelerated tests, the PCA found that by and large, the coatings based on a methyl methacrylate formulation provided better protection on exposed surfaces than other types of coatings. The laboratory test results were confirmed by the outdoor weathering exposure. Similarly, on smooth concrete surfaces, methyl methacrylate coatings with a higher solids content gave better protection. Generally, the polyurethanes, polyesters, and epoxies tended to cause a glossy appearance and created a yellowing or darkening effect.

PERFORMANCE REQUIREMENTS

When selecting, designing, specifying and constructing in concrete, it would be advantageous to refer to Chapter 1 to ensure that the pertinent performance requirements are reviewed. An example for concrete would be the following analysis.

STRUCTURAL SERVICEABILITY

Concrete is excellent in compression and can be designed for tension loads by conventional reinforcement or by prestressing. Prestressing may also be used to introduce stresses in the material by opposing stresses from the service loads whereby the tensile stresses may be practically eliminated.

For architectural concrete, rather than being simply an appendage, the concrete should be designed for load bearing or other structural functions to reduce the cost of construction, by serving both as the structural element and the architectural element.

FIRE SAFETY

Concrete is not combustible; therefore it does not develop any of the products of combustion associated with fire. However, concrete should be designed for the required hours of fire rating based on ASTM E119, and also by rational design taking into account aspects of fire resistance such as heat transmission, flame penetration, and the maintenance of structural capability. Where penetrations or joints occur in the concrete, there are now materials available such as incombustible foam and gasket materials to provide adequate hourly fire resistance ratings for the penetrations and joints.

HABITABILITY

Thermal Properties

While concrete does not possess insulating qualities, its bulk does provide it with a heat or cold reservoir since it gives off heat (or cold) rather slowly. Consideration should be given to the use of insulation on the inside face of walls, or below floors of exposed overhangs. In precast wall panels insulation can be introduced between the inner and outer wythe.

Acoustic Properties

Noise transmission through concrete walls is reduced due to its bulk and density. For floors however, impact or tapping noises require sound deadening through the judicious selection of floor covering materials. Stair elements may have neoprene bearing pads at supports to reduce sounds from impact loads.

Water Permeability

Properly designed and constructed, concrete is usually impervious to water. However the introduction of waterproofing, dampproofing, waterstops, or other design elements should be considered by an investigation of the proposed design and use.

Hygiene, Comfort, Safety

Walks, steps, and ramps subjected to water from rain should have broomed finishes or applications of alundum or carborundum to prevent slipping. Exposed concrete walkways or stairs on interiors should be hardened through proper curing to inhibit dusting.

DURABILITY

While structural concrete in foundations may be subjected to attack by sulfates in the soil and concrete used for work in seawater may be subject to attack by saline salts, our concern is for the durability of exposed architectural concrete. The durability of such concrete exposed to the weather may be subject to freeze–thaw cycling and may be affected by chemical deicing salts.

Environments may be harsh in nature and may exert internal forces on concrete containing moisture. The use of deicing chemicals heighten the problems by increasing these forces.

ACI Standard 301, Specifications for Structural Concrete for Building, requires the use of air entrainment and a limitation on the water-cement ratio to control durability.

COMPATIBILITY

Differing materials may interact with one another as outlined in Chapter 1. In the first instance the ingredients used to make concrete must be compatible. Since new coarse aggregates often are used for the first time to obtain a unique architectural effect it is essential to run a petrographic test to insure that the aggregate is suitable for use in concrete.

In addition, the detailing of concrete on a drawing may be such that rain water drains from a concrete surface onto a bronze or gray solar tinted glass. The alkalies leached from the concrete may etch the glass vividly as a result of the detailing.

One must be alert to all of those possibilities, and a check for compatibility with adjacent materials must be made to assure a problem-free solution.

CONCRETE FLOORS

The effect of well designed and executed concrete on the vertical surfaces and ceilings of a building is sometimes marred by poor concrete floor surfaces—inside and outside. The designer has several options by which floors can be brought to the same level of quality as architectural concrete. See Table 3-4 for terminology and brief descriptions of slab finishes recognized by ACI 301.

INTERIOR SLABS ON GRADE

Support slabs on compacted, permeable fill that drains moisture to well compacted, permeable soil below. An ideal fill material is crushed stone with a top course of fine particles to provide a surface that will take construction traffic without rutting, that will not puncture the moisture (or vapor) barrier, and that will permit the lateral migration of moisture beneath the slab. The slab should not be restrained from settling slightly in service; it is better to allow for some settlement than to invite fracture.

TABLE 3-4
CONCRETE SLAB FINISHES IN ACI 301

		Term	Paragraph	
Slab finishes	Integral finishes	Scratched finish	11.7.1	Default finish: Surfaces receiving bonded cementitious material. Class C levelness tolerance.
		Floated finish	11.7.2	Default finish: Surfaces receiving roofing, waterproofing, sand bed terrazzo. Class B.
		Limestone textured troweled finish	Not in 301	Same as floated, but with coarse crushed ice under float. Class B or A.
		Troweled finish	11.7.3	Default finish: Floors intended as walking surfaces and receiving floor coverings. Class B or A.
		Broom (belt) finish	11.7.4	Default finish: Sidewalks, garage floors, and ramps. Class B.
		Exposed aggregate finish	11.7.9	Level, seed with aggregate. Class B.
	Dry shake finishes	Mineral aggregate finish	11.7.6	Float-in aggregate in 2 passes. Trowel. Class B.
		Metallic aggregate finish	11.7.6	Float-in aggregate in 2 passes. Trowel. Class B.
		Nonslip (abrasive aggregate) Finish	11.7.7	Default finish: Exterior platforms, steps, and landings; interior and exterior pedestrian ramps. 2.5 lb./sf. min. Class B.
	Two course Slab finishes (depress slab ¾ to 1 in.)	Heavy duty topping, same day	11.7.5.3	Spread topping when slab is partly set. Compact, float, and trowel. Class B or A.
		Heavy duty topping, deferred	11.7.5.4	Scratch slab. Wet cure 3 days. Dampen, apply bonding agent. Spread topping, compact, float, & trowel. Class B or A.

Finishing Tolerances:
Class C: Plane within ¼ in. in 2 ft.
Class B: Plane within ¼ in. in 10 ft.
Class A: Plane within ⅛ in. in 10 ft.
      (difficult to obtain)

An effective moisture barrier should be placed over the compacted fill. Not only should the membrane material have a moisture transmission rating of less than 0.30 perms, but also a strong, sealable material must be chosen that will resist moisture migration after punishing work has been done over it. In undemanding work, wide sheets of 0.006 in. (0.15 mm) polyethylene, lapped at least 4 in. (25 mm) at sides and ends, will stay in place reasonably well during concrete placement. Precautions must be taken to seal penetrations and to ensure that punctures are not made as the concrete is placed, moved, and vibrated. Heavy asphalt-impregnated board material with asphalt-sealed lap joints is used in more demanding situations. These situations include floors that are to receive sensitive finishes such as wood or marble as well as floors over which sensitive objects such as

wood furniture or electronic equipment will be placed.

Although not common practice, the Portland Cement Association (PCA) recommends that a 3-in. (75-mm)-thick layer of sand be placed over the moisture barrier to minimize slab warping, to allow some downward moisture loss from the wet concrete, to reduce drag friction as the concrete contracts, and to protect the moisture barrier from puncture.

For slab-on-grade concrete, American Concrete Institute's ACI 301 recommends that the designer specify higher than the ordinary $f'_c = 3000$ psi compressive strength—and stiffer slump values. See Table 3-5 for typical slab uses and recommended higher strengths.

According to PCA's "Concrete Floors on Ground," reinforcing is generally not needed in slabs that are

TABLE 3-5
CONCRETE FOR SLABS-ON-GRADE
FOLLOWING ACI 301

Use	Minimum f'_c, psi	Maximum slump, inches
Offices, churches, schools, hospitals, residences	3500	4
Garage floors	3500	4
Light industrial, commercial	4000	3
Single course industrial floors, integral topping	4500	3
Topping for steel-tire vehicles, and conditions of severe abrasion	5000–8000	1

uniformly supported on a well compacted base. The primary purpose of steel or plastic fiber reinforcement is to hold together any cracks that may occur. The reinforcing does not itself prevent cracking, nor does it significantly increase the strength of a well supported floor.

EXTERIOR SLABS ON GRADE

Exterior concrete slabs over the ground are constructed similarly to interior slabs in terms of concrete strength, but more attention is given to jointing because of wider variations in service temperature and exposure to water.

An exterior slab does not need porous fill or a moisture barrier beneath; uniformly graded fill without rocks, well compacted, is sufficient. In freezing climates it is important to keep water from entering the subgrade either from the top or under the slab edges. This is usually accomplished by selecting a joint sealer that will not admit water even after years of joint flexure and by blocking moisture entry at the slab edge by turning it down or erecting some other sort of barrier.

The finish of an exterior slab is always more rough than would be suitable at the interior. ACI 301 specifies *default* finishes for slip-prone surfaces, outside or inside. These are required of a contractor unless otherwise specified:

- Sidewalks   Broom finish
- Garage floors   Broom finish
- Vehicular ramps   Broom finish
- Steps, landings, and platforms   Nonslip finish
- Pedestrian ramps   Nonslip finish

In addition, the designer will usually want to specify that the broom finish be applied to all vehicular surfaces on the site such as roads, pads, and approaches.

Nonslip finish is specified by ACI 301 as a dry shake application of metallic aggregate to the already floated concrete surface. The dry shake aggregate is applied in two passes that total at least 25 pounds per 100 square feet, with additional floating after each pass. At that point the surface is given a fourth finishing operation: either a brooming, a troweling, or another floating, which choice must be specified in the contract documents.

CONTROL, ISOLATION, AND CONSTRUCTION JOINTS

The three basic types of joints in interior and exterior concrete slabs on grade are usually planned and positioned as analyzed by the structural engineer. The chapter "Jointing Practice" in PCA's "Concrete Floors on Ground" provides a summary of materials and good practice.

Control Joints

Control joints (sometimes called *contraction joints*) are the basic defense against random shrinkage cracking and are the most common joint type. If control joints every 20 to 30 feet on centers each way are unacceptable, reinforcing should be used in the slab. The column grid spacing in the structure can be used as a convenient control joint interval. Control joints are often sawed to one-fifth the green slab thickness then later blown clean and filled with soft material to keep the kerf from filling with dirt. They can also be formed with key-profile steel or fiber strips as described later for construction joints.

Isolation Joints

Isolation joints are placed around penetrating columns and at slab perimeters. Isolation extends through the full thickness of the slab and is usually executed with preformed, resilient joint filler material. Perimeter isolation usually accounts for the second greatest total joint length in the work. In exterior work, isolation joints are often termed *expansion joints* since they protect slabs from heaving in hot weather. The filler strips for isolation (expansion) joints can be of seven basic compositions, listed here roughly in ascending order of cost:

1. Unfaced asphalt-impregnated cane or wood fiber (ASTM D1751, Nonextruding Type)
2. Asphalt impregnated wood fiber or glass fiber felt-faced sandwich, filled with mineral filler and/or fibered asphalt mastic (ASTM D994; tends to permanently extrude in service)
3. Unfaced cork (ASTM D1752, Type II)
4. Unfaced self-expanding cork (ASTM D1752, Type III)
5. Unfaced sponge rubber (ASTM D1752, Type I)
6. Asphalt wood fiber or glass fiber felt-faced sandwich, filled with asphalt-bound cork granules (ASTM D1751, Resilient Type)
7. Coal tar or glass felt-faced sandwich, filled with fibered coal tar mastic (also included in ASTM D994, but with no Type distinction made; tends to permanently extrude in service)

Designers have a hard time remembering these joint filler classifications, one of the most confused areas of American standard making. It is often necessary to search through ASTM standards to identify and specify the level of quality needed for a project.

Construction Joints

Construction joints are formed at "cold joints"—lines where concrete placement stops for the day. A construction joint is often formed with 16 gage or 18 gage steel—or ⅛-inch-thick stiff fiber—with a key-shaped profile. The joint form is installed either the full thickness of the slab or ¼ inch less with a removable cap for later joint sealing. Alternatively, isolation joint filler material, suitably supported, can be used to form a construction joint, but the resulting concrete-to-concrete interface will have no key-shaped profile to restrain differential vertical movement.

Joint Filling

The method of filling sawed or formed control joint kerfs, and the tops of isolation joint and construction joint fillers which have properly been held ¼ to ½ inch below the surface of the concrete deserves the designer's attention. For floors which will receive only foot traffic, a sealant such as urethane with an ASTM D2240 Durometer A Scale hardness of 40 to 60 is adequate. But where hard-wheeled vehicles use the slab, the edges of the kerf or recess will crumble. In the past, loose sand has been swept in the joints, but this creates an ongoing clean-up problem. Pouring molten lead had been tried, but the solid lead has no resilience or healing property. The most effective material is one with a hardness and resilience midway between urethane and lead, such as a semirigid epoxy formulated especially for this purpose and marketed by several producers. This semirigid epoxy has an ASTM D2240 Durometer A Scale hardness of approximately 80.

FLATNESS AND LEVELNESS

American Concrete Institute's Specification for Structural Concrete for Buildings, ACI 301-84(88), defines three classes of finish tolerance in Chapter 11, Slabs, each class of flatness (or smoothness) determined by a 10-ft straightedge placed anywhere on the slab in any direction:

Class A must be planed to within ⅛ in. in 10 ft.
Class B must be planed to within ¼ in. in 10 ft.
Class C must be planed to within ¼ in. in 2 ft.

Architects often specify Class A, which contractors and the ACI have pointed out for years is difficult to attain in all work. Even when attained, Class A flatness is not flat enough for all building functions—factory floors and rolling file room floors being among them.

F-Number System

ASTM and ACI came up with a procedure and a measure for floor flatness and floor levelness in the 1980s which, though time consuming and expensive to execute, can ensure flatter, more level floors. The ASTM E1155 Test Method for Determining Floor Flatness and Levelness Using the F-number System requires that test sections and measurement paths be laid out, that special instruments be used to take measurements, and that a prescribed statistical procedure be used to rate each part of the floor for F_F, flatness, and F_L, levelness.

F_F expresses the maximum floor curvatures, up and down, allowed over 24 in. (610 mm). It is computed on the basis of successive 12-in. (305-mm)-elevation differentials, usually obtained by running a small, self-propelled robot over a prescribed course.

F_L expresses the relative conformity of the floor surface to a horizontal plane as measured over a 10 ft (3 m) distance.

Flatness and Levelness Norms

Of F_F, or flatness, values, ACI has reported that from nationwide feedback, F_F45 appears to be about the maximum flatness that a knowledgeable contractor would agree to deliver on a large floor with a hardened surface. A superflat floor, which is needed for slabs such as those for high-bay, narrow-aisle, mechanized warehouses, may require a flatness of F_F100 or higher. In buildings with hardened slab surfaces, the majority have been measured to fall between F_F25 and F_F40 with equally satisfactory results and service. For high-quality floor slabs in offices, classrooms, and industrial space a flatness of F_F20 and F_F35 is often going to be sufficient to the needs of the occupant. In the interest of practicality and economy, arbitrarily high F_F numbers should be avoided.

Wyndham Hotel, Dallas, TX: granite—Sunset Red, polished finish. Dahl/Braden & Chapman, Architects. *(Courtesy of Cold Spring Granite Company.)*

4

MASONRY

Masonry has been generally defined as an assembly of brick, stone, concrete masonry units, structural clay tile, architectural terra cotta, glass block, gypsum block, or similar material bonded together with mortar to form walls and other parts of buildings. However, since modern-day technology is outpacing the redefinition of terms, it might be more practical, for our purpose, to discuss and review these materials by dividing them into two basic categories: (1) unit masonry and (2) stone.

Unit masonry materials are primarily manufactured units of a size that are generally handled and erected by one mason. However, there are exceptions to this simple definition in that prefabricated panels of brick and concrete masonry units require several masons to erect them. Unit masonry includes such materials as:

Brick	Architectural terra cotta
Concrete block and	Ceramic veneer
concrete brick	Glass block
Structural clay tile	Gypsum block
Structural facing tile	Adobe brick

Stone is primarily a natural quarried material that can be assembled with mortar or which in modern-day technology can be erected and installed with metal anchors and fasteners and jointed with sealants, without the use of mortar. Stone materials that are used for building applications include:

Granite
Limestone
Marble
Sandstone
Slate
Travertine

MASONRY STANDARDS

Basic building code requirements for masonry structures covering their engineering and construction are contained in a document jointly developed and endorsed by the American Concrete Institute, American Society of Civil Engineers, and The Masonry Society. The document, commonly referred to as ACI 530, is often given its full designation: ACI530/ASCE5/ TMS402. The Brick Institute of America, Mason Contractors Association of America, National Concrete Masonry Association, National Lime Association, and Portland Cement Association supported the development of this standard, which brings together the major masonry associations in an unprecedented joint effort toward documenting sound masonry construction on the basis of engineering principles.

An additional document, ACI 530.1 (ACI530.1/ ASCE6/TMS602) provides actual specifications for masonry materials placing, bonding, and anchoring. ACI 530.1 can be used as the basis for the engineering aspects of masonry specifications. Additional information must be provided for the specifications—some of a structural and some of an appearance nature.

For instance, one of the four types of ASTM C270 mortar must be selected. If a lintel-bearing dimension of more than 4 in. (100 mm) is desired, that too must be specified. Architectural information that must be supplied by the specifier is the insulation of cavity

walls, weep hole and flashing design, bond patterns, mortar joint profile, belt courses, and brick lintels. Workmanship expectations—such as that vertical joints in a wall line up, or the maximum number of closers allowed in any one course—must also be added.

BRICK

MANUFACTURE

Brick is made from clay or shale that is finely ground, mixed with water, molded to the desired shape, dried, and fired in a kiln. Three processes are used in the manufacture of brick today.

Stiff-Mud process. About 12 to 15 percent water is added to the clay. After thorough mixing, the mixture is extruded through a die and cut with a tightly stretched wire.

Soft-Mud process. About 20 to 30 percent water is added to the clay to produce a uniform plastic mass. The mixture is placed in molds by hand or machine. To prevent the mix from sticking to the molds, the molds are either wetted or sanded. If water is used as the lubricant the brick is called *water-struck;* if sand is used it is called *sandstruck.*

Dry-Press process. Using clays of low plasticity and the addition of up to about 10 percent water, the mixture is placed in steel molds and subjected to pressures of 500 to 1500 psi, producing the most accurately formed brick.

SIZES

Brick is manufactured in a number of sizes. Few manufacturers make all sizes, and new sizes are added and less popular ones are removed as design requirements change. For example, with the advent of high-rise apartments, econo and jumbo sizes were introduced to provide a face size of a scale consistent with the

TABLE 4-1
BRICK SIZES

	Width (in.)	Height (in.)	Length (in.)
Standard	3¾	2¼	8
Modular	3¾	2½	7⅝
Roman	3¾	1⅝	12
Norman	3¾	2¼	12
Econo	3⅝	3⅝	7⅝
Jumbo	3⅝	7⅝	7⅝

scale of the building, to reduce the cost of masonry construction, and to keep masonry competitive with other facing materials. Some of the more common sizes are shown in Table 4-1.

Since size and availability vary in many localities, it is wise to check sizes before proceeding with a design or specifying.

SPECIAL SHAPES

Where special shapes are required to fulfill a design requirement, as for moldings, completing an unusual opening, or for cladding circular columns, consult brick manufacturers being considered for the project to determine whether they can produce the shapes required or the modifications to be made to the design to stay within the limitations of their manufacturing capabilities.

Quite often brick can be cut or clipped to fit certain conditions of the design. However, more refined shapes may have to be specially molded. See Figure 4-1 for special shapes. Color variation may occur due to separate firing of special shapes. Consult with manufacturers and obtain samples to verify color variation.

BUILDING BRICK

Formerly called *common brick,* building brick is manufactured to meet the requirements of ASTM C62. In many instances building brick has been utilized intentionally as facing brick, depending upon its color after firing and whether its face has been textured by scoring, combing, wire cutting, or otherwise

treated to provide a unique surface appearance.

Building Brick is classified under ASTM C62 as to durability in accordance with the following criteria:

Grade SW. Severe weathering for exposure to heavy rainfall and freezing

Grade MW. Moderate weathering for exposure to average moisture and minor freezing

Grade NW. Negligible weathering for exposure to moisture and freezing

A Weathering Index Map of North America shown in Figure 4-2 indicates those areas subject to severe, moderate, and negligible weathering.

Building brick, the commonplace red brick, is widely used for foundations and for backup for exterior solid walls. It is also used as a facing brick when its face texture and color are desirable.

FACING BRICK

Facing brick is made from clay, shale, fire clay, or mixtures thereof, under controlled conditions. Its quality is governed by ASTM C216, which sets forth standards as to durability (weathering) and appearance. Durability consists of two grades, SW and MW, as explained under Building Brick. Appearance is governed by three types, described in Table 4-2.

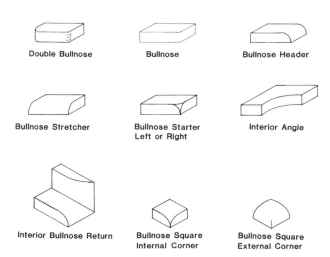

FIGURE 4-1 Special brick shapes. (*Reprinted from Hornbostel, Construction Materials, New York: John Wiley & Sons, Inc., 1978.*)

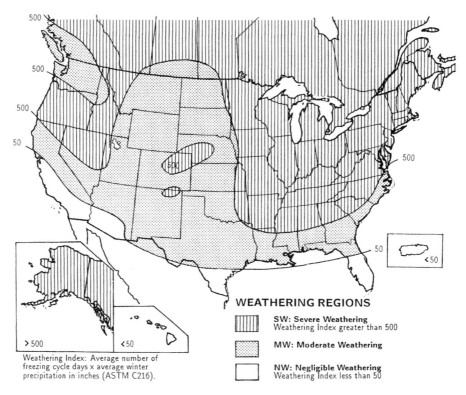

WEATHERING REGIONS

| | **SW: Severe Weathering**
Weathering Index greater than 500 |
| **MW: Moderate Weathering** |
| **NW: Negligible Weathering**
Weathering Index less than 50 |

Weathering Index: Average number of
freezing cycle days x average winter
precipitation in inches (ASTM C216).

FIGURE 4-2   Weathering Index Map of North America.

GLAZED FACING BRICK (GLAZED BRICK)

Glazed facing brick is made from a combination of clay, shale, fire clay, or mixtures thereof similar to the requirements set forth for facing brick, and with a finish consisting of a ceramic glaze fused to the body at above 1500°F. Many colors, textures, and degrees of sheen are available from various manufacturers. When glazed facing brick is intended for exterior use, consult the manufacturer as to suitable material.

Units are produced to meet requirements of ASTM C126. One of the requirements governs grades for tolerances of face dimensions as follows:

Grade S (select). For use with comparatively narrow mortar joints

Grade SS (select size or ground edge). For use where variation of face dimension must be very small

The other requirements are concerned with the properties of the finish with respect to imperviousness, resistance to fading, resistance to crazing, flame spread, toxic fumes, and hardness and abrasion resistance.

TABLE 4-2
BUILDING BRICK APPEARANCE TYPES

Type	Use
FBS	For general use in exposed exterior and interior masonry walls and partitions where wider color ranges and greater variation in sizes are permitted than are specified for Type FBX.
FBX	For general use in exposed exterior and interior masonry walls and partitions where a high degree of mechanical perfection, narrow color range, and minimum permissible variation in size are required.
FBA	Brick manufactured and selected to produce characteristic architectural effects resulting from nonuniformity of the individual units.

BRICKWORK

Brickwork involves the assembly of masonry units including mortar, jointing, bond, tieing, and workmanship to ensure performance, appearance, strength, and weathertightness. Other factors which influence heat transmission, sound transmission, and fire resistance are a function of the design of a masonry wall.

Mortar

The primary function of mortar is to bond masonry units together so that the mortar joint is durable and acts as a seal against the entrance of water. Other important properties of mortar are workability, water retentivity, strength, and its ability to heal minor cracks.

The primary ingredients of mortar are cementitious material, aggregate, and water. Two standards for mortar are available: ASTM C270 and Brick Institute of America (BIA) M1-88. Essentially, the BIA standard restricts the cementitious ingredients to portland cement and lime, whereas the ASTM standard also allows the use of masonry cement as one of the cementitious ingredients. Canadian Building Digest 163 states: "It is difficult to predict the properties of masonry cements since their composition is not always published. Their use should therefore be based on the basis of known local performance."

BIA standard M1-88 lists four types of mortar as shown in Table 4-3.

Portland cement-lime mortars are proportioned by volume in accordance with information shown in Table 4-4.

As stated at the outset, the most important functions of mortar are its bonding or adhesive qualities and its durability. Bonding is increased by:

TABLE 4-3
MORTAR TYPES

Type	Compressive strength	Use
M	2500 psi	A high-compressive strength mortar specifically recommended for masonry below grade and in contact with earth
S	1800 psi	A mortar recommended for use in masonry where maximum flexural strength is required
N	750 psi	A medium strength mortar suitable for general use in exposed masonry above grade and specifically recommended for parapets, chimneys, and exterior walls subjected to severe weathering
O	350 psi	A low-strength mortar suitable for use in nonload-bearing walls of solid masonry units, load-bearing walls of solid units in which the axial compressive stresses developed do not exceed 100 psi, and where the masonry wall will not be subject to severe weathering

1. Mixing mortar to the maximum flow (ASTM C109) compatible with workmanship. This means using maximum amount of water and retempering.

2. Wetting clay units whose suction rate exceeds 30 g/min · 19,400 mm^2.

Architect-engineer design teams often lose sight of the importance of mortar in providing weathertight construction. Some engineers concern themselves only with mortar's compressive strength, ignoring the advice of ASTM Committee C-12 on Mortars for Unit Masonry that "mortars should typically be weaker

TABLE 4-4
MORTAR PROPORTIONS BY VOLUME

Type	Portland cement	Hydrated lime	Sand measured damp loose condition
M	1	¼	Not less than 2¼ and not more than 3 times the
S	1	over ¼ to ½	sum of the volumes of cement and lime used
N	1	over ½ to 1¼	
O	1	over 1¼ to 2½	

than the masonry units." The reason for the emphasizing bond strength over compressive strength is explained at length in ASTM C270 X1.6.3.

ASTM's argument for not making compressive strength in mortar selection the sole criterion is that bond strength and flexural strength of the mortar are more important, the latter because it gives mortar the ability to resist cracking. The presence of a significant amount of lime in the mortar increases bond strength, workability, water retentivity while setting, flexural strength, and adds a self-healing property to any cracks that occur in the mortar. Lime in mortar promotes crack healing by the fact that this $Ca(OH)_2$ in the mix carbonates over the years by reacting with CO_2 in any air that penetrates a crack, forming $CaCO_3$ and sealing that crack against water penetration.

ASTM states that this micro-cracking and subsequent self-healing of mortar is a desirable feature in water-resistant construction and that for this reason the mortar's compressive strength should be designed to be slightly weaker than the compressive strength of the block or brick. The micro-cracking should occur in the mortar, where it can heal, not in the masonry units where cracks will not heal. A typical ASTM C90 masonry unit has a compressive strength of 1900 lb/in^2 average which is almost identical to the 1800 lb/in^2 (12.4 MPa) figure for Type S mortar. Thus the next weaker mortar, Type N, meets ASTM's recommendation. There is however little danger in specifying Type S; if the block is up to standard, Type S will not introduce excessive compressive strength and compromise the other desirable properties of the mortar. Type S is safe for brick, which generally test 40 to 55 percent stronger than block.

The specifying of self-healing mortar is particularly important in single wythe masonry construction or when there is a likelihood that damp masonry units will find their way into exterior wall construction. For this reason, ASTM recommends Type N mortar for exterior load-bearing walls above grade and Type O for non-load-bearing.

ASTM goes on to say that retempering mortar to replace water lost by evaporation is an important step in keeping the bond strength and flexural strength high, along with the maintaining workability under the trowel. Mortars can and should be retempered for 2 hours or more after leaving the mixer, depending on climatic conditions—with the usual gauge of sufficient water being the mason's own on-the-spot judgment in keeping the mix workable.

It is remixing of mortar—returning mortar more than a few hours old to the mixer, or trying to retemper mortar after a few hours—that should be prohibited by the specifications.

Joints

The aesthetics of a brick joint are determined by its size, color, and the manner in which it is tooled. The method by which a joint is tooled also contributes to the watertightness of the wall. The tooled concave joint which compresses the mortar tightly against the masonry units produces the best resistance to water penetration by densifying the surface of the mortar. Joints should be tooled after the mortar has received its initial set; this compensates for any initial shrinkage.

Joints that are rubbed or that are made by cutting with a trowel run the risk of admitting water because they do not compress the mortar surface against the units at the side of the joint and against the mortar body itself. Likewise, struck and raked joints do not shed water; this can promote leaking and frost damage. The use of stripped joints and joint profiles that do not shed water should be limited to interior walls, walls in arid climates, and to cavity walls where there is a mortar parge coat to protect the building from water intrusion.

Joint sizes are a function of the masonry unit size and type. Glazed brick joints are generally ¼ inch; facing brick joints, ⅜ to ½ inch; and building brick joints ½ inch. Typical joints are shown in Figure 4-3.

Bond Patterns

While masonry bonding is the laying of units in rows or courses to tie the units together, bonds are also designed to enhance the appearance of a masonry wall. Depending upon the wall design (i.e., solid wall, cavity wall, or faced wall), either masonry bonding or metal ties are employed to bond the units into a solid mass. Each course of brick is one continuous horizontal layer bonded with mortar. The course can consist of brick laid end to end (stretcher) and/or with headers (short dimension). In a solid or cavity wall, each continuous vertical section of masonry one unit in thickness constitutes a wythe. The manner in which the wythes are bonded or tied creates a bond pattern. See Figure 4-4 for bond patterns.

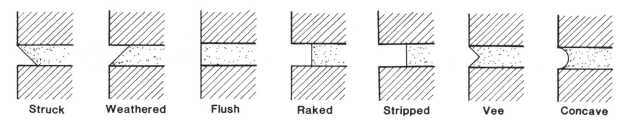

FIGURE 4-3 Brick mortar joints.

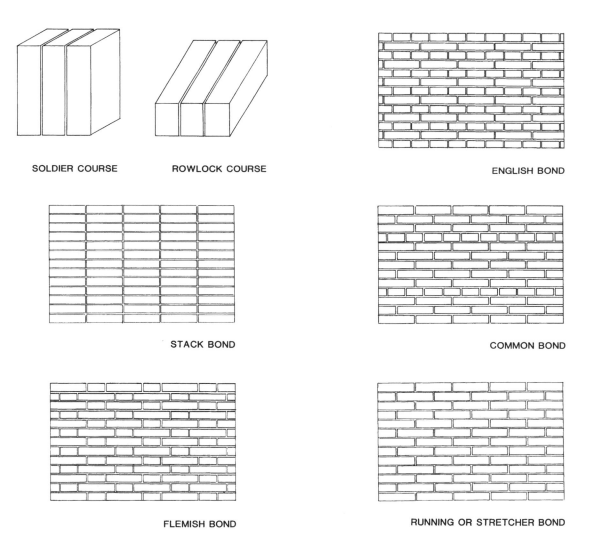

FIGURE 4-4 Brick bond patterns and courses.

Stretcher or running bond. A pattern created by laying brick end to end (long dimension) with each course breaking joints at the midpoint of the course below.

Common bond. A pattern consisting of stretcher or running bond courses, six or seven courses high with a course of headers (short dimension) laid perpendicular to the stretcher course and thus bonding into the inner wythe.

English bond. A pattern consisting of alternating courses of stretchers and headers.

Flemish bond. A pattern created by using one header followed by one stretcher in a course and with each course offset so that a header in one course is centered over the stretcher below.

Stack bond. A pattern of brick stretchers laid so that horizontal and vertical joints are all in line.

Soldier course. Brick laid on end with the face showing; used essentially for belt courses or flat arches.

Rowlock course. Brick laid on face edge with end showing; used for sills or belt courses.

Header bond. A pattern created by all headers in all courses, with each brick breaking joints over the midpoint of the unit below.

Sailor course. Brick laid on end with the broad side of the brick showing. Such brick must be determined beforehand to have a weatherproof broad face without frog or perforations.

Ties and Anchorage

Masonry walls of the solid type are bonded together with either brick bonds or metal ties. Cavity walls and faced walls (against concrete or brick veneer) are tied to the backing with various types of metal ties. Intersecting walls may be bonded with masonry or metal ties.

Metal anchors and ties are usually of zinc-coated steel or other noncorrodible metal, and include a variety of types such as wire mesh, wire, corrugated metal, dovetail slots with flat dovetail anchors, rigid steel straps, cavity-wall anchors, and continuous horizontal reinforcement. See Figure 4-5 for masonry wall ties.

A study made by the Armour Research Foundation in 1960 concluded that continuous horizontal reinforcement is as effective as brick headers in tying

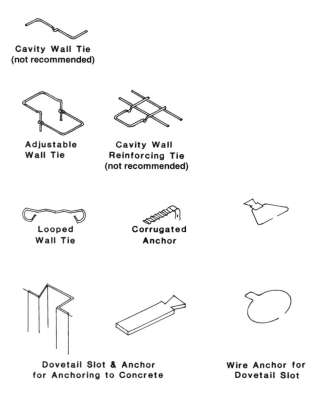

FIGURE 4-5 Masonry wall ties.

walls against lateral wind loading. A similar study noted that solid walls bonded with metal ties had significantly greater resistance to water penetration than masonry-bonded walls. Refer to ACI 530 for additional design requirements.

Quality of Work

Leaks in masonry walls are the result of the penetration of water through openings between mortar and brick rather than through mortar or brick. Therefore workmanship, rate of absorption of masonry units, and water retentivity of mortar are the controlling factors affecting the construction of watertight masonry walls. To achieve this end result, do the following:

1. Lay brick in a full bed of mortar without furrowing.

2. Head joints of stretcher courses should have end of each unit fully buttered with mortar.

3. Header courses should have each side fully buttered with mortar.

4. Shove each brick into place so that the mortar oozes out at the top of joints.

In solid masonry construction, lay heavy back-up units first, parge its outer face, then lay face units. Tool face joints as previously noted under joints.

Since units with high rates of absorption will suck the water from the mortar, reduce the bond, and induce shrinkage cracks, it may be necessary to wet the units prior to laying. Brick with high suction rates can be determined as follows: Draw a 1-inch-diameter circle with a wax crayon on the bed of the unit. Place 20 drops of water inside the circle. If the water is absorbed in less than 1½ minutes, the units should be wetted prior to laying, since their suction rate is high.

Water retentivity of mortar is a measure of the flow and workability of a mortar. It is also the property of a mortar which prevents bleeding or water gain when the mortar is in contact with relatively impervious units. To ensure the proper water retentivity, specify that the mortar have a flow after suction of not less than 75 percent of that immediately after mixing as determined by ASTM C91.

Efflorescence

The white soluble salt that sometimes appears as a deposit on masonry is known as efflorescence. This deposit is due to the entrance of water into the brickwork, the dissolving of salts (primarily sodium and potassium carbonates and sulfates), and their migration to the outer surface and deposition there in the form of a white soft powder.

All of the ingredients used in masonry construction (brick, mortar, and water) may contain the salts described above. For face brick, ASTM C216 requires that brick not effloresce when tested according to ASTM C67. Therefore, mortar ingredients and water may be the unknown source of these salts. The use of lime and portland cement of low-alkali content will greatly reduce the capacity of mortar to contribute to efflorescence. Water and sand can be checked by laboratory analysis for alkalinity to reduce the possibility of efflorescence.

MASONRY WALL DESIGN

Individual masonry units have certain physical properties relating to compressive strength, flexural strength, and water absorption. Mortar also has certain physical characteristics such as bond strength and tensile strength. While the properties of masonry walls are affected by the physical characteristics of the individual units and mortar, they are also influenced to some degree by other factors, such as quality of work and bonding, which have a bearing on lateral loading, water resistance, thermal and other properties.

Solid Masonry Walls

Masonry walls may be constructed using two or more wythes of solid brick or by using an outer wythe of brick and concrete masonry unit back-up. Prior to the current increased use of concrete masonry units as a back-up unit, hollow clay tile was used. The masonry wythes may be tied together using brick bonding or metal ties. The spacing of brick bonding units or metal ties is governed by ACI 530 and local building codes.

Glazed face brick should not be used in solid masonry wall construction. Since water may enter a completed masonry wall, it must have an opportunity to escape, generally by evaporation from the face. When glazed brick is used in noncavity wall construction, the face glaze may pop off from the forces exerted by the pressure buildup of the water in the form of water vapor.

Cavity Wall Construction

The cavity wall has been used in the construction of many types of structures in Great Britain and Europe for at least 100 years, primarily because of its resistance to rain and water penetration. This resistance to water penetration is based on its unique air space that serves as a break in the transmission of water from the outer face of the exterior wythe to the inner face of the interior wythe.

A cavity wall consists of two walls or wythes separated by an air space (generally 2 inches) and joined together by means of metal ties. Three elements are essential to ensure the success of a cavity wall: (1)

drainage weep holes at its base to release water entering the system, (2) corrosion-resistant ties to unite the wythes structurally, and (3) a cavity free of mortar or other material that might form a bridge by which water can migrate to the inner wythe.

Additional advantages over solid wall construction include reduced weight, increased thermal efficiency, and protection against water infiltration into the structure. While water may enter the exterior wythe, it will run down the inside face of the exterior wythe at a flashing gutter and then exit out at weep holes, as shown in Figure 4-6.

Veneered Walls

A veneered masonry wall is one in which an outer wythe of masonry is tied to a structural backing. It is most commonly used in conjunction with wood-frame construction, with an air space between the masonry and the sheathing and tied to it with noncorrosive metal ties. Veneered masonry may also be used as an architectural finish where structural concrete is used. It has also been adapted for use with an exterior framing system of metal studs and gypsum sheathing, veneered

with brick secured to the system with metal ties. See Figure 4-7 for a typical veneered masonry wall.

FIRE RESISTANCE

One of the more important provisions of building codes is the regulation governing fire safety. How walls, floors, columns, and other building elements perform in the presence of fire conditions is of major concern to the architect and the public.

The fire resistance of walls, partitions, columns, and other enclosures is based upon the ASTM standard for Fire Tests of Building Construction and Materials E119. While it does not measure the fire hazard in terms of actual performance in a real fire situation, it gives a comparison of the measure of performance between assemblies tested under similar conditions.

Various configurations of masonry construction will develop certain fire-resistance ratings. Tables 4-5 and 4-6 illustrate fire resistance ratings for typical load-bearing walls and for a fireproofed column, respectively.

When designing for fire resistance requirements, check pertinent local building codes and the Fire

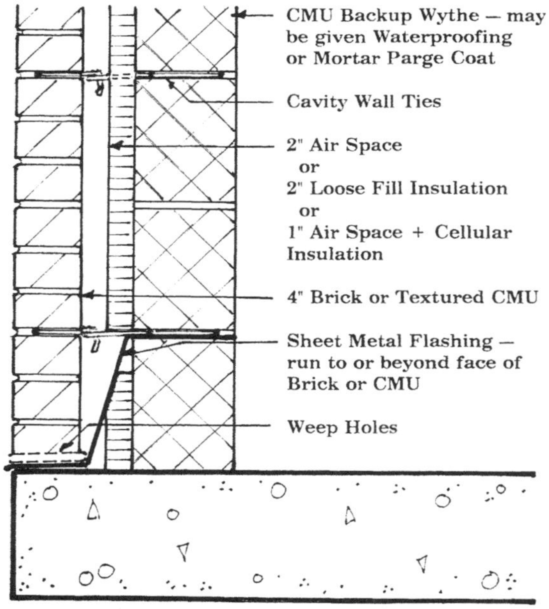

FIGURE 4-6 Brick or textured CMU cavity wall. 4½ in. maximum cavity depth.

CMU Backup Wythe — may be given Waterproofing or Mortar Parge Coat

Cavity Wall Ties

2" Air Space
or
2" Loose Fill Insulation
or
1" Air Space + Cellular Insulation

4" Brick or Textured CMU

Sheet Metal Flashing — run to or beyond face of Brick or CMU

Weep Holes

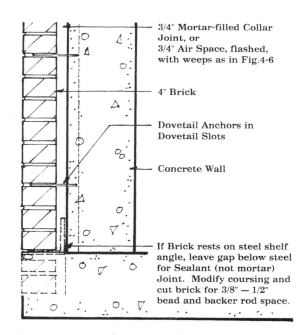

FIGURE 4-7 Veneered masonry wall, wtih alternative detail for shelf angle support.

3/4" Mortar-filled Collar Joint, or
3/4" Air Space, flashed, with weeps as in Fig.4-6

4" Brick

Dovetail Anchors in Dovetail Slots

Concrete Wall

If Brick rests on steel shelf angle, leave gap below steel for Sealant (not mortar) Joint. Modify coursing and cut brick for 3/8" — 1/2" bead and backer rod space.

TABLE 4-5
LOAD-BEARING BRICK WALLS

Wall thickness (in.)	Wall type	Ultimate fire resistance (hr)
4	Solid	1¼
8	Solid	5
12	Solid	10
10	Cavity	5

TABLE 4-6
FIREPROOFED COLUMN

Construction	Rating
Steel Column, 6 × 6 inches or larger	
3¾-inch brick with brick fill	4 hours
2¼-inch brick with brick fill	1 hour

TABLE 4-7
U-VALUES AND R-VALUES—EXTERIOR MASONRY

Wall type	U-value	R-value
Solid		
8-inch brick	0.48	2.1
12-inch brick	0.35	2.9
Cavity		
10-inches (2-inch air space)	0.33	3.0

Resistance Ratings published by the American Insurance Association.

THERMAL CHARACTERISTICS

The characteristics concerning heat flow are explained in Chapter 1, under the heading Thermal Properties—Thermal Transmittance and Resistance.

The thermal transmittance of masonry walls may be expressed in U-values and the thermal resistance in R-values, as shown in Table 4-7. The R-values or thermal resistances shown in Table 4-7 are quite low or negligible as compared to current requirements limiting heat loss through exterior walls. However, by adding insulation to the back of exterior solid walls, or by installing insulation in the air space of cavity walls, increases in R-values can become quite significant, depending on the type and thickness of insulation.

SOUND INSULATION

The sound transmission loss of a wall or partition is that property which enables it to resist the passage of sound from one side of the construction to the other. See Chapter 1 and the discussion on Acoustics for more definitive explanations.

Insofar as sound absorption is concerned, brick masonry is a poor absorber of sound energy. However, there are perforated and/or slotted structural glazed facing tiles that do have the capacity to absorb sound energy; this material is discussed later in this chapter.

The sound transmission loss of a number of brick masonry walls together with their sound transmission class (STC) and construction are shown in Table 4-8.

EXPANSION AND CONTRACTION

Masonry walls contract and expand with changes in temperature and moisture, and these factors must be taken into account during the design of the structure. The average coefficient of thermal expansion for a clay or shale brick is 0.0000036 inches per inch per °F. For each 100 linear feet of brick wall for a 100°F temperature rise, it will expand 0.43 inch or about ⁷⁄₁₆ inch.

One of the principal causes of masonry cracking is differential movement between masonry and the various elements of the structure with which the

TABLE 4-8
STC VALUES FOR VARIOUS MASONRY WALLS

STC values	Construction
45	4-inch brick, solid
50	10-inch brick, cavity wall, 2-inch air space
52	8-inch brick, solid
59	12-inch brick, solid

masonry abuts. The skeleton-frame, both steel and reinforced concrete, moves at different rates than the masonry as a result of differing coefficients of thermal expansion and contraction. Differential thermal movement also occurs between masonry walls and concrete foundations, between parapet walls and enclosing walls, and at offsets in walls and intersecting walls. Each building design must be analyzed to determine potential movements and provision made to relieve excessive stress by the introduction of expansion joints at locations noted in Figure 4-8 and elsewhere as determined.

Details for these typical expansion joints may be found in BIA Technical Notes—Series 18 and 18A.

While the above differential thermal movements occur horizontally and require vertical expansion-relieving joints, there is also a masonry failure that is induced by the shortening of structural frames that requires the use of horizontal relieving joints. In high-rise buildings, plastic flow, especially in lightweight concrete columns, may cause a vertical shortening of the frame. Since the exterior masonry is usually carried on shelf angles, there is the possibility of masonry failures characterized by bowing, or by spalling of the faces at shelf angles and lintels. The introduction of horizontal expansion joints at these angles is critical; BIA Technical Note 18A recommends a detail for this condition.

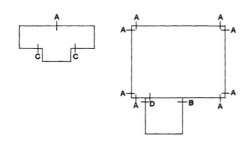

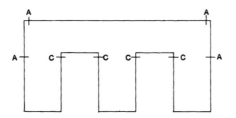

FIGURE 4-8 Typical expansion joint placement.

REINFORCED BRICK MASONRY

Reinforced brick masonry (RBM) is a system consisting of brick, mortar, grout, and reinforcing steel, designed and placed in such a manner that resultant masonry construction will have greatly increased resistance to forces which produce tensile, shearing, and compression stresses. Natural phenomena which produce these forces are earthquakes and strong winds such as hurricanes, tornadoes, and cyclones. RBM may also be used for isolated elements of a building, such as chimneys, beams, girders, piers, floors, roofs, and lintels.

The principles used in the design of RBM are essentially the same as those used and commonly accepted for reinforced concrete; therefore, similar formulae may be used. Standards used in the design of RBM may be found in ACI 530 and in the Brick Institute of America "Technical Notes" Series 17. Mortar and grout used in the RBM system are governed by ASTM C476.

In the 1950s a method of construction known as the "High Lift Grouting System" was developed in the San Francisco Bay Area. This technique has improved over the years and evolved into a more sophisticated and economical solution in its application to both low- and high-rise structures using RBM. In this system the outer wythes of masonry are built up around the vertical reinforcement and allowed to set for a minimum period of 3 days; after that, the grout is pumped into the space containing the reinforcement. Figure 4-9 illustrates a typical wall constructed by the high-lift grouting technique.

PREFABRICATED BRICK MASONRY

Prefabricated brick masonry is a relatively new masonry system that has certain advantages over conventional in-place brick laying.

Developed in Europe in the 1950s, the system was adapted in the United States in the early 1960s. Begun initially to mechanize the panelization of brick to overcome cold weather construction, it has grown in scope to include the fabrication of complex shapes.

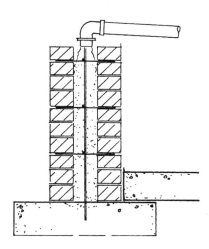

FIGURE 4-9 High-lift grouting for RBM wall. *(Courtesy Brick Institute of America.)*

The advantages of prefabrication include:

1. Elimination of scaffolding
2. Fabrication of complex shapes
3. Factory prefabrication year-round under controlled weather conditions
4. Elimination of enclosing and winterizing the structure under construction
5. Reduction in construction time

FIGURE 4-10 RBM panel, 39 feet long, being hoisted into place. *(Courtesy Brick Institute of America.)*

Prefabricated brick masonry has been made possible by the development of high-bond mortars, a rational design method for brick masonry, and improved brick units. In addition, a standard for prefabricated panels has been established in ASTM C901, Specifications for Prefabricated Masonry Panels.

Prefabricated panels are also possible with thin brick facing units in conjunction with concrete, fiberboard, or other backing materials. Figure 4-10 shows a representative example of prefabricated masonry element being hoisted into position.

CONCRETE MASONRY UNITS

HISTORY

Modern-day concrete block or concrete masonry unit (CMU) dates back to 1882. Today, with increased automation and the benefit of long-term use, experience, and research, concrete masonry units have become not only a standard structural building material but also a product having aesthetic architectural applications. This latter quality has been achieved through the incorporation of color, texture, surface treatment, and shapes of various configurations.

MANUFACTURE

Concrete masonry units are manufactured using portland cement, graded aggregates, and water. When required, the mix may also contain air-entraining admixtures, coloring pigments, and pozzolanic materials. The manufacturing process utilizes machine molding of a rather dry, no-slump concrete. Automatic machinery consolidates and molds thousands of units each day.

Curing, which is absolutely essential to control shrinkage, is performed in a number of ways. Air drying, which requires about 2 to 4 weeks of open-air drying with weather protection, is not as desirable as two types of accelerated curing. The more prevalent type of accelerated curing requires heating the units in a steam kiln at atmospheric pressure, with steam temperature at about 120 to 180°F for about 12 to 18 hours. The other accelerated method is autoclaving or high-pressure steam curing. This latter method subjects the units to saturated steam at about 375°F and a pressure of 170 psig for about 12 hours.

Types

There is one concrete masonry block and one concrete brick ASTM standard as follows:

ASTM C90—Hollow Load-Bearing Concrete Masonry Units

ASTM C55—Concrete Building Brick

A hollow unit is defined as having a net concrete area (in plan) of less than 75 percent.

Since concrete masonry units are subject to shrinkage and expansion, for architectural purposes it is

TABLE 4-9
MOISTURE CONTENT REQUIREMENTS

% Linear shrinkage	% Moisture content*		
	Humid	Intermediate	Arid
0.03 or Less	45	40	35
0.03 to 0.045	40	35	30
0.045 to 0.065	35	30	25

* Humid—average annual RH above 75%. Intermediate—average annual RH 50 to 75%. Arid—average annual RH less than 50%.

best to limit use to the moisture-controlled units, designated as Type I under the ASTM standards and as shown in Table 4-9.

Aggregate Selections and Block Weight

Aggregate selection has an influence not only on the weight of the block but also on the textural quality, including the split-face units and on the block's insulating value, as shown in Table 4-10. There are three weight gradations of CMU, as shown in Table 4-11.

TABLE 4-10
R-VALUES OF BRICK/CMU CAVITY WALLS

Wall construction: 4 in. brick (R = 0.44)* with cavity at least 1 in. wider than insulation to permit air circulation and water weepage from back of brick wythe. Bonding by hot dip galvanized steel pintle and eye horizontal reinforcing with plastic ring drip, spaced 16 in. oc vertically, with at least 1 tie every 1.77 ft². ASTM C90 block at inner wythe with density of either 115 or 135 lb/ft³.

Calculations: Following ASHRAE 90.1-1989.

Thickness and lb/ft³ of block inner wythe	8 in. CMU		4 in. CMU	
	115	135	115	135
2 in. cavity: clear; no insulation	3.8	3.5	3.3	3.0
2 in. cavity: filled with loose WP vermiculite†	7.4	7.1	6.9	6.6
2 in. cavity: 1 in. XPS styrene board, R = 5.0 + 1 in. clear space‡	8.8	8.5	8.3	8.0
2 in. cavity: 1 in. isocyanurate board with reflective surface, R = 7.2 + 1 in. clear space	12.7	12.4	12.2	11.9
3 in. cavity: 2 in. XPS styrene board, R = 5.0 + 1 in. clear space‡	13.8	13.5	13.3	13.0
3 in. cavity: 2 in. isocyanurate board with reflective surface, R = 7.2 + 1 in. clear space	19.9	19.6	19.4	19.1

* If scored, fluted or split-face CMU is used, add 0.5 to each value.
† If perlite is used in place of vermiculite, add 1.7 to each value.
‡ If expanded instead of extruded styrene board is used, deduct 0.8 from each value.

TABLE 4-11
BLOCK WEIGHTS AND AGGREGATES

Weight designation	Unit weight (pcf)	Aggregates types
Normal weight	Over 125	Sand and gravel Crushed stone and sand
Medium weight	105–125	Air-cooled slag
Light weight	Less than 105	Coal cinder Expanded slag Expanded clay, shale, slate Pumice Cellular concrete

Sizes and Shapes

Concrete block dimensions are usually given in modular nominal sizes, with the face size normally stated as 8 × 16 inches. Since joint dimensions are typically ⅜ inch thick, the actual face size is 7⅝ × 15⅝ inches. Block is commonly available in thickness (width) of 4, 6, 8, 10, and 12 inches. Solid "soaps" are usually 1, 1½, 2, or 3 inches thick.

Concrete brick is likewise sized to be laid with a ⅜-inch joint, resulting in modules of 4-inch widths and 8-inch lengths. The typical concrete brick is 2¼ × 3⅝ × 7⅝ inches.

SURFACE FINISHES

For architectural purposes, concrete block is now being produced with a variety of textures which are influenced by the type and grading of aggregates, with color by the addition of various pigments, and with prefaced units having surface-applied resinous materials and ceramic or porcelainized glazes in various colors.

Textured Surfaces

The surface textures available for concrete masonry units may be classified as fine, medium, and coarse and are achieved by various aggregates, their grading, the mix proportions, and the wetness of the mix. For large projects some manufacturers may produce spe-

cial textures to suit the architect's needs. See Figure 4-11, Surface Texture.

A smooth-faced block is available that is produced by grinding the exposed faces approximately ¹⁄₁₆ to ⅛ inch. Ground-face units show aggregates of varying colors, sizes, and types to good advantage. With the addition of coloring pigments, these ground-face units are used in walls and partitions as a finishing material without further treatment.

Colors

The natural color of concrete masonry depends upon the color of the aggregates and the cement used. This can vary from the typical shades of gray to the earth tones of brown. Since these colors are achieved by the use of the locally available materials, the resulting colors will be more uniform and easier to duplicate in the

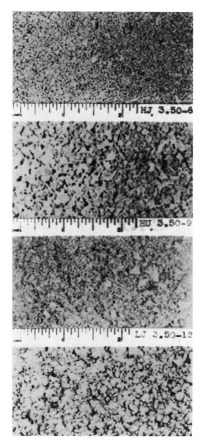

FIGURE 4-11 Examples of textures of concrete masonry units. *(Used with permission of Portland Cement Association.)*

event of additional work at the same project. Mock-ups of such units should be erected to ascertain the maximum degree of variation that will be permitted.

In addition to the natural color variations available, artificial colors can be obtained through the addition of mineral oxide pigments in the concrete mix. However, when used on the exterior, the colorfastness of some mineral oxides such as blue are questionable. Another problem associated with the exterior use of some of these units is the possibility of efflorescence marring their appearance.

Prefaced Units

Concrete block may also be prefaced with a resinous mixture of resin, sand, or portland cement with integral colors, to produce smooth or dappled surfaces approximately ¼ inch thick. The resinous facings form an integral bond with the concrete masonry units and are cured by a heat process.

The facings are about ¹/₁₆ inch longer than the block face and return ¼ inch into the joint. The resulting bed and head are ³/₈ inch thick, but the face joint becomes ¼ inch thick. Double-faced units are also available along with such features as caps, sanitary bases, returns, and scoring. The resinous facings are produced to meet the requirements of ASTM C744.

Split-Face Units

Block and bricks may be split or fractured to produce a rough finish. The appearance of the face when split will be irregular, and the aggregate within the face will be fractured to provide interesting variations of texture. By varying the cement aggregates and their gradation and by adding color pigments, a host of possibilities is available for architectural expression.

Sculptured and Screen Units

Sculptured or patterned block are produced by providing raised or recessed geometric forms cast into the faces, thus providing the architect with a wide palette from which to select. In addition, patterns and profiles may include ribbing, fluting, and scoring, all

as shown in Figure 4-12. The sculptured surfaces provide a display of striking shadow effects which can be varied by the specific pattern in which the units are laid.

Screen or pierced units are used for a variety of purposes such as solar screens, wind breaks, diffusion of strong sunlight, and decorative dividers. They offer privacy with a view and airy comfort with wind control. However some designs are only available in certain areas and some designs are restricted by copyright. Construction of walls and partitions using these units requires specific structural analysis, the use of a framing system, vertical and horizontal joint reinforcement, and anchorage of the wall to a framing system. See Figure 4-13, Screen Walls.

Acoustical Units

Special units providing sound-absorbing qualities are produced with vertical-slotted faces. The sound absorption is derived from the fact that the cavity within the unit acts as a sound resonator. Other units have the cavity filled with fibrous material or an energy-absorbing septum. Each type offers sound absorption at differing frequencies and is useful in reducing noise in such applications as gymnasiums, natatoriums, and industrial applications. See Figure 4-14 for an application involving acoustical units.

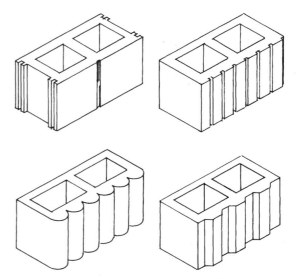

FIGURE 4-12 Scored, fluted and ribbed block. *(Used with permission of Portland Cement Association.)*

FIGURE 4-13 Screen walls provide privacy. *(Used with permission of Portland Cement Association.)*

BLOCKWORK

Masonry unit walls and partitions are usually constructed as one wythe thick. However, when exterior walls are designed in locations where rain penetration may be a factor it would be prudent to consider a cavity wall design. See Wall Design, Weathertightness, in this Chapter.

Units delivered and stored at the job site should be protected from rainfall or moisture gain in humid areas by canvas or polyethylene tarpaulins. During construction it is essential that the tops of walls be covered with tarpaulins to prevent entry of rain or snow. Concrete masonry units should never be wetted before setting, since moist block will shrink as the excess moisture evaporates. It is essential that the block be stored and erected below the maximum moisture content permitted in the specifications.

Mortars

Mortar for concrete block masonry is similar in most respects to that used for brickwork as described in this chapter. When erecting composite walls of brick and block, the mortar specified for the brick is used throughout.

When colored mortar is desired, the desired results may be achieved by the use of white cement and pigments, colored masonry cement, or colored sand.

Joints

Mortar joints are normally ⅜ inch thick. Two types of mortar beds are used: full bedding (webs and face shells are bedded in the mortar) and face-shell bedding (only the face shells are bedded in mortar). Full bedding is used where strength is an important factor (i.e., first course on a foundation, solid units, piers, columns, and pilasters) and in reinforced masonry. For all other concrete block, face-shell bedding is sufficient. See Figure 4-15 for types of mortar bedding.

To obtain more watertight construction, a concave joint or a Vee joint should be used. (See Figure 4-3, mortar joints.) Concave and Vee joints compress the

FIGURE 4-14 Acoustical units employed to improve acoustics. *(Used with permission of Portland Cement Association.)*

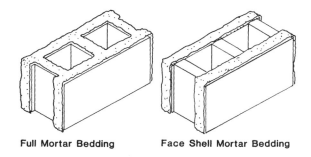

Full Mortar Bedding   Face Shell Mortar Bedding

FIGURE 4-15 Types of mortar bedding on block. *(Used with permission of Portland Cement Association.)*

mortar and offer better resistance to water penetration than other types of joints.

Crack Control

While a number of factors will cause concrete masonry walls to move (e.g., thermal change and change in moisture content), shrinkage due to moisture loss is quite significant and should be addressed by the designer to introduce measures to inhibit crack formation.

Four factors influence the degree of drying shrinkage: (1) type of aggregate, (2) curing method, (3) method of storage, and (4) protection of freshly set walls from rain and dew. Units made with sand and gravel shrink less than other types. High-pressure steam curing reduces shrinkage best. Moisture-controlled units when installed at or below the relative humidity of the locality will exhibit less shrinkage. Insofar as moisture content is the controlling factor affecting shrinkage, masonry units should be stored and kept dry until setting.

Two methods can be utilized to accommodate shrinkage. One is to introduce control joints, the other is to provide joint reinforcement. Figure 4-16 shows typical control joints.

Location of control joints as recommended by ACI 531, Concrete Masonry Structures Design and Construction, are shown in Table 4-12.

For more detailed descriptions of locations of control joints see the *Concrete Masonry Handbook for Architects, Engineers & Builders* published by the Portland Cement Association.

Joint reinforcement is utilized to control cracking caused by drying shrinkage. While reinforcement does not eliminate cracks, it controls the formation of highly visible cracks. The stresses which do occur are transferred to the reinforcement; as a consequence there is an even distribution of stresses, and hairline cracks result which are barely visible.

Joint reinforcement should consist of a minimum of 9 gage side rods and 9 gage cross rods, complying with ASTM A82 and located as follows:

1. In the first two courses above and below all openings, and extending a minimum of 2 feet on both sides of opening
2. In the first two or three joints above floor level, below roof level and near top of the wall
3. As shown in Table 4-12

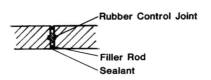
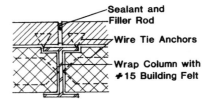
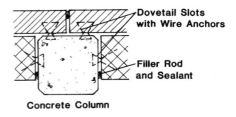

FIGURE 4-16   Control joints in block.

For additional information on sizes, galvanizing, and locations of joint reinforcement, review the current literature of the manufacturer of these materials.

Bond Patterns

Exposed concrete block can be used quite effectively architecturally by creating numerous bond patterns to achieve various effects. Long, low expressions may be

TABLE 4-12
MAXIMUM SPACING OF CONTROL JOINTS IN NONREINFORCED MASONRY

Maximum spacing of joint reinforcement (inches)	Maximum spacing of control joints	
	Panel length/height	Panel length (feet)
None	2	40
24	2.5	45
16	3	50
8	4	60

obtained with the use of 2-inch-high units laid horizontally. Height may be expressed by vertical stacking of 8 × 16-inch units. Sculptured and patterned block can create rhythmic sequences. The variety of bond patterns that can be achieved depends only upon the imagination of the architect.

Ties

Bonding of concrete masonry units in composite wall construction is best accomplished with metal accessories. While masonry bonding is possible, there are certain risks. Rain penetration is more likely with masonry bonds than with metal ties. Metal ties also allow the flexibility of differential movement when composite construction is used, thereby relieving stresses and limiting cracking.

Ties for exterior use must be fabricated of hot dip galvanized steel, stainless steel, or other types of corrosion-resistant rods or wire. For cavity walls, a plastic disk may be introduced in the wire that is centered over the cavity to act as a drip. For composite walls of block and brick facing, an adjustable tie system is used that allows for adjustment of the difference in levels between the wythes. Continuous metal ties are more commonly referred to as joint reinforcement. See Figure 4-17 for representative metal ties.

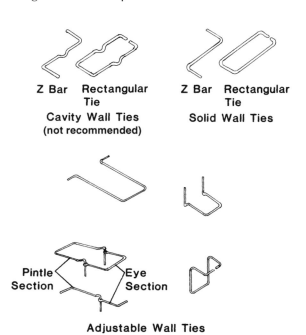

Z Bar   Rectangular
Tie
Cavity Wall Ties
(not recommended)

Z Bar   Rectangular
Tie
Solid Wall Ties

Pintle
Section

Eye
Section

Adjustable Wall Ties

FIGURE 4-17 Concrete unit masonry ties. (*Used with permission of Portland Cement Association.*)

WALL DESIGN

Concrete walls and enclosures possess certain physical properties, as well as the aesthetic. They have the ability to handle thermal problems, the ravages of fire, noise, and rain penetration, all if properly addressed and designed.

Thermal Characteristics

While masonry is a poor insulator of heat, the addition of insulation in a cavity wall or the use of insulation in the cores will greatly enhance the thermal efficiency of a concrete masonry wall. Table 4-13 illustrates the U-values of various walls.

Fire Resistance

Fire-resistant assemblies are tested in accordance with ASTM E119, Fire Tests of Building Construction and Materials. Fire-resistive ratings of concrete block depend upon the type of aggregate used and the *equivalent thickness* (ET) of the block, where the ET is the average thickness of solid material. Blocks with pumice aggregate provide the highest hourly ratings. Most building codes will state the required fire resistance of concrete masonry units in terms of the ET.

Sound Insulation

Sound transmission (the passage of sound from one space to another) and sound absorption (the property

TABLE 4-13
U-VALUE FOR VARIOUS MASONRY WALLS

Wall construction	Insulation	U-value
8 in. sand and gravel	none	0.53
" "	loose fill-in core	0.35
8 in. expanded clay, shale	none	0.33
" "	loose fill-in core	0.18
10 in. cavity wall, 4 in. heavyweight block, 4 in. brick	none	0.34
" "	poured fill-in cavity	0.13

TABLE 4-14
SOUND TRANSMISSION LOSS OF CMU WALLS

Construction	STC value
8-in. hollow, lightweight aggregate	49
8-in. hollow, stone aggregate	52
10-in. cavity, 4-in. brick, 4-in. lightweight hollow units	54
8-in. hollow, lightweight aggregate with ½-in. gypsum board on resilient channels	56
10-in. cavity, 4-in. brick, 4-in. lightweight aggregate with ½-in. gypsum board on resilient channels	59

Note how cavity-type walls enhance the STC value and how the addition of resilient channels and ½-in. gypsum board likewise reduces the sound transmission.

of a material or construction to absorb sound energy) are factors to be considered in designing intervening walls and partitions.

Exterior walls at airports, major highways, and similar noise-generating sources can be designed with masonry walls that will effectively reduce the sound transmission. Table 4-14 shows some masonry constructions and their sound transmission loss values.

For interior partitions where sound absorption is desirable, as in gymnasiums, swimming pool areas, and auditoriums, the use of acoustical block will provide increased sound absorption characteristics. Lightweight aggregate block will have noise reduction coefficients (NRCs) in the range of 0.40 to 0.45, whereas some acoustical blocks with slotted faces and fibrous fillers have NRCs of 0.60 to 0.70. However, when paint is applied to CMU the NRC will be reduced considerably.

Weathertightness

Rain can penetrate blockwork between mortar joints and the masonry units, or through shrinkage cracks in the block. In solid composite concrete block wall construction it is essential to back parge the vertical collar joint between the interior and exterior wythes, including filling of all mortar joints. However, a well-designed and constructed cavity wall will outperform a solid wall in the resistance to rain penetration. As noted previously, concave or Vee joints are best suited to resist water penetration.

Paints, coatings, and stucco are sometimes used to reduce water penetration of uncoated block walls. To determine the effectiveness of these applications, a test procedure for ascertaining the resistance to leakage of unit masonry walls subjected to wind-driven rain may be utilized. ASTM E514, Water Permeance of Masonry, may be used to measure the appearance of moisture or visible water on the back of a panel that has been coated. The degree to which the coating prevents or permits the passage of water under these test conditions will indicate its effectiveness as a waterproofer.

REINFORCED CONCRETE MASONRY

Reinforced concrete masonry, like reinforced brick masonry, consists of block, mortar, reinforcing steel, and grout so designed and constructed that the assemblage works in unison to resist forces associated with seismic conditions and heavy winds.

Units are laid so that unobstructed vertical cells are aligned to form a continuous core in which reinforcing steel and grout are placed. Mortar and grout used in connection with reinforced concrete masonry are specified in ASTM C476.

Two techniques are used to erect reinforced concrete masonry: (1) low-lift grouting and (2) high-lift grouting. The low-lift grouting procedure is much more simple and more widely used. In low-lift grouting for a single wythe wall, the masonry units are laid to a height of 5 feet and the grout poured into the cores embedding the steel reinforcement. In high-lift grouting, the units are laid story high and then filled with grout by pouring or pumping.

Standards used in the design of reinforced concrete masonry are contained in ACI 530.

PREFABRICATED CONCRETE MASONRY PANELS

Masonry unit panel walls are being fabricated both on-site and off-site by a variety of methods. More sophisticated developments include the use of machines that lay block and fill the head, face, and cross-web joints with mortar.

The advantages of this mechanized production are: (1) an all-weather operation, (2) quality control and uniformity of production, and (3) speed of erection.

STRUCTURAL GLAZED FACING TILE

Structural glazed facing tiles are made from clay, shale, fire-clay, or mixtures thereof. They have a finish consisting of a ceramic glaze fused to the body at above 1500°F. A wide choice of colors is available.

The clay tile body is produced to meet ASTM C212, Structural Clay Facing Tile, for a load-bearing tile. The ceramic glazed facing is produced to comply with ASTM C126, Ceramic Glazed Structural Clay Facing Tile. Two grades are available: Grade S (select) for use with comparatively narrow joints and Grade SS (select size or ground edge) for use where variation of face dimension must be very small. Units are also available as single-faced or two-faced.

Two-face sizes are produced: a nominal $5\frac{1}{3} \times 12$ inches and a nominal 8×16 inches, with bed depths of 2, 4, 6, and 8 inches.

Acoustical units having perforated faces and with NRCs of 55 to 50 are produced for use in such locations as indoor swimming pools, gymnasiums, and laboratories.

Units may be laid with joints as thin as $\frac{3}{16}$ inch, either in stretcher bond or stack bond.

ARCHITECTURAL TERRA COTTA

Architectural terra cotta was a widely used material up until the late 1920s. A striking example of its use is the facade of the Woolworth Building in New York City.

Architectural terra cotta is generally custom made, hard burned, glazed, or unglazed clay building units, plain or highly ornamental, and hand molded or machine extruded. The units are hollow or open back with ribs, finished in a variety of glazes and complex shapes, and designed primarily for ornamentation and decoration. A more modern version is ceramic veneer, an architectural terra cotta characterized by large face dimensions and thin sections.

Architectural terra cotta is anchored to backing materials with metal ties. Ceramic veneer is adhered to backing with mortar. More recent developments in the use of precast panels incorporates the use of key-backs, which permits concrete to flow into the key-back and to create a mechanical bond.

GLASS BLOCK

Glass block was first introduced as a building material in the early 1930s, and its use has been somewhat erratic. Overused inappropriately in some cases, its use declined. In recent years, however, physical changes in styles, colors, sizes, and light transmission, and more innovative use by architects have stimulated the reuse of this building material.

Glass block is generally produced as a hollow unit by fusing two halves together and creating a partial vacuum during the process. Varying the pattern by pressing into either the inner or outer surfaces of the block face will cause light striking the surface to be diffused, reduced, or reflected differently. Solid units are also available.

Fibrous glass inserts can be installed within the unit to control glare, brightness, and solar heat gain and to increase thermal transmittance. Solar reflective units have a highly reflective, thermally bonded, oxide surface coating that reduces both solar heat gain and transmitted light.

Units are generally square, nominally 6, 8, and 12 inches, with some rectangular sizes 4×8 inches and 6×8 inches. Bedding widths are $3\frac{1}{8}$ inches and $3\frac{7}{8}$ inches. For styles, sizes, and patterns, it is best to consult the most recent manufacturer's literature. Since the units cannot carry more than their own weight, wall panels are restricted as to length, height, and square foot area. The current literature of manufacturers should be consulted with respect to these limitations and also for precautions that should be taken to accommodate expansion at heads, jambs, and sills.

Glass block is laid in stack bond with ¼-inch mortar joints. Joints must be reinforced as recommended by manufacturers and as required by building codes.

STONE

BUILDING STONE

Rock Classification

Rock is a geological term referring to the solid material that forms the earth's crust and is composed of an aggregate of grains of one or more minerals. Dimensional stone is rock selected for building use and processed by shaping, cutting, or sizing. It is also the commercial term applied to quarry products.

Rock or stone is divided into three classifications based on its geologic origin: igneous, sedimentary, and metamorphic.

Igneous rock is formed from the solidification of molten rock such as that caused by volcanic activity and pressure caused by the shifting of the earth's surface. The igneous rock most widely used as a building stone is granite.

Sedimentary rock is formed from silt, marine life, and disintegrated rock that has been deposited in place or as sediment by running water in rivers or seas. These deposits have been layered and solidified through pressure induced by overlying materials and by cementing together through chemical action such as gases contained in water. Some examples of building stones derived from sedimentary rock are limestone, sandstone, and travertine.

Metamorphic rock may be either igneous or sedimentary rock whose character and structure have been further changed by subsequent pressure, heat, moisture, or combinations of these forces. Examples of metamorphic rock are marble and slate.

Stone Selection

Rock used in building construction is known as building stone. Its use encompasses many aspects of a building: (1) as a structural material in load-bearing walls, (2) as a finish material for exterior and interior walls, and (3) as a flooring and paving material.

With new techniques for quarrying, and with new equipment for finishing, the search for new sources of stone to provide a wider range of colors has ensued. Some stone is available in limited quantities and in limited areas, while others are plentiful worldwide.

Whenever domestic or foreign stone is considered for use on the exterior of a building, care must be exercised in its selection. Stones indigenous to the locality where they are quarried have generally withstood the ravages of their environment and may be used in similar climatic environments without trepidation. However, occasionally when stone is used in a new locale without proper investigation, unforeseen problems arise. The brownstone materials used for exterior steps and facades of residences in New York City deteriorated badly. The ravages of water, wear, and temperature that the brownstone had to endure in New York were completely different from those conditions prevalent at the quarries from whence these stones were taken. One would not use adobe brick in a wet climate, but it endures in the arid Southwest.

Similarly, building stone that has endured on structures through the ages in its native environment is beginning to show the effects of acid rain caused by industrial fumes and automobile engine exhaust gases, a problem that the designers selecting the building stone could not envisage at that time. The chief culprits in the disintegration of stone are oxides of carbon, sulfur, and nitrogen, the important deleterious ingredients found in the combustion of fossil fuels.

Stone Masonry Set in Mortar

Stone masonry construction, as noted previously, has undergone dramatic changes as architectural styles have changed, and the curtain wall stone panel or veneer panel has come into vogue. The traditional stone masonry wall set in mortar and used for fine residences, religious buildings, public buildings, banks, and other load-bearing walls is classified as to shape and finish as being either rubble or cut stone. Rubble is essentially the crude, uncut stone that is collected as fieldstone having rounded, natural faces or angular, broken faces. When laid in a wall, the pattern can be random or coursed. See Figure 4-18 for fieldstone elevations.

For cut stone, there are essentially no standard definitions. The terms cut stone, ashlar, and dimension stone have been used with varying degrees of differences among producers of marble, granite, and limestone. The term ashlar refers both to (1) a stone that has been cut generally square or rectangular and with either a finished or unfinished face and (2) a stone masonry wall construction utilizing ashlar stone. See Figure 4-19 for ashlar construction.

ASTM has but one definition for dimension stone: "a natural building stone that has been selected, trimmed or cut to specified or indicated shapes or sizes, with or without one or more mechanically dressed surfaces."

Bonding of Stone Masonry

Where stone masonry is laid up with a backing of either stone, concrete block, or brick, the bond between the facing and the back-up may be accomplished by use of bond stones, anchors, bond courses, or a combination of these elements.

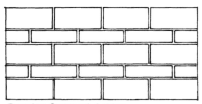

Regular Coursed Ashlar

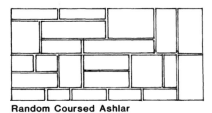

Random Coursed Ashlar

FIGURE 4-19 Ashlar wall construction.

Bond stones are facing stones generally cut to twice the bed thickness of the material used for facing stones. The percentage of stone used as bond stones is usually defined by building codes. Figure 4-20 shows a typical wall bonded with bond stones.

Veneer Stone

With the advent of new construction techniques and architectural styles, a change has occurred in the manner in which building stone is used on the

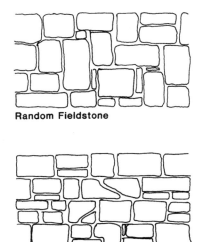

Random Fieldstone

Coursed Fieldstone

FIGURE 4-18 Rubble or fieldstone coursing.

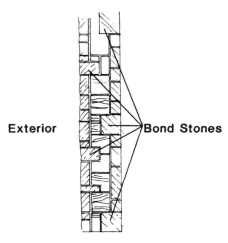

Exterior **Bond Stones**

FIGURE 4-20 Bonding of stone masonry.

facades of high-rise structures. The introduction of skeleton frame construction has almost eliminated the need for thick, massive, load-bearing stone masonry walls. The trend has been toward building stone panels or veneers less than 2 inches thick (50 mm), for granite, marble, travertine, and slate. To accomplish these ends, special anchoring systems have been developed to support these thin veneers. In some instances veneers of granite, marble, travertine, and slate measuring 40 mm (1.57 in.) and 30 mm (1.38 in.) have been utilized for exterior facings using standard and newly patented anchoring systems.

The Zibell Anchoring System is a patented product of the Georgia Marble Company. The system includes galvanized steel struts that can be anchored to either concrete or steel back-up and extruded aluminum members and aluminum fastening clips, all of which form a metal grid that carries the stone veneer facade. It is also adaptable to renovations and interiors. The system lends itself to simple and rapid installation.

The ISR System is a development of the Vermont Marble Company. This system is designed for rapid installation of prefabricated panels of marble, granite, serpentine, or other natural building stones from 7/8 inch to 1½ inches thick. Stainless steel angles are bolted to a back-up structural grid or masonry wall. The angles support the stone veneer panels by engaging grooves at the edges of the panel.

ASTM C1242 is a standard guide for design, selection, and installing of exterior stone anchors and anchoring systems.

The architect or designer must investigate the thickness of the particular species of stone that is under consideration with respect to face size, modulus of rupture, flexural strength, compressive strength, and handling stresses to ensure that the thickness is structurally adequate for the intended use.

With the introduction of thin veneers there has also been a reduction in the joint width, and sealants have replaced mortar in the joints. This replacement of mortar by sealants has occurred because narrower mortar joints have a tendency to powder out. Sealant technology has improved to the point where sealants provide a jointing material far superior to mortar. To assure nonstaining of stone by sealants, use test method ASTM C510.

Typical Building Stones and Uses

While exotic stone such as Mexican onyx and other rare stones have been used in building construction, this book is concerned with the most commonly used building stones. Table 4-15 lists these stones, their characteristics, and areas of use.

Physical Properties

Since building stone is one of the earliest building materials, a wealth of information has been accumulated on its physical and chemical properties. Building stone was used early on as a structural material in wall-bearing construction, and a good deal of data are available on thicknesses, sizes, and details associated with this type of construction. However, since World War II, more and more veneer-type panel construction has been used. Designers must therefore be extremely careful in selecting stone

TABLE 4-15
TYPICAL BUILDING STONES AND USES

Building stone	Type	Color	Major use	Minor use
Granite	Igneous	Wide range	Exterior and interior wall facings	Paving, flooring
Limestone	Sedimentary	Buff, gray	Exterior wall facings	Copings, sills, interior wall facings
Marble	Metamorphic	Wide range	Exterior and interior wall facings, flooring	Countertops
Sandstone	Sedimentary	Yellow, brown, reds, tan	Exterior wall facings	Paving
Slate	Metamorphic	Blue, gray, green, red, black	Paving, roof shingles	Wall facing
Travertine	Sedimentary	Tan, buff, gray	Exterior and interior wall facings	Flooring, paving

species, thicknesses, and panel sizes before making decisions on these characteristics. The factors of weathering, wind loads, and seismic conditions where these prevail must be taken into account since there is not yet a sufficient long-term history of thin, veneer-type building stones under these conditions of use.

There are a number of ASTM test methods available to ascertain certain physical characteristics that are pertinent when designing with building stone as follows:

ASTM C241	Abrasion Resistance
ASTM C170	Compressive Strength
ASTM C97	Density
ASTM C880	Flexural Strength
ASTM C99	Modulus of Rupture
ASTM C510	Staining of Stone by Sealants
ASTM C97	Water Absorption
ASTM C217	Weather Resistance of Slate

Structurally, building stones used for building construction are amply strong, especially in compression. When used as a soffit or ceiling, the thickness may have to be increased to accommodate anchors, which reduce the section.

Durability (see Chapter 1) is a most important performance characteristic, and weathering is the chief factor. Local stones may be used in the same locale if a history of their use there shows successful applications over a period of time. In addition, durability may be judged by examining open quarries or outcroppings to see how the stone has fared when exposed to the elements over a long time. That specific type of stone may also be expected to perform well in similar climatic environments far removed from its original source. However, as has been stated

previously, industrial, chemical, and automobile engine exhaust fumes may reduce the life expectancy. If a public building or a monument is contemplated with a life expectancy of several hundred years, then a more searching examination should be conducted to determine durability. If the structure is to have a life expectancy of 75 to 100 years, the risks of deterioration are much less.

For interior walls, most building stones, including the exotic marbles, will have no durability problems. However, when used as countertops, or when used in toilet rooms as walls, wainscots, or partitions, there may be evidence of staining or discoloration. Proper maintenance or the use of protective sealers may inhibit staining.

Table 4-16 shows some of the physical characteristics of typical stones used in building construction.

The National Building Granite Quarries Association recommends for granite the following standards for physical characteristics:

Water absorption	0.4% max.	ASTM C97
Density	160 lbs/cu ft	ASTM C97
Compressive strength	19,000 psi min.	ASTM C170
Modulus of rupture	1,500 psi min.	ASTM C99

The Indiana Limestone Institute recommends these values when designing with oolitic limestone:

Water absorption	7½% max.	ASTM C97
Modulus of rupture	700 psi max.	ASTM C99
Compressive strength	4,000 psi min.	ASTM C170

ASTM has developed a set of standards for the major building stones that set forth the requisite working characteristics as follows:

TABLE 4-16
PHYSICAL CHARACTERISTICS OF TYPICAL BUILDING STONES

Stone	Compressive strength	Modulus of rupture	Absorption
Granite	20,000–36,000 psi	1,480–3,240 psi	0.08–0.22
Limestone	4,000–20,000 psi	700 psi min.	7.5% max.
Marble	6,000–17,000 psi	—	0.069–0.609
Sandstone	4,000–64,000 psi	1,500 psi	—
Slate	10,000–15,000 psi	12,000 psi	.01–.02%

Physical property	Test req.	ASTM test
Granite—ASTM C615, Architectural Grade		
Absorption	0.4%	C97
Compressive strength	19,000 psi	C170
Modulus of rupture	1,500 psi	C99
Limestone—ASTM C563, Medium Density		
Absorption	7.5%	C97
Compressive strength	4,000 psi	C170
Modulus of rupture	500 psi	C99
Marble—ASTM C503		
Absorption	0.75%	C97
Compressive strength	7,500 psi	C170
Modulus of rupture	1,000 psi	C99
Sandstone—ASTM C616, Quartzitic		
Absorption	3%	C97
Compressive strength	10,000 psi	C170
Modulus of rupture	1,000 psi	C99
Slate—ASTM C629		
Absorption	0.25%	C97
Modulus of rupture	9,000 psi	C120

In some instances, particularly for nondomestic stone, some physical characteristics may fall below the working criteria established by the ASTM standards. The prospective user may be enthralled by the exotic stone being investigated and must decide whether the deficient characteristic is sufficient to rule out the choice of material or whether the deficiency can be compensated for by some other means, such as increased thickness.

Anchors and Anchorage

Anchors are metal ties used to secure stone in place. Anchors include straps, rods, dovetails, expansion bolts, cramps, and wire ties. Most anchors are designed to hold stone in its vertical position rather than support its gravity loads.

Under the heading of thin veneer stone, examples of proprietary and some standard metal anchoring systems for thin veneers are discussed. Stone exceeding 2 inches in thickness generally requires the types of anchors shown in Figure 4-21.

The metals used for anchors should always be noncorrosive, (1) so that they do not fail by virtue of cor-

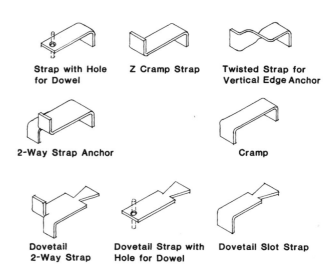

FIGURE 4-21 Typical anchors for stone.

rosion and (2) so that they do not stain the stone they are securing. Stainless steel for anchors offers many attributes. It is not too costly. It has high tensile strength. It is practically noncorrosive and most enduring. Other metals used are zinc alloys, yellow brass, and commercial bronze, with the least desirable being galvanized steel.

Whenever metal anchoring systems are used to support stone, care should be exercised to avoid galvanic action in unlike metal connections. See Chapter 1, Compatibility.

Staining

Building stone does have a tendency to absorb some moisture. When this moisture migrates from back-up materials, anchorage systems, and from ground-level sources, the moisture entering the stone may carry contaminants or soluble salts that may stain the stone. A major source of soluble salts is the concrete or masonry back-up.

To prevent staining, a number of precautions must be observed. By introducing weep holes above shelf angles and at base courses, the accumulation of water is reduced. Dampproofing treatments provided at base courses will act as a barrier to moisture migration into the stone. See Figure 4-22.

The best defense against staining is to prevent moisture from entering the wall. The most vulnerable areas are the stone joints. In veneer work, the use of

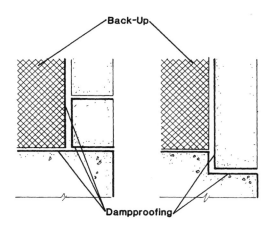

FIGURE 4-22 Dampproofing stone at grade.

FIGURE 4-23 Wyndham Hotel, Dallas, TX: granite—Sunset Red, polished finish. Dahl/Braden & Chapman, Architects. *(Courtesy of Cold Spring Granite Company.)*

sealant joints in lieu of mortar joints effectively reduces the entrance of water. When mortar joints are used, nonstaining cement offers the best protection against staining.

GRANITE

Physical Characteristics

Granite is a crystalline igneous rock composed mainly of feldspar and quartz with lesser amounts of mica and hornblende. Among building stones, granite is one of the hardest and most difficult to cut and finish. However, for exterior applications it is one of the most enduring. See Figure 4-23 for granite installation.

Colors

Depending on the quarry, domestic granite can be obtained in the following colors: white, gray, buff, beige, pink, red, blue, green, brown, and black. Granite in varying colors is likewise available from Canada and abroad.

When a block of granite is taken from a quarry it may be cut parallel to one of three axes. Depending upon which axis it is cut, slight variations in the appearance will result.

Classification

The National Building Granite Quarries Association classifies architectural granite as follows:

Building granite. Granite used either structurally or as a veneer for exterior or interior wall facings, steps, paving, copings, or other building features

Masonry granite. Granite used in large blocks for retaining walls, bridge piers, abutments, arch stones, and similar purposes

Finishes

Finishes that are most commonly available are as follows:

Polished. Mirror gloss, with sharp reflections.

Honed. Dull sheen, without reflections.

Fine rubbed. Smooth and free from scratches; no sheen.

Rubbed. Plane surface with occasional slight "trails" or scratches.

Shot ground. Plane surface with pronounced circular markings or trails having no regular pattern.

Thermal. Plane surface with flame finish applied by mechanically controlled means to ensure uniformity. Surface coarseness varies, depending upon grain structure of granite.

Sand-blasted coarse stippled. Coarse, plane surface produced by blasting with an abrasive; coarseness varies with type of preparatory finish and grain structure of granite.

Sand-blasted, fine stippled. Plane surface, slightly pebbled, with occasional slight trails or scratches.

8-Cut. Fine bushhammered; interrupted parallel markings not over $3/32$ inch apart; a corrugated finish smoother near arris lines and on small surfaces.

6-Cut. Medium bushhammered finish, similar to but coarser than 8-cut, with markings not more than $1/8$ inch apart.

4-Cut. Coarse bushhammered finish with same characteristics as 6-cut, but with markings not more than $7/32$ inch apart.

Sawn. Relatively plane surface with texture ranging from wire sawn, a close approximation of rubbed finish, to shot sawn, with scorings $3/32$ inch in depth. Gang saws produce parallel scorings; rotary or circular saws make circular scorings. Shot-sawn surfaces are sandblasted to remove rust stains and iron particles.

Special finishes of many kinds are also available from some producers to meet special design requirements. Samples should be obtained to ascertain how the granite species will appear with the special finish.

Minimum Thickness

The thickness of exterior veneer panels has been discussed under Veneer Stone. For bushhammered or pointed finish, a minimum thickness of 4 inches is required.

When granite is cut into panels (or tiles) less than 1 inch (25 mm) thick there is danger that the inherent discontinuities of granite's structure will bridge the thickness of the panel, permitting water passage from the face, or staining from the back-up. This susceptibility to staining or efflorescence from back-up materials is particularly likely to occur when very thin granite tile, $1/2$ in. (13 mm) or less, is set in mortar in exterior locations. Thin granite set in mortar in exterior locations should have its back face and edges coated with a good grade of nonstaining cementitious waterproofing, just as is customarily done with limestone and marble panels.

Joint Widths

Granite joints are usually $1/4$ inch thick. Smaller joint widths where desirable for design purposes may be obtained, but the costs will increase to achieve this end result.

Setting

In addition to the proprietary systems noted under "Veneer Stone," granite veneer can be set and anchored with the anchors described under "Anchors and Anchorage," and Figure 4-21.

When granite veneer is set, the vertical loads are typically carried on discontinuous angle supports arranged so that the angle is centered at the vertical joint between adjacent stones. Pads or buttons of plastic, neoprene, or lead, generally 1×1 inch by the joint thickness, are used at each horizontal joint to maintain the joint width until the sealant or mortar sets.

Checklist

1. The quarry must have sufficient stone of the color selected to satisfy the needs of the project.
2. The stone selected must be capable of withstanding the rigors of the weather at the project site.

3. Veneer thickness is a function of panel size especially with regard to handling, transportation, erection, and structural adequacy.

4. Detail the installation to inhibit moisture movement. Use waterproofing on back-up materials to prevent staining. At bases, detail the waterproofing as shown in Figure 4-22.

5. Mortar when used should be a nonstaining type.

6. Obtain sample to verify color, finish, and texture variations.

7. Specify shop and erection drawings together with structural calculations where necessary for anchorage system.

8. When storing stone at project site prior to setting, make certain that temporary wood strips or other parting devices do not stain or disfigure the stone.

9. During construction, unfinished stonework should be protected from rain or snow by plastic or nonstaining coverings.

LIMESTONE

Physical Characteristics

Limestone is a sedimentary rock composed chiefly of calcium carbonate. The chief varieties are oolitic limestone and dolomitic limestone. The latter has a high magnesium carbonate content.

Oolitic limestone, which is quarried mainly in Indiana, is a finely divided calcium carbonate formed of shells and shell fragments that were broken, crushed, and ground, and then redeposited in a shallow sea. Oolitic limestone is characteristically a freestone (a stone that may be cut freely in any direction without fracture or splitting) without pronounced cleavage planes, possessing a remarkable uniformity of composition, texture, and structure. This attribute lends itself to ease in machining and provides flexibility of shape and texture at low cost.

Dolomitic limestone is richer in magnesium carbonate (about 10 to 15 percent MgO) and frequently somewhat crystalline in character. It has higher compressive and modulus of rupture strengths than oolitic limestone. The dolomitic varieties are mined mainly in Minnesota and contain a broader range of color

and texture than oolitic limestone. Some of these stones are classified as marble by the Marble Institute of America.

Colors

Oolitic limestone is available in two colors as classified by the Indiana Limestone Institute—buff and gray. Buff varies from a light, creamy shade to a brownish buff. Gray varies from a light, silvery gray to shades of bluish gray.

Dolomitic limestone is available in gray tones, pinks, light to dark brown, and bluish-gray.

Classification and Uses (Oolitic Limestone)

The Indiana Limestone Institute classifies oolitic limestone by the degree of fineness of the grain particles and other natural characteristics that make up the stone. Structurally, the grades are essentially identical.

Oolitic limestone contains a few distinguishable calcite streaks or spots, fossils of shelly formations, pit holes, reedy formations, open texture streaks, honeycomb formations, iron spots, travertine-like formations, and grain-formation changes. Based on these characteristics, oolitic limestone is graded by the Indiana Limestone Institute as follows:

1. *Select.* Fine- to average-grained stone having a controlled minimum of the above characteristics

2. *Standard.* Fine- to moderately large-grained stone permitting an average amount of the above characteristics

3. *Rustic.* Fine- to very coarse-grained stone permitting an above-average amount of the above characteristics

4. *Variegated.* An unselected mixture of Grades 1 through 3, permitting both the buff and gray colors

Select Grade is generally used and confined to those areas of a building where: (1) cost is not a prime factor; (2) smooth machine finishes are desired; and (3) molded, carved, and sculptured detail is intended. As such it is well suited for lower-story work, entrances, and similar details where it is readily observed.

Standard Grade is most commonly used where a general uniformity of texture is desired, and cost is a consideration. It is particularly useful for commercial and monumental building for the ashlar stone work where Select Grade is neither appropriate nor warranted and where the slight variation in texture does not detract from the overall design intent. Standard Grade is also adaptable to the smooth finishes.

Rustic Grade is adapted to the less formal types of architectural design where a wide range of color tone (either buff or gray) and texture are appropriate.

Variegated Grade is used where mixtures of color tones (buff and gray) and texture are appropriate, especially for the rougher finishes such as chat-sawed, shot-sawed, and sand-sawed.

Finishes (Oolitic Limestone)

Smooth. Produced by a planer or grinder, or by a circular sander using a carborundum-faced sanding disk. Produces a relatively smooth surface with a certain amount of texture.

Plucked. A machine finish obtained by rough planing the surface, thus breaking or plucking out small particles and resulting in an interesting rough texture.

Machine-tooled. Parallel concave grooves are cut into the stone, in 4, 6, or 8 bats (grooves) to the inch. Depth of groove varies between $1/32$ to $1/16$ inch.

Chat-sawed. This finish is produced during the gang-sawing operation using a coarse pebbled surface resembling sand blasting.

Shot-sawed. By using steel shot in the gang-sawing operation, a coarse, uneven finish is produced, ranging from a pebbled surface to one ripped with irregular, roughly parallel grooves. The steel shot rusts during the process, allowing a certain amount of rust stains to develop and adding permanent brown tones.

Split face. A rough, uneven, concave convex finish is produced through a splitting action.

Rock face. Similar to split face except that the face of the stone is dressed by machine or hand to produce a bold, convex projection along the face of the stone.

Finishes (Dolomitic Limestone)

Split face.   Same as oolitic limestone

Gang sawed.   Consists of nearly parallel striations up to about $1/16$ inch deep

Shot-sawed.   Same as oolitic limestone

Carborundum.   Same as oolitic limestone

Planer.   Similar to Smooth Finish of oolitic limestone

Sand-rubbed.   Fine sand used as abrasive to produce a smooth finish

Honed.   Smoothest flat plane finish without a surface shine

Polished.   Shiny and reflective surface

Tapestry.   A heavy, sand-blasted finish that emphasizes the petrified plant life of the stone

Split rusticated finish.   Produced by a combination of sawing and splitting

Panel Sizes and Thicknesses

Dolomitic limestone has greater crushing and tensile strengths than oolitic limestone. With oolitic limestone, the Indiana Limestone Institute (ILI) recommends certain panel sizes and thicknesses for efficient fabrication and handling, as shown in Table 4-17.

Thin veneers under 2 inches in thickness are not usual with oolitic limestone. It is best to review the design requirements of a project with a producer to properly engineer the panel dimensions, after considering finishes, transportation, handling, and fabrication techniques.

TABLE 4-17
ILI MAXIMUM PANEL SIZES

Height (feet)	Width (feet)	Thickness (inches)
5	3	2
9	4	3
11	5	4
14	5	5
18	5	6

Checklist

See Checklist under Granite.

MARBLE

Physical Characteristics

Marble is a metamorphic rock, generally a meta-morphosed limestone composed of crystalline and compact varieties of calcium carbonate and/or magnesium carbonate. Its crystalline structure permits polished marble to gleam, since light penetrates a short distance and is then reflected from the crystalline structure. See Figures 4-24, 4-25, and 4-26 for marble installations.

Marble varies greatly in its ability to withstand atmospheric durability. Acid rain, industrial pollution, and automobile exhaust fumes may cause severe deterioration to the point where the material will be etched, flake, and ultimately crumble and disintegrate.

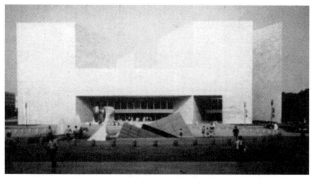

FIGURE 4-24   National Gallery of Art, East Building, Washington, DC: Tennessee marble. I.M. Pei & Partners, Architects.

Colors

The intrusion of other substances and impurities during the formation of marble results in a very colorful and veined stone that makes marble one of the more desirable decorative building stones that can take a high polish to reflect these characteristics.

Marble can range from white to black. Domestic marble colors include tan, pink, rose, red, brown,

FIGURE 4-25   Beinecke Rare Book & Manuscript Library, Yale University: white marble. Skidmore, Owings & Merrill, Architects. *(Photographer, Ezra Stoller © ESTO.)*

FIGURE 4-26 Interior view of Figure 4-25 showing translucent characteristics of marble. *(Photographer, Ezra Stoller © ESTO.)*

green, gray, and blue-gray. Marble is also available from foreign countries in a multitude of colors.

Classification

Marble is classified by groups by the Marble Institute of America (MIA) as follows:

Group A. Sound marbles and stones with uniform and favorable working qualities.

Group B. Marbles and stones similar in character to Group A, but working qualities somewhat less favorable; occasional natural faults; limited amount of waxing* and sticking† necessary.

Group C. Marbles and stones of uncertain variation in working qualities: geological flaws, voids, veins, and lines of separation common; which require repair by waxing,* sticking,† and filling; liners‡ and other forms of reinforcement freely employed when necessary, before or during installation.

---

* Waxing: Finishing by filling the natural voids in marble with color-blended material.
† Sticking: Process of cementing together broken slabs or pieces of marble.
‡ Liners: Structurally sound sections of marble that are cemented to the back of marble veneer to give strength or additional bearing surface.

Group D. Marbles and stones similar to Group C but with a larger proportion of natural faults and maximum variations in working qualities. This group comprises many of the highly colored marbles prized for their decorative qualities. The same methods of repair as used for Group C are required.

The classification of marble into these four groupings is based on experience gained over the years by marble suppliers and installers. The basis of this classification is the characteristics encountered solely in finishing and indicates what method of finishing is considered proper and acceptable.

While the C and D groups of marbles are more decorative by virtue of their veining and geological flaws, they are not necessarily suited for all building applications, especially exteriors. The Group A marbles are the soundest of all and are the ones most usually used for exterior applications.

Finishes

Marble can be finished in a variety of ways to enhance its appearance; this can range from polished to rough, as noted in Table 4-18.

Applications

Since marble is one of the most colorful of the building stones, it is widely used in all types of building applications. However, the veining and geological faults which create the beauty of marble inhibit its exterior use. Repair by way of sticking, waxing, and reinforcement allows Groups C and D marble to be used for interiors but rarely for exterior applications.

Polished finishes are restricted to a handful of marbles when used for exteriors. A honed finish is recommended for flooring.

In addition to the use of marble for exterior and interior walls, it can be used for copings, sills, saddles, treads and risers, paving, flooring, toilet partitions, and countertops.

Split-face finished marble is used for masonry ashlar work where the cut stone may have a bed about 4 inches deep, a height of from 2 to 8 inches, and lengths of about 12 to 48 inches.

TABLE 4-18
MARBLE FINISHES

Polished	A mirrorlike, glossy surface that brings out the full color and character of the marble. Produced by polishing a honed surface with a textile buffer and fine abrasives.
Honed	A velvety-smooth surface with little or no gloss produced by machine or hand rubbing with special abrasives.
Grit	A smooth, dull finish obtained by rubbing with an abrasive grit.
Sand, blown	A smooth, matte surface achieved by a light sandblasting.
Sand, wet	A smooth surface obtained by rubbing with a machine using sand and water as abrasives.
Sanded	A smooth, dull finish produced by rubbing with sand.
Natural	A moderately rough, textured face produced by sawing with sand and water as abrasives.
Split Face	A rough natural face of stone produced by machine splitting.

Thin Veneer Panels

Marble exterior facings can vary in thickness from $7/8$ to 2 inches. The required thickness will depend on the panel size, anchoring provisions, the handling requirements, and the local building code. In general, the greater thicknesses are desirable for high-rise structures, or where the panel faces are large, or where the weather is severe. Thinner panels are adequate where the panel sizes are small or for low storefront work. However, it is prudent to check the thickness to be detailed with several marble suppliers and installers.

Checklist

1. See checklist for Granite.
2. For thin veneers, provide a space between marble and back-up for air circulation.
3. Where solid grouting is required between marble and back-up, use nonstaining, waterproofed mortar utilizing portland cement.

SANDSTONE

Physical Characteristics

Sandstone is a sedimentary rock usually consisting of quartz cemented with silica, iron oxide, or calcium carbonate. Sandstone is durable and has a very high crushing and tensile strength. Bluestone and brownstone are sandstones named for their colors.

Colors

Sandstones come in a variety of colors. Sandstones of pure silicon dioxide are white. With the iron oxide impurities, sandstone colors are available in grays, yellows, browns, reds, tans, and pinks.

Finishes

Sandstone is available in split-face, rustic-face, pitched-face, chat-sawed, sand-sawed, and smooth-sawed finishes.

Sizes and Uses

A good deal of sandstone is used as rubble stone masonry and as split-face ashlar stone masonry in sizes varying in bed width from 3 to 5 inches, in height from 2 to 12 inches, and in length from 8 to 36 inches.

Veneer panels are available from some suppliers in the sizes shown in Table 4-19.

TABLE 4-19
MAXIMUM FACE SIZE AND
THICKNESS OF SANDSTONE

Face size	Thickness
2 × 4 feet	2¼ inches
6 × 3½ feet	3 inches
8 × 3½ feet	3½ inches
8 × 3½ feet	4 inches

Rubble stone masonry and split-face masonry are set in mortar and are usually wall bearing. Veneer stone panels are generally installed with conventional stone anchors and mortar joints.

SLATE

Physical Characteristics

Slate is a very fine-grained metamorphic rock derived from sedimentary rock shale. It is characterized by an excellent parallel cleavage entirely independent of the original bedding, by which cleavage the rock may be split easily into relatively thin slabs.

Color

Slate owes its colors to ingredients other than shale. Carbonaceous or iron sulfides produce the dark colors of black, blue, and gray. Iron oxide accounts for the reds and purples and chlorite the green.

Select slate is uniform in color. Ribbon slate contains bands or ribbons of darker color and sometimes ribbons of different colors. The colors may be unfading or weathering (color changes with exposure of weather).

Finishes

Slate is available in several finishes as follows:

Honed.　A semipolished finish, smoother than sand-rubbed but without a high sheen surface.

Sand rubbed.　Surface is rubbed to remove all natural clefts using the equivalent of a 60-grit abrasive.

Natural cleft.　This is the natural split or cleaved face. It is moderately rough with some textural variation.

Semi-rubbed.　Approximately 50 percent of natural cleft face removed.

Gauging.　A grinding process used on backs of natural cleft surfaces to produce a more even thickness for better fit.

Uses

Slate is used for a variety of building areas both interior and more recently as exterior wall and column facings. Some areas of use are as follows:

Interior walls	Shelving
Flooring	Blackboards
Paving	Electrical panel boards
Flagging	Fireplaces
Treads and risers	Bases
Stools	Roofing shingles

Sizes and Thicknesses

Slate is not used for ashlar or rubble masonry. Black slate is used primarily as a facing veneer on exterior and interior walls. All varieties are used as flooring (see Chapter 9) and paving (see Chapter 2). For exterior face veneers, sizes of up to 5 feet × 8½ feet × 1½ inches have been used successfully. Smaller exterior panels have utilized 1-inch thick slate. Limitations for individual panels are not over 9½ feet in length and not over 5 feet in width.

Setting

Exterior wall panels. Each slate panel should be anchored separately by nonferrous ¼-inch diameter wire turned down 1 inch into a ⅜-inch round, 1½-inch deep hole in the edge. A minimum of four anchors is recommended for panels up to 12 square feet, with two additional anchors for every additional 6 square feet of panel. Doweling natural cleft slate to slate is not recommended. Relief angles and occasionally liners are recommended at normal floor-line distances. The back of the slab should be a minimum of 1 inch from back-up, with an air cavity, and with portland cement spots 6 × 6 inches centered 18 inches apart.

Exterior jointing. For natural cleft finishes, exterior joints should be ⅜ to ½ inch wide because of the variation in the texture and lippage of adjacent panels.

Interior wall panels. Setting is similar to exterior panels except that in some cases, small panels ¼ inch thick may be set in mastic and with butt joints.

TRAVERTINE

Physical Characteristics

Travertine is a sedimentary rock and a variety of limestone, which is deposited from solution. It is a product of chemical precipitation from hot springs. Travertine is cellular with the cells usually concentrated in thin layers that display a stalactic structure. Some that take a polish are sold as marble and may be classified as travertine marble under the class of commercial marble. As a result of its manner of formation, travertine is characterized by many irregular cavities. Figure 4-27 shows the travertine facade of the LBJ Library, Austin, Texas.

Colors

Travertine is available in grays, pinks, rose, and shades of tan. Some travertine has large fissures and others less noticeable fissures.

Travertine is produced in the United States, but the more exotic colors and formations are quarried near Rome in Italy. However, for a major project it would be essential to visit the quarries or obtain 2½- × 5-foot samples to select the specific material desired. One need only examine the many structures at Lincoln

FIGURE 4-27 LBJ Library, Austin, TX: travertine facade. Skidmore, Owings & Merrill, Architects. *(Photographer, Ezra Stoller © ESTO.)*

Center in New York to visualize the differences between various travertines from different quarries.

Finishes, Uses, Setting

Travertine can take a high polish and is finished, used, and set like marble. When travertine is used for structures such as countertops, the fissures may be filled with chips of travertine and colored mortar to match the adjacent areas.

Checklist

1. See checklist under Granite.
2. For large projects, an inspection of the quarry to make selections and ensure an adequate supply is recommended.
3. Verification of specified material by submission of large panel samples (2½ × 5 feet) is suggested.

John F. Kennedy Library, Boston, MA: interior view illustrating space frame. I.M. Pei & Partners, Architects. (© *Mona Zamdmer 1979, Photographer.*)

5

METALS

FABRICATION PROCESSES

Good architectural design and detailing require not only a knowledge of the characteristics of the metals used in ornamental metalwork but also an understanding of how they are worked, shaped, and formed in the fabrication process. Each metal by virtue of its physical characteristics has its own peculiarities, and the ease or difficulty in forming is reflected in its cost-in-place. Obviously, by understanding fabrication processes, economies may be introduced by proper selection of standard sizes and shapes and by detailing.

The following definitions of shaping and forming terms will aid in understanding the fabrication process:

Blanking. In sheet metalwork, the cutting out of a piece of metal, usually by means of a press.

Braking. A mechanical bending operation usually performed on sheets and plates.

Broaching. Finishing the inside of a hole to a shape other than round.

Casting. An article formed by solidification of molten metal in a mold.

Cold drawing. Drawing metal through a die without the application of heat.

Cold-rolled. Metal rolled at room temperature, below the softening point, usually harder, smoother, and more accurately dimensioned than hot-rolled material.

Cold working. The process of changing the form or cross section of a piece of metal at a temperature below the softening point.

Countersinking. Beveling the edge of a hole for the reception of the head of a bolt, rivet, or screw.

Drawing. Forcing metal to flow into a desired shape without melting by pulling it through dies.

Embossing. Development of a raised design on a metal surface by die pressure or by stamping or hammering on the reverse surfaces.

Extrusion. Forcing a molten metal through a die by pressure.

Fluting. Formation of a semicircular groove or series of grooves in sheet metal.

Forging. Heating and hammering or pressing metal into a desired shape.

Forming. Pressing metal into shape by mechanical operations other than machining.

Hot-forming. Working operations such as bending, drawing, forging, piercing, and pressing performed at temperatures above the recrystallization temperature of the metal.

Lost-wax process. A process using patterns of wax which are melted and drained from the mold before the metal is poured; used in the making of castings involving undercuts and other complications.

Milling. Removal of metal to develop a desired contour by means of a revolving cutting tool.

Perforating. Punching or drilling multiple holes in sheet metal, blanks, or formed parts.

Pressing. Forcing metal to conform to the shape of a die by means of pressure.

Punching. Forcing a punch through metal into a die, forming a hole the shape of the punch.

Reaming. Enlarging a round hole in a piece of metal by means of a revolving edged tool.

Riveting. Forming a connection between two or more pieces of metal by passing a rivet through aligned holes and upsetting to form a head.

Rolling. Shaping metal, either hot or cold, by passing it between revolving rolls set to a predetermined distance apart. Rolls may be flat or shaped as desired.

Seaming. Uniting the edges of a sheet or sheets by bending over or doubling and pinching the edges together.

Shearing. Cutting metal by the action of two opposing passing edges.

Spinning. Shaping sheet metal by bending or buckling it under pressure applied by a smooth hand tool or roller while the metal is being revolved rapidly.

Stamping. Bending, shaping, cutting out, indenting, embossing, or forming metal, either hot or cold, by means of shaped dies in a press or power hammer.

Straightening. Eliminating deformations by pressing, rolling, or stretching.

Stretcher leveling. A process of stretching a metal sheet to produce a straight, flat surface.

Swaging. Surface working of a forging (either hot or cold) by means of repeated blows, usually between dies.

Tapping. Cutting internal threads in a punched or drilled hole.

Tempering. A heat treatment whereby metal is brought to a desired degree of hardness and elasticity.

Tumbling. A process of cleaning metal articles by placing them in a revolving container, with or without cleaning material.

Turning. Removal of metal by means of an edged cutting tool while the piece is being revolved about its axis.

Upsetting. Building up or thickening the section of a piece of hot or cold metal by shortening the piece by axial compression.

Work hardening. The increase in hardness developed in a metal as a result of cold working.

STANDARD STOCK MILL PRODUCTS

For most architectural applications there are standard stock metal items, produced in the form of sheet, plate, strips, bars, rods, wire, or extrusions, that are used to develop either simple shapes and forms or combinations of these mill products that are used to develop complex shapes and forms. The following definitions are representative of standard stock items of most metals.

Angle. A section of metal rolled, drawn, or extruded through L-shaped rolls or dies.

Bar. Round, square, rectangular, hexagonal, or other solid stock of drawn, rolled, or extruded metal. A rod.

Channel. A rolled, drawn, or extruded metal section having a U shape.

Flat. A rectangular bar whose width is greater than its thickness.

Pipe, round. A hollow, round section of metal, the size of which is determined by the nominal inside diameter in inches.

Pipe, square. A hollow, square section of metal, the size of which is determined by the nominal outside diameter in inches.

Plate. A flat piece of metal. Various metals are defined as plate by the following thickness criteria:

Aluminum	¼ inch or more
Copper	0.188 inch or more
Steel	3/16 inch or more
Stainless steel	3/16 inch or more

Rod. See Bar.

Round. A cylindrical rod (see Bar).

Sheet. A thin, flat piece of metal, the thickness of which is thinner than plate (see Plate).

Strip. Narrow metal sheets either produced in coil form or cut to length and finished flat.

Tubing. A hollow section of metal which may be round, square, rectangular, hexagonal, octagonal, or other shape, measured by the external size in inches and wall thickness by gage or decimals of inches.

Wire. A small-diameter rod measured by gage, produced by a drawing process (see Bar).

JOINING

Both ornamental and utilitarian metalwork are fabricated in units and assembled or joined in the shop into sections. The sections are joined together in the field into the finished work. Joining is an important aspect of metalwork and may be performed in a number of different ways, depending upon the type of metal and the specific problem. Typical joining procedures include bolting and riveting, welding, brazing, and soldering.

Bolting and Riveting

Bolting and riveting are similar operations where two or more pieces of metal are connected by a bolt or rivet that passes through holes. Bolting may be temporary or permanent. Riveting is a permanent connection where one end of the shank is upset by hammer blows to form a head. During this process the shank expands to fill the holes fully, thus forming a strong, tight joint. Riveting is rarely used now for structural steel.

Welding

Welding is a process of joining metals by applying heat and pressure, with or without filler material, to produce an actual union through fusion. There are a number of welding processes employed as follows:

Carbon arc. An electric arc process wherein a carbon electrode is used, and fusion is produced by heating. Pressure may or may not be applied, and filler metal may or may not be used.

Electric arc. A process wherein a metal electrode is used which supplies the filler material in the weld and the heat to produce the fusion.

Forge welding. A process wherein fusion is produced by heating in a forge or furnace and applying pressure or blows to the work.

Fusion welding. A process of welding without pressure in which a portion of the base metal is melted. It is usually accomplished by gas flame or electric arc heating.

Gas welding.   A process of welding wherein fusion is produced by heating with gas (acetylene, hydrogen), with or without pressure and with or without filler material.

Resistance welding.   A process of welding accomplished by placing the work to be joined under pressure in a machine, then applying an electric charge through the joint, the resistance of which produces heat to fuse the joint.

Welding sometimes imparts distortion, brittleness, or changes in strength and ductility at the joint. To overcome these deficiencies, cold working and annealing are often necessary to restore the original working characteristics. With nonferrous metals such as aluminum the factor of color may have an important bearing upon the choice of the proper welding process and the proper electrode or filler metal.

Brazing

Brazing is a process wherein a molten filler metal is used to join metal parts. The filler metal has a melting point below that of the metals to be joined. Brazing is accomplished at temperatures above that of soldering (800°F) and below that of welding. Heating for brazing may be accomplished by dipping the parts into a bath of the molten alloy, by heating with torches, furnace heating, or by electrical resistance.

Brazing materials must be selected to offer corrosion resistance between base metals and filler, or, where a color match is required, between the base metal and the brazing metal, or where the strength of the joint will not be impaired by the brazing metal.

Brazing materials consist of the following:

Aluminum-silicon.   For brazing aluminum

Copper-phosphorus.   For brazing copper and copper alloys

Silver.   For brazing ferrous metals, copper, and copper alloys

Copper and copper zinc.   For brazing ferrous metals, copper, and copper alloys

Heat-resisting alloys.   For brazing ferrous metals

Soldering

Soldering is a process similar to brazing with the filler metal having a melting temperature range below 800°F. Since soldering temperatures are low, there is no alloying of the base metal and the solder. As a result the base metals are usually stronger than the joint. Where the strength of the joint in sheet metalwork is to be improved, it is advisable to reinforce the seams by crimping, interlocking, riveting, or bolting before soldering, depending upon the solder to make the joint tight. Aluminum is not easily soldered. See Aluminum for further information.

HEAT TREATING

Heat treating is employed in metalworking to induce certain properties or to relieve stresses and strains after certain metalworking processes have been performed. Heat-treating processes include the following:

Annealing.   A heating and cooling operation performed on metal in the solid state involving cooling at a relatively slow rate. The process generally results in reducing hardness, improving machinability, facilitating cold working, removing stresses, and altering the ductility and toughness of metals. The temperature of the operation and the rate of cooling will depend upon the specific metal and the purpose of the annealing process.

Tempering.   A specific heat treatment whereby metal is brought to a desired degree of hardness or softness.

SURFACE WORKING

Surface-working processes involve the application of certain operations to the surface of metals to alter their appearance and include the following:

Blasting, cleaning.   Obtaining a mottled or pebbled surface by means of blasting the surface with sand, grit, or steel shot through a nozzle by air pressure.

Brushing, buffing, polishing. Producing smooth, satin, bright, or buffed finishes by means of wheels on high-speed lathes, by belts on sanding wheels, or by disks and wheels on hand buffers and grinders.

Etching. A process of chemical etching the surface by means of acid or alkali solutions to obtain decorative architectural effects.

Grinding. A surface texture is obtained by varying the grit in a grinding wheel or disk.

Hammering. Metal surfaces can be altered by indentation through hammering or peening to obtain the desired degree of surface alteration.

ALUMINUM

Aluminum is a nonmagnetic silvery white metal that is easily formed in the fabrication process by extrusion, rolling, drawing, stamping, casting, and forging. It is light in weight (about one-third the weight of iron) and has a melting point of about 1200°F. The thermal coefficient of expansion is 0.0000128, and the tensile strength is 22,000 psi.

Since aluminum unalloyed is deficient in strength and soft, it is rarely used in building construction in its refined state. By alloying it with other elements, its physical characteristics are enhanced considerably.

Aluminum alloys are available in the form of bar, castings, extrusions, forgings, pipe, plate, sheets, structural shapes, tubes, and wire. Aluminum provides a high degree of corrosion resistance; since the products of corrosion are white, staining of adjacent surfaces is reduced.

ALUMINUM ALLOYS

Alloy Classification System

The Aluminum Association classifies aluminum alloys on the basis of the major alloying metal. The most widely used wrought aluminum alloys in building construction are shown in Table 5-1.

TABLE 5-1
ALUMINUM ALLOYS

Alloy	Major alloying metal
Series 2000	Copper
Series 3000	Manganese
Series 4000	Silicon
Series 5000	Magnesium
Series 6000	Magnesium and silicon
Series 7000	Zinc

ALLOY SELECTION GUIDE

The following is a guide to the selection of aluminum alloys.

Sheet and Plate

3003	Most widely used for roofing sheet metal applications where anodizing is not required. Assumes a slight yellowish cast when anodized.
Alclad* 3004	A clad aluminum sheet used for standard corrugated, ribbed, or V-beam section and various embossed patterns for industrial roofing and curtain wall sheets.
5005	Commonly used for low-cost, all-purpose sheets with good formability and finishing characteristics. Has good anodized appearance match with alloy 6063 extrusions.
5050	An alloy with good corrosion resistance and stronger than alloys 3003 and 5005. Produces a comparatively clear, white appearance after anodizing.
5052	Good workability and excellent corrosion resistance. Assumes yellowish cast when anodized. Used for venetian blinds and weatherstripping.

* The term *alclad* refers to a protective cladding of aluminum that is applied to thin sheets of a core alloy to improve its corrosion resistance. When buffing clad products, exercise care not to wear through cladding. Do not grind. The cladding may be of the same or different alloy than the core.

6061   Most economical and versatile of the heat-treatable alloys. Used for roll-formed structural shapes and applications requiring high strength. Good anodized appearance match with alloy 6061 extrusions, but may take on yellowish cast when anodized.

Extrusions

6061   Used principally for extruded structural shapes, pipe and tubing, or applications requiring high strength. For color anodizing matching, use in conjunction with alloy sheet 6061.

6063   Most commonly used extrusion alloy for building and ornamental metal products. For anodized color matching, use alloy sheet 5005.

Castings

43   Used for hardware and ornamental metalwork where strength is not critical; turns gray after anodizing.

214   Stronger than alloy 43. Best appearance match with 6063 extrusions and 5005 sheets, when anodized.

356   High-strength casting alloy; turns gray after anodizing.

Special Alloys

For proprietary alloys (both sheet and extrusions) designed for quality applications where excellent anodized appearance is critical, it is best to consult with the major aluminum producers.

Porcelain Enamel Alloys

1100
Sheet   A commercial pure aluminum, with low mechanical properties and good workability. Specify PE grade.

3003
Sheet   Higher mechanical properties than 1100 alloy. Has excellent framing characteristics. Use PE Grade 3003.

6061
Sheet & extrusion   Stronger and harder than alloys 1100 and 3003, combines good mechanical properties with good resistance to corrosion.

7104
Extrusion   Allows maximum freedom of design for extruded shapes. It combines the extrusion characteristics of alloy 6063 with

higher mechanical properties and good workability.

Casting
Alloy43   A general-purpose casting alloy.

Casting
Alloy356   Good casting characteristics and heat treatable to develop maximum mechanical properties.

Specialty Porcelain Enamel Alloys

Improved alloys are constantly being discovered as a result of research, commercial practice, and metallurgical advances. Consult porcelain enamel fabricators for most recent development of porcelain enamel aluminum alloys.

TEMPER AND HEAT TREATMENT

The tempering of aluminum alloys is achieved by mechanical or thermal treatment or by a combination of both, to improve strength or hardness. By alloying aluminum with other elements, strength and hardness are imparted to the pure aluminum. Further strengthening is achieved by classifying the alloys into two categories: non-heat-treatable and heat-treatable.

Non-heat-treatable alloys, Series 1000, 3000, 4000, and 5000, are further strengthened by cold working, denoted by the H series of tempers.

Heat-treatable alloys, Series 2000, 6000, and 7000, which contain copper, magnesium, zinc, and silicon either singly or in various combinations, will respond to pronounced strengthening when heat treated.

Heat treatment or solution heat treatment is an elevated temperature process designed to put the soluble alloying elements in solid solution. This is followed by rapid quenching, usually in water, which momentarily freezes the structure and for a short time renders the alloy very workable.

Artificial aging or precipitation hardening is achieved by heating for a controlled time at slightly elevated temperatures.

TABLE 5-2
BASIC TEMPER DESIGNATIONS

F	As fabricated—Applies to products of shaping processes in which no special control over thermal conditions or strain hardening is employed.
O	Annealed—Applies to wrought products which are annealed to obtain the lowest-strength temper, and to cast products which are annealed to improve ductility. The O may be followed by a digit other than zero.
H	Strain-hardened (wrought products only)—Applies to products which have their strength increased by strain hardening, with or without supplementary thermal treatment to produce some reduction in strength; always followed by two or more digits.
W	Solution-heat-treated—Unstable temper, applies to alloys which spontaneously age at room temperature after solution heat treatment.
T	Thermally treated to produce stable tempers other than F, O, or H; followed by one or more digits.

TABLE 5-4
SUBDIVISION OF T TEMPERS

T1	Cooled from an elevated temperature-shaping process and naturally aged to a substantially stable condition
T2	Cooled from an elevated temperature-shaping process, cold worked, and naturally aged to a substantially stable condition
T3	Solution heat-treated, cold worked, and naturally aged to a substantially stable condition
T4	Solution heat-treated and naturally aged to a substantially stable condition
T5	Cooled from an elevated temperature-shaping process and artificially aged
T6	Solution heat-treated, then artificially aged
T7	Solution heat-treated and then stabilized
T8	Solution heat-treated, cold worked, then artificially aged
T9	Solution heat-treated, artificially aged, then cold worked
T10	Cooled from an elevated temperature-shaping process, cold worked, then artificially aged

Basic Temper Designations

A temper designation system, based on heat treatment, aging, and annealing, has been formulated consisting of letters and number designations. Table 5-2 shows the basic temper designations which are usually added as a suffix to the alloy type, for example, 6063-T5. Table 5-3 shows the subdivision of H tempers, and Table 5-4 shows the subdivision of T tempers.

For fabricated products, manufacturers usually purchase aluminum stock shapes that are tempered to the requirements necessary for the specific products. When designing building components, consult with the aluminum producer and fabricator to ascertain the required alloy tempers for the specific needs.

TABLE 5-3
SUBDIVISION OF H TEMPERS

H1	Strain hardened only. The digit indicates degree of strain hardening.
H2	Strain hardened and partially annealed.
H3	Strain hardened and stabilized.

CLEAR AND COLOR-ANODIZED FINISHES

Aluminum is unique among the architectural metals with respect to the wide variety of finishes including the integral clear and color-anodized finishes available as a result of research and development.

There are two important advantages of finished aluminum to the architect: (1) appearance and (2) protection. These are derived on the basis of certain pretreatments which include: (1) mechanical finishes (ranging from polished to satin, bright, matte, and pebble-textured) and (2) chemical finishes (ranging from caustic etch to acid etch, brightened, and chemical conversion coatings). Following these pretreatments (except for chemical conversion coatings), the aluminum may then be anodized to obtain a clear coating or an integral color-anodized coating.

Aluminum may be used without an anodized finish since exposure to the air will result in the formation of a thin, protective oxide film. Prolonged exposure to the weather, however, will result in roughening of the surface with attendant chalkiness.

Anodizing, which is a controlled oxidizing process, produces a thicker, denser, and harder oxide coating that adds to the durability of the metal. It is recommended that for exterior architectural applications, only aluminum which has been anodized be used unless a high-quality coating is factory-applied.

Mechanical Finishes

Mechanical pretreatment is a process whereby the surface characteristics of the metal are induced by mechanical means. These characteristics may be achieved by the original mill production processes such as rolling and extruding or by subsequent polishing, grinding, brushing, or blasting techniques. The mechanical processes used and their designations have been classified by the Aluminum Association and are shown in Table 5-5.

The mechanical finishes are performed on individual parts or components, generally a hand operation, although mechanical equipment is involved. These operations may include buffing wheels, belt polishers, sanders, and blasting equipment.

Prior to specifying any mechanical finish, it is best to consult the aluminum producer and product fabricator to ascertain whether certain items are capable of receiving specific mechanical finishes. For example, small-radius inside corners and inaccessible areas on extruded or formed shapes cannot be buffed on a belt polisher. Where these surfaces are finished by hand, they may not match the belt finish.

Buffed finishes should be reserved for narrow, flat surfaces, since application of this process to broad surfaces will result in oil-canning as a result of the high reflectivity. In addition the belt width limitation will result in overlaps on a broad surface, thereby reducing uniformity of finish and appearance.

Alloys that have an alclad surface may in some instances not be capable of receiving a mechanical finish because the cladding is too thin to withstand such an operation.

A sample of the mechanical finish desired should be examined and the cost and suitability verified prior to making a commitment on the mechanical finish to be used. In addition, the mechanical finish should receive the proposed chemical finish and anodic treatment so that the ultimate finished product can be visualized.

TABLE 5-5
MECHANICAL FINISHES (M) ON ALUMINUM

As Fabricated	
M10	Unspecified
M11	Specular as fabricated
M12	Nonspecular as fabricated
M1X	Other (to be specified)
Buffed	
M20	Unspecified
M21	Smooth specular
M22	Specular
M2X	Other (to be specified)
Directional Textured	
M30	Unspecified
M31	Fine satin
M32	Medium satin
M33	Coarse satin
M34	Hand rubbed
M35	Brushed
M3X	Other (to be specified)
Nondirectional Textured	
M40	Unspecified
M41	Extra-fine matte
M42	Fine matte
M43	Medium matte
M44	Coarse matte
M45	Fine shot blast
M46	Medium shot blast
M47	Coarse shot blast
M4X	Other (to be specified)

Chemical Finishes

Chemical pretreatments serve three principal purposes: (1) to clean the aluminum surface in preparation for subsequent finishes, (2) to provide surfaces of uniform electrochemical reactivity to receive anodic coatings, and (3) to etch the surface to obtain specific light reflectance characteristics.

From the standpoint of equipment used and processing time required, chemical treatments are among the least expensive finishing procedures. Mechanical finishing usually involves several operations, with the work performed on individual components or assemblies. Chemical treatment is performed in batches; the finished products are loaded into chemical baths that are part of the anodizing line and sequence of operations.

Several types of chemical treatments are used, and these are classified as: (1) general cleaning treatments (nonetched); (2) etched treatment, which results in a matte finish (most popular of architectural finishes, especially on broad flat surfaces); (3) bright finishes ranging from mirror bright to diffuse bright; and (4) chemical conversion coatings (used for paints, coatings, and laminations, but not to receive anodic finishes). Table 5-6 shows the Aluminum Association classifications of the various chemical treatments.

Since most chemical finishes are achieved by immersing the assembled product in a bath which is usually one of the baths in an anodizing line, the size of the tank may often be the limiting factor in the design of the size of the units to be treated, such as column covers, spandrels, or window frames.

When specifying chemical treatments, care must be exercised that the texture to be obtained is harmonious. For example, because of differing metallurgical

TABLE 5-6
CHEMICAL FINISHES (C) ON ALUMINUM

Nonetched Cleaned

C10	Unspecified
C11	Degreased
C12	Inhibited chemical cleaned
C1X	Other

Etched

C20	Unspecified
C21	Fine matte
C22	Matte
C23	Coarse matte
C2X	Other

Brightened

C30	Unspecified
C31	Highly specular
C32	Diffuse bright
C3X	Other

*Chemical Conversion Coating**

C40	Unspecified
C41	Acid chromate-fluoride
C42	Acid chromate-fluoride phosphate
C43	Alkaline chromate
C4X	Other

* Chemical conversion coatings are shown as part of the chemical finishes. However, they are not a pretreatment for anodic coatings. They result in gray or green colors but are intended as a preparation of the surface to receive organic paint coatings.

characteristics of sheet, extrusions, and castings, the same alloy in these differing forms may not have exactly matching textures following similar chemical treatment. The texture-matching quality may also not be quite the same when similar alloys having different tempers are chemically treated by the same process. It is recommended that samples be obtained to ensure texture-matching quality whenever various forms, tempers, and alloys are used in the same configuration or in close proximity to one another.

Anodic Finishes

Definition

Anodizing is an electrolytic process in which the aluminum to be anodized is immersed in a specific acid solution through which a direct electric current is passed between the aluminum and the solution, with the aluminum acting as the anode. This causes negatively charged oxygen anions to combine chemically with the aluminum, forming an aluminum oxide film. This electrolytic process results in the controlled formation of a relatively thin but durable anodic coating on the surface of metal, as compared to natural weathering of aluminum, which results in a very thin, soft, and sometimes chalky oxide coating.

Types of Anodizing Processes

While there are several anodizing processes that result in aluminum oxide formations, there are essentially three processes used in architectural applications.

1. *Sulfuric acid anodizing.* This process is the oldest and one of the most widely used anodizing processes. In this process sulfuric acid is used as the electrolytic solution. The most notable finishes are the typically clear, transparent coatings. With the advent of newer processes, the sulfuric acid is now often referred to as the conventional process. While coloring dyes and pigments are also available with this method, it has limited architectural applications. At present only gold-color mineral pigments are suitable for colorfast exterior applications. As noted in Table 5-7, anodic coatings A31 and A41 are typical clear coatings of this sulfuric acid process. A33 and A43 represent the impregnated colors. Integral colors

TABLE 5-7
ARCHITECTURAL ANODIC FINISHES (A)

Designation	Description	Methods of finishing
Architectural Class II Finishes (0.4 to 0.7 mil)		
A31	Clear coating	15% H_2SO_4, 70°F at 12 A/ft^2 for 30 min
A32	Coating with integral color	Color dependent on alloy and anodic process
A33	Coating with impregnated color	15% H_2SO_4, 70°F at 12 A/ft^2 for 30 min followed by dyeing with organic or inorganic colors
A34	Coating with electrolytically deposited color	15% H_2SO_4, 70°F at 12 A/ft^2 for 30 min followed by electrolytic deposition of inorganic pigment in the coating
Architectural Class I Finishes (0.7 mil and over)		
A41	Clear coating	Same as Class II except 60 min electrolysis
A42*	Coating with integral color	Color dependent on alloy and anodic processes
A43	Coating with impregnated color	Same as Class II except 60 min of electrolysis
A44	Coating with electrolytically deposited color	Same as Class II except 60 min of electrolysis

* Since the A42 finish is obtained by either the conventional or the hardcoat process, the type of process must be specified.

noted in Table 5-7 as A42 may also be obtained with the conventional method using certain controlled alloys to produce color. If the hardcoat integral color is desired, it must be so specified.

2. *Integral color hardcoat anodizing.* In this process, special patented acid electrolytes are used and the integral color is obtained by means of the electrolyte, the aluminum alloy, higher electric current densities, higher voltages, and more accurate control of the electrolyte composition and temperature. The oxide coatings developed through this method are more dense and have higher resistance to abrasion than the conventional anodic coatings. The colors range from the light bronzes to medium and dark bronze, and from light grays to dark grays and black. As noted in Table 5-7, anodic coatings A32 and A42 are typical coatings derived by this process.

3. *Electrolytically deposited colors.* A proprietary method known as *Analok,* licensed by the Aluminum Company of Canada Ltd., produces a range of lightfast colors similar to those produced by the integral color hardcoat process. In this method, noted in Table 5-7 as A34 and A44, stable metallic compounds are electrolytically deposited at the base of the pores in a previously formed oxide coating.

Designation of Anodic Finishes

Table 5-7 shows a modified Aluminum Association designation system for anodic finishes that are used primarily for architectural purposes: Class I and Class II.

Architectural Class I finishes are those more than 0.7 mil thick and weighing more than 27 mg/sq in. They are appropriate for interior use where they are subject to normal wear and for exterior use where they are subject to the effects of weathering.

Architectural Class II finishes are those with thicknesses of between 0.4 and 0.7 mils with corresponding weights of from 17 to 27 mg/sq in. They are utilized for interior items that are not subjected to excessive wear or abrasion and for exterior surfaces that are within easy reach and can be maintained on a regular basis.

Sealing the Anodic Coating

The final step in the anodizing process, and one that must be specified, is the sealing of the porous oxide coating. The coating has literally billions of microscopic pores, and these must be closed to prevent absorption of contaminants that will stain and corrode the surface. Both clear and integrally colored anodic coatings are generally sealed in pure or deionized boiling water to seal the pores and prevent further absorption, as shown in Figure 5-1.

Standard Finish Designations

The Aluminum Association Designation System for aluminum finishes involving clear and color-anodized coatings consists of a letter designating the mechanical treatment (M), the chemical treatment (C), and anodic (A) finishes, and two-digit numbers indicating the specific finish, all of which are shown in Tables 5-5, 5-6, and 5-7.

Examples of how the system is used are illustrated as follows. The designation is preceded by the letters AA to identify it as an Aluminum Association designation.

AA-M21 When this designation is specified, a smooth specular finish is obtained by mechanical treatment.

AA-M32 C12 A31 When this designation is specified, a medium satin finish (M32), an inhibited chemical cleaning (C12), and a clear anodic coating using a sulfuric acid bath for 30 minutes (A31) is obtained.

Quality Control of Anodic Finishes

There are three basic qualities of the anodic coating that must be ensured and these are: (1) the coating weight, (2) the coating thickness, and (3) the resistance of the coating to staining. These qualities can be ascertained by testing of random samples.

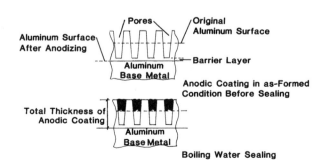

FIGURE 5-1 Sealing mechanism of anodic coatings. *(Courtesy of Aluminum Company of America.)*

Coating weight. ASTM B137 is a method of test for coating weight which is determined by stripping the coating in phosphoric-chromic acid solution and weighing the sample prior to and after the test procedure.

Coating thickness. ASTM B244 is a method of test for coating thickness which is determined by the lift-off effect of a probe coil that contacts the coating and generates eddy currents in the metal substrate.

Resistance to staining. This property is obtained by proper sealing of the anodic coating described previously and is ascertained by one of the following test methods:

ASTM B136 Standard Method for Measurement of Stain Resistance of Anodic Coatings on Aluminum

ASTM B457 Standard Method for Measurement of Impedance of Anodic Coatings on Aluminum

International Standard ISO-2931 Assessment of Quality of Sealed Anodic Oxide Coatings by Measurement of Admittance of Impedance. A minimum impedance of 100 kilohms is required.

International Standard ISO-3210 Assessment of Sealing Quality by Measurement of the Loss of Mass after Immersion in Phosphoric-Chromic Acid Solution. The maximum dissolution weight loss should be no more than 2.6 mg/sq in.

Color and Color Matching of Color-Anodized Aluminum

The color and degree of color matching of color-anodized aluminum are of the utmost concern to the architect. The problem concerns not only the architect's design selections but also the architect's specifications and the agreed-upon method of ascertaining the degree of color acceptability and color matching between the architect and the finisher.

When designing a structure, the architect should break up the panel design, using projections or reveals at panel joints that reduce or eliminate undesirable appearance because of slight variations in color of adjacent panels. The architect must also recognize that it is difficult to color-match extrusions and sheet and may want to accentuate the differences.

The selection of matte chemical finishes and bright chemical finishes likewise have an effect on color.

Matte finishes will result in a lighter apparent color, and bright finishes will result in a darker apparent color. These apparent color variations result from the reflectivity of the metal substrate as well as from the anodic coating. Only controlled alloys should be specified for color-anodized finishes.

As an additional control, representative samples should be obtained from a finisher or the major producers. Two samples should be selected to establish the light-and-dark range of colors that will be permitted on the project. During erection, the extreme colors should not be placed adjacent to one another but kept separated by an intermediate color.

During production, an inspection procedure can be specified that is mutually agreeable to the architect and finisher. This may include visual comparison of previously approved color range standards under certain indoor lighting arrangements or outdoor inspection in natural light.

Steps in the Anodizing Process

Since anodic coatings reflect the surfaces under them, the pretreatment of these surfaces by mechanical, chemical, and electrochemical techniques is essential to the attainment of a good anodic coating. The basic steps in the anodizing line after mechanical and chemical pretreatment are shown in Figure 5-2.

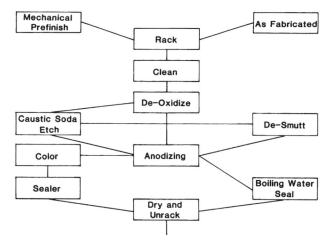

FIGURE 5-2 Steps in the anodizing process. *(Courtesy of Aluminum Company of America.)*

APPLIED COATINGS

In addition to the electrochemical anodic finishes, four other types are provided under the Aluminum Association designation system. These coating types are designated resinous-organic, vitreous, electroplated, and laminated.

The fabricator of the aluminum normally has to ship the cut or partly fabricated components to a finishing plant for application of the coatings discussed below, unless coil-coated stock is being used. This, of course, is also true of anodizing—for all but the largest aluminum fabricators. This extended total fabrication time for aluminum components with quality finishes must be taken into account in costing, scheduling, and changes to the work.

Resinous-Organic Coatings

For use in architectural applications, only those organic coatings with life expectancies of at least 10 years are described in detail here: the fluoropolymers, powder coatings, siliconized acrylics and siliconized polyesters, and the plastisols.

Paints can be applied to cleaned and etched aluminum surfaces, but their satisfactory service in sunlight, rain, and polluted air is limited—some kind of repainting would have to be done every 5 to 10 years—a very expensive proposition for slender framing containing much glass and sealants that would have to be masked. Thus, no paints—only coatings—are discussed here.

To qualify as high-performance coatings, standards have been established by the American Architectural Manufacturers Association (AAMA). AAMA 605.1, "Specification for High Performance Organic Coatings for Architectural Extrusions and Panels," and AAMA 605.2, "Specification for Premium High Performance Organic Coatings for Architectural Extrusions and Panels," are specifications that describe test procedures and requirements for factory applied resinous coatings that are formulated to give long service under severe conditions.

Resinous-organic coatings are generically designated AA R10 in the Aluminum Association system. There is no current agreement on assigning numbers such as R11, R12, etc., to any of the coatings that are described here.

Fluoropolymers

Polyvinylidene fluoride (PVDF) resin is the only fluoropolymer that is in commercial use as a finish on architectural aluminum. Polyvinyl fluoride (PVF) is too hard to apply, and polytetrafluoroethylene (PTFE) cannot be applied in a solvent formulation and has a porous structure when sintered in place on a surface. PVDF, like the other fluoropolymers, is a highly inert substance, almost totally unaffected by ozone, and is the most ultraviolet-resistant coating available. Abrasion and chemical resistance is high. PVDF is not chemically related to the chlorofluorocarbons (CFCs) that wreak havoc with the atmosphere and cause high-altitude ozone depletion.

Fluoropolymers used to be referred to as "fluorocarbons," a term that is now generally limited to fully fluorinated polymers such as Teflon. The common acronym PVDF was once commonly written PVF2.

PVDF color coats can be applied over prepared aluminum, galvanized steel, aluminized steel, and glass surfaces, most often as part of a multi-coat system. Aluminum provides a very smooth surface either for direct application or for application over a prime coat or prime plus barrier coat. A clear top coat is sometimes specified over the primary color coat. PVDF can be used to coat coil sheet stock or it may be used to electrostatically spray (ESP) extruded sections. The resin is normally baked at approximately 245°C (475°F) although an air-curing formulation is also available, primarily for touch-up. The resin is optimally used at 70 percent strength, tests having revealed no benefit to higher concentrations of PVDF. Lower strengths of the PVDF resin component of the coating definitely do not perform as well as 70 percent strength for longevity in normal exposed use. Applied at optimal concentration, PVDF provides excellent color fastness and resistance to gloss change (some 20-year warranties are offered) and adhesion to substrate.

There are two basic producers of PVDF architectural resins in North America. A dozen or more formulators of architectural coatings supply the metal finishing industry with proprietary products based on Hylar 5000 or Kynar 500 resins. Both qualify as AAMA 605.2 coatings.

In budgeting, realize that price breaks occur between standard solid colors, custom solid colors, and metallic colors.

Powdered Coatings

Like some other high-performance coatings, these were largely developed in Europe for a more narrow range of climatic conditions. While remaining a major presence there, they have been adapted to North American conditions and have found a place in the market in part because they provide some practical advantages: excellent application characteristics (heavier buildup at edges rather than equal thickness or starving) and lack of volatile organic compound (VOC) emissions to the atmosphere.

In composition they are basically polyesters that have been formulated and augmented to provide good resistance to color change and chalking.

Siliconized Polymers

Siliconized acrylic and siliconized polyester are less expensive coatings that provide a solid middle level of performance. Their color retention, resistance to chalking, chemical resistance, abrasion resistance, and flexibility are not as great as that of other high-performance coatings, but they have become the standard of the highly competitive residential and commercial window industry.

The desirable properties of the silicone family of resins (which include the siloxanes) prompt these mixtures, since silicones by themselves cannot be formulated as film-forming coatings. There is no industrywide agreement on the amount of silicones that should be present. Spray formulations usually run about 50 percent maximum, coil coatings about 30 percent. The spray version can be brittle for some applications. The siliconized polymers can mildew and can be difficult to touch up or recoat.

Because of their ease of application and curing, they are often applied in the aluminum fabricator's plant, without the need for shipping to finishing operators. Although silicone-acrylics and silicone-polyesters are used in coil coating sheet aluminum, their most frequently encountered application is by electrostatic spray (ESP), which ensures that even the deepest crevasses of the aluminum extrusion receive the coating before baking. In fact, with many fabricators "ESP paint" has become a kind of code word on their shop drawings for a silicone-acrylic or silicone-polyester coating.

The wise design professional asks just what material is being provided when ESP—which is merely the method of application—is being offered.

Plastisols

Plastisols are dispersion coatings based on high molecular weight polyvinyl chloride (PVC) homopolymer resins dispersed in a plasticizer. They provide good corrosion, scuff, and mar resistance. Their color retention and chalk resistance is not as good as that of PVDF films. Vinyl plastisols are resistant to a wide range of reagents and are frequently used in chemical processing plants.

Other Organic Resins

Fluorocarbons (toxic, very costly) and polyurethanes (less toxic, difficult to apply) can also be applied to aluminum. Epoxies (excellent adhesion and chemical resistance, but brittle) are recommended for interior use only. All three are very hard and can give a high-gloss finish.

Vitreous Coatings

Most vitreous or ceramic coatings are inorganic, porcelain enamel coatings bonded to aluminum by fusion at a temperature of at least 425°C (800°F). Porcelain enamel is an alumina-borosilicate glass mixed with other ingredients to provide color and other desirable characteristics such as resistance to heat, abrasion, and corrosion. In light and pastel colors it resists color change from ultraviolet degradation well. It is the hardest coating put on aluminum and the easiest to wipe clean, but is also the most brittle.

The Porcelain Enamel Institute (PEI) has long been active in promoting quality standards for architectural porcelain enamel and has produced standards for quality control, alloy selection, and test methods. PEI publishes a specification for the exterior use of porcelain enamel on aluminum: ALS-105.

Vitreous coatings are generically designated AA V10 in the Aluminum Association system. There is no current agreement on assigning numbers such as V11 or V12 to subcategories.

Electroplated and Laminated Coatings

Electroplating and laminating coatings to aluminum are not commonly encountered in commerce, but constitute generic categories E10 and L10 in the Aluminum Association system of finish designation. Laminated coatings are usually applied directly over the substrate, without intervention of a primer.

Fluoropolymers, particularly polyvinyl fluoride (PVF or Tedlar), lend themselves to film formation. These films of uniform color can be directly laminated to aluminum with good adhesion and constant film thickness. PVF and PVDF films can also be laminated directly to steel, vinyl, and ABS plastic substrates.

At least one acrylic film is marketed for coil application only. The film is of good quality and bonds well to the substrate. Acrylic films have limited scratch, stain, and solvent resistance.

EXTRUSIONS

One of the advantages of using aluminum for architectural purposes is the comparative ease with which it may be extruded. This allows the designer freedom of choice in fashioning a detail that would involve more intricate metalworking with other architectural metals.

When aluminum is extruded, a heated ingot is placed in an extrusion press and forced through a shaped opening. The dies can create a limitless variety of one-piece shapes with external and internal ribs, channel curves, flats, slots, grooves, and oddly shaped openings. The extrusion die is comparatively inexpensive, and this feature too allows the designer to utilize this technique of extrusion more frequently. At present, aluminum extrusions are produced with circle sizes ranging from ¼ inch to 31 inches.

METALLURGICAL JOINING PROCESSES

For a comprehensive discussion on the subject of welding, brazing, and soldering, see *Welding Aluminum*, published by the American Welding Society.

Welding

Aluminum is readily joined by welding, and most welding techniques may be used. When appearance is of primary importance, fusion welding using the gas tungsten-arc and gas metal-arc produce the best as-welded appearance.

Welded parts may also receive chemical pretreatments and electrochemical anodic finishes. Resistance, ultrasonic, and pressure welds are least noticeable after these treatments.

Brazing

Brazing forms joints of excellent appearance that require little or no finishing. When anodizing is required, brazing filler metals darken during the finishing. To avoid this problem, complete flux removal is required prior to anodic treatment.

Soldering

Soldering of aluminum is not the best solution to joining of aluminum. Welding and brazing are preferable for joints requiring good strength. Other techniques that can be used to avoid soldering include adhesive bonding, mechanical fastening, or epoxied joints. Soldering is not recommended for sheet metal joining.

COPPER

Copper and its alloys (principally zinc) are probably the oldest metals used for ornamental metalwork in building construction. This is undoubtedly due to the fact that, of all architectural metals, copper and its alloys provide the inherent advantage of integral color. The different alloys have varying colors and, as

will be explained later, problems can arise in otherwise well-executed architectural detailing because of failure to select proper alloys for color match and color harmony.

The copper alloys primarily used for ornamental metalwork have been and still are called bronzes. They are, however, truly brasses except for some of the casting alloys. The wrought sheet, plate, and extrusion copper alloys are essentially alloys of copper and zinc, which is the definition for brass. Only some of the casting alloys containing 2 percent or more of tin can be classified as bronzes.

PHYSICAL PROPERTIES

When cold worked, copper alloys may exhibit tensile strengths ranging from 36,000 to 70,000 psi for some silicon bronze alloys. Tensile values for red brass 230, Muntz metal 280, and architectural bronze 385 fall in the range of 40,000 to 60,000 psi. These strengths compare favorably with those of aluminum and carbon steel. The modulus of elasticity for copper alloys in tension ranges from 14 million to 17 million.

The thermal coefficient of expansion of copper alloys is approximately 0.00001 per °F. A useful approximation allows ⅛ inch expansion per 10 feet of length for each 100°F temperature change.

Since the cost of copper is high as compared to aluminum and steel, light structural steel core members are used to stiffen an element using sheet copper alloys as a covering.

COPPER AND COPPER ALLOYS

Alloy Designation System

The major copper alloys, their composition, natural color, and final weathered colors are shown in Table 5-8. The final weathered colors are achieved in about six years.

**TABLE 5-8
PRINCIPAL COPPER ALLOYS**

Alloy number & name	Composition	Natural color	Weathered colors
110 copper	99.9% Cu	Salmon red	Reddish brown to gray-green
122 copper	99.9% Cu 0.02% P	Salmon red	Reddish brown to gray-green
220 commercial bronze	90% Cu 10% Zn	Red gold	Brown to gray-green
230 red brass	85% Cu 15% Zn	Reddish yellow	Chocolate brown to gray-green
260 cartridge brass (yellow brass)	70% Cu 30% Zn	Yellow	(Not for exterior use)
280 Muntz metal	60% Cu 40% Zn	Reddish yellow	Red-brown to gray-brown
385 architectural bronze	57% Cu 3% Pb 40% Zn	Reddish yellow	Russet brown to dark brown
655 silicon bronze	97% Cu 3% Si	Reddish old gold	Russet brown to mottled dark gray-brown
745 nickel silver	65% Cu 25% Zn 10% Ni	Warm silver	Gray-brown to mottled gray-green
796 leaded nickel silver	45% Cu 42% Zn 10% Ni 2% Mn 1% Pb	Warm silver	Gray-brown to mottled gray-green

Principal Forms, Standards, and Uses

The various copper alloys are available in a variety of forms, such as rods, bars, tubes, and sheets. Table 5-9 illustrates the principal forms that are available, the standards to which they are produced, and typical end uses.

Color Matching of Copper Alloys

Color match and color harmony are prime considerations for the architect when using copper alloys. It is not unusual to find as many as four alloys in combination for some designs to achieve color match and harmony. Table 5-10 shows color matching of various forms of copper alloys as equated to sheet and plate forms.

STAINING AND CORROSION

Sulfur compounds, stemming from combustion of fossil fuels and combined with water in the form of acid rain, are the chief atmospheric corrosive agents of copper and its alloys. The weathering of copper alloys over the years is attributable to this corrosive action. Concentrated attack may result in thinning of the metal to failure. Moderate weathering produces the patinas that enrich the coloring of copper alloys.

Wherever dissimilar metals are in direct contact in the presence of moisture, galvanic corrosion of the less noble metal in the couple may occur (see Chapter 1, Table 1-5). Under such conditions, provision should be made to insulate the materials to avoid corrosion by using paint primers, sealants, or tapes.

Where copper roofing or flashing shed water onto porous stonework such as limestone or marble, the detailing of such installations should be refined to prevent such run-off directly onto these surfaces, since it may cause significant disfigurement.

TABLE 5-9
FORMS, STANDARDS, AND USES OF COPPER ALLOYS

Alloy no.	Forms available	Standards*	End uses
110	Strip, sheet	B152	Roofing metal
122	Tube	B75	Roofing metal, doors, lighting fixtures, railings
		B88	
220	Strip	B36	Unlimited use
	Wire	B134	
	Bar, rod	—	
230	Strip	B36	Unlimited use
	Pipe	B43	
	Tube	B135	
260	Strip	B36	Interior use, interior-lighting fixtures, signs
	Tube	B135	
	Pipe	—	
280	Plate, sheet	Fed. spec.	Curtain walls, entrance doors
	Strip	QQ-B-613	
385	Extrusions	B455	Curtain walls, entrance doors
655	Plate, sheet	B97	Artwork, entrance doors, windows
	Pipe, tube	B315	
745	Sheet, strip	B122	Artwork, bank equipment, elevator cabs
	Bar	B151	
	Rod	B206	
	Tube	—	
796	Bar extrusions, rod	—	Artwork, bank equipment, elevator cabs

* Standards are ASTM except when noted Fed. Spec.

TEMPERING AND HEAT TREATMENT

In the copper alloy family, tensile and yield strengths are increased primarily by means of alloying and cold working. Although heat treating finds some limited use as a strengthening mechanism, it is not applicable to any of the principal architectural copper alloys.

FINISHING

Standard designations for copper alloy finishes are published by the Copper Development Association, in the *Copper, Brass, Bronze Design Handbook.* These consist of mechanical finishes—M, chemical finishes—C, organic coatings—O, and laminated fin-ishes—L. A summary of these standard designations is shown in Table 5-11.

Chemical Coloring

Some of the chemical finishes hasten the natural weathered effect that generally results from exposure to the weather. The verde antique finishes are developed using acid chloride treatment or acid sulfate treatments.

Statuary (oxidized) finishes are produced in light, medium, and dark colors, depending upon both the concentration and the number of applications of the chemical coloring solutions. Two to ten percent aqueous solutions of ammonium sulfide, potassium sulfide (liver of sulfur) or sodium sulfide (liquid sulfur) are used to produce statuary finishes.

TABLE 5-10
COLOR MATCHING COPPER ALLOYS*

Sheet and plate alloys	Extrusions	Castings	Fasteners	Tube & pipe	Rod & wire	Filler metals
Alloy 110 **Alloy 122** Copper	**Alloy 110** Copper (simple shapes)	**Copper** (99.9 min.)	**Alloy 651** Low-silcon bronze (fair)	**Alloy 122** Copper	**Alloy 110** Copper	**Alloy 189** Copper
Alloy 220 Commercial bronze, 90%	**Alloy 314** Leaded commercial bronze	**Alloy 834**	**Alloy 651** Low-silicon bronze	**Alloy 220** Commercial bronze, 90%	**Alloy 220** Commercial bronze, 90%	**Alloy 665** High-silicon bronze
Alloy 230 Red brass, 85%	**Alloy 385** Architectural bronze	**Alloy 836***	**Alloy 651** Low-silicon bronze (fair) **Alloy 280** Muntz metal	**Alloy 230** Red brass, 85%	**Alloy 230** Red brass, 85%	**Alloy 655** High-silicon bronze (fair)
Alloy 260 Cartridge brass, 70%	**Alloy 260** Cartridge brass, 70% (simple shapes)	**Alloys 852,** **853**	**Alloy 260** Cartridge brass, 70% **Alloy 360** **Alloy 464** **Alloy 465**	**Alloy 260** Cartridge brass, 70%	**Alloy 260** Cartridge brass, 70%	**Alloy 681** Low-fuming bronze (poor)
Alloy 280 Muntz metal	**Alloy 385** Architectural bronze	**Alloys 855*** 857	**Alloy 651** Low-silicon bronze (fair) **Alloy 280** Muntz metal	**Alloy 230** Red brass, 85%	**Alloy 280** Muntz metal	**Alloy 681** Low-fuming bronze
Alloy 655 High-silicon bronze	**Alloy 655** (simple shapes)	**Alloy 875**	**Alloy 651** Low-silicon bronze **Alloy 655** High-silicon bronze	**Alloy 651** Low-silicon bronze **Alloy 655** High-silicon bronze	**Alloy 651** Low-silicon bronze **Alloy 655** High-silicon bronze	**Alloy 655** High-silicon bronze
Alloy 745 Nickel-silver	**Alloy 796** Leaded nickel-silver	**Alloy 973**	**Alloy 745** Nickel-silver	**Alloy 745** Nickel-silver	**Alloy 745** Nickel-silver	**Alloy 773** Nickel-silver

Source: Courtesy, Copper Development Association, Inc., New York, NY.
* Alloys to be used in various forms, for best color match with certain sheet and plate alloys. Color of surfaces compared after identical grinding or polishing.

DESIGN CRITERIA

Sheet and Strip

When designing in sheet, it is necessary to avoid oil canning or buckling. With thinner gages, distortion becomes more pronounced. Broad, bright, reflective surfaces accentuate minor variations in flatness and become apparent. Distortion can be reduced by increasing the gage or by using a backing material to increase rigidity. Natural weathering, chemical coloring, and texturing tend to mask minor distortions by reducing surface reflectivity.

Unsupported broad, flat areas such as spandrels or column covers usually require a metal thickness greater than 0.100 inch to avoid oil canning. By introducing patterns or textures, the increased rigidity may permit gage reductions to the range of 0.064 to 0.100 inch. These reduced thicknesses are also suitable for metals laminated or bonded to suitable substrates.

TABLE 5-11
SUMMARY OF STANDARD DESIGNATIONS FOR COPPER ALLOY FINISHES*

Mechanical Finishes (M)			
As fabricated	Buffed	Directional textured	Nondirectional textured
M10-unspecified mill finish	M20-unspecified	M30-unspecified	M40-unspecified
M11-specular as fabricated	M21-smooth specular[†]	M31-fine satin[†]	M41-(unassigned)
M12-matte finish as fabricated	M22-specular[†]	**M32-medium satin**	**M42-fine matte**[†]
M1x-other (to be specified)	M2x-other (to be specified)	**M33-coarse satin**	M43-medium matte
		M34-hand rubbed	M44-coarse matte
		M35-brushed[†]	M45-fine shot blast
		M36-uniform	M46-medium shot blast
		M3x-other (to be specified)	M47-coarse shot blast
			M4x-other (to be specified)

Chemical Finishes (C)	
Nonetched cleaned	Conversion coatings
C10-unspecified	**C50-ammonium chloride** (patina)
C11-degreased	**C51-cuprous chloride-hydrochloric acid** (patina)
C12-cleaned	**C52-ammonium sulfate** (patina)
C1x-other (to be specified)	C53-carbonate (patina)
	C54-oxide (statuary)
	C55-sulfide[†] (statuary)
	C56-selenide (statuary)
	C5x-other (to be specified)

Coatings			
Clear organic (O)	Laminated (L)	Vitreous and metallic	Oils and waxes
AIR DRY (general architectural work)	L90-unspecified	Since the use of these finishes in architectural work is rather infrequent, it is recommended that they be specified in full, rather than being identified by number.	These applied coatings are primarily used for maintenance purposes on site. Because of the broad range of materials in common use, it is recommended that, where desired, such coatings be specified in full.
O60-unspecified	L91-clear polyvinyl fluoride		
O6x-other (to be specified)	L9x-other (to be specified)		
THERMOSET (hardware)			
O70-unspecified			
O7x-other (to be specified)			
CHEMICAL CURE			
O80-unspecified			
O8x-other (to be specified)			

Source: Courtesy, Copper Development Association Inc., New York, NY.
* In this listing, those finishes which are printed in boldface type are the ones most frequently used for general architectural work; those marked [†] are commonly used for hardware items.

Extrusions

As a general working guide, extruded shapes are limited in cross section to shapes having a greatest diagonal dimension which can be contained within the perimeter of a 6-inch circumscribed circle and as shown in Table 5-12.

FABRICATING PROCESSES

Forming

Architectural copper alloys lend themselves to a variety of forming processes as shown in Table 5-13.

Joining

Fasteners

The use of fasteners (screws, bolts, rivets) to join architectural copper alloys is the simplest and most common joining method. Color matching of fastener to metal alloy is important and is shown in Table 5-14.

Adhesive Bonding

Copper alloys can be bonded to steel, plywood, hardboard, and similar substrates. As a result, thinner gages can be used, resulting in cost reductions and in panels having flat, broad surfaces without oil canning. Alloy 110 can be used in such applications in gages ranging from 0.002 to 0.032 inch. Muntz metal 280 can be applied in gages as low as 0.032 inch.

For exterior applications, thermosetting or high-quality thermoplastic adhesives are used. Since moisture may enter at edges, edge design and detailing are crucial to prevent peeling and moisture entry.

TABLE 5-12
EXTRUSION DESIGN CRITERIA

Diameter of circumscribing circle (inches)	Minimum gage of extrusion (inches)
2	0.064
3	0.080
4	0.093
5	0.108
6	0.125

TABLE 5-14
COPPER MECHANICAL FASTENERS

Fastener alloy	Color match
260	Color matches alloy 260
280	Matches alloy 385
360	Matches alloy 260
464 and 467	Fair color match with alloy 385
485	Fair to good color match with alloys 280 and 385
745	Color matches with alloy 745 and 796

TABLE 5-13
COPPER ALLOYS SUITABLE FOR FABRICATING PROCESSES

Alloy	Bending	Brake forming	Extrusion	Cold forging	Hot forging	Rollforming	Spinning
110	X			X	X	X	X
122	X						
220	X	X		X	X	X	X
230	X	X		X	X	X	X
260	X	X		X	X	X	X
280	X	X			X		
385			X		X		
655	X	X		X	X	X	
745	X	X		X		X	X
796			X				

Adhesive Joining

Railings, intersecting members, and similar details can be joined by the use of bonding adhesives and sleeved connections with concealed pins and fasteners.

Metallurgical Joining Processes

Copper alloys employ brazing, soldering, and welding in joining metal parts. Brazing is the preferred method in terms of adequate joint strength and soundness. However, blind or concealed joints are preferred with brazing, since color matching is fair to poor.

Soldering is used primarily for roofing and flashing to seal joints. These joints are mechanically reinforced to ensure adequate strength. Soldering should be confined to concealed joints, since solders do not color match with the copper alloys.

Welding of copper alloys should be restricted to the silicon bronzes that are readily welded and produce good color matches and sound welds.

STAINLESS STEEL

Stainless steels make up a family of corrosion- and rust-resistant iron-base alloys containing a minimum of 12 percent chromium. The corrosion resistance is improved by adding more chromium. Nickel and manganese when alloyed with the chromium-iron-base metal produces special characteristics such as strength, toughness, and ease of fabrication.

Stainless steel is the strongest, most durable, and most corrosion resistant of all the architectural metals. It is likewise nonstaining and can therefore be used with other materials such as stone, metals, and clay tile products without the danger of staining or deterioration.

Because of its strength, lighter gages can be used as compared to other metals, thereby effecting economies. Also, because of its corrosion-resistant properties, minimal maintenance is required of stainless steel.

ALLOY CLASSIFICATION

Classification

While there are over 40 different stainless steel alloy compositions, only seven are commonly used in architectural metalwork. In addition, stainless steels are divided into three groups according to metallurgical structure: austenitic, martensitic, and ferritic. While this classification is of interest chiefly to metallurgists, there are basic differences that are of import to architects.

1. *Austenitic stainless steels* (AISI 200 and 300 Series) contain nickel and are essentially nonmagnetic. They are hardened by cold working but not by heating. They are ductile and can be fabricated and welded easily. The types used primarily in architectural metalwork are 201, 202, 301, 302, 304, and 316.

2. *Ferritic stainless steels* (AISI 400) contain chromium as the primary alloying element and are magnetic. They are hardened only slightly by heat treating and can be hardened moderately by cold working. The type used primarily in architectural metalwork is 430.

3. *Martensitic stainless steels* contain a magnetic alloy with a limited application in architectural uses.

Types

The various types of stainless steel are usually employed as follows.

For sheet, strip, plate, bars, tubing, and extrusions that find application in both exterior and interior architectural metalwork such as column covers, doors, fascias, mullions, panels, windows, and trim, and for roofing metalwork:

TYPE 301	Contains less chromium and nickel than types 302/304 and has slightly higher work-hardening characteristics; also slightly higher tensile strength than 302/304
TYPE 302/304	The most popular and most widely used alloys architec-

turally, referred to as 18–8 stainless (18% Cr–8% Ni); often used interchangeably

TYPES 201 and 202   Lower in nickel content and higher in manganese content than the 302/304 types but a little more difficult to form

For applications at or near marine or saltwater atmospheres and in industrial applications where corrosive conditions obtain:

TYPE 316   A modification of types 302/304 with a higher nickel content and the addition of 2 to 3 percent molybdenum that adds to corrosion resistance and pitting resistance

For interior architectural applications where less resistance to corrosion is tolerable:

TYPE 430   A ferritic chrominum stainless steel alloy with no nickel and less costly than austenitic types described above

For fasteners in either exposed or protected locations:

TYPE 305   Used for bolts, nuts, screws, and other fasteners, compatible with types 302/304 insofar as appearance, corrosion, and durability are concerned

For fasteners in locations protected from weather:

TYPE 410   Used for mechanical fasteners where less corrosion resistance is required

Physical Properties

Yield strength of stainless steel alloys is between 30,000 and 50,000 psi, tensile strength between 75,000 and 115,000 psi, and modulus of elasticity about 28 million psi. The coefficient of thermal expansion is 0.0000094.

FINISHES

Stainless steel sheet and strip are supplied from the mill in various standard finishes. Polished finishes (Nos. 3, 4, 6, 7, and 8) can be applied to plate, bars, sheet, tubular products, and extrusions. Table 5-15 shows the extent of the standard mill finishes. Since architectural finishes have a directional appearance, specify panels to be erected with the grain parallel and in the same direction.

Proprietary Finishes

In addition to the standard mill finishes, many proprietary finishes are available from individual producers. It is best to obtain samples and explanations as to cost, availability, and efficacy of these proprietary finishes on specific shapes and forms.

TABLE 5-15
STANDARD STAINLESS STEEL FINISHES

Type	Description
Sheet-Rolled	
No. 1	A dull finish, nonarchitectural
No. 2D	A dull, nonreflective finish
No. 2B	A bright, moderately reflective finish
Bright annealed	A bright, highly reflective finish
Sheet-Polished	
No. 3	An intermediate polished finish
No. 4	A bright machine-polished finish with a visible grain, the finish most frequently used for architectural applications
No. 6	A dull satin finish
No. 7	A bright, highly reflective finish
No. 8	A bright mirror finish
Stainless Steel Strip	
No. 1	Similar to No. 2D for sheet
No. 2	Similar to No. 2B for sheet
Bright annealed	Similar to bright annealed for sheet

FABRICATING PROCESSES

Forming

Stainless steels for architectural applications may be cut by shearing and sawing. They may be blanked, nibbled, punched, and drilled—also brake formed, roll formed, cast, and extruded.

Castings are used for hardware and for ornamental purposes in sculpture and plaques.

Extrusions of stainless steel are likewise available in angles, railings, stiles, thresholds, and other shapes. There are limitations on sizes based on the extrusion technique. Since extrusion is a constantly evolving procedure, designers should consult the extruder or fabricator to obtain information on the latest capabilities in the extrusion process.

The high ductility of stainless steel permits the use of sharp bends and moderately deep stamped patterns. Sheets of 18 gage or thinner can be bent 180° and flattened without cracking.

Joining

Stainless steel can be assembled or joined by metallurgical means (welding and soldering) and by mechanical fasteners (bolts, screws, rivets).

Welding of stainless steel is readily performed by all the common fusion and resistance methods. In most instances, grinding and polishing of welds removes any trace of the weld, which blends with the adjacent surface.

Soldering is accomplished with phosphoric fluxes that will not corrode stainless steel. Soldering should be used to seal or fill a joint, but not to provide structural strength.

Mechanical fastening of all-stainless-steel assemblies should be accomplished with stainless steel screws, bolts, and rivets, to ensure a permanent noncorroding attachment.

Adhesive bonding of stainless steel to plywood and hardboard in the production of veneer panels and sandwich panels is possible with the development of structural adhesives such as epoxies and polyurethanes.

STEEL

Steel, an alloy of iron, is used by architects not only as an integral part of structural systems in buildings but also, when exposed, as part of the architectural ornamental expression. Exposed structural systems used architecturally include space frames and arches to span large, unobstructed floor areas such as convention halls, exhibition spaces, or sports arenas. Others include cable-supported structures, and still others include low buildings where fireproofing is not mandated by building codes and the steel frame may be left exposed.

Steel is also used for ornamental metalwork to enhance the appearance of buildings. Some structures are famed for their beautiful grille work, stairs, railings, sculpture, and ornamental metalwork.

The classification and identification of steel is rather complex and involves, among other things: (1) chemical composition, (2) method of manufacture, (3) mechanical properties, (4) heat treatment, and (5) reference to a recognized standard.

For architectural purposes, carbon steel and high-strength, low-alloy steel (HSLA or weathering steel) are the primary steels used to produce such effects. Stainless steel is a steel alloy, but for purposes of singular identification as an ornamental metal, it is discussed separately in this chapter.

CARBON STEEL

Classification

Steels are classified as carbon steels when: (1) no minimum content is specified or required for the alloying elements, (2) the amount of carbon does not exceed 2 percent, and (3) the amount of iron exceeds 95 percent.

Carbon steels are likewise classified by grade on the basis of their carbon content. Amounts of up to 0.8 percent carbon increase the strength and hardness of carbon steel and decrease the ductility.

Table 5-16 shows types of carbon steel based on the percentage of carbon.

Physical Properties

Carbon steel used for architectural purposes includes mild steel, medium steel, and very mild steel. Of these, the mild steels are the most widely used and are generally carried in stock by warehouses and fabricators. Mild steels have a tensile strength in the range of 36,000 to 65,000 psi, form easily, and retain true sections when fabricated.

Shapes

Bar sizes of carbon steel include channels, angles, Tees, Zees, and rolled sections having a maximum dimension of the cross section of less than 3 inches.

Structural size shapes are rolled, flanged sections having at least one dimension of the cross section 3 inches or greater.

Most bar size shapes and structural size shapes of carbon steel are covered by ASTM A36 for chemical requirements, tensile properties, and bend test requirements.

Pipe and Tubing

Pipe and tubing as defined earlier in this chapter under Standard Stock Mill Products are available for a variety of architectural design purposes. They may be

obtained in standard weight, extra-strong, and double extra-strong.

Several ASTM standards are available by which to specify pipe and tubing as follows:

ASTM A53	Welded and Seamless Steel Pipe; covers black and hot-dipped galvanized products
ASTM A500	Cold Formed Welded and Seamless Carbon Steel Structural Tubing in Rounds and Shapes
ASTM A501	Hot-Formed Welded and Seamless Carbon Steel Structural Tubing
ASTM A512	Cold-Drawn Buttweld Carbon Steel Mechanical Tubing
ASTM A513	Electric Resistance-Welded Carbon and Alloy Steel Mechanical Tubing
ASTM A618	Structural Tubing, Hot Formed, Welded and Seamless

See Figures 5-3 and 5-4 for illustrations of pipe and tubing used for space frames.

Sheet and Strip

Sheet and strip are used architecturally for components of buildings such as curtain walls and fascias, roofs, for interior walls and partitions, doors and windows, floors and ceiling systems, and signage.

Steel sheet and strip are made up of carbon steels; high-strength, low-alloy steels; and full alloy steels.

Hot-rolled sheet and strip are produced by squeezing hot steel ingots with huge rolls repeatedly until the desired thickness is reached. Cold-rolled sheets

TABLE 5-16
CARBON STEEL TYPES

Type	Carbon steel content	Description
Very mild	0.05–0.15	An extra-soft steel, tough, ductile and used for sheets, wire, pipe, and fastenings
Mild	0.15–0.25	Strong, ductile, machinable, used for buildings, bridges, boilers
Medium	0.25–0.35	Harder and stronger than mild steel, used for machinery, shipbuilding, and general structural purposes
Medium-hard	0.35–0.65	Used where wear and abrasion is encountered
Spring	0.85–1.05	Used for spring manufacture
Tool	1.05–1.20	Hardest and strongest grade

FIGURE 5-3 East Wing, National Gallery of Art, Washington, DC: interior view illustrating space frame. I.M. Pei & Partners, Architects. *(Photographer, Ezra Stoller © ESTO.)*

FIGURE 5-4 John F. Kennedy Library, Boston, MA: interior view illustrating space frame. I.M. Pei & Partners, Architects. *(© Mona Zamdmer 1979, Photographer.)*

are formed by further rolling hot-rolled sheets after they have been allowed to cool and have been pickled to remove scale.

The most popular steel sheet and strip for architectural purposes are as follows:

Hot-rolled carbon steel

Cold-rolled carbon steel

High-strength, low-alloy weathering steel

Sheet for porcelain enameling

Zinc-coated steel

These can be further identified by reference to ASTM standards as follows:

ASTM A570	Sheet and Strip, Hot Rolled, Structural Quality
ASTM A611	Sheet and Strip, Cold Rolled Structural Quality
ASTM A424	Sheet for Porcelain Enameling
ASTM A446	Sheet, Hot Dipped Galvanized Structural Quality
ASTM A591	Sheet, Electrolytic Zinc Coated
ASTM A606	Sheet and Strip, Hot Rolled and Cold Rolled, Improved Atmospheric Corrosion Resistance

Metallic Coated Steel Sheet

Aluminum. Aluminum-coated steel sheet, Type II, consists of steel sheets, factory finished on both sides, with a coating of commercially pure aluminum. These sheets combine the strength of steel with the corrosion resistance of aluminum and are used for roofing, siding, and other building products.

Terne metal. A mixture of 85 percent lead and 15 percent tin used as a coating on both sides of steel sheet. Coating weights are typically 20 pounds and 40 pounds. Used primarily for roofing, terne metal has long-term permanence when painted and maintained. The standard for terne-coated steel sheet is ASTM A308.

Other metallic coatings. Steel sheet is frequently plated with other metals such as brass, copper, chromium, or tin, to combine the qualities of the coating (such as color and texture) with the strength of steel and a reduction in cost.

Fabrication

Carbon steels can be hot rolled, cold rolled, forged, cast, welded, punched, blanked, and cut, but not extruded.

Hot-rolled steel has a thin, tight scale over a smooth-rolled surface; corners are usually slightly rounded.

Cold-rolled steel is produced by passing cleaned or pickled metal between heavy rolls or dies to work the metal while it is cold. The process hardens and stiffens the steel, increases its tensile strength, and improves the surface. Cold-rolled or cold-finished products are more accurate as to size and gage than hot-rolled products and are free from scale.

HIGH-STRENGTH, LOW-ALLOY STEEL (WEATHERING STEEL)

Weathering steel is a high-strength, low-alloy steel that is remarkably resistant to corrosion from normal atmospheric exposure and attains a tight oxide coating of varying colors that are architecturally pleasing. The color of weathered steel can be described as russet brown with an intermixing of browns, reds, and blues.

In ordinary carbon steel, rust begets rust. The corrosion resistance of high-strength, low-alloy weathering steel depends upon the formation of a dense, stable layer of rust that prevents oxygen and other contaminants from continued reaction with the base metal. The corrosion resistance of weathering steel is approximately 4 times that of carbon steel.

The action of continued wetting and drying of the surface is essential to develop this tight oxide covering over a period of about 3 years. An indoor environment or an arid climate are not conducive to the full development of this oxide coating.

Careful design is essential in the detailing of various building elements utilizing weathering steel. Surfaces must drain properly to permit drying; otherwise, normal, loose rusting occurs. Water that drains or drips from the steel must not be allowed to impinge on other materials that will show rust stains or streaking. Porous materials are vulnerable to such absorption and discoloration.

In designing with weathering steel for the first time, it is essential that the architect allow the producer to review the details of design to ensure that the components weather properly and that adjacent materials are not subject to water run-off from the weathering steel.

To obtain a uniform weathering that is pleasing in appearance, mill scale must be removed by cleaning, sanding, scraping, or wire brushing. Blast cleaning is perhaps the best preparation. Oil, grease, and chalk marks must also be removed, or else these areas will not weather uniformly.

Weathering steel structural shapes and sheet metal that may be specified to ASTM standards are as follows:

ASTM A242	High-Strength Low-Alloy Structural Steel
ASTM A588	High-Strength Low-Alloy Structural Steel with 50 ksi Minimum Yield Point
ASTM A606	Steel Sheet and Strip, Hot Rolled and Cold Rolled, High Strength, Low Alloy

Fasteners of high-strength structural bolts that are made of these alloys should be used so that uniform weathering will result. Welding should be performed with compatible welding electrodes.

Elements of weathering steel that are not boldly exposed to the atmosphere—such as glass rebates in lights or such other connections, including contact surfaces of overlapping steel—should be painted to prevent formation of loose rust.

One of the earliest examples of a unique design employing weathering steel is the John Deere Company administration building in Moline, Illinois, designed by

FIGURE 5-5 Ruan Center, Des Moines, IA: example of an unpainted exterior plate wall using weathering steel. Kendall, Griffith, Russel, Artiaga, Architects-Engineers. *(Courtesy of U.S. Steel Group, a unit of USX Corp.)*

FIGURE 5-6 U.S. Steel Building, Pittsburgh, PA: example of exposed weathering steel facade. Harrison & Abramovitz & Abbe, Architects. *(Courtesy of U.S. Steel Group, a unit of USX Corp.)*

Eero Saarinen. See Figures 5-5 and 5-6 for typical examples of buildings utilizing weathering steel.

STEEL DECKING

Steel decks, especially acoustical decks, are sometimes a part of the visible building fabric—as viewed from the interior. More importantly, they serve as concrete forms, completing the description of formwork in Chapter 3. The selection of steel deck is critical in the success of roofings and roof insulations described in Chapter 7.

Historically, some stainless steel and aluminum decks have been custom fabricated for unique purposes, but all stock deck is steel alone. Roof deck profiles are generally different from floor deck profiles—reflecting the different purposes they serve. A more important distinction exists between composite and noncomposite deck sections, the former having integral lugs rolled into the deck profile to increase its bond to concrete. Deck also can be categorized as single sheet or cellular, the latter consisting of two sheets welded together to provide raceways for electrified floors, perforated acoustical ceilings, canopies, and similar construction that will be seen from below—as well as simply to provide stronger sections for long spans.

Some steel decks are tested with various concrete fills, gypsum board, sprayed fireproofing, and as unprotected deck to qualify as components in fire-rated designs that range in their UL rating from ¾ hr to 4 hr.

Steel Decks as Formwork

Steel deck is made in depths up to 3 in. for use under concrete floor fill, composite deck usually being the choice. For additional shear strength over supporting structural steel, steel studs are often resistance welded on the worksite at critical locations in the deck pans. The deck-concrete system must be designed not just for its composite strength when dry, but also for minimal deflection in the steel deck alone during concrete placement. The way in which the concrete is placed and struck off *after* full wet-load deflection in the floor has taken place will determine whether a flat floor or one with hills and valleys results.

For undemanding work, floor decking can be replaced by form decks (or centering) which are as shallow as %16 in. and which are made in metal thicknesses as little as 0.015 in. (0.4 mm) or approximately 28 USS gage. Steel forms do not act compositely with the concrete. Such a form can practically disappear, except for some nasty staining, if corrosion should set in.

Unprotected or painted decks can be used if the atmosphere at the underside of the deck will assuredly be dry—always. If there is any likelihood of dampness, the deck should be galvanized. Where the underside is exposed to view, a prime-coated or galvanized deck should be selected for field painting later.

Electrified Decks

It seems simple to select a cellular deck to carry wiring beneath the floor. However, the execution of such work is complicated by the need to segregate power and communications conductors, to incorporate trench header ducts for lateral runs, and to design a suitable way of providing riser fittings over the deck in order to locate, tap, abandon, and close outlets according to varying occupant needs. Precise dimensional control of the concreting is essential. This specialized design, shop drawing preparation, and execution is often handled under a separate section of the specifications.

Steel Roof Decks

The workhorses of steel roof deck are the 1½ in. deep wide rib, intermediate rib, and narrow rib types. Deeper sections of 2, 3, 4½, 6, and 7½ in. are also made. In 1993 it was reported that 41 percent of all the roof decks over which insulation was applied during the preceding 10 years had been steel. Steel roof decks with concrete fill may have accounted for another 5 to 10 percent.

Breakdowns in design team effort frequently occur when the architect does not insist that the structural engineer incorporate several qualities into the structural design (qualities that some engineers pass off as not directly related to strength of structure and therefore not important):

- Roof deck must have proper slope for drainage.

- Roof deck must be stiff enough not to flex insulation and roofing under imposition and removal of loads.

- Steel thickness must be sufficient to hold mechanical roof fastenings.

- Roof deck must not corrode from atmospheric or other conditions below or above the deck.

The slope, of course, comes not from the deck but the structure supporting it. It is usually, but not always, less expensive to slope structure than to use tapered board insulation.

The success of the insulation and roofing above a steel deck depends on the deck's stiffness. Deck should be selected for limited deflection, 1/480 maximum, controlled by the moment of inertia—not just strength as measured by the section modulus.

More and more mechanical fastening of all or part of roofing and roof insulations is being called for. In high wind locations, the areas behind parapets and in roof corners are subject to extremely high negative pressures. A thickness of 22 gage is minimal in such situations. Each 2-point reduction in gage designation adds about 100 lb to the withdrawal strength of typical screwed fasteners.

If a lightweight concrete fill is to be used over the steel deck, ASTM A525, G90 galvanizing should be required. G60 weight is not sufficient.

If phenolic insulation is to be used over the steel deck, protection from leached acids must be provided over the steel. Although G90 galvanizing is helpful, the acid from phenolic foam will destroy the zinc in time, as it starts work on the steel. An acid-resisting vapor barrier is more effective. Since vapor may be trapped under the roof membrane, the insulation course must be vented.

Acoustical Decks

Deep sections of single-sheet deck and all depths of cellular deck can be obtained perforated to admit sound energy from spaces below. The fiber insulation that is placed in the acoustical cavity is installed with the deck.

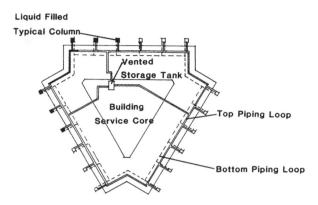

FIGURE 5-7 U.S. Steel Building. Schematic plan of fire-proofing system including liquid-filled exterior columns. *(Courtesy of U.S. Steel Group, a unit of USX Corp.)*

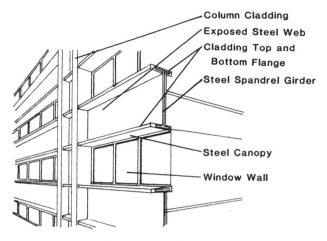

FIGURE 5-8 One Liberty Plaza, New York, NY. Cladding attached to top and bottom flanges form a fire canopy, protecting the exposed steel web of the girder. (See also Figure 8-20.)

FIRE SAFETY OF STEEL STRUCTURES

Unprotected steel at temperatures above 1000 F° loses about half its ultimate strength. As a result, steel framing in most structures is encased in concrete, masonry, or gypsum board, or covered with cementitious and fibrous sprayed-on fireproofing or intumescent coatings.

Limiting the temperatures that exposed steel structures may reach during a fire requires designing the system in such a manner as to preclude this temperature rise. One example is the U.S. Steel building in Pittsburgh, PA. The building has liquid-filled columns to circulate water heated by fire away from the affected columns and replace it with cooler water from storage tanks or city water supplies (see Figure 5-7). Another example is the use of flame shields that deflect heat and flames from a burning building away from exterior structural steel spandrels. This design is used in the One Liberty Street building in New York City, as shown in Figure 5-8.

A design aid for exposed steel introduced by the American Iron and Steel Institute is *FS-3, Fire Safe Structural Steel.* It is a calculation procedure intended for exterior spandrel beams and exterior columns which may be protected from a building fire by geometry of space and distance. While this method is still in its infancy, it is a rational approach and may open the way for designing some structures utilizing exposed framing that is fire protected by space and geometry.

METALLIC PROTECTIVE COATINGS

General

Carbon steels are often coated with metallic protective coatings to inhibit corrosion of the base metal. To ensure sound protective coatings, they must be of uniform density and free of pinholes or other discontinuities.

Zinc Coatings

Zinc coatings protect steel based on the galvanic reaction between zinc and steel which causes the zinc to corrode in favor of the steel. See Chapter 1, Compatibility. Zinc is applied to steel products by several different methods as follows:

Hot-dip galvanizing. A process of coating steel products by immersing them in a bath of molten zinc after cleaning them. This process provides the surface with a tightly adhering coat of zinc, which is one of the most effective agents in protecting steel from rust. Several ASTM standards are available for hot-dip galvanizing procedures as follows:

ASTM A123   On steel fabricated products, (rolled/pressed/forged shapes) and assembled steel products

ASTM A153   On iron/steel hardware

Several classes of hot-dip zinc coatings are available relating to the weight of coating per square foot of surface. The weight of coating to be used is proportional to the severity of the corrosion potential to be expected.

Electrogalvanizing. A process produced by an electric current. By immersing a steel product in the electroplating solution of zinc sulfate or zinc cyanide, a pure zinc coating is deposited whose thickness can be controlled. Heavy coatings such as those provided by the hot-dip method cannot be obtained in the electrolytic process.

Sherardizing. A zinc cementation process wherein the steel product to be coated is surrounded by zinc dust and then heated in an oven. A thin zinc coating is produced over the steel product. This process is limited to small products of complex shape.

Spraying. A process whereby zinc is fed in the form of a wire into a spray gun, where it is melted and projected by air pressure in a hot, atomized spray against the object to be coated.

Painting. Application of a zinc-rich paint on prepared surfaces of steel. Zinc-rich paint is produced to meet the requirements of Steel Structures Painting Council SSPC-PS 12.

East Wing, National Gallery of Art, Washington, DC: interior view illustrating space frame. I.M. Pei & Partners, Architects. *(Photographer, Ezra Stoller © ESTO.)*

ARCHITECTURAL WOODWORK

This chapter is intended and limited to discuss only wood and wood products that are utilized in architectural woodwork. For this purpose architectural woodwork includes millwork, cabinetwork, paneling, and structural glued laminated timber and decking.

The subject matter contained in this chapter is confined to those materials such as solid wood, plywood, particleboard, fiberboard, solid surfacings, and plastic laminate, which in turn are generally used to produce end products that result in architectural woodwork.

STANDARDS AND REQUIREMENTS

CLASSIFICATION OF WOOD

Trees that provide lumber for architectural woodwork are divided as a matter of convenience into two groups—softwoods and hardwoods. The softwoods, in general, are the coniferous or cone-bearing evergreen trees such as the pines, hemlocks, firs, spruces, and cedars. The hardwoods are the deciduous or broad-leafed trees such as the maples, oaks, and birches.

The terms hardwood and softwood refer primarily to the above breakdown of groups and not to the fact that one group is hard and the other is soft.

The softwoods are more commonly used for framing purposes, such as studs, joists, rafters, and posts. The hardwoods are primarily used for interior finishes, flooring, paneling, cabinetry, and furniture where natural finishes are desired.

MOISTURE CONTENT AND SEASONING

Moisture content is defined as the weight of water contained in wood, expressed as a percentage of the weight of the oven dry wood. As wood dries and its moisture content decreases, wood shrinks; conversely, as wood absorbs moisture, it swells.

When equilibrium for moisture content is reached for a condition where the wood will be in service, its tendency to shrink, expand, or warp will be diminished. However this condition never remains constant in actual service because of normal changes in atmospheric moisture. It is therefore important that an approximate equilibrium moisture content be reached.

It is essential that lumber be seasoned until the moisture content is similar to the conditions under which the wood will be used. Lumber is seasoned or dried by natural air drying or by kiln drying. Air drying takes place outdoors where wood is stacked and allowed to season over a period of about two months. Kiln drying takes place in a large oven where the rate of seasoning of lumber is controlled and requires only two or three days to accomplish.

The Wood Handbook, published by the Forest Products Laboratory of the Department of Agriculture, recommends the moisture content values for interior woodwork as shown in Table 6-1.

LUMBER GRADES

Grading of lumber refers to its quality. Since wood is a natural material, uniformity is hard to come by. The term grading is best summed up in the U.S. Department of Commerce Product Standard PS-20, American Softwood Lumber Standard, as follows:

The grading for lumber cannot be considered an exact science because it is based on either a visual inspection of each piece and the judgement of the grader or on results of a method of mechanically determining the strength characteristics of structural lumber.

To indicate the grade, the lumber manufacturing associations of softwood lumber stamp the grade on each piece.

Softwood lumber grades are based on PS-20 (identified above) which establishes voluntary guidelines through the American Lumber Standards Committee for the softwood industry associations. Each softwood association classifies softwood lumber according to size, use, and manufacturing.

Hardwood lumber grades are established by the National Hardwood Lumber Association which measures the percentage of usable material in each piece.

TABLE 6-1
PERCENT AVERAGE MOISTURE CONTENT

Dry southwestern states	Damp southern coastal states	Remaining states in continental United States
6	11	8

There are five basic hardwood grades as follows: First and Seconds (FAS), Selects, No. 1 Common, No. 2 Common, and No. 3 Common.

Woodwork institutes in the United States recommend that their own more detailed lumber grade descriptions be used for architectural woodwork. Each grades hardwood and softwood species as to the clear areas required, the type and number of defects allowed, and other qualities. Woodwork Institute of California (WIC) identifies Premium, Custom, and Economy grades; Architectural Woodwork Institute (AWI) identifies Grades I, II, and III.

FIRE-RETARDANT TREATMENT

The model building codes and most state and municipal codes restrict the use of combustible materials in places of occupancy such as assembly, educational, mercantile, business, institutional, and residential. Since plywood and lumber used for architectural woodwork can be pressure treated with fire-retardant chemicals making them noncombustible, they are acceptable under most codes for these applications.

Fire-Retardant Chemicals

The salts used for impregnating lumber and plywood through pressure treatment so that they may later receive a transparent finish include ammonium phosphate, ammonium sulfate, borax, boric acid, and zinc-chloride.

Since these salts are hygroscopic they cannot be used in locations where the relative humidity exceeds 80%. In addition, some species of lumber such as white oak tend to darken when impregnated with these salts. The pressure treatment plant should be consulted before wood selections are made to ascertain the effect of the fire-retardant chemicals on the specific wood species when a clear finish is required.

Since these chemicals are water soluble, redrying by kilns is necessary after treatment to obtain the required moisture content. The retention of these fire-retardant chemicals in the wood makes sawing, drilling, and woodworking extremely difficult.

Exclusions from Code Requirements

A study commissioned by the Architectural Woodwork Institute (AWI) to analyze the four major model codes with respect to fire resistance requirements for interior architectural woodwork disclosed that certain items were exempt from these requirements.

The four model codes analyzed were as follows:

BOCA	National Building Code—1990
ICBO	Uniform Building Code—1991
SBCCI	Standard Building Code—1991
NFPA 101	Life Safety Code—1991

The exclusions of architectural woodwork from the fire resistance requirements under these codes are the following:

Cabinetry and casework. These items are considered as furniture or furnishings whether freestanding or fixed or attached and therefore do not require fire resistance treatment.

Interior finish. Items such as wall and ceiling covering $\frac{1}{28}$ inch or less in thickness do not require fire resistance treatment. Paneling that is composed of plywood or particleboard with a wood veneer facing can meet this fire resistance requirement if the core material is impregnated with a fire-resistant chemical and an untreated wood veneer, $\frac{1}{28}$ inch or less in thickness, is applied to the surface.

Trim. Items such as mouldings, baseboards, railings, and door and window trim may be used without fireproofing if the area of trim and interior finish is 10 percent or less of the total wall and ceiling area in a room as per the following formula:

$$A = \frac{2H(L + W) + (L \times W)}{10}$$

where A = area of interior finish within room
H = ceiling height
L = length of room
W = width of room

Flame Spread Ratings

The model codes and most state and municipal codes refer to ASTM E84 as the test method to determine flame spread requirements (see Chapter 1) for architectural woodwork. There is no unanimity among the codes as to the flame spread ratings for exits, corridors, and other spaces in the various occupancies previously noted. Each model code or state and municipal code must be reviewed for its requirements.

In addition some insurance companies may require more restrictive flame spread ratings than are required by the model codes or state and municipal codes. ASTM E84 procedures require a 10-minute flame spread test. Factory Mutual and other insurance organizations require that fire-resistant lumber meet American Wood-Preservers' Association (AWPA) Standard C20 and that plywood meet AWPA Standard C27. These standards require that lumber and plywood be subjected to the ASTM E84 test for 30 minutes in lieu of 10 minutes, that the flame spread be not over 25 minutes, and that each piece treated be identified with a label by an approved agency such as UL.

PRESERVATIVE TREATMENT

The need for preservative treatment is not frequently encountered in interior architectural woodwork, although some millwork, paneling, parts of casework in damp locations, or backup wood construction may require it.

STANDARDS

Preservative treatment in recent years has almost always used the pressure vessel process. The general standard for pressure preservatives for wood is AWPA C2, for plywood AWPA C9. These preservatives are waterborne salts of such chemicals as acid copper chromate (ACC), ammoniacal copper arsenate (ACA),

and chromated copper arsenate (CCA) that are forced into the structure of the wood in such a way that little leaching out will occur over repeated cycles of wetness and dryness.

The USDA Forest Service estimates that 95 percent of all preservative treated (PT) wood in the United States is pressure treated with CCA—producing the familiar green cast that is seen on the surface of PT lumber and that extends considerable distance below the surface. Southern Pine takes treatment particularly well. Western woods are generally less receptive, and in the case of timbers, many species have to be incised to retain preservative.

The process, end product, and grade for wood treatment using these preservatives should follow the American Wood Preservers Bureau (AWPB) LP2 standard for above-ground items. (Treatment for wood that will be in contact with soil or fresh water should follow AWPB LP22.) When the proper AWPB treatment is specified, an appropriate AWPA preservative will be provided.

Wood items that will benefit from LP2 pressure preservative treatment are:

- Wood furring and blocking at exterior walls
- Wood framing and blocking, including cabinet bases, within 18 in. (460 mm) of a slab on earth
- Wood paneling that extends within 18 in. of a slab on earth
- Wood plates and sills on slabs on earth
- Wood behind or under roofing, flashing, and waterproofing, such as cants, nailers, blocking, edge strips, curbs, and equipment supports

The quantity of preservative that is retained varies with the preservative, often 0.25 or 0.30 lb/ft^3 (400 or 480 kg/m^3) for LP2 treatment, and 0.40 or 0.50 lb/ft^3 (770 or 960 kg/m^3) for LP22 treatment. All wood should be kiln dried after treatment to bring its moisture content back to no more than 19 percent (15 percent for plywood).

It is possible to preservative treat wood and plywood by dipping and brushing, but these methods do not penetrate the wood nor do they leave much preservative salt in the cells of the wood. However, after PT wood has been sawed or otherwise cut in the course of fabrication or erection, a brushed application should be specified following the AWPB M4 standard.

The corresponding abbreviation for pressure applied fire retardant treatment is FRT. This qualifies wood to receive a UL FR-S label.

For architectural woodwork that is to receive a natural finish, it is best to obtain samples of the proposed wood species that have been treated with the specified preservative. The samples should be step-finished to show the sequence of coatings that bring each piece to the final finish. Unexpected results from this combination of materials can often be corrected by adjusting one or two of the materials.

Environmental Concerns

All methods of wood preservation involve the use of toxic chemicals or heavy metal salts. The use of solvent-borne pentachlorophenol—formerly widely used in preservative treating millwork, doors, and windows, and certain parts of casework—is no longer permitted. Creosote—with its odor, color, unfinishability, and toxicity to skin and lungs—is totally unsuitable for interior use.

The heavy metal salts—which contain such elements as chromium, copper, arsenic, and zinc—have little potential for leaching out into the environment when applied by the pressure treatment process and when their use is limited to concealed work. All the same, CCA and other heavy metal poisons, with their discoloration of the wood or plywood to which they are applied, are not favored for interior use. For interior work, it is desirable to use waterborne poisons, not ones carried into the wood by petroleum distillates that release themselves slowly into the ambient atmosphere.

Colorless solvent-borne preservatives such as pentachlorophenol which were formerly favored for interior work and work that might be touched have been largely replaced by less toxic formulations. Some of the replacement poisons employ methylene thiocyanate, benzothiozoles and phosphorothates—which are less toxic than pentachlorophenol—and are carried in a light, volatile, almost odorless solvent. This reduces danger to human beings yet poisons termites and fungus. The formulations penetrate well, are somewhat water-repellent, and can be stained or painted.

Borates

A still newer technology, even more friendly to man and environment, is the waterborne borate approach.

Disodium octaborate, in combination with wetting agents, is applied to the surface of dry wood, preferably wood with less than 8 percent moisture content. The chemical migrates into the wood's structure without application of pressure. Borates are poisonous to termites, wood-boring beetles and ants, and to fungi, but not to human beings and animals at several times this concentration. The aqueous carrier gives off no fumes. Borates are colorless and can be painted when dry.

STRUCTURAL GLUED LAMINATED TIMBER (GLULAM)

DEFINITION

The term structural glued laminated timber (*glulam*), refers to an engineered, stress-rated product of a timber laminating plant comprising assemblies of specially selected and prepared wood laminations securely bonded together with adhesives. The grain of all laminations is approximately parallel longitudinally. The separate laminations must not exceed 2 inches net thickness. The laminations may be comprised of pieces that are joined to form any length, placed or glued edge-to-edge to make wider ones, or bent to curved form during gluing.

ANSI/AITC A190.1 is a standard for the production, inspection, testing, and certification of glulam. AITC refers to American Institute of Timber Construction.

LUMBER

Lumber used for glulam is structurally graded in accordance with standard grading provisions for the species and supplementary requirements of laminating specifications. Some species of lumber used include Douglas Fir, Southern Pine, Hemlock, and Larch.

FIRE SAFETY

An advantage of glulam is that the self-insulating qualities of heavy timber sizes cause the assembly to be slow-burning. By proper detailing, fire safety is increased, as in the elimination of concealed spaces and the use of fire-stops to interfere with the passage of flames up or across a structure.

Building codes generally exempt heavy timber framing from interior finish flame spread requirements, and numerous transparent finishes are available to enhance the color and texture of the wood species selected for glulam construction.

Where fire-retardant chemicals are contemplated, the following factors should be investigated: strength reduction, compatibility of treatment and adhesives, gluing procedures, and fabricating procedures.

WOOD PRESERVATION

Where decay due to fungi, insects, borers, or exposure to high humidity is expected, consideration must be given to pressure preservative treatment. For the treatment to be effective the proper chemicals must be used and the degree of retention and penetration known. For members exposed to weather and not protected by overhanging roofs or eaves, treatment must be provided or woods resistant to decay must be used.

Pressure preservative treatment must be used within buildings subject to high humidity levels where the glulam may reach a moisture content in excess of 20 percent.

Information on pressure preservative treatment is available in the American Institute of Timber Construction publication AITC 109.

APPEARANCE GRADES

There are three appearance grades for glulam—Industrial, Architectural, and Premium. These grades apply to the surfaces of the glulam members and include such items as growth characteristics, inserts, wood fillers, and surfacing operations.

Industrial appearance grade is intended for use in industrial plants, warehouses, garages, and other uses where appearance is not of primary concern.

Architectural appearance grade is suitable for construction where appearance is an important factor.

Premium appearance grade is used for structures that demand the finest appearance.

Detailed information on appearance grade specifications is contained in AITC 110-83, Standard Appearance Grades for Structural Glued Laminated Timber.

SHAPES

Glulam design and construction make possible the use of structural timbers in a wide variety of sizes and shapes and permit the architect to exercise a wide latitude in the creation of architectural forms which express the structure's function and use.

Glulam timber members may be straight or curved to meet design requirements and specifications and include shapes shown in Figure 6-1.

DESIGN DATA

Design values, data, and standards relative to the design of glulam are contained in the following publications:

Adhesives	ASTM D2559 and D4689
Appearance grades	AITC 110-83 Standard Appearance Grades for Structural Glued Laminated Timber
Design values Softwood	AITC 117, Standard Specifications for Glulam Softwood Species
Hardwood	AITC 119, Standard Specifications for Glulam Hardwood Species
Testing and inspection	ANSI/AITC A190.1
Timber construction	*Timber Construction Manual,* published by John Wiley & Sons, Inc.

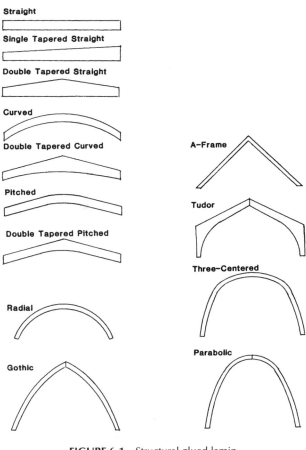

FIGURE 6-1 Structural glued lamin.

Solid decking is T&G, kiln-dried timber available in select quality grade and commercial quality grade. Wood species include Douglas Fir, Larch, Southern Pine, Hem-Fir, and Western Cedar. The AITC has a publication No. 112 for "Tongue and Groove Heavy Timber Roof Decking" which provides detailed information on solid decking.

HARDWOOD VENEERS

GENERAL

The architect wishing to utilize wood in a design has an infinite variety of wood species from which to select. This is especially true when the architect chooses the veneers of hardwoods which have endless varieties of grain and figure patterns, colors, and textural interest. Some woods have ever-changing highlights and shadows, and others are strong, sturdy, and rugged in character.

Even within a species, the architect can select from a wide range of figure and grain patterns. Like fingerprints, the grain patterns of any two trees are never exactly alike. This individualism is perhaps one of the most appealing factors when one selects a natural material such as wood as opposed to a synthetic material. Further refinement is achieved by the manner in which the wood is cut, finished, and matched. See Figure 6-2.

Wood-preservative treatment	AITC 109, Treating Standard for Glulam

DECKING SYSTEMS

Timber decking is comprised of both laminated and solid timber members. Either system may be employed with glulam beams or arches to complement an architectural expression. Decking is available in a variety of textural exposed surfaces including smooth, saw textured, grooved, striated, and wire-brushed. These may be prefinished in a variety of stains.

Glue laminated decking is assembled from three or more individual kiln-dried laminations into single decking members with T&G patterns. It is available in several thicknesses and appearance grades.

HARDWOOD SPECIES

Hardwood can be utilized both as a veneer or in the solid form, although for some species the amount of wood is so limited that solid members cannot be obtained in the size and quantity required.

More than 200 species are available from more than 99,000 varieties of hardwoods for use in architectural designs. Hardwood trees, their botanical names, place of origin, characteristics, and uses are shown in Table 6-2.

FIGURE 6-2 Mahogany reception desk. W.C. Morgan & Associates, Architects.

Environmental Concerns

The number of hardwoods listed in Table 6-2 could easily be doubled if other woods, primarily from the tropical rainforests of South America, Africa, Southeast Asia, and the East Indies, and imported in commercial quantities, were counted. Many of these tropical hardwoods are being harvested at rates totally out of scale with any possible replenishment rate. The fact is that little or no attention is being paid to replenishment. A tropical forest has to be in place for centuries for the slow building of a canopy to take place—a canopy that will cause slow-growing hardwoods to reach for the sun—generating long straight boles without branching short of the top limb cluster. Of course many trees are not being harvested for their wood; the forest is being cleared for settlement and agriculture and the cleared timber is marketed as an afterthought—or burned. Many of today's building owners, and many of their architects, are aware of the environmental price that hardwood harvesting and hardwood clearing entail: not just lack of replenishment, but soil destruction, river pollution and silting, displacement of original inhabitants and their cultures, and in many cases air pollution and extinction of plant and animal species.

Within the list in Table 6-2 there are temperate zone hardwoods that are also in short supply. We have cut deeply into our Black Walnut supply. It is harder for mills to obtain Red Oak, White Ash, and Butternut in suitable lengths and bole diameters. Redwood could be cut to extinction if the harvesting levels of a few decades ago were to be resumed.

The architect is in a good position to make globally sensitive choices in setting up his palette of materials. Often today's client will approve and reinforce the architect's approach.

Frank Lloyd Wright saw buildings as properly embracing the site, not overwhelming or destroying it. Today Wright might go on to say that our building sites extend far beyond the property line—perhaps as far as the groves of Humboldt County and the basin of the Amazon.

VENEER TERMS

Veneers from Different Parts of Trees

Veneers are generally cut from the trunk, but some species produce choice and unusual figures from other portions of the growth. See Figure 6-3. Commercially, the various portions of a tree which produce veneers are as follows: longwood, stumpwood, crotchwood, and burl.

Longwood

Longwood or trunkwood is cut from the trunk and may be rotary cut, half-round rotary, back-cut rotary, flat or quarter sliced, or sawn.

Stumpwood

Stumpwood or butt is produced from the stump of a tree. The figure is produced by the wood fibers which, compressed in growth, tend to wrinkle as they twist and fold over each other at the point where the roots join the trunk. Stumpwood is generally half-round rotary cut.

TABLE 6-2
HARDWOOD (DECIDUOUS) TREES

Species	Location	Color	Use	Pattern
Alder, Red (*Alnus rubra*)	West coast of U.S.	Pale pink, brown	Stained furniture	Not distinct
Ash, Black (*Fraxinius nigra*)	Lake states	Warm brown	Furniture, cabinets, doors	Clusters of eyes
Ash, White (*Fraxinus americana*)	Eastern U.S.	Cream to very light brown	Furniture, paneling, trim	Moderately open grain
Avodire (*Turraenthus africana*)	Liberia, Cameroon	From white to light golden cream	Paneling, furniture, cabinets	Largely figured with a mottle
Birch, Black or Sweet (*Betula lenta*)	Adirondacks	Brown, red-tinged	Paneling, cabinets, furniture	Grain distinct
Birch, Yellow* (*Betula alleghaniensis*)	Eastern U.S., Canada	Cream or light brown	Paneling, doors, cabinets, furniture	Plain mild pattern
Butternut (*Juglans cinerea*)	Appalachians	Pale brown	Veneers	Soft to medium texture
Cherry, Black (*Prunus serotina*)	Eastern and central U.S.	Light red-brown	Furniture, cabinets, paneling	Straight grained
Elm, American (*Ulmus americana*)	Eastern and central U.S.	Light brownish	Furniture, cabinets	Mild grain
Elm, Carpathian Burl (*English Elm*) (*Ulmus campestris*)	France, England, Carpathian Mts.	Brick red to light tan	Fine cabinetry	Burl
Gum, Red (*Liquidamber styraciflua*)	Eastern and central U.S.	Reddish brown	Cabinetry	Figured
Lauan, Red "Philippine mahogany" (*Shorea negrosensis*)	Philippines	Red to brown	Furniture, doors, cabinets	Ribbon stripe
Mahogany, African (*Khaya ivorensis*)	Africa	Light pink to reddish brown	Paneling, furniture, cabinets, doors	Figured
Mahogany, Tropical American (*Swietenia macrophylla*)	Central and South America	Light reddish to a rich, dark red	Paneling, furniture, cabinets, doors	Figured
Maple, Hard (*Acer saccharum*)	Lake states, Appalachia	Cream to light reddish brown	Furniture, floors, paneling, cabinets, doors, trim	Usually straight, birds eye
Maple, Soft (*Acer saccharinum*)	Lake states, Appalachia	White to reddish brown	Furniture, paneling, cabinets	Straight

* Sapwood marketed as White Birch, heartwood as Red Birch.
† Sapwood marketed as White Maple.

(Continued)

TABLE 6-2 (CONTINUED)
HARDWOOD (DECIDUOUS) TREES

Species	Location	Color	Use	Pattern
Oak, English Brown (*Quercus robur*)	England	Light tan to deep brown	Paneling, furniture	Noticeable figure and grain
Oak, Red (*Quercus borealis*)	Eastern U.S.	Reddish tinge	Paneling, furniture, cabinets, floors, doors, trim	Flake figure, open pores
Oak, White (*Quercus alba*)	East or Rocky Mountains	Light brown, grayish tinge	Paneling, furniture, cabinets	More pronounced than red
Poplar, Yellow (*Liriodendron tulipifera*)	Eastern U.S.	Canary-to-green with dark streaks	Stained furniture	Straight grain, little figure
Rosewood, Brazilian (*Dalbergia nigra*)	Brazil	Dark brown to violet	Paneling, cabinets	Coarse, even grain
Satinwood, Ceylon (*Chloroxylon swietenia*)	Sri Lanka, India	Pale gold	Paneling, furniture	Rippled, straight stripe
Teak (*Tectona grandis*)	Southeast Asia, Indonesia	Tawny yellow to dark brown	Paneling, furniture	Mottled fiddleback
Tigerwood (*Lovoa klaineana*)	West Africa	Gray-brown to gold	Paneling, furniture	Ribbon stripe
Walnut, American Black (*Juglans nigra*)	Midwestern U.S.	Light gray-brown to purplish brown	Paneling, furniture	Plain to highly figured
Walnut, Circassian (*Juglans regia*)	Europe	Tawny colored	Paneling, furniture	Variegated, streak of black or brown
Zebrawood (*Brachystegia*)	West Africa	Straw and dark brown	Paneling	Striped

Crotchwood

Crotchwood veneers are obtained from the portion of the tree just below the point where it forks into two limbs. Here the grain is crushed and twisted, creating a great variety of plume and flame figures, often resembling a well formed feather. Crotches are sliced parallel to the trunk line, and the outside of the block produces a swirl figure that changes to full crotch figure as the cutting approaches the center of the block.

Burl

Burls come from a warty growth generally caused by some injury to the growing layer just under the bark. This injury causes the growing cells to divide abnor-

mally, creating excess wood that creates little humps. Succeeding growth follows these contours. Cutting across these humps by the half-round method brings them out as little swirl knots or eyes. See Figure 6-4.

Types of Veneer Cuts

Two logs of the same species but with their veneers cut differently will have entirely different visual characteristics, even though their color values are similar. Six principal methods of veneer cuts are used as follows:

1. *Rotary.* The log is mounted centrally in a lathe and turned against a stationary razor-sharp blade, in a manner similar to the unwinding of a roll of paper.

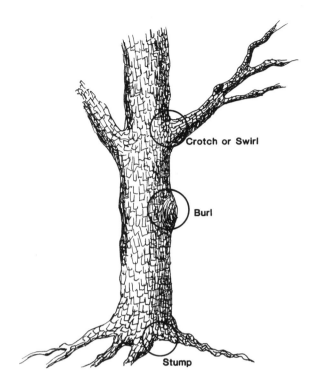

FIGURE 6-3 Veneers from different parts of trees.

FIGURE 6-4 Burl, Carpathian elm.

Since this cut follows the log's annular growth rings, a bold, variegated grain marking is produced. Rotary-cut veneer is exceptionally wide, and cannot be sequenced matched.

2. *Half-round.* This is a variation of rotary cutting in which segments of the log are mounted off center in the lathe. It results in a cut slightly across the annular growth rings, and shows modified characteristics of both rotary- and plain-sliced veneers.

3. *Back-cut.* The log is mounted as in half-round cutting, except that the bark side faces in toward the lathe center. The veneers so cut are characterized by an enhanced striped figure and sapwood along the edges.

4. *Plain or flat-slicing.* The half log is mounted in a movable frame with a stationary knife. The heartside of the log is placed flat against the guide plate and the slicing is done parallel to a line through the center of the log, producing a variegated figure.

5. *Quarter-slicing.* The quarter log is mounted as in plain slicing, except that the growth rings of the log strike the knife at approximately right angles, producing a series of straight stripes in some woods and varied stripes in others.

6. *Rift cut.* This is generally produced from oak species that have medullary ray cells which radiate from the center of the log like the curved spokes of a wheel. The rift or comb grain effect is obtained by cutting perpendicularly to these medullary rays either on a lathe or a slicer.

Figure 6-5 shows the six principal methods of cutting.

Figure and Pattern

Figure in veneers is produced by growth rings, flakes or rays, irregular grain pigments, or a combination of two or more of these factors. Typical examples are:

1. Growth rings—flat cut oak
2. Rays—quartered oak or sycamore
3. Irregular grain—crotch or stripe mahogany
4. Pigment—zebrawood and Macassar ebony

Figure and pattern terms include the following:

Bird's-eye. This is due to local sharp depressions in the annual rings, accompanied by considerable fiber distortions. Rotary veneer cuts the depres-

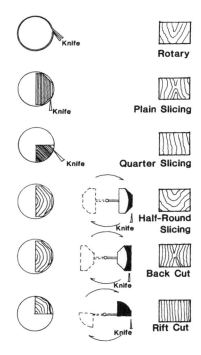

FIGURE 6-5 Methods of veneer cutting.

sions crosswise and shows a series of circlets called bird's eyes.

Blister. This figure is produced by an uneven contour of the annual rings and not to blisters or pockets in the wood. The veneer must be rotary cut or half-round cut to produce the blistered effect.

Chain. A succession of short cross markings of uniform character remotely suggesting cross links of a chain.

Cross fire. Figures which extend across the grain as mottle, fiddleback, raindrop, and finger roll are often called cross figure or cross fire. A pronounced cross fire adds greatly to the beauty of the veneer.

Curly. Distortion of the fibers produces a wavy or curly effect in the veneer, found mostly in maple or birch.

Fiddleback. A fine, strong, even, ripply figure as frequently found on the backs of violins, found mostly in mahogany and maple.

Finger roll. A wavy pattern in which the waves are about the size of a finger.

Mottle. A variegated pattern which consists principally of irregular, wavy fibers extending for short distances across the face. If a twisted, interwoven grain also has some irregular cross figure, the broken stripe figure becomes a mottle.

Raindrop. When the waves in the fibers occur singly or in groups with considerable intervals between, the figure is called raindrop, as it looks like streaks made by drops striking a window pane at a slant.

Rope. If the twist in the grain of a broken stripe is all in one direction, a rope figure results.

Stripe, broken. Broken stripe is a modification of ribbon stripe, the markings tapering out and producing a broken ribbon. If the log described in ribbon stripe also has a twist in the grain, the stripes are short or broken.

Stripe, plain. Alternating lighter and darker stripes, running more or less the length of a flitch and varying in width. It is produced by cutting on the quarter a log that shows growth rings.

Stripe, ribbon. Wide unbroken stripes, produced by cutting on the quarter, a log from a tropical tree, principally mahogany with interwoven grain.

See Figure 6-6 for typical examples of figure characteristics of veneers.

VENEER MATCHING

Veneers are matched by utilizing veneers cut from the same log or a segment of a log. The log that produces these veneers is known as a flitch. A *flitch* is a hewn or sawed log or a section of a log made ready for cutting into veneers. A flitch is also the series of resulting veneer sheets laid together in sequence or as they were sliced or sawn, so that they may be matched and joined to make panel faces.

The joining of veneers is accomplished by means of a tapeless slicer which glues the long edges of the veneers together in whatever pattern is to be employed. Certain standard matching patterns are available as described in the following sections.

Types of Matching Between Individual Veneer Pieces

Book match. Every other sheet is turned over, as are the leaves of a book. Thus, the back of one veneer meets the front of the adjacent veneer, producing a matching joint design.

Slip match. Each sheet is joined side by side and conveys a sense of repeating the flitch figure. Most commonly used in quarter-sliced veneers.

FIGURE 6-6 Figure characteristics of some veneers. (a) Fiddleback, (b) ribbon stripe, (c) cross-fire, (d) mottle.

Random match. A deliberate mismatch by random selection of pieces from one or more flitches, creating a casual or boardlike effect.

End match. When the panel height exceeds the veneer length, it may be matched vertically as well as horizontally by book matching, thus achieving a uniform grain progression in both directions.

Special matching effects. Herringbone, diamond, diamond reverse, V, inverted V.

Assembling Veneers Within a Panel

Running match. Each face is made from as many veneer pieces as necessary. The portion left over is used to start the next panel.

Balance match. Each face is made with equal width veneers using odd or even pieces. This type of matching may be used in sequence matched panels.

Center match. Each face is made with an even number of equal-width veneers, which results in a balance of grain and figure on each side of a center line of the panel.

Matching Panels

For architecturally matched panels, either sequence matched panel sets or blueprint matched panels and components should be selected. These types of matching are defined as follows:

Sequence matched panel sets. These panels are manufactured for a specific installation to a uniform panel width and height. If more than one flitch is required to produce the panels, similar flitches should be used. Doors occurring within the panel run are not sequence matched.

Blueprint matched panels and components. This arrangement produces maximum figure and pattern continuity since all panels, doors, and other veneered components are made to the exact sizes and in exact veneer sequence. The flitch selected should yield sufficient veneers to complete the work.

Figures 6-7 and 6-8 show the various types of veneer matching previously discussed.

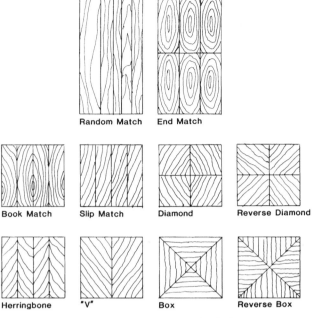

Random Match · End Match · Book Match · Slip Match · Diamond · Reverse Diamond · Herringbone · "V" · Box · Reverse Box

FIGURE 6-7 Matching between individual veneers.

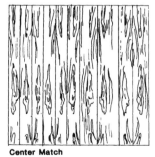

Center Match

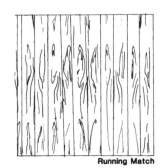

Running Match

Balance Match

FIGURE 6-8 Assembly of veneers within a panel.

ARCHITECTURAL PLYWOOD

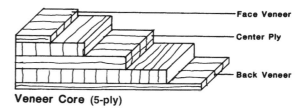

Veneer Core (5-ply)

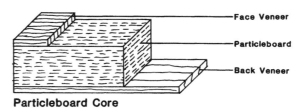

Particleboard Core

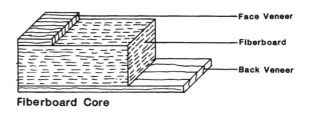

Fiberboard Core

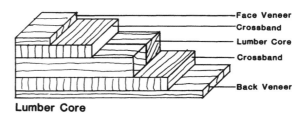

Lumber Core

FIGURE 6-9 Types of plywood cores.

PLYWOOD

Construction

Plywood for architectural woodwork purposes is a general term used to describe a panel made up of an odd number of plies of wood or wood products, cross-bonded and laminated to one another with adhesive. The outer plies are wood veneers called the face and the back. The grain of these two faces must be parallel to provide stability. This gives the panel nearly equalized strength and minimizes dimensional changes.

For lumber core plywood the plies immediately adjacent to the outer faces are called crossbandings. The grain of these plies is usually laid at 90° to the face plies.

Plywood Cores

The cores of plywood can be made of four distinctive types of material as shown in Figure 6-9 and as follows:

1. *Veneer core.* This type of core consists of veneers of wood. Panel thicknesses vary from ⅛ to 1 inch and more and with as little as 3 plies to as many as 11 plies or more. This type of core is used primarily for construction and industrial plywood, utilizing softwood lumber and some hardwood species.

2. *Lumber core.* This core is essentially composed of strips of lumber edge glued into a solid slab using woods of a uniform texture such as bass and poplar. Lumber core plywood is used primarily for panels, countertops, and panelings. Panels are generally ¾ inch thick but are also available in thicker sizes. The exposed faces are generally hardwood veneers. This core is gradually being phased out.

3. *Particleboard core.* A core of medium-density particle board (approximately 40 to 50 lb/ft³) con-

forming to ANSI A208.1 comprises the core for plywood. The face veneers are glued directly to the core. Particleboard core plywood is used for furniture, paneling, and countertops.

4. *Fiberboard core.* A core of medium-density fiberboard (approximately 40 to 50 lb/ft³) conforming to ANSI A 208.2. It can be used for cabinetry and paneling.

Woodwork Institute Standards

Architectural Woodwork Institute and Woodwork Institute of California standards for interior hardwood plywood are governed by three grades—Premium, Custom, and Economy.

In identifying hardwood veneer grades within these categories, WIC cites the Hardwood Plywood Manufacturers Association's ANSI/HPMA 1991 Interim Standard, which has several features in common with the PS 51-71 standard. Veneer grades are:

AA	Highest
Specialty	For species with unique grains such as Wormy Chestnut, Birdseye Maple and English Brown Oak
A	Few characteristics and repairs
B, C, D	Descending levels of quality
E	Greatest number of characteristics and repairs

Plywood water resistance types under ANSI/HPMA 1991 (Interim) are:

Technical	Waterproof bond for specific technical uses
Type I	Waterproof bond for limited exterior use
Type II	Water resistant bond for interior use

AWI, in contrast, cites Hardwood Plywood & Veneer Association's HP-American Standard for Hardwood and Decorative Plywood as a standard. AWI's grades under this standard are:

AA	Highest, described in detail in AWI Architectural Woodwork Quality Standards, Section 200
A	Midquality
B	Greatest number of variations, natural growth characteristics and repairs.

Veneer grades are independent of overall woodwork grades. A Custom grade piece of cabinetry can be specified to have AA grade hardwood veneers.

Hardwood Panel Sizes

Hardwood panels are normally available in 48-inch widths and 6- to 12-foot lengths in increments of 1 foot. Thicknesses are normally available in dimensions of ⅛, ¼, 5/16, ⅜, ½, ⅝, and ¾ inch. Special sizes up to 5 feet wide and 30 feet long can be fabricated. Availability of sizes in excess of these dimensions should be ascertained from architectural woodwork suppliers prior to detailing and specifying these requirements.

Special Plywood

Several additional special plywoods are manufactured having certain surface patterns that are of architectural interest. These patterns include the following:

Grooved. An exterior-type fir, cedar, or pine plywood with grooves or kerfs; available factory finished with stains or paint.

Brushed. An exterior or interior plywood produced by subjecting the panels to wire brushing; also available with grooves and factory finish.

Scratch sanded. A plywood panel with exposed surfaces scratch sanded to expose texture; available with grooves and factory finish.

PARTICLEBOARD

Particleboard is defined as a panel material composed of small, discrete pieces of wood or other lignocellulosic materials that are bonded together in the presence of heat and pressure by a synthetic resin adhesive or other suitable binder. Other materials are added during its manufacture to improve certain properties such as finishing, abrasion resistance, strength, and durability.

Particleboard is manufactured in three densities as follows:

Low density.   Less than 40 lb/ft³
Medium density.   40 to 50 lb/ft³
High density.   Over 50 lb/ft³

Particleboard has exceptional dimensional stability, surface flatness, and glue-bonding characteristics. Since it can be manufactured from wood chips, shavings, slivers, strands, sawdust, and other by-products of wood, it may ultimately replace veneer core plywood and lumber core plywood as a panel material. Because particleboard has excellent dimensional stability, it is being utilized more than ever for hardwood veneer architectural paneling, cabinet work, and countertops.

ANSI A208.1 is a standard for particleboard. A medium density core is normally used for hardwood plywood and with plastic laminate. Particleboard cores can be fireproofed to receive a Class I or Class A rating.

FIBERBOARD

Fiberboard is made of wood particles that have been converted to fibers that have been bonded together in the presence of heat and pressure by a synthetic resin adhesive or other suitable binder. Fiberboard is manufactured in three densities as noted above for particleboard.

It is flat, smooth, and uniform and lends itself to overlays of wood veneers and plastic laminates. It is one of the more rapidly growing mat-formed panel products. At present there is no fire-resistant core.

ANSI A208.2 is a material standard for fiberboard. A medium density core is normally used for hardwood veneers.

PLASTIC LAMINATES

TYPES

The general term *plastic laminate* covers high- and low-pressure types, as well as some more recently developed products. The terminology is not universal: the terms *high-pressure decorative laminate* (HPDL) and *thermoset decorative (TD) panels* appear in the Woodwork Institute of California (WIC) standards. The term *low-pressure decorative laminate* (LPDL) is used by Architectural Woodwork Institute to describe thermoset decorative panels.

There are two other types of laminates for woodwork: liquid acrylic radiation-cured laminates and vinyl overlay laminates.

HIGH-PRESSURE DECORATIVE LAMINATES (HPDL)

The qualities of high-pressure laminates are set forth in the National Electrical Manufacturers Association ANSI/NEMA LD3 standard. (Before World War II, plastic laminates were produced primarily for electrical insulation.)

Manufacture

Sheets of HPDL are made as sandwiches of phenolic resin-impregnated kraft papers surfaced with a melamine-impregnated decorative sheet and an almost clear protective overlay—usually melamine. The number of kraft/phenolic layers determine the sheet thickness. See Figure 6-10. Textures—from high gloss through matte, orangepeel, and stippled—can be imparted to the top surface by the impression of a textured steel plate. The back of the sandwich is sanded to aid adhesion.

High-pressure in the name reflects the 500 to 1200 lb/in^2 (3450–8300 MPa) pressure, at temperatures greater than 265°F (130°C), that are used to bond all layers of the sandwich.

Varieties

In addition to the many textures available, there are solid colors, numerous shades of white, and woodgrains. Marbled, textile, and other patterns are also offered—bold and subtle. Photographic processes are used to bring new colors and patterns to the marketplace each year.

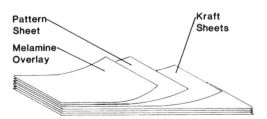

Pattern Sheet
Melamine Overlay
Kraft Sheets

FIGURE 6-10 High-pressure plastic laminate sheet.

A postforming grade of HPDL is made by all producers to allow no-drip, bullnose, single-, and double-radius counter edge profiles to be formed. Postforming grade can also be applied to furniture and other simply curved fabrications. A list of grades appears in Table 6-3.

Abrasion- and scuff-resistant surfaces can be obtained on HPDLs. Fire-rated, static-dissipative, and heavy-duty laminates are made as well as thick, factory-fabricated HPDL floor tile.

Fire ratings depend on the nature of the adhesive and the backing material and range from a flame spread rating 20 to 25, and a smoke developed rating from 0 to 75, as tested following ASTM E84. This qualifies the fire-rated grades as Class 1 finishes if they are used over fire-rated particleboard.

0.63 mm (0.025 in.) aluminum sheets and feature strips, anodized to the colors of brass, chrome, and copper—in bright and brushed finish—are available laminated to the kraft/phenolic backings. A strippable clear plastic sheet protects the surface of these metallics during fabrication and installation.

Tambours—laminates scored in narrow strips and held together by strong backings—are made for wrapping curved surfaces such as columns, counter fronts, and table bases.

HPDL sheets are generally available in 30, 36, 48, and 60 in. widths, from 96 to 144 in. long (762, 914, 1219, and 1524 mm wide; 2438 and 3657.6 mm long).

THERMOSET DECORATIVE (TD) PANELS

Standards for thermoset decorative panels are set in the specifications for a trademarked product Permalam, which is manufactured by licensed United States and Canadian members of the American Laminators Association (ALA). TD (also called low-pressure decorative laminate, LPDL) panels may be

TABLE 6-3
GRADES OF HIGH-PRESSURE DECORATIVE PLASTIC LAMINATE (HPDL)

Grade	Grade and thickness designations*	Uses
General purpose	GP 50 GP 38 GP 28 GP 22	Thicker grades are for surfaces that receive heavy use, as in countertops. Thinner grades are for vertical surfaces such as panels and doors.
Postforming	PF 42 PF 30 PF 22	This grade permits simple bends to be made by heating. The heavy grade can be used to wrap counter edges and make integral backsplashes.
Cabinet liner	CL 20	Cabinet interiors, where less wear resistance and color choice is needed.
Backer	BK 50 BK 20	Balancing sheets for undersides of counters and backs of panels. Very limited color availability.
Special purpose	SP 125 SP 62	For higher degree of resistance to impact.
High wear	HW 120 HW 80 HW 62	For access floor panels (as in studios) where resistance to scuffing, gouging, and heel marks is essential.
Fire-rated	FR 62 FR 50 FR 32	For use where a flame spread <25 is needed.

From NEMA LD-3-91

* Thicknesses are designated in thousandths of an inch. Thus 62 represents $\frac{1}{16}$ in. or 1.6 mm.

either melamine or polyester clad. Like all laminated plastics, they are designed for interior use.

Manufacture

A typical thermoset decorative panel starts with a particleboard, medium density fiberboard, or some other dense cellulose board. A decorative melamine or polyester web overlay is thermally fused in a press, either to both sides of the board, or to one side with a backer (balancing) sheet on the other. Matte or stippled textures are imparted to the surfaces by the steel plates of the press.

The pressure exerted in the process ranges from 175 to 200 lb/in², at temperatures of 275 to 350°F for polyester overlays (1200 to 1380 MPa at 135 to 180°C), or to pressures from 300 to 400 lb/in², at temperatures of 300 to 400°F for melamine overlays (2070 to 2760 MPa at 150 to 205°C).

Performance characteristics of the surfaces are similar to those of high-pressure decorative laminates.

TD/LPDL Varieties

As with HPDL sheets, thermoset decorative panels can be made in a range of textures, colors, and patterns. Because of TD panels' sandwich construction, different finishes can be provided on the two faces of the panels if so ordered in production run quantity.

Thermoset decorative panels are available with flame spread ratings of 25 and 75, as tested following ASTM E84.

As a rigid, factory clad panel ranging from ¼ to 1⅛ in. (6 to 29 mm) in thickness, TL panels cannot be postformed. They are usually cut and edged to form drawer bodies, interior cabinet panels, wardrobe doors, shelves, paneling, and other interior woodwork that will not be subjected to abrasion or impact. TD panels are not used for countertops but are widely used for cabinet doors, displays, and furniture that will not be subjected to heavy wear.

TD panels are available in typical particleboard or fiberboard sizes. They are edged in wood veneer, solid hardwood, PVC or metal tee-moldings, melamine, or polyester strips.

Thermoset decorative panels are frequently used in combination with high-pressure decorative laminates

in producing casework. In this hybrid construction the counters and other heavy-use parts are constructed in HPDL while the interior parts are done in TD panel material. Both WIC and AWI recognize the appropriate use of TD/LPDL panel material in Premium, Custom, and Economy grades of casework.

OTHER PLASTIC LAMINATES

Liquid acrylic radiation-cured laminates have much the same appearance as thermoset decorative panels. They are factory laminated from liquid resins applied to particleboard or fiberboard, and are textured as they are cured by radiation to produce a tightly bonded surface that withstands moderate wear.

Vinyl overlay laminates are factory laminated from sheet vinyls adhered to particleboard or fiberboard. Like the other plastic laminates, the surfaces are harder than paints and varnishes, with greater possible variety in color, pattern, and texture.

PLASTIC LAMINATE ASSEMBLIES

A plastic laminate assembly or panel is very much like plywood, having a laminate face and back, a core, and glue lines to create the assembly.

HPDL Adhesives

Several varieties of adhesives are in use to bond laminates to various substrates. These include: (1) thermosetting rigid adhesives such as resorcinol and epoxy adhesives, (2) contact type adhesives such as neoprene, and (3) hot-melt glues.

Thermosetting adhesives require the use of pressure to insure adherence and are limited to flat pressable elements. The epoxy adhesives are used primarily for bonding to impervious cores such as steel.

Contact adhesives are suitable for wood and metal surfaces. Both the substrate and the plastic laminate are coated with the adhesive. Care must be exercised in positioning the two surfaces to be bonded, since the components cannot be realigned once contact has been made. Contact adhesives are used on curved surfaces or those not adaptable to press gluing.

Hot-melt glues are primarily for the application of laminate edges using high temperatures and then subjecting the laminate to pressure.

Substrate Materials

The prime requisites for a substrate material to which plastic laminate is adhered are dimensional stability, uniform density, and smooth surface characteristics.

Since high-pressure plastic laminate is a cellulosic material, it behaves very much like wood and has a grain direction and dimensional characteristics similar to wood. As humidity decreases, plastic laminate tends to contract, and as humidity increases, the plastic laminate tends to expand. As a result the following wood substrates offer the best core material for plastic laminate facings: particleboard, fiberboard, and hardwood-faced veneer core plywood.

Particleboard, because of its engineered properties, results in a flat core material with the finer chips at the surface, which provides a smooth surface to receive plastic laminate facings. The use of medium-density (40 to 50-pound) particleboard complying with ANSI A208.1 is recommended.

Hardwood-faced veneer core plywood utilizing a Philippine Mahogany–faced-veneer provides a smooth, grain-free surface for laminating purposes.

Fir plywood is not recommended as a core for plastic laminate since the pronounced grain of the fir may result in the telegraphing of the grain into the plastic laminate. This is particularly true of press-glued laminations.

Fiberboard of medium density complying with ANSI A208.2 is recommended because it provides a smooth surface to receive plastic laminate.

FABRICATION AND INSTALLATION

The fabrication of plastic laminate components such as panels, cabinets, and countertops should be performed in accordance with NEMA LD-3 requirements and with those of the AWI Architectural Woodwork

Quality Standards. Both standards provide quality of work guidelines for gluing, application of edges, cutting, drilling, sawing, and routing.

SOLID POLYMER SURFACINGS

NONLABORATORY TYPES

Solid polymer surfacings are most often associated with countertops for vanities and kitchen cabinets and the bowls that are a part of them. However, the versatile materials are also widely used for shower walls, wainscots, interior signs, tabletops, and in store fixture construction. *Solid surfacing* is the name commonly used for these products within the woodworking industry and among bath and kitchen builders: it has largely replaced synthetic marble. The use of the term solid surfacing reflects the widespread practice of fabricating items from sheet material, while synthetic marble often brings to mind one-piece cast countertops complete with sinks and backsplashes.

Properties

Acrylics and polyesters, and various copolymers of these, filled and unfilled, are the staples of solid surfacing technology. The most important qualities in solid surfacings are stain resistance, resistance to chemicals, resistance to boiling water, low absorption, hardness, and impact resistance. Producers provide information on these and other qualities following tests set forth in the NEMA LD3 standard and various ASTM test procedures.

Fabrication

Sink bowls of the same material as a counter can either be integrally cast in the countertop material or manufactured separately and sealed to the underside of a precise cutout. Bowls of other materials can be adhered to the underside or set in the countertop with either flush or raised rims.

LABORATORY TYPES

For resistance to reagents and general abuse, the most common upgrades of high-pressure plastic laminates and domestic or commercial solid surfacings are:

- Cast epoxy, ¾, 1 and 1¼ in. thick
- Mineral-filled or -fibered calcium silicate panels, usually with a fused inorganic finish, ¾ and 1¼ in. thick
- ⅛-in. glass reinforced polyester surfacing laminated to a plywood base

Stone, usually slate, soapstone, or bluestone, is another class of laboratory countertop or sink material that departs from the solid polymer surfacing category completely.

AWI AND WIC WOODWORK STANDARDS

The Architectural Woodwork Institute and Woodwork Institute of California are associations of architectural woodwork producers who publish standards for the detailed design, fabrication, and finishing of casework, trim, paneling, and wood doors: "All woodwork exposed to view in the finished building except flooring, exposed decking, trusses and rafters." Each association maintains quality control programs, WIC

TABLE 6-4
GRADES OF WOODWORK QUALITY, AS DESCRIBED BY AWI AND WIC

Both the Architectural Woodwork Institute and the Woodwork Institute of California have established levels of quality that apply to casework, trim, paneling, doors, other millwork, and ornamental wood fabrications. The details of each quality level for each category of woodwork are shown in AWI Architectural Woodwork Quality Standards and WIC Manual of Woodwork.

Grade	AWI definition	WIC definition
Premium	The grade specified when the highest degree of control over the quality of workmanship, materials, installation, and execution of the design intent is required. Usually reserved for special projects or feature areas within a project.	This grade is a superior quality of materials and craftsmanship with a corresponding increase in cost. It is intended primarily for the best of hardwood construction, but any species of wood may be specified.
Custom	The grade specified for most conventional architectural woodwork. This grade provides a well-defined degree of control over the quality of workmanship, materials, and installation of a project. The vast majority of all work produced is Custom Grade.	This grade includes all the requisites of high-quality millwork and is suitable for all normal uses in high-grade construction, such as higher quality residential, school, and commercial building.
Economy	The grade which defines the minimum expectations of quality, workmanship, materials, and installation within the scope of AWI Standards. When AWI Quality Standards are referenced as part of the contract documents and no grade is specified, AWI Custom Grade standards will prevail.	This grade establishes a standard to meet the requirements of lower cost residential and commercial construction wherein economy is the principal factor and for use in storage rooms and utility areas.

primarily in California and Nevada—serving 20 percent of the United States population–and AWI primarily in states to the east.

Both associations have defined three levels of woodwork quality, Premium, Custom, and Economy—Custom being the commonly specified standard for high-quality, conventional work. The three quality levels for AWI and WIC are described in Table 6-4.

Custom Grade is the default quality level if the standards of AWI are cited without further specification. One pattern has emerged as the use of AWI and WIC standards has gained popularity with architects and interior designers: there is a tendency to over-specify, specifically to call for Premium Grade on ordinary construction of good quality. Custom Grade offers a high-quality standard and need not be upgraded except in the most monumental and costly commissions. When in doubt, check a few of the fabrication differences between Custom and Premium. Decide if the upgrade is worth the expense.

Terminology and detailed quality requirements are similar in AWI and WIC standards but are by no means identical. Where AWI recognizes three styles of cabinet construction (flush overlay, reveal overlay, and exposed face frame), WIC recognizes four (flush overlay, reveal overlay, lipped, and flush).

The Woodwork Institute of California also sets standards for wood laboratory furniture and appropriate laboratory counter materials.

Both institutes maintain compliance programs which permit disputes over the quality of fabricated woodwork to be submitted, for a fee, to AWI or WIC for analysis and written report of adherence to the published standards. Woodwork Institute of California, in addition, offers a certification service for the installation of fabricated woodwork items.

American Republic Building, Des Moines, IA: gray marble flooring on interior carried into outdoor courts. Skidmore, Owings & Merrill, Architects. *(Photographer, Ezra Stoller © ESTO.)*

THERMAL AND MOISTURE PROTECTION

In large part, the products used for thermal and moisture protection are either concealed (waterproofing, insulation, firestopping), not generally visible (membrane roofing, roof curbs, and hatches) or inconspicuous (flashings and joint sealants). However, some architectural designs cannot be fulfilled without the intelligent use of these products.

Thermal and moisture protection is also provided by highly visible building components such as sidings, EIF assemblies, panel assemblies, shingles, and tile roofing. Some functional properties of these high-visual-impact components will be covered here. Hopefully, the designer can then survey and select from among the wealth of exterior claddings, having been made aware of aspects such as resistance to wind and water, insulation against heat and cold, strength, and durability.

WEATHER PROTECTION STRATEGY

MODES OF WEATHER PROTECTION

There are three basic modes of weather protection that can be employed:

- Membrane erection
- Water diversion
- Pressure balancing

In Chapters 7 and 8 of this book, one, two, or three of these modes furnishes the principle on which each product or system functions. Waterproofings, water repellents, vapor retarders, insulation, roofings, flashings, and sealants are but isolated tools in a complex matrix of technologies by which we find protection from all forms of wind, water, ice, vapor, heat, and cold.

DESIGN, NOT MATERIALS ALONE

Some of the ravages of unwanted moisture in buildings cannot be combatted by products alone—the emphasis must be on thoughtful strategy and detailing. Rising damp in masonry walls is dealt with by skillfully locating impermeable cutoffs in walls at grade. Repelling rain from masonry surfaces, dealing with condensation within wall cavities, the collecting and expelling of in-wall moisture to the exterior, taking precautions against spalling from the freezing of absorbed water, and preventing the trapping of moisture or the buildup of vapor pressure—these are subjects that must be shared in books on construction details and execution.

One strategy is so widely recognized in good moisture-control design that it must be mentioned here: Never trap moisture. Sooner or later moisture trapped within a waterproof envelope will have to escape. For this reason, installing two parallel waterproof membranes in wall or roof construction—the belt and suspenders approach—can be less effective than one properly placed membrane. A double membrane can fail from intense water vapor pressure generated on a sunny day, thus actually endangering the entire program of moisture control in a building.

Another fact of life is that all parts of the building's envelope admit water to some degree at various times. Rather than attempt to build a hull, it is usually better to devise methods of controlling this water intake and to devise methods of expelling the water before it can do damage.

WATERPROOFING

PRINCIPLES

The term *waterproofing* is defined in ASTM D1079 as the "treatment of a surface or a structure to prevent the passage of water under hydrostatic pressure." Dampproofing is treatment to prevent the passage of moisture not under pressure. "Prevent" is a strong word: *retard* is more realistic. The types of waterproofing that are available can be classified as shown in Table 7-1.

Positive and Negative Faces

Most waterproofings are designed for application to exterior surfaces since they form a barrier to the entrance of water. The walls and floors provide the support system to counterbalance the force of a hydrostatic head of water. Where reservoirs, tanks, or pools are waterproofed to contain water, the waterproof linings are likewise installed on the water side—or pressure side—of the structure. In all of these cases the waterproofing is said to be applied to the positive side or positive face.

However, some waterproofing systems can be applied to the side opposite the potential or actual

TABLE 7-1
WATERPROOFINGS AND DAMPPROOFINGS

Waterproofing Coatings
Acrylic modified cement
Liquid applied
  Urethane
  Coal tar modified urethane
  Asphalt modified urethane
  Rubberized asphalt
Crystalline
Metal Oxide
Bituminous
  Asphalt
  Coal Tar Pitch

Sheet Waterproofings
Built-up Bituminous
  Asphalt
  Coal Tar Pitch
Lead
Preformed Panels and Rolls
  Modified Bitumen
  Elastomeric
    EPDM, neoprene, CSPE, PIB, NBP
  Thermoplastic
    PVC, EIP
Bentonite
  Panels
  Sheet

Dampproofing below Grade
Acrylic Modified Cement
Bituminous
  Asphalt
  Coal Tar Pitch
Built-up Bituminous
Simplified use of other waterproofing methods as damp-
  proofing

Dampproofing Above Grade
Asphalt
Acrylic Modified Cement

source of the water—the negative face—the side which is not directly under pressure.

Membranes

The term *membrane* is often applied to moisture protection materials once they are in place. Since almost all moisture protection and roofing products ulti-mately form some sort of membrane, the term is redundant and has been used sparingly in descriptions here. Instead, distinguishing terms such as *sheet, roll, trowel applied* and *sprayed* have been used— terms which buyers, lenders, contractors, and appliers look for to determine what type of material the designer has in mind.

Like *waterproof,* which is commonly used to describe materials that are at best water resistive, *membrane* might be thought to imply impermeability. However, permeable membranes are a part of nature; a membrane of zero permeability is a rare thing.

Language Traps

In this litigious age, it is better not to bestow qualities such as "fireproof" or "waterproof" on products. No product has ever been made that does not fail at some level of stress. All the same, our common language, by long tradition, uses terms such as *fireproofing* and *waterproofing* simply to communicate the existence of products that can make construction more fire-resistant and more resistant to the intrusion of moisture when selected and applied intelligently. These terms are not dangerous when used as nouns describing common articles of commerce such as bituminous dampproofing or Acme Dampproofing Compound.

It is when *-proof* words are used in a way that imply perfection that trouble may follow. These -proof words, used as verbs and adjectives in some instructions and descriptions, can be misunderstood by those who wish to misunderstand them. "Make wall fireproof" or "apply fireproof mastic" can be cleverly turned against the specifier. It is better to say "construct 1 hour fire-rated wall" or "apply fireproofing mastic."

This discussion will not try to change English usage. It will however use -proof words as little as possible lest misunderstandings arise.

MATERIALS AND SYSTEMS

Various types of waterproofing and dampproofing systems are listed in Table 7-1. Keep in mind that much of a building's structure and envelope is designed to be watertight in the first place. These waterproofings are often introduced to act as suspenders when the belt fails. Good concrete work and good masonry work in the building's skin are the first line of defense. The waterproofing is selected in part by predicting precisely under what conditions the concrete and the masonry may be expected not to keep all the water out.

Selecting Waterproofings

In selecting the type of waterproofing, the designer should understand the likely nature of the waterproofing problem, its location in the structure, and its relation to the local climate—then assess available materials and systems to arrive at a solution.

A structure may be subject to water infiltration at a number of vulnerable locations. It may be at foundations below grade due to a hydrostatic head of water. It could occur at a plaza with occupied spaces below that need protection. The structure could be vulnerable due to internal equipment such as pumps in mechanical spaces or plumbing fixtures in toilet rooms. Areaways, fountains, and elevator pits will need special solutions. Under some climatic or construction conditions it may be desirable to apply above-grade dampproofing or a water repellent to the walls. Figure 7-1 shows a hypothetical building section and how each problem might be handled.

For instance, in Figure 7-1—at the basement below grade—if the water table were above the basement floor level, C- and S- types of waterproofings could be applied to the exterior face of the foundation wall

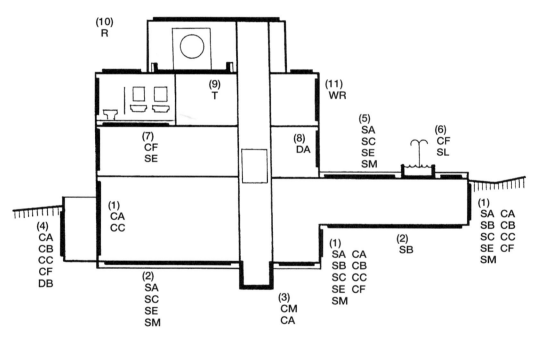

Waterproofing codes for this figure:

C =	Waterproofing coatings	S =	Sheet waterproofings	DA	Above-grade dampproofing
CA	Acrylic-modified cementitious	SA	Built-up bituminous	DB	Below-grade dampproofing
CB	Bituminous	SB	Bentonite	WR	Water repellent
CC	Crystalline	SC	Preformed panel/roll	R	Roofing
CF	Fluid-applied	SE	Elastomeric	T	Traffic coating
CM	Metal oxide	SL	Lead		
		SM	Modified bitumen		

For conditions where no head of groundwater pressure will be exerted against the foundations, many of the waterproofings here can be applied in reduced quantity as dampproofings, or other dampproofings described in this chapter may be substituted.

FIGURE 7-1   Selecting waterproofings.

(1) if excavation makes the walls accessible from the exterior. Without access, only CA, CC, and CM types can be considered. It would be advantageous to find out what methods local waterproofers are using and with what success.

For the basement slab (2), most of the S- types of waterproofings can be placed over a mud slab to block water from upward entry. If a mud slab is impractical, there are ways in which the SB type can be used, or the CC type might be elected.

With a head of water in the ground, the CM type is often selected for the negative faces of the elevator pit walls and floor (3). With little or no water, CA or CC types might be chosen.

Areaways and basement stairwells (4) may receive a C- type of coating or a DB type dampproofing if the foundation wall behind them is waterproofed against water under pressure.

At the plaza level (5) SA, SC, SE or SL types will permit paving materials to be placed over. However, at a pond or fountain (6) an SL type or a heavy CF system (protected from sunlight) might be considered.

At toilet room floors (7) the waterproofing must be carefully analyzed to find a product that will permit thinset tile to adhere. With a mortar setting bed a wider range of C- and S- type products can be considered.

In some climates, masonry walls (8) may benefit from the application of DA type dampproofing inside. Not so frequently in new construction, but in existing construction where a water problem exists, WR type water repellents may help.

Traffic toppings, T types, are frequently put below mechanical equipment (9) that may leak water or oil to areas below. A low concrete curb is often built around the area and its interior face waterproofed with the same material.

Roof areas (10) receive roofing systems.

Surface Preparation

Moisture control products—especially waterproofings, insulations, and roofings—that are applied over structural elements must be placed over smooth, hard, dry, oil-free concrete, or masonry surfaces if they are to function properly.

As much as possible, their installers must be made primarily responsible for the condition of the concrete or masonry surfaces. The waterproofing applier should then be required to check the surface for holes, projections, severe cracking and roughness, and for sufficiently low moisture content (usually below 10 percent), and should report defects to the contractor. It is not realistic to expect appliers to do extensive concrete or masonry repair before they can start their waterproofing, insulating, or roofing. Only the most simple smoothing, filling, or cleaning should be the responsibility of the applier.

However it is accomplished, the surface must be smooth, hard, dry, and free of bond-breaking substances.

Contact

Promoting full contact is wise waterproofing strategy. A product that is 100 percent adhered to its substrate is a product that will not permit water to penetrate at some point of damage and then flow laterally—perhaps meters distant—to an opportune crack or joint in the deck or foundation. Products that are held in place by dots of adhesive can be maddening to analyze when trying to locate a leak.

Protecting Waterproofing

Many waterproofings, dampproofings, and vapor retarders are soft, especially in the days immediately following application. It is good practice to specify a protection board over all of these products—one that can remain in place and be covered over.

A common protection course material for horizontal surfaces is a thin sandwich of asphalt-saturated felts, polyethylene film, and modified asphalt with mineral fillers. These sheets can be lapped and adhered in place. They will withstand limited traffic as well as backfilling and concreting operations. Their loss of thickness from compression and decay is limited, and they do not attract termites.

Common protection courses for vertical surfaces include inexpensive ½-in. expanded polystyrene beadboard and ¾-in. asphalt-impregnated cellulose board (often held in place by the tacky surface of the waterproofing they protect). On horizontal waterproofed surfaces the choice is often asphalt sandwich sheets which withstand light traffic well. Plain cellulose board and plywood have less long-term dimensional stability and insect resistance.

Metal oxide waterproofing receives a mortar or concrete protective course. Bentonite must always be restrained by hard-packed earth or by several inches of concrete to perform its waterproofing function as it wets and expands.

Special Warranties

For waterproofing and dampproofing in walls, the producers of the materials generally do not offer warranties. However, the appliers of wall waterproofing and dampproofing are not unfamiliar with supplying, at a cost, warranties of their work that extend beyond the one-year correction-of-work period customary with the AIA and EJCDC General Conditions. Thus building owners and design professionals often request that contractors provide 2-year or 5-year special warranties on the letterhead of the applier and endorsed by the contractor.

With roofing systems, warranties by the producer of the materials are more common. These are discussed under the Roofing heading of this chapter.

WATERPROOFING COATINGS

Acrylic Modified Cement

Portland cement, modified with admixtures, is in wide use for waterproofing against heads of water 10 ft (3 m)—and much greater. For undemanding situations, these cementitious mixtures are brushed neatly into place. For heavier coats sand is added to the mix for troweling in place. For demanding waterproofing situations, a troweled coat may be followed by a brushed coat. An acrylic admixture in the water improves both bond and waterproofing performance.

The quantities of cement, water, and sand—and the amount of acrylic admixture in the mixing water—for each type of coat can be found in each producer's instructions.

Because these modified cement coatings can be finished to a smooth surface and then painted, they are often used on the negative face of an exterior wall or foundation. They can also be used on negative faces for remedial waterproofing, thus saving the cost of excavation and protection at the exterior (positive) face of the foundation.

Special procedures must be followed for the filling of cracks.

Except for heavy parge coats, cement waterproofings are not shown or specified by coating thickness. Rather, they are commonly specified by the number of coats of each type, the mix for each coat, the method of applying, the spread rate, and curing times. ANSI A118.4, the standard developed for latex-cement tile mortars, applies to cement waterproofing.

Liquid Applied Coatings

Although liquid-state products such as polysulfide, epoxy, polychloroprene (neoprene), and chlorosulfonated polyethylene (Hypalon) have been used in waterproofings, the only commonly marketed liquid applied elastomeric products are urethane-based coatings and rubberized asphalt.

Liquid applied coatings can be applied to the positive face of vertical wall surfaces or between concrete slabs.

The advantages of a liquid applied waterproofing are:

- There is continuity of the membrane between horizontal and vertical planes, around projections and penetrations.
- The membrane adheres to every part of the substrate, which causes leaks to be found more easily, and can then be isolated, since there can be no lateral travel of water beneath the membrane.

Urethane-Based Coatings

Straight urethane and asphalt modified urethane can be specified in two-part formulation. These two products, as well as coal tar pitch modified urethane, are also available as one-part formulations.

Two-part formulations are useful for cold weather application since they cure rapidly, but they may cure too rapidly in very hot weather. The higher the solids content, the less chance there will be that leak-inviting bubbles in the waterproofing film will form during application. Most producers make two versions of each product, one for horizontal and one for vertical application.

Coal tar pitch formulations should not be used in confined spaces, near food preparation, or in areas where fumes may be objectionable. On the other hand, pitch-bearing products are naturally fungicidal, do not deteriorate under water, and perform well in the earth.

In 1976, ASTM C836 was published, appearing to be an industry consensus for liquid applied waterproofings. However, as of 1995 only five producers cite it, while nine major producers—equally prestigious—still describe their products in terms of older test standards that were developed for rubber, such as ASTM D412, D624, D746, D2240, and E96.

ASTM C898 sets standards for both materials and the application of urethane waterproofings. The standard requires that concrete have no more than 4 to 8 percent moisture content. This is difficult to achieve with lightweight aggregate concrete which generally runs 5 to 20 percent in moisture content in the months after placement. Standard weight concrete soon cures to 3 to 5 percent moisture content in temperate weather.

Horizontal applications of waterproofing are often pond tested for 24 to 48 hours under 2 to 4 in. (50 to 100 mm) of water to ensure early detection of any leaks.

Liquid applied waterproofing must not be exposed to the sun for more than a few days. A protection course is customarily installed above horizontal surfaces to protect from traffic and sunlight. It is not wise to use unprotected waterproofings of this type in pools and fountains since they become exposed to the sun for long periods.

Table 7-2 is a general guide to the complex availability situation for the basic formulations of liquid applied urethane and modified urethane waterproofing materials.

Specifying Urethane Coatings

To specify these waterproofings for competitive bidding, one must know the curious ways in which the industry is fragmented—if apples-to-apples competition is the goal. It is as if there were four urethane coating industries, each with its own standards and way of doing business. Only producer-backed warranties of waterproofing performance were considered in compiling this list: limited warranties on

TABLE 7-2
LIQUID APPLIED URETHANE-BASED WATERPROOFINGS

Formulations and installed-product warranties available from fourteen major producers, with published notice of ASTM C836 compliance, arranged roughly in descending order of cost.

Urethane-based waterproofing formulation	Solids content, percent	Follows ASTM C836?		Producer warranties offered
		Yes	No	
Two-part	100	—	2	3-year
	100	—	1	2-year
	100	—	3	none
	80	1	—	none
One-part	100	1	—	none
	88	—	1	3-year
	83	—	1	3-year
	80	1	—	none
Two-part asphalt modified	88	1	—	none
One-part coal tar pitch modified	80	3	—	none
	80	—	2	none
One-part asphalt modified	88	1	—	none
	83	1	—	none
	80	1	—	none

materials and applier guarantees that may be obtainable were not counted.

Warranted, Two-part, 100 percent solids urethane. Three producers offer this product, with warranties up to 3 years. A fourth producer makes a 3-year warranted, one-part, 88 percent urethane. All require trained, authorized appliers. None claims to follow ASTM C836.

Two-part, 100 percent solids urethane. Four other producers offer this product without warranty or citation of ASTM C836. None mentions applier training or licensing.

One-part, 80 percent solids coal tar pitch modified urethane. Five other producers offer this product, without warranty. Three cite ASTM C836. None mentions applier training or licensing.

One-part, 80 to 88 percent solids asphalt modified urethane. Three other producers offer this product, without warranty. All follow ASTM C836. None mentions applier training or licensing.

To specify competition, one must start with one of these four categories. A specification cobbled together to call for a one-part, 100 percent urethane with 3-year warranty by an authorized applier, following ASTM C836, is mythical.

One of these producers in the last category also offers one-part straight urethanes, an 80 percent solids two-part urethane, and an 88 percent solids two-part asphalt modified urethane, all without warranty but following ASTM C836.

Rubberized Asphalt Coatings

Rubberized asphalt is a combination of ground, reclaimed rubber, and asphalt. It is usually applied hot to a thickness of 0.180 in. (4.6 mm). Its advantage over urethane-based coatings is that it is less sensitive to moisture and cold at the time of application. It sets up softer, however, and must be protected.

Crystalline Waterproofing

Several compounds, applied in aqueous solution, penetrate concrete and react with it to form insoluble crystals that fill the small cracks and capillaries and become an integral part of the concrete, thus blocking the transmission of water. A moist cure is essential to their success. Crystalline compounds may be placed on either the positive or negative faces of the structure. These compounds do not act as bond-breakers between the concrete and most other materials. This permits painting and remedial work to be done where crystallines are present. Since these products have no body, cracks and joints must be filled with another material, usually a cement.

Crystalline waterproofings cannot be shown or specified by coating thickness—they are dimensionless. Designers must specify mix, method of applying, application rate, and curing time for various situations from the information found in producers' instructions. There are no standards for crystalline waterproofings.

Metal Oxide Waterproofing

A time-honored method of waterproofing is to mix iron filings and an oxidizing agent with cement (and often sand), which is then brushed in or troweled on as a thick coat. This is sometimes referred to as metallic waterproofing. The iron rusts and expands, making for a very tight coat—not pretty, but a barrier to moisture that can be given a cement plaster coat (on vertical surfaces) or covered with a concrete topping for traffic-bearing slabs.

The treatment of cracks before waterproofing is critical. A deep, rectangular rabbet is routed out along the length of each crack or joint. The rabbet is then wetted, primed, and filled with the coating material. The circumference of each pipe penetration is treated in the same way.

Metal oxide waterproofing can be used on both vertical and horizontal surfaces. The actual iron-filled cement waterproofing coat is not likely to be damaged by casual contact, but it should be protected from damage by repeated foot traffic. Metal oxide waterproofing can be used on the exteriors of foundation walls, but its widest use has been on the interior, negative faces and floors of elevator pits, concrete tanks, wet rooms, areaways, and other relatively small, critical elements of buildings. It is also used on the negative face of party walls where adjacent construction makes access to the positive face impossible.

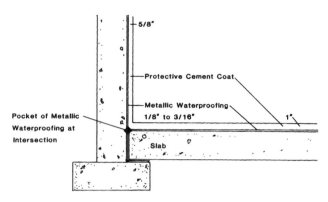

FIGURE 7-2   Metallic waterproofing.

Metal oxide waterproofing with its bond coat, waterproofing coat and thick protection coat may total more than ½ in. Its thickness, however, is not dimensioned on the drawings. Instead, it is left to the specifications to describe the mixes, the method of applying each coat, the application rate of each layer, and each coat's curing time, as compiled from the differing information found in various producers' instructions.

See Figure 7-2 for a typical metal oxide waterproofing detail. Typical proportions for coats are shown in Table 7-3.

There are no published standards for metal oxide waterproofing systems or for its metal oxide component.

Bituminous Coatings

Some troweled, fibered dampproofings (listed under the Dampproofing heading) are sufficient, in cases where the head of water is very low, to serve as waterproofing.

Sprayed and brushed dampproofings are not suitable for holding back ground water under pressure. No tables provided by either dampproofing producers or industry associations state at what point a troweled dampproofing coating, unreinforced by felt or fabric, can be trusted to serve as waterproofing.

SHEET WATERPROOFINGS

The advantage of components that are applied in sheet form is that they are factory-fabricated, which means that the work products are more likely to be of uniform weight and free of bubbles and thin spots. This factory quality control puts the thickness and completeness of the waterproofing assembly less at the mercy of the worker who wields the nozzle, brush, or trowel late Friday afternoon.

However, all sheet waterproofings still require attention to temperature and moisture conditions, to good and full adhesion, to instructions, and to care with penetrations and terminations.

TABLE 7-3
TYPICAL PROPORTIONS FOR METAL OXIDE WATERPROOFING MIXES

Coat	Metal	Cement	Sand	Mixing & other requirements
Prime or bond coat, for either joint filler or waterproofing coat	1	1	—	Wet to heavy paint consistency. Apply to damp surface.
Joint filling mix	1	2	3	Wet to troweling consistency.
Waterproofing (slurry) coat	2	1	—	Wet to brushing consistency.
Protection (parge) coat	—	1	2.5	Wet to troweling consistency.
Topping mix 1 to 2 in. (25 to 50 mm) thick	—	1	2	Plus 3 parts pea gravel; wet to stiff mix; 1 to 3 in. (25 to 75 mm) slump.
If topping is not used, provide, as part of concrete work:				
Traffic slab 3 to 4 in. (75 to 100 mm) thick	—			$f'_c = 3500$ psi concrete with pea gravel; 1 to 3 in. (25 to 75 mm) slump.

Built-Up Bituminous Assemblies

Hot coal tar pitch, hot asphalt, solvent-bound (cutback) asphalt, and asphalt emulsions, combined with layers of sheet goods, are the ingredients of built-up bituminous waterproofing assemblies. The longest lasting bitumen for underground use is coal tar pitch; the least trustworthy over time are asphalt emulsions which tend to reemulsify if wetted persistently. The use of cutback asphalts and hot pitch is limited because of the fumes they emit; there may be health hazards to workers in trenches or violation of volatile organic compound (VOC) release limits. In extremes of heat and cold, the hot-applied products are less subject to problems since they do not sag or delaminate from heat once in place. They do not freeze or become difficult to work in extreme cold.

The choice of sheet goods used in reinforcing is governed by budget. Glass fabrics and felts—the more expensive products—do not decay, are stronger, and bond well with the bitumen. Less expensive cotton fabrics, burlap, and paper felts are not as strong and are subject to biological attack, although their absorption of bitumen is a plus. Polyester fabrics fall between the two in cost, strength, bonding, and longevity.

Fabrics are more pliable and conform to irregularities, while felts are easier to lay up. Fabrics and felts used in waterproofing are usually coated or saturated with asphalt or pitch. Uncoated fabrics and felts do not lay up easily and are not as common.

Fabrics and felts may be shingled to provide 2-, 3-, 4-, or 5-ply assemblies. They may also be layed up ply-on-ply—one ply at a time, lapped 3 in. (75 mm) at roll ends and sidelaps. The joints in each course should be broken 12 in. (300 mm) from the previous course. After smoothing and priming the surface, an initial coat of bitumen is applied. Bitumen is applied between each ply of fabric or felt, and a final coat is applied overall. Alternating layers of felt and fabric may be employed.

Asphalt emulsions must dry thoroughly between coats, and each coat must be applied under fully dry conditions.

Top edges of waterproofing must be held on the wall by means of a continuous preservative-treated nailer strip or must be disc nailed 8 in. (200 mm) on centers. Special provision must be made to support the assembly in hot weather until backfilling can take place.

The number of plies is selected according to the head of water to be withstood, as shown in Table 7-4.

A deep installation can be incremental: one ply added for each depth step shown.

Bitumen is applied so that each coat contains at least the quantity for each unit area as shown in Table 7-5, the number of coats always being one greater than the number of plies.

Detailed guidelines for the construction of built-up waterproofing membranes are found in the NRCA *Waterproofing Manual.* Standards for built-up bituminous waterproofing materials are listed in Table 7-6.

How Waterproof?

Built-up bituminous assemblies are waterproofing classics. The practice of applying successive layers of asphalt or coal tar pitch with reinforcing felt or fabric has been a staple of building construction for well over a century. The name waterproofing has stuck to the practice, but such construction is not absolutely waterproof. When water, under pressure, is present for prolonged periods, moisture will find its way into the structure—perhaps only in the form of a damp basement wall. Asphalt is not fully waterproof: it will absorb water. It can also deteriorate under the influence of organisms in soil, water, and air. Asphalts applied as aqueous emulsions can reemulsify.

TABLE 7-4
NUMBER OF FABRIC PLIES IN BITUMINOUS WATERPROOFINGS

Head of water at bottom of wpfg. (ft/m)	Plies of fabric in hot-mopped coal tar pitch or asphalt	Plies of fabric in cutback asphalt or emulsified asphalt
1–3 / 0.3–1.0	2	2
3–10 / 1.0–3.0	3	3
10–25 / 3.0–7.5	4	4
25–50 / 7.5–15.0	5	—

TABLE 7-5
BITUMEN FOR BUILT-UP BITUMINOUS WATERPROOFINGS

Bitumen	Quantity, each coat
Hot coal tar pitch	28 lb/100 ft^2 (1.4 kg/m^2)
Hot asphalt	23 lb/100 ft^2 (1.1 kg/m^2)
Cutback asphalt	4 gal/100 ft^2 (1.6 l/m^2)
Asphalt emulsion	4 gal/100 ft^2 (1.6 l/m^2)

TABLE 7-6
STANDARDS FOR WATERPROOFING WORK

Quality standards that can be cited for the components of built-up bituminous waterproofing assemblies. Some of these standards will be of use in specifying bituminous dampproofing.

Bitumens

Coal tar pitch primer (creosote)	ASTM D43
Coal tar pitch	ASTM D450, Type II
Asphalt primer (for use under hot mopped asphalt, cutback asphalt, or asphalt emulsion)	ASTM D41
Asphalt, for hot mopping	ASTM D449, Type I
Cutback asphalt (solvent-borne, for cold application)	ASTM D491
Emulsified asphalt	ASTM D1187

Fabrics

Pitch-saturated glass	ASTM D1668, Type II
Pitch-saturated woven burlap	ASTM D1327, coal tar pitch
Pitch-saturated cotton	ASTM D173, coal tar pitch
Asphalt-saturated glass	ASTM D1668, Type I
Asphalt-saturated woven burlap	ASTM D1327, asphalt
Asphalt-saturated cotton	ASTM D173, asphalt

Felts

Pitch-saturated organic felt	ASTM D227
Asphalt-impregnated glass mat, heavy duty, 44 lbf/in. (7.7 kN/m) breaking strength, 0.060 lb/ft² (293 g/m²) weight	ASTM D2178, Type IV
Asphalt-impregnated glass mat, standard, 22 lbf/in. (3.85 kN/m) breaking strength 0.084 lb/ft² (410 g/m²) weight	ASTM D2178, Type III
Asphalt-saturated organic felt	ASTM D226

Very few membranes can be made absolutely waterproof. A lead pan, perfectly executed, can turn out to be waterproof over the long run. Coal tar pitch construction, adequately designed and perfectly executed, can keep out water for a long time because of the inherent water resistance of coal tar pitch. Two or three other constructions described in the chapter have a high probability of resisting water penetration for 20 years or more. But to build an envelope either below ground or on the roof that will keep out water the way the hull of a ship does is almost impossible. And even ships have bilges.

Lead

Lead waterproofing—most often employed for pools, fountains, planters, and decks with paving—has the advantage of long service with almost no maintenance. If water is retained over an occupied area, lead should be considered regardless of expense.

The most permanent construction uses the largest available 6- or 8-lb (25- or 34-kg/m²) lead sheets, which are lapped 1½ in. (38 mm) and burned (welded) together full seam width. With 5-lb (21-kg/m²) sheets, sometimes used for planters and less demanding work, the seams can be lapped 1½ in. and soldered.

Several precautions must be taken to ensure satisfactory work:

• Lead must never touch concrete. Coat concrete with asphalt or an elastomer before adhering the lead sheets in place.

• Mortars and other cementitious materials must not be used over lead. A coat of asphalt or an elastomer must coat the lead before any tile or pavers or wear slabs are put over the lead waterproofing.

• Both faces of the lead at each seam must be shaved bright before applying lead burning rod material and flame. Soldering requires even more preparation.

Preformed Panels and Rolls

Preformed panel and adhered roll waterproofings perform at very low permeability ratings, often less than 1.0 perm.

Often a choice must be made between preformed waterproofings and liquid applied waterproofings. Their physical characteristics may be similar, but there are important differences. In making any choice consider these aspects:

Preformed and Roll Waterproofings

- Less affected by moisture in substrate, up to about 10 percent or 12 percent.
- Membrane able to span small cracks, up to ⅛ in. if water pressure is not great.
- Membrane able to span soft joints only if joints are small and water pressure is not great.
- Membrane will not conform to projections.
- Membrane will bridge bugholes safely if pressure is not great. Tie holes and honeycomb must be filled.
- Membrane may not be adhered to 100 percent of the surface if work quality is normal. Chance for lateral transmission of water.
- Membranes tend to be hard, without need for curing; resist compression by rock particles in the backfill. Protection board course still highly desirable.
- Mixing errors almost nonexistent.
- Thin spots less likely.
- No bubbles; but possibility with some panel products for leakage at a defective lap.

Liquid Applied Waterproofings

- Not recommended over concrete with greater than 4 to 8 percent moisture content.
- Membrane able to fill small cracks. Safe up to ⅛ in. if water pressure is not great.
- Membrane not able to span soft joints. Provision must be made for hard joint cover if membrane is to go over.
- Membrane will conform to small projections, tie holes, bugholes, and honeycomb, but may lose thickness and strength at edges.
- Membrane will likely adhere to 100 percent of the surface being waterproofed if work quality is normal. Easier to pinpoint leaks.

- Membranes may be soft or not fully cured at time of backfill. A rock particle can pinch to zero thickness. Protection board course is a must.
- Mixing error can occur; two-part product may not set up.
- Possibility of thin spots.
- Possibility of air bubbles almost the size of the finished membrane thickness and inviting leakage.

Modified Bitumen Sheet Waterproofing

One common preformed *mod bit* product is supplied as a stiff but flexible panel approximately ⅛ in. (3 mm) thick. This sandwich panel has facings of asphalt-impregnated organic and glass felts (plus a polyethylene antistick surface) over a multilayered core of straight and modified asphalts. The panel is almost impermeable to water vapor transmission: one product has tested to 0 perms.

Modified bitumen sandwich panels are adhered in place, usually in a full coating of asphalt. The panels are sturdy, not easily dented, and can be backfilled without protection board in soils that are free of sharp stones. In fact, a protection course material, patterned on this waterproofing panel, is often used to protect other waterproofings.

Elastomeric Sheet Waterproofing

Elastomeric waterproofing products include a number of polymers as listed in Table 7-7. The elastomeric sheets are supplied as roll goods.

As with the panel types of waterproofing, elastomeric sheets are lapped and set in a full bed of asphalt or other organic adhesive.

Vulcanized (thermoset) elastomeric sheets are joined by use of adhesive. Nonvulcanized (uncured) elastomeric sheets can be heat welded (in effect vulcanized) or joined with adhesive.

The elastomerics are not degraded by fungi or bacteria and resist attack by most substances that are ordinarily found in soils. EPDM and NBP are degraded by aromatic hydrocarbons, EPDM by aliphatics also. PIB is degraded by petroleum-based solvents, oils, and coal tar.

TABLE 7-7
ELASTOMERIC WATERPROOFING PRODUCTS

Acronym and chemical name		Thickness produced	ASTM standard	Approximate no. of U.S. producers
Vulcanized (Thermoset) Elastomers				
EPDM	Ethylene propylene diene monomer	0.040–0.068	D4637	17
Neoprene	Polychloroprene	0.055–0.060	D4637	2
Nonvulcanized (Uncured) Elastomers				
CSPE,				
Hypalon	Chlorosulfonated polyethylene	0.039–0.045	D5019	11
CPE	Chlorinated polyethylene	0.036	D5019	1
PIB	Polyisobutylene	0.100	D5019	1
NBP	Butadiene-acrylonitrile (nitrile alloy)	0.040	D3083	1
Thermoplastics				
PVC	Polyvinyl chloride	0.030–0.050	D4434, D3083*	5
EIP	Ethylene/PVC interpolymer	0.033–0.060	†	2
CPA	Copolymer alloy PVC alloyed with high molecular weight plasticizer	0.040–0.050	†	4

* Waterproofing standard
† EIP and CPA should exceed D4434 standard.

Thermoplastic Sheet Waterproofing

Thermoplastic waterproofing roll goods include a number of polymers as listed in Table 7-7.

Thermoplastic sheets are lapped and set in a full bed of organic adhesive. Sheets are heat welded or joined with adhesive. PVC cannot be set in or sealed with asphalt.

The thermoplastics are not degraded by fungi or bacteria and resist attack by substances that are ordinarily found in soils.

Bentonite Waterproofing

Bentonite is a highly expansible clay composed principally of the mineral montmorillonite and small amounts of feldspar, mica, and volcanic ash. Bentonite clays swell to many times their dry volume when wet, forming a gel that water cannot pass through. When confined by a concrete foundation and earth or backfill, bentonite panels or sheets are compressed into an impervious, gelatinous mass as a result of their own expansion. They form these gel barriers by reacting to the slow action of ground moisture as well as by reacting to free water.

Bentonite in the corrugated flutes of biodegradable kraft boards or bentonite mixed with soft butyl rubber and bound into a fabric sandwich are the most common forms of this waterproofing medium. Joints at vertical surfaces are made by lapping. Pervious cardboard tubes of the material are placed at penetrations, foundation joints, and other critical lines to complete the seal.

Bentonite encapsulated in butyl strips is often used in sealing concrete joints in place of vinyl waterstops.

Bentonite is one of the few materials that is effective in waterproofing the underside of slabs on grade. In that use, the panels are often butted and stapled to avoid double swelling at laps, which can cause lifting in slabs less than 6 in. (150 mm) thick. Bentonite can also be used in planters and beneath terrace paving. Details must be carefully researched and worked out with producers' representatives to ensure that bentonite's sensitivity to moisture, and the enormous pressures generated by its expansion, are used to protect the construction and not create problems.

For use below 10 m (33 ft) a double thickness of panels is installed to resist hydrostatic pressure.

Salty or highly alkaline ground water will not activate ordinary bentonite. A special formulation for use near the sea or in desert sites must be specified.

DAMPPROOFING

Dampproofing should simply be thought of as performing either of two functions:

- Keeping moisture from entering through the foundations (exterior underground dampproofing)
- Blocking moisture passage at walls above grade (in-wall dampproofing and exterior water repellents)

Almost any waterproofing previously discussed can be used as dampproofing—usually in the thinnest form since it does not have to withstand a head of water, merely the slow release of moisture, often moisture vapor, from the ground or from the external atmosphere. The following dampproofing products form moisture barriers that are generally not sturdy enough or effective enough to withstand standing water or water under pressure: below-grade and above-grade dampproofing coatings.

BELOW-GRADE DAMPPROOFING COATINGS

Acrylic Modified Cement

Acrylic modified cement, because of its economy in thin, brushed coat applications, is often used. An advantage is the convenience of application: if brushed on, there is no need for specialized equipment. There are no odors or fumes.

Bituminous Types

Asphalt and coal tar pitch are the oldest dampproofing coatings and are still much in demand. Specialty appliers often perform dampproofing using these products, especially on large work, but the technology is simple enough that general labor sometimes applies cold-applied dampproofings on small work that is not complex.

These dampproofing products release hydrocarbons that are classified as volatile organic compounds (VOC) to the atmosphere as they dry. Urban areas that have VOC controls in place such as California's half dozen Air Quality Management Districts; Maricopa County AZ (Phoenix); Harris County TX (Houston); Chicago and East St. Louis, IL; the state of New Jersey; and Metro New York City (including Suffolk, Nassau, Westchester, and Rockland Counties), severely limit the amount of VOCs that can be present in bituminous dampproofing products sold or used within their jurisdictions.

Where VOC restrictions exist, consider the use of emulsified bituminous products. These waterborne products are not as effective gram for gram and year after year as solvent-borne or cutback products, but adequately specified and applied they can limit moisture penetration.

A drawback of emulsions is that they tend to reemulsify slightly if water is continuously present in quantity. An advantage of emulsions is that they breathe slightly and permit the out-migration of dampness in the foundation walls to the surrounding soil when the soil is dry.

Virtually all bituminous dampproofing products have been free of asbestos for a number of years. All the same, asbestos-free products should be specified, and producers should be required to attest to the fact.

Sprayed, brushed, and troweled asphalts, sometimes fibered, comprise the bulk of bituminous dampproofing coatings. The election of coal tar pitch is limited due to the tendency of irritating fumes to collect in the limited spaces in which dampproofing is usually carried on.

Bituminous dampproofings on concrete block foundations are often applied over a thin, hard troweled, cured parge coat of cement plaster. The cement plaster has waterproofing qualities of its own, especially if the mixing water contains an acrylic admixture. The great advantage of this cement-sand coat is that it offers a superior surface for application and adhesion and allows a cove to be formed at footing tops and internal corners.

Primer coats, usually a thinned version of the dampproofing material, are often desirable but not always necessary. Where the substrate is in good condition and receptive to dampproofing, it is acceptable not to prime unless the dampproofing producer clearly warns to the contrary. Published manufacturer's instructions are almost nonexistent with basic bituminous products.

Asphalt Dampproofing Below Grade

The designer who wants to protect work below grade with asphalt must choose among the following:

- *Choose cold or hot application.* Does the work location and extent justify the expense of bringing in a kettle or heated tanker? If cold applied, then choose either solvent (solvent-borne, solvent-bound, cutback) products, or emulsified (water-borne) products. Consider VOC regulations, dryness of substrate, fumes, freezing conditions, continuousness, and pressure of water present in the soil.

- *Choose spray, brush, or trowel application.* Unfibered or lightly fibered products can be applied by spraying or brushing to a specified area per unit volume of material—ft²/gal or m²/l. Unless the work is so small as to make spray equipment impractical, appliers usually spray. Heavily fibered or mineral-filled products must be troweled, likewise to a specified area per gallon or liter. Average thicknesses are not commonly specified, although a minimum, field-checkable thickness may be.

- *Choose to prime coat or not to prime.* Primers are not always needed.

- *Choose one coat or two.* Two is better than one, picking up skips, bridging bubble holes, and covering thin spots. Cost and desired performance determine this choice.

Coal Tar Pitch Dampproofing

Coal tar pitch dampproofing is carried out much the same way as asphalt dampproofing. In the past, pitch has been hot applied, but recently cold-applied products have been marketed.

The fumes from coal tar pitch limit its use in confined areas, near food preparation, and in VOC-sensitive jurisdictions.

ABOVE-GRADE DAMPPROOFING COATINGS

To limit the passage of water vapor through masonry walls above grade, especially in areas that regularly experience both cold and wet weather, a fibered coat of asphalt is often sprayed over the walls before furring and applying gypsum board.

Coal tar pitch is never used since its fumes would affect indoor air quality.

Thin coats of acrylic modified cement may also be used to dampproof masonry walls above grade. The great advantage of a cementitious coating is the cleanliness and convenience of the operation: if brushed on, there is no overspray to clean up and no need for specialized equipment. There are no odors or fumes. If brushed on carefully the cementitious coating may be painted.

TRAFFIC COATINGS

Traffic bearing coatings, when left exposed, waterproof slabs that will receive:

- Pedestrian traffic
- Limited vehicular traffic
- Clean water leakage or flooding from indoor mechanical equipment

For heavy vehicular traffic these coatings should be protected by a heavy wearing course of concrete. These traffic coatings are not intended for industrial use under intense traffic and steel-wheeled vehicles: heavy toppings—resinous or cementitious (6 mm or thicker)—are available for such heavy-duty functions.

For safety, the coatings usually incorporate fine aggregate to reduce the likelihood of slipping when wet. Where traffic coatings are used in the presence of vehicles and indoor mechanical equipment, an oil-resistant formulation should be sought. Outdoor coatings must be UV-resistant and must often withstand months of attack from water contaminated with de-icing salts.

Over the years, various urethane and epoxy materials have been marketed as traffic coatings, usually in the 1- to 2-mm-thickness range. Published results of laboratory testing must be analyzed before selecting a coating for the purpose at hand. Consider the location of the coating, frequency of traffic, expected abuse, and the nature of the wear and tear that the coating must endure.

WATER REPELLENTS

Water repellents are products sold primarily to remedy leakage in masonry construction. Acting at the surface of the construction being protected, they become part of a complex web of events and interactions that extend the full depth and the full height of a building's skin. They can help or hinder the correction of leaks.

Repellents serve other functions also: cutting down dirt pickup, more rapidly restoring a dry look to masonry or concrete after rain, or preserving stone and other masonry materials from disintegration. But their main employment remains countering leaks and moisture buildup.

WHOLE WALL DESIGN

Unless the surface of the building envelope is metal or glass, persistent wind-driven rain will penetrate—often more than half the thickness of the wall. Water diversion and pressure balancing are the first design strategies against penetration, followed by the selection of relatively impermeable products and product assemblies. Forgotten sometimes is the fact that sooner or later trapped water must be made to leave the wall before it does damage. For this reason devices such as weep holes, cavities, drainage channels, and flashings are built into the envelope.

Much can be done to design concrete, masonry, and stucco as relatively impermeable materials. Good design includes a proper concrete or stucco mix, proper placement and curing, use of dense masonry units, and selecting mortars that bond and heal well.

Seemingly small defects in construction, or defects that accumulate with age, can negate the basic water-resistant quality of concrete, masonry, and stucco. Small discontinuities, surface crazing, and shrinking can make the skin permeable. A remedial coating for such walls should fill voids and cracks, reduce absorption, and repel water, yet permit trapped moisture and salts to escape—maintaining good appearance all the while. The truly ideal remedy for leaks would be to build the wall properly in the first place.

TYPES OF REPELLENTS

Two basic types of repellents are offered: film-forming types and penetrating types. Both are clear. The penetrating types add less sheen to the wall surface.

Film Forming

The film-forming repellents include water- and solvent-borne acrylics (which dry) and silicones (which moist cure) mainly on the host surface, with no significant penetration. Stearates form films by reacting with salts at the surface of the host material, with little visible surface build.

Penetrating

The penetrating repellents include silanes, siloxanes, and other silicon compounds that enter whatever porous structure the host offers, coating or blocking the pores to the depth of a few millimeters at most. Silanes and siloxanes operate by reducing surface tension in the pores, making it difficult for capillary absorption of water into the host material to take place.

The chemistry and the mode of action of these silicon compounds is complex; rather than detail it here, the reader is referred to articles listed in the bibliography, each of which in turn contains its own bibliography on this disputed subject.

PRACTICAL CONSIDERATIONS

All repellents share a short service life. One may be effective three times as long as another, but we are talking about a few years, not decades. It is hard to know when to recoat, and recoating with another repellent can bring problems.

Selecting a repellent for natural building stone can be tricky. Specialists who have had actual experience with repellents and their effects are the place to start. Actual tests on the particular stone is a necessary next step, but even this may not reveal long-term effects. Sometimes a simple stearate or silicate is effective for a few years, where a more complex chemical will harm the stone.

Repellents are widely used to limit water and waterborne salt intake in reinforced concrete paving. Only penetrating types are effective due to wheel wear. Still the water has to escape in dry weather, leaving a high salt concentration for the next wet cycle. Repellents should never be thought of as waterproofings, whether on horizontal surfaces or walls.

Clayford Grimm's article, listed in the bibliography, counts the long-term cost of successive water repellent treatments. Since crack repair *before* treatment is necessary, Grimm makes the point that an economical solution is to repair the masonry and skip the treatment. Which returns the discussion to the point made earlier: proper concrete, masonry, and stucco design and execution at the outset makes the application of remedial material to new construction unnecessary.

WATER VAPOR TRANSMISSION

For a discussion of the general problems of air and moisture penetration and of water vapor transmission, see the heading Water Permeability in Chapter 1.

MOISTURE STRATEGIES

In older buildings, air—and the water vapor that it carries—moved more freely through the roof, walls, and ground floor. This was because the buildings were put together differently—more loosely one could say—using materials such as shingles, seamed metal sheets, brick, wood studs, plaster on wood lath, flags on soil, and elevated wood floors which allowed relatively free passage of air. With today's tighter buildings, airborne water vapor can be stopped, can build up pressure, and can condense within roof, wall, and floor assemblies while indoor-outdoor temperature differentials shift.

But vapor retarders do not provide a solution by themselves. First, their very location within the building shell must be carefully analyzed so that they do not stop and condense water where it can do damage. Second, many of the components inside or outside of a vapor retarder must breathe to vent trapped water vapor. The outside skin often has the toughest job: it must initially bar water from entering, but must breathe when the water attack stops—a dual function which not every material can perform. Third, buildings are not built like ships; buildings do not work efficiently if an impermeable skin is the sole separation of inside from outside. Shingled weather protection—rather than a calked hull—is as old as thatched roofs, shingles, and lap siding. Fourth, in recent decades we have recognized that certain void spaces in exterior walls stop water from entering by interplay of external and cavity pressures. We have learned to engineer cavity construction (also called pressure-relief or pressure-balanced design).

Controlling Water Vapor

In the field of vapor transmission control the four major areas of activity are:

- Water vapor entering the building from the ground, through slabs on grade and crawl spaces
- Water vapor entering the building from wet soil through the foundation walls
- Water vapor passing through the structural roof deck of buildings that have moist internal atmospheres, then condensing in the roof insulation or exerting pressure on the underside of the roof membrane
- Water vapor condensing inside wall assemblies as the balance of wetness and dryness, inside and out, shifts with the season

Locating the Vapor Retarder

The tactics employed in dealing with water vapor differ according to climatic conditions.

- *Temperate and cold climates.* These are climates in which more than a few freezing nights can be predicted in the course of a year. Here a vapor retarder should be installed near the interior face of each exterior wall to keep building moisture from living occupants, food preparation, and the combustion of fossil fuels from penetrating the wall cavity. If it were to penetrate the wall it could condense (and even freeze). The outer face of exterior walls should repel water but should breathe to permit any penetrating moisture to escape in warm or dry weather.
- *Warm, humid climates.* In climates such as those found in Hawaii, the Caribbean, and the coastal states from Texas to Florida, any vapor retarder should be installed near the outer face of exterior walls to keep moisture on the outside from penetrating to the point where it can be condensed by mechanically cooled air at the interior of the building. Impermeable materials should not be installed on the inner faces of these walls.
- *Hot, dry climates.* In the southwestern desert states of the US and similar areas, an added vapor retarder is of little help, and can even cause harm,

since the air, inside and out, is dry most of the time. Interior moisture generated by occupants and processes should be encouraged to vent itself to the exterior.

- *In all climates.* If drained wall cavities are created to reduce the penetration of wind-driven rain—pressure equalization cavities—any vapor retarder should be kept between the cavity and the interior face of the wall.

VAPOR RETARDERS

Vapor retarders of various types (some of which qualify as vapor barriers) are designed to limit the passage of moisture in each of the conditions listed above. Common materials and locations are:

- Preformed modified bitumen sandwich panels or polyethylene sheets are installed beneath slabs on grade or on top of earth in crawl spaces.
- Waterproofings or dampproofings known to be impermeable to water vapor are placed around the foundation.
- In many roofs, water- and vapor-tight roof materials are placed over all construction to keep out rain. Where moisture can build up beneath these membranes, any insulation is vented in some way to the exterior. For extreme buildups of water vapor at the interior—as in paper plants, natatoriums, and some textile mills—built-up bituminous membranes or impermeable papers sealed and adhered to the roof deck are used to protect insulation and roofing from interior moisture.
- Plastic sheets or backed metal foil sheets or panels are placed in one face of the exterior wall framing at the appropriate location for the climate and building function.
- Insulation at exterior walls is faced with impervious paper or metal foil (inside face or outside as appropriate to the climate).
- Masonry in exterior walls in cold climates is often given a bituminous coating before the interior finish is furred out and installed.

Some of the materials used to control vapor transmission are coatings, membranes, foils, and impervious papers as listed above. Other vapor retarders come to the worksite as part of the insulation or gypsum board. Many vapor retarders are specified as part of other work, such as polyethylene sheets under concrete slabs, dampproofing on foundations, and vapor retarder courses under some roofing assemblies. Specific vapor retarder products include such construction as:

- 0.00035 in. (0.009 mm) aluminum foil, ¼ × ½ in. (6 × 12 mm) mesh glass fiber scrim, and 30-lb kraft
- Metallized polypropylene, glass fiber scrim, kraft
- PVC film, glass fiber scrim, and aluminum foil
- Polypropylene film, glass fiber scrim, and aluminum foil
- PVC film, glass fiber scrim, and metallized polyester film
- Asphalt-saturated felt and polyethylene film
- Asphalt-saturated felt, glass fiber scrim, and polyethylene film
- Asphalt-saturated felt, glass fiber scrim, and aluminum foil

Where a separate membrane is needed to hinder the passage of water vapor, there are numerous reinforced papers, films, and foils on the market. These specialized, freestanding vapor retarders are sturdy enough to span framing intervals and do not tear easily.

Vapor Barriers and Vapor Stops

The general term *vapor retarder* has two subterms, *vapor barrier* and *vapor stop,* that define elevated levels of performance.

Any vapor retarder that has a permeance of 1 perm or less qualifies as a vapor barrier. A tenth of a perm, or less, is frequently specified for demanding situations. Many products are made with this <0.1 perm rating.

Where vapor can leak into insulation over a period of time, negating its insulating value and likely deteriorating the insulating material, a zero-perm vapor barrier material must be specified. This is a vapor stop. Vapor stops are frequently placed over insulation for refrigerated cabinets and rooms.

AIR SHIELDS

Air shield materials—also called draft barriers or building wraps—resist air infiltration, convection currents, and air loss. However, unlike vapor retarders, air shields are permeable to water vapor. Barring unwanted exchange of inside air with outside air is fundamental to energy conservation in buildings.

Air shields that have developed since 1980 are generally light sheets of olefin fibers such as polyethylene that are described by their makers as "cross-laminated" or "spunbonded". They are highly tear-resistant, stretch-resistant, almost translucent, and are available in rolls up to 9 ft wide. Several ultraviolet-resistant air barriers are now marketed for use over the sheathing in wood-framed buildings. As breathing fabrics, the water vapor transmission of air barriers is several times greater than that of vapor retarder material.

INTERIOR INSULATION

PRINCIPLES

Insulating materials that are commonly used to insulate the exterior walls of buildings are also employed in insulating horizontal surfaces through which thermal transfer may take place such as top floor suspended ceilings, ceilings below attics, exposed framing in pitched roofs, exterior soffits, and floors over crawl spaces, garages, open ground floors, and cantilevered floors.

Interior thermal insulations, which tend to be the lightest, least rigid insulations made, cannot be used for specialized tasks such as firesafing, roof insulation, and curtain wall insulation. For such uses see the headings for Firestopping, Roof Insulation, and Metal Curtain Walls.

Light, nonrigid interior thermal insulations use the air that they entrap in their fibrous or cellular structure to impede the flow of heat. These insulations must be used in such a way that they never quite fill the space allotted to them—they must never be allotted less depth than their nominal fluffed out thickness. Compressing insulation decreases its R-value.

Wetness in the insulation will also decrease its insulating value. Its location in the building must be one that will stay dry.

BLANKET INSULATIONS

Blanket insulation is often furnished in rolls. Batts are short lengths of blanket insulation. A few of the products described here are relatively inflexible and qualify as semirigid insulation.

Commonly available thicknesses of blanket insulations and their R-values are shown in Table 7-8.

Mineral Wool

Mineral wool, derived from molten slag, is the only one of the earliest fibrous insulating materials to remain a market factor today. It is still one of the most fire resistant, starting to disintegrate at not less than

2000°F (1090°C), as compared to about 1050°F (570°C) for glass fiber blankets. Mineral wool has a slightly higher insulating value than ordinary glass fiber insulation in the same thickness, but high-density glass fiber insulation (the same weight fibers but packed more closely) exceeds mineral wool in R-value/unit thickness.

Basalt

Basalt insulations have the same resistance to fire damage that slag-based mineral insulations do. Basalt blankets can be supplied in 2.5, 4.0, 6.0 and 8.0 lb/ft³ densities. The facing options for mineral wool and basalt are much the same as those for glass fiber.

Glass Fiber

Glass insulation is sold with a variety of facings or no facing. Kraft on one side is most common. A kraft-aluminum foil facing is available to retard vapor transmission. Generally installation is by friction-fit rather than by staples or nails. High-density glass fiber blankets derive their higher thermal efficiency not only from the denser packing of the fibers (smaller air spaces) but also from the reduction of wasteful convection currents within the blanket.

TABLE 7-8
R-VALUES OF FIBROUS SEMIRIGID AND BLANKET INSULATIONS

| Thickness (inches) | Densities in lb/ft³ and kg/m³ | | | |
| | 2.5/40.2 | 0.7/11.2 | 1.0/16.0 | 0.6/9.6 |
	Semirigid basalt fiber	Mineral fiber	High-density glass fiber	Glass fiber
2.0	8.0	7.4		
3.0	12.0	11.0		
3.5		13.0	15.0	11.0
4.0	16.0			
5.25		19.0		
5.5			21.0	
6.0		22.0		
6.25				19.0
8.25			30.0	
9.5				30.0
10.25			38.0	
12.0				38.0

Comparative figures for thermal resistance (R-values) for commonly marketed thicknesses of blanket insulations are shown in Table 7-8.

Claims that glass fiber particles from insulation may cause lung cancer have not met with success, and efforts to ban the material have failed for lack of documented cases, much less proof. All the same, the industry has taken the precaution of labeling the product with a warning, recalling the history of asbestos awareness and later claims. Installing unfaced glass fiber material can be irritating to skin and eyes, so producers have introduced totally wrapped blankets in some markets. The wraps are minutely perforated to allow some compression and air transfer.

Cotton

Faced loose cotton insulating blankets are made in the most widely used thicknesses of glass fiber blankets. The fill is recycled from textile scraps and is non-irritating. The R-values of the blankets are comparable to standard glass fiber products.

LOOSE FILL INSULATIONS

These are most often loose forms of insulation that are commonly provided in blanket or spray-applied form.

Glass fiber, mineral fiber, recycled paper cellulose, and scrap cotton are the most common loose fill for wood-framed attic installation, and can be installed in wood-framed walls as well. These loose fills are commonly blown in place. The lower the density of the loose fill—as with glass fiber type and to a lesser degree, mineral fiber—the more the R-value of the fill will be reduced when there are very low temperatures outside. Convection currents induced when the Δt between top and bottom reaches 80°F (44°C) will reduce the previously-published R-values of glass fiber loose fill 50 percent. Recycled paper cellulose loose fill insulation is sometimes installed damp, with a binder, to produce an installation that neither settles, shifts, nor permits significant convection within the fill.

Loose vermiculite and perlite, treated against water absorption, are commonly used for masonry in-wall insulation.

Foamed styrene inserts are designed to be snugly fitted in the cells of concrete masonry units. These inserts insulate the wall without fear of insulation settling or of insulation runout when penetrations are made in the masonry cells.

SPRAYED-IN-PLACE INSULATIONS

Sprayed cellulose, in the form of recycled newspaper combined with binders and fire-retardant salts such as sodium borate and ammonium sulfate, is the most commonly encountered sprayed-in-place insulation. It is light, inspectable, reasonably durable until it can be covered, fills in well around conduit and pipes, and the overspray sweeps up easily when dry. Its disadvantages are the possibility of starved areas; the fact that late installation of other trades' work will knock off areas with little likelihood of replacement (no touch-up kits are seen); mildly corrosive effect on metal studs, conduit, and wiring devices; and the adding of dampness and free water at the point of application. Some recent formulations address the wetness problem by providing a much drier spray mix.

Sprayed cellulose is for wall surfaces; it is not suitable for filling cells in masonry.

Questions have been raised about the permanency of its fire retardancy and the health effects of the borates, the sulfates, and lead-bearing inks in the paper, but studies have not definitively shown any of these to be a problem. The salts are not toxic in small quantities and the amount of lead in printing ink lessens each year.

A number of products that are primarily used for fireproofing of steel can also be used to provide insulation. These spray-on products are basically vermiculite- or mineral-fiber-based, cementitious mixes that harden to form an insulating layer that is hard to remove without a tool. The expense of these fireproofing products makes them uneconomical as ordinary thermal barriers, but some of the variants that have been developed specifically for use as insulation can solve a problem where an insulation must be exposed, as high in a field house or auditorium. Formerly these materials contained asbestos, now they do not.

FOAMED-IN-PLACE INSULATIONS

The popularity of earlier urea-formaldehyde insulations, foamed in place in wall cavities, has declined as concern for indoor air quality increased. Today there are phenolic-based polymeric foams and icynene foams that do not release formaldehyde. Both the phenolics and icynenes are fire-resistant and have R-values of 4.6 per in. or higher. Neither uses forbidden chlorofluorocarbon (CFC) blowing agents.

There is at least one magnesium oxide based, compressed air-blown foam insulation that gives off few emissions and is fire-resistant.

These insulations can be foamed in almost any stable, confined space: metal and wood stud walls, block cells, and wall cavities among them. Some tests have been made that indicate enhancement of the rating in specific fire-rated split wall constructions amounting to 1 or 2 hours. Like most other thermal insulations, they have the side effect of reducing sound transmission.

Some foamed in place insulations have bearing values of approximately 35 lb/in^2, but all are fragile.

BOARD INSULATIONS

The wide choice of board-type insulations, primarily developed for use above roof decks, is covered under the Roof Insulation heading in this chapter. These insulating products, which have dimensional stability, some load-bearing capacity, and rigidity, are often employed in insulating foundations, cavity walls, cold rooms, curtain walls, and as cores in wall sandwich panels. Some are inherently vapor-impermeable and water-resistant: they can be used in direct contact with soil, surfaces likely to sweat, or in the layer of a wall assembly where water vapor condensation is likely to occur when the dew point is reached.

Semirigid Board Insulations

Where crushing is not likely to occur, fibrous insulating materials are marketed for use in semirigid board form. By providing higher fiber densities and by applying facings, elevated R-values are obtained.

REFLECTIVE INSULATIONS

Most insulations are designed to stop heat transfer by conduction and convection. Reflective films stop the radiant transfer of energy. They depend to a large degree, but not entirely, on the presence of air cavities on at least one side.

Some aluminum foil reflective insulations are shipped in folded, compressed form and are pulled open at the point of installation to produce many layers of foil, separated by air spaces of ½ in. (13 mm) or more. These foil packs were developed primarily for installation between wood rafters, wood studs, or wood furring strips, and have flanges for stapling.

Other reflective products include heavy plastic films with bright vacuum-deposited metallic surfaces that can be fastened across the faces of studs or rafters, often creating enclosed air spaces where none existed before. In such a case, reduction in thermal transfer by convection as well as by radiation is accomplished.

EXTERIOR INSULATION AND FINISH (EIF)

PRINCIPLES

Exterior insulation and finish assemblies are so widely known by the abbreviation, EIF, that producers have changed the name of Exterior Insulation Manufacturers Association to EIF Industry Members Association (EIMA).

The elastomeric or modified cement plaster finish that is the final coat of an EIF assembly can also be extended—without the insulation—to cover adjoining concrete and concrete masonry units. Thus, EIF assemblies and stand-alone EIF finishes are often specified together, as when an EIF-clad building has ancillary walls and parapets that must have the same appearance and watertightness as the EIF-clad portions.

Two classes of exterior finishes are standard with the industry: polymer-based (PB), which is the thinner, elastomeric coating system, and polymer-modified (PM), which is cement-based, thicker, and heavier. Since PB and PM can confuse, one occasionally hears the older terms *softcoat* and *hardcoat*. The stuccolike hardcoat systems are certainly hard (although the polymer modification makes them less brittle than traditional stucco). The so-called softcoat systems are actually quite hard and can be designed to be as impact-resistant as the hardcoats. The range of structural substrates and insulations that lie beneath either PB or PM finishes is similar but must be selected with important functional differences in mind.

MAKING AN EIF ASSEMBLY WORK

An EIF assembly on an exterior wall should not be continued below grade, at least not without a full isolation joint to prevent ground water from wicking upwards. It is wise to detail the assembly as stopping 8 to 12 in. (200 to 300 mm) above grade: ordinary lawn care and pavement cleaning equipment and materials can ruin the appearance and the watertight integrity of the finish in a short time.

Horizontal assemblies should not be detailed at a slope less than 6 in 12 inches, whether the condition is a coping, a sill, or a ledge. Even a ½-in. (13 mm)-deep decorative reveal should have its bottom sloped to drain outward. One of the advantages of an EIF installation is that it is a breathing assembly that effectively repels rain, but on the other hand vents any condensed, leaked, or accumulated moisture to the exterior when the weather is dry. But this breathing quality dictates that water must never stand on the surface of an EIF assembly.

Building expansion joints should be designed to pass through the entire EIF assembly's substrates and supports whether they consist of gypsum board, cement board, wood, steel framing, masonry, concrete, or some combination of these. Panel joints in the insulation and finish components should also be designed to extend at least through the substrates of gypsum board, cement board, and wood. Panel joints include those joints needed to break the assembly into panels whose size is limited by thermal movement, as well as any joints made necessary by panelized construction. See Figure 7.3

Panels in assemblies with a polymer-modified (PM) finish should be limited to 120 to 150 ft² (13 to 16 m²) each. Panels in polymer-based (PB) assemblies can be larger than those in PM assemblies, but must still be positioned and structurally analyzed to accommodate the type and severity of movement that a PB assembly can withstand.

Shop fabricated panels may be made for lifting into place if care is taken in all measuring of building frame and openings: A ½-in. (13 mm) or ¾-in. (20 mm) joint leaves little margin for poor fit if uniform appearance is to be maintained. The extra steps that have to be taken to shop fabricate panels are justified if the building must be closed in early. All the same, a building should have highly repetitive panel sizes and generally should be at least three stories tall before the panelized strategy is considered.

EIF BASE AND SUBSTRUCTURE

Since the base panels that are in the center of an EIF assembly are not structural in the sense that a masonry substrate is, the choice of the base material to which the insulation is to be attached is important. The base must be strong, waterproof, durable, suitable for fastening to the structure, and must provide a suitable substrate over which to fasten the insulation. Historically, the base's paper and its moisture-sensitive bond to the gypsum board was the weakest point in the assembly. Today, glass fiber faced gypsum boards have been developed that offer improved bond and resistance to moisture deterioration. Where this base is not deemed to have sufficient permanent strength and bond, glass-reinforced cement board and plywood boards can be used. Also, mechanical fastening can be added over any base to resist delamination due to penetrated moisture and wind loads. See Table 7-9.

This base should be designed and specified as part of an overall EIF assembly specification. When the base panels are placed over lightgage steel framing, the base's fastenings must be of type, size, and corrosion-resistance to ensure permanence. The steel framing must be designed with proper strength, resistance to deflection under wind load, and corrosion resistance. The gage of the framing metal must be sufficient to allow adequate screwing or welding into structural units. The gage must be heavy enough to retain the screws holding the base over many years in

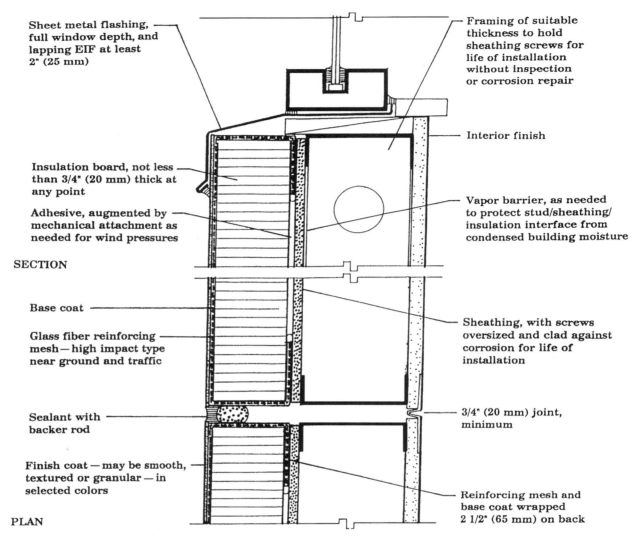

Sheet metal flashing, full window depth, and lapping EIF at least 2" (25 mm)

Framing of suitable thickness to hold sheathing screws for life of installation without inspection or corrosion repair

Interior finish

Insulation board, not less than 3/4" (20 mm) thick at any point

Adhesive, augmented by mechanical attachment as needed for wind pressures

Vapor barrier, as needed to protect stud/sheathing/insulation interface from condensed building moisture

SECTION

Base coat

Glass fiber reinforcing mesh—high impact type near ground and traffic

Sheathing, with screws oversized and clad against corrosion for life of installation

Sealant with backer rod

3/4" (20 mm) joint, minimum

Finish coat—may be smooth, textured or granular—in selected colors

PLAN

Reinforcing mesh and base coat wrapped 2 1/2" (65 mm) on back

FIGURE 7-3 Exterior insulation and finish.

a potentially corrosive environment without any opportunity for inspection or preventive maintenance.

Precautionary steps toward permanent structural integrity do not stop there. Whatever construction underlies the base panels must be analyzed for migration of water vapor from inside the building, for condensation, and from water intruding through joints or other routes from the outside or construction above. Barriers or escape routes for all internal moisture sources must be built in. In preventing condensation, it is desirable to design the entire wall assembly so that the dew point falls within closed cell plastic insulation where moisture cannot enter.

EXTERIOR INSULATION

Board insulations are commonly expanded polystyrene (EPS board) although isocyanurate and extruded polystyrene are also used. Board material and thickness is selected on the basis of overall R-value, water vapor transmission, and the presence or absence of reveals cut in the board. The denser isocyanurate and extruded boards can be used where high impact resistance is needed.

Insulation boards should be offset 4 in. (100 mm) vertically and horizontally from joints in supporting sheathing.

TABLE 7-9
SHEATHINGS FOR POLYMER BASED EIF ASSEMBLIES

From information collected by the authors. Additional information can be found in EIMA Tech Notes WC-101.

Type	Exposure*	Standard
Cementitious boards		
Type A, sun/rain/snow resistant	OK	ASTM C1185 and C1186
Type B, not rain/snow resistant	Not OK for rain or snow	ASTM C1185 and C1186
Wood		
APA Exterior plywood	OK	PS 2-92
APA Exposure 1 plywood	OK for 6 months	PS 2-92
APA Exposure 2 plywood	Do not use	
APA OSB†, Exposure 1	OK for 6 months	PS 2-92
APA OSB†, Exposure 2	Do not use	
Gypsum boards		
Glass mat faced‡	OK for 6 months	ASTM C1177
Paper faced	OK for 1 month without severe weather	ASTM C79

* Allowable exposure before applying insulation. *OK* sheathings will deteriorate in time; they should not be left uncovered indefintiely. If rain, freezing, or intense sun is expected while any sheathing is exposed longer than 1 month, the sheathing should be protected with lapped waterproof paper or film, or the work should be tented.
† Oriented strand board.
‡ EIMA considers products complying with ASTM C1177 as the preferred gypsum based sheathings.

Boards are almost never more than 4 in. (100 mm) thick; ¾-in. (20 mm) board thickness is the minimum recommended for EIF, measured to the bottom of any reveals that will be made in the boards. For instance, if ½-in. (13-mm) reveals are designed, use at least 1¼-in. (32 mm) board.

Small reveals or rabbets are practical and economical only in PB assemblies: a heavy PM finish coat will fill in and soften the visual impact of small rabbets unless expensive hand work is undertaken.

Projecting belt courses, quoins, sills, and window trim are often made of the same material as the boards—sculpted by hot wires to the desired profile in the shop. At the worksite these are adhered to the insulating boards or the EIF assembly substrate.

Adhesive fastening of insulation to substrate is common in ordinary cases, but mechanical fastening must either augment or replace adhesives in a number of situations:

- When PM assemblies, which are heavier than PB assemblies, are used
- When wind loads will be high
- When moisture may enter insulation or substrate and break bond
- When a producer recommends or code requires

REINFORCING THE FINISH

In PB assemblies, the insulation is given a base coat—either straight acrylic-based or acrylic-modified portland cement—in which open weave glass fiber mesh is embedded. A standard or high standard mesh weight (see Table 7-10) is used for ordinary away-from-traffic areas that are not subject to abuse or unusual loads. The mesh is wrapped around board edges and in back of the edges for about 3 in. (75 mm), especially at joints, copings, and openings. The mesh pieces should be lapped sheet-to-sheet about 3 in. (75 mm). Many producers recommend that a heavier corner weight mesh be used at external corners.

In PM assemblies, the insulation is likewise given a base coat, usually of modified portland cement, in which a heavier glass fiber mesh is embedded. The

TABLE 7-10
GLASS FIBER MESH WEIGHTS FOR EIF WORK

Descriptive names for mesh weights will vary from producer to producer; EIMA has no weight classification standard.

Rarely do the offered range of mesh weights match from producer to producer: Specify actual numerical weight ranges for purposes of competitive bidding.

Description	Weight oz/yd^2	Weight g/m^2	Use
Standard or light	4.0–5.0	135–170	Standard for PB nonimpact areas.
Standard, high or plus	6.0–8.0	200–270	An upgrade of the industry standard.
Medium or intermediate	10.0–12.0	335–405	Often used with PM systems.
Medium plus or strong	14.0–17.0	470–575	Use within 8 ft (2.5 m) of normal public traffic.
High impact or armored	20.0–24.0	675–810	Use for high traffic, expected abuse, and for thick PM systems.
Corner	7.0–9.0	235–305	Required by many producers in place of standard weight within 8 in. (200 mm) of external corners.

mesh weight will run from medium to armor weight, wrapped as in PB assemblies but butted sheet-to-sheet and the joint covered with a wide strip of lighter mesh.

Armor-weight glass fiber mesh is used where impact forces are expected, as at walls fronting sidewalks or playgrounds.

FINISHES OVER EXTERIOR INSULATION

In PB systems the fully embedded glass fiber fabric is covered with a variety of finishes which vary from $\frac{1}{16}$ to $\frac{1}{8}$ in. in thickness. The finishes range from relatively smooth, pigmented acrylics, through sanded and textured acrylic surfaces, to acrylic matrices into which marble or quartz granules are embedded.

In PM systems the initial, polymer-modified cement finish coat is thicker, starting at about $\frac{1}{4}$ in., but is generally held below $\frac{1}{2}$ in. (6 to 13 mm) so that finish does not become too heavy for the supporting components. Any texture that can be executed in conventional cement-lime-sand stucco can be executed in a PM EIF finish. The second and final coat is polymer-based and is about $\frac{1}{16}$ in. (1.6 mm) thick. This coat may be pigmented.

All finishes are continued, untextured, and without any added aggregate around concealed edges of the EIF assembly.

Because sealants often have bonding problems with the final polymer-based finish, that last coat is better deferred until joint sealants have been installed to adhere directly to the more cementitious base coats.

EIF JOINT SEALING

Good quality sealants over proper joint backing material are essential to the proper performance of an EIF assembly. Every aspect of joint design must be carefully worked out beforehand, from spacing and width to provisions for corners, terminations, changes of substrate, pressure equalization, weeping, and window installation.

Urethane sealants have not proved universally successful in sealing joints in EIF assemblies. With failed urethane joints, retrofit with silicone has been successfully performed. In at least one major repair, the expense of removing the hardened urethane in the joint caused the original sealant to be left in the joint, which was then gone over with silicone tape.

The sealants should be applied by experienced waterproofing specialists. Ideally these mechanics would be part of the EIF installing team, but frequently the work is separated and later arguments about the performance of the entire system develop. Under standard AIA and EJCDC general conditions the contractor may split up the work any way he wishes. However, many architects and engineers make an effort to specify unified overall responsibility for everything that goes into the curtain wall system that contains the EIF assembly, from the studs and the screws in the studs to the interface with doors and glazing, as is commonly done with metal curtain wall systems.

EIF VAPOR RETARDERS

In many conditions the location of a vapor retarder behind the EIF assembly is just as important to the success of the entire wall system as well-designed, well-executed joints. Not all moisture attacking the bond between insulation board and sheathing enters through the face of the wall or its joints. Building moisture, if not checked, will migrate outward, and, if it meets the impermeable barrier of the board insulation at a below-dew-point temperature, will condense and soften the adhesive. Even in mechanically fastened EIF assemblies, condensation where the screw threads enter the steel studs can cause corrosion and failure.

To combat moisture attack from the rear, locating a vapor retardant membrane inboard of the adhesive, fasteners, and even the studs or masonry support must be studied. Year-round variations in outdoor and indoor temperatures and RHs must be predicted, and vapor pressures and locations of the dew point plane must be computed.

EIF METAL FLASHINGS

Where an EIF assembly includes a window sill, a ledge, or a coping, the condition should be sloped outward to shed water and a sheet metal flashing should be introduced to lap the EIF components at least 2 in. (25 mm). This flashing must be sealed to the surface of the PB or PM finish with a compatible sealant. Although joint sealants and vapor barriers are wisely made a part of single-installer responsibility for the EIF assembly, sheet metal flashings often end up

being provided by another party. It is easy to overlook this critical material interface both in detailing and in specifying. Figure 7-3 shows correct installation of metal flashing.

GENERATING A TRUE ENVELOPE

Metal framed curtain walls are customarily specified and subcontracted as single-source responsibility items of work. Most other vertical portions of the building envelope are fragmented by comparison. Storefronts-and-masonry, windows in stuccoed block construction, and strip windows with an EIF assembly all challenge the designer and the builder to make the parts fit together and perform as a unit. Wind and rain know no jurisdictional boundaries.

In the absence of subcontract or prime contract firms that will execute all parts of the vertical building envelope, the skill of the specifier and the skill of the general contractor make the difference between a coordinated, functioning installation and a monumental problem. In addition, the competence of the designer's analysis of temperatures, expansion/contraction, wind and other imposed forces, condensation, air movement, trapped water release, and corrosion are crucial.

The various parts of the envelope system (structure, panels, insulation, vapor retarders, subframing, fasteners, window and door frames, glass, glazing, joints, water diversion devices, sealants, and finishes) must be made the responsibility of the smallest number of parties possible—one party being the ideal. Unfortunately masons, window installers, waterproofers, plasterers, and the EIF-installing trades never organize as a single entity in today's trade practices. One precaution applies particularly to construction management projects: The packaging of the project should at least avoid splitting the envelope work into potential areas of conflict.

There is no universally observed scope to the EIF component of a building envelope. However, the more that matters of substructure support, fastening, moisture control (barriers, joints, weeps, etc.), water diversion devices such as flashings, and inset or interfaced items such as windows, doors, and storefronts can be made the responsibility of one party, the greater the likelihood of satisfaction both in the construction and the correction of the work.

ROOF INSULATION

PRINCIPLES

For buildings with roofs insulated from the inside, the choice of insulation is made much the same way as the choice of wall insulation—frequently resulting in the use of loose or soft fibrous materials such as glass fiber and cellulose fiber that do not have to support traffic or resist weather.

Placing a building's insulation as far as practicable to the exterior of its structural skin makes for thermal efficiency. Thus, buildings are most often designed either with insulated decks or with insulation placed outside the roof structure. This section reviews insulation strategies used both at and outside the roof plane.

In the tables of roof insulations that follow, some types of decks, fills, and boards that are not commonly available are listed. The roof insulation industry seems to undergo change even more frequently than other segments of the building products market. Some products that are sleepers today may find wider acceptance tomorrow, and some products that have been on the market until recently may regain favor. In any case, those recent dropouts will be encountered for years to come as our building inventory is recycled. Their properties should be known.

STRUCTURAL INSULATING DECKS

Structural decks that have integral insulating value include several types of structural plank which are supported by concrete, steel or wood beams, or purlins. Commonly used structural insulating decks are listed in Table 7-11. For comparison during early design, some of the common structural materials that these insulating decks replace can be seen in Tables 7-11 and 7-12.

ROOF INSULATING FILLS

Where insulation is not applied to a roof as individual boards, the insulation is almost always applied as fill. The consistency of fills at time of application run from highly fluid slurries to semisolid, nonflowing material that has to be floated or compacted. One seeming exception is urethane foam, which is sprayed rather than pumped. But the result is the same with all types: a smooth surfaced, continuous sheet of insulating material results, ready for roofing and foot traffic when cured or dried.

Water-bound insulating fills must be brought to no more than 25 percent moisture content before roofing can proceed, or the roofing must be vented to allow vapor from the excess liquid water to escape. With all of the portland cement-containing roof fills listed in Table 7-13, one or more of the following precautions must be designed into the work:

1. Water vapor must be permitted to escape downward, as through slots in metal deck. Clearly this will not work for a concrete structure.

2. Water vapor must be encouraged to migrate to the perimeter of the roof deck and an escape route upward must be ensured.

3. Water vapor must be permitted to escape through vents in the roofing membrane itself. If not done carefully to prevent entry of rainwater this can negate the function of the roof.

4. The insulating fill must remain exposed to sun in dry weather until its moisture content is 25 percent or less as recommended by the roofing producer. Good weather may be easy to specify but is hard to enforce.

The first two fills listed in Table 7-13 contain no water and need no dryoff time. A third—the cellular concrete type—has less water in its mix than other cementitious types, and much of this water goes to hydrate the large proportion of cement in the mix. Observation has shown that cellular concrete can attain a suitably low moisture content in a relatively short time.

It is not surprising that cement-based and gypsum-based wet fill insulations are more widely used below the 40th parallel than above it. The southern and Sun Belt states have more sunny days that permit these water-laden fills to dry out in time for scheduled roofing application.

TABLE 7-11
STRUCTURAL INSULATING DECKS

Roughly in order of thermal efficiency

Type	Description	Density lb/ft³	R-value/in. @ 75°F
Cement-wood fiber plank	Coarse wood strands, bound with portland or oxychloride cement, 2 to 4 in. thick	30.0 21.0	2.00 1.75
Lightweight concrete plank	Reinforced concrete with cellular or lightweight coarse aggregate, 2 to 4 in. thick	40.0	1.90
Gypsum board roof panels	Gypsum deck units, 2 in. thick (mainly in East)	50.4	0.90
Comparison with normal weight (135 to 160 pcf, ACI 301 1.3) structural concrete:			
	Quartz gravel aggregate	150	0.07 avg.
	Quartz gravel aggregate	140	0.08 avg
	Limestone aggregate	140	0.09
Comparison with lightweight (<115 pcf, ACI 301 1.3) structural concrete:			
	Expanded shale/clay aggregate	115	0.14
	Expanded shale/clay aggregate	100	0.18
	Foam/cellular concrete	80	0.33
	Foam/cellular concrete	60	0.48
	Foam/cellular concrete	30	0.90
Comparison with earth fills (at 10 percent moisture content) that may replace insulation over underground roofs:			
	Sandy clay, packed	100–110	0.14–0.10
	Topsoil, loose	75–80	0.25–0.16

Foamed-in-place sprayed urethane is included as a roof insulation fill since it directly supports a sprayed or roller-applied roof membrane, usually also a urethane although some silicone coatings have been used. ASTM C1029 lists urethane foam as coming in four compressive strength grades: Type I, 15 lb/in²; Type II, 25 lb/in²; Type III, 40 lb/in²; and Type IV, 60 lb/in². The R-value/in. for all Types is 6.2.

BOARD ROOF INSULATION

Board insulations are adhered or mechanically fastened to all varieties of decks from ribbed steel to cast-in-place concrete. Some boards, expanded polystyrenes, and glass fiber, especially, are fabricated into tapered units that can be assembled on flat roofs to slope water to the drains. See Figure 7-4.

Table 7-14 describes board-type roof insulations. One insulation, urethane, has been almost totally replaced by its chemical relative, isocyanurate (iso

board). Phenolics have been withdrawn from the North American markets; the problems of corrosion that installed phenolics cause must be addressed.

Cellular Plastic Insulations

Cellular insulations are often faced with felts, foils, and other barriers to prevent hot bitumen damage and vapor transmission. Most cellular plastics are also available with wood or fiberboard facings for nailing or mopping.

All exposed cellular plastic insulations are degraded by hot bitumens used in adhering built-up and modified bitumen roofing. For this reason the industry associations generally recommend that a course of ½-in. wood fiber board or of ¾-in. perlite board be fastened or adhered over the cellular material before applying hot bitumens.

Closed or open cell networks are formed in plastic insulations by the use of thermally efficient blowing

TABLE 7-12
THERMAL EFFICIENCY OF BUILDING ENVELOPE COMPONENTS

For comparison and for use with values for insulating materials given in other tables.

Description	Thickness	Weight, pounds, in thickness shown	R-value of full thickness shown
Cast-in-place concrete	4 in.	48	0.32
	8 in.	96	0.64
Face brick	3¾ in.	35	0.44
Common brick	3¾ in.	33	0.75
Slag block, 120 pcf	7⅝ in.	38	1.46
140 pcf	7⅝ in.	42	0.98
120 pcf	11⅝ in.	60	1.81
140 pcf	11⅝ in.	66	1.16
Concrete block	11⅝ in.	90	1.28
Slag block, 120 pcf, with lightweight fill	7⅝ in.	39	3.79
Slag block, 140 pcf, with lightweight fill	7⅝ in.	43	1.98
Limestone	4 in.	48	0.34
Granite	4 in.	55	0.30
Mortar coat	½ in.	5	0.10
Softwood plywood	¾ in.	2.3	0.93
Gypsum board	½ in.	2.1	0.44
Wood bevel siding	¼–¾ in.	1.0	0.81
Felt, 15 lb		0.1	0.06
Clear glass	6 mm	3.0	0.14
Insulating glass, clear, nonreflective, two ¼ in. panes with ½ in. air space	25 mm	6.0	1.92
Cement plaster (with or without metal lath)	¾ in.	6.5–7.5	0.18–0.10
Acoustical ceiling panels, suspended	⅝ in.	1.0	1.25
	¾ in.	1.2	1.50
Plaster on gypsum lath	⅞ in.	6.7	0.40
Ribbed steel roof deck	20 gage	1.5	0.0014
Single ply roofing, without gravel	⅛–¼ in.	1.0–2.0	0.10–0.08
3 or 4 ply BUR + gravel	⅜–½ in.	5.0–7.0	0.36–0.30
Asphalt shingles with underlayment	¼–½ in.	3.5	0.55–0.45
Air space, in furring	¾ in.		0.97
in studwall	3½ in.		0.97
in rafters	5½–9½ in.		0.85
Air space above suspended ceiling	12–36 in.		0.85

agents, which remain in the cells. Over the years, diffusion of atmospheric nitrogen and oxygen into the outer cell layers occurs, replacing some of the original gas used in blowing.

Two problems that have arisen with some cellular plastics are their loss of R-value and their release of ozone-depleting or smog-forming gases to the atmosphere.

Thermal Resistance Values

In reading Table 7-14 the controversy that has gone on for a decade about the true thermal insulating efficiency of urethanes and isocyanurates must be understood so that credible, defensible R-values are selected in designing for energy conservation. The

TABLE 7-13
ROOF INSULATING FILLS

In order of thermal efficiency

Type	Description	Density lb/ft³	R-value/in. @ 75°F	ASTM designation
Sprayed	Foamed urethane	2.0	6.20	C1029
Lightweight aggregate concrete, wet fill	Expanded perlite aggregate concrete with portland cement binder, 6:1 mix, cast in place*	30.0 @ 25%MC	2.50	
Asphalt bound-perlite, dry fill	Lightweight aggregate with asphalt binder, spread and rolled in place as a thermo-setting hot mix (marketed on limited basis)	25.0	2.04	
Lightweight cellular concrete, wet fill	Portland cement concrete with foaming agent, cast in place*	30.0 @ 25%MC	1.20	
Lightweight aggregate concrete, wet fill	Expanded vermiculite aggregate concrete with portland cement binder, 3.5:1 mix, cast in place*	38.0 @ 50%MC	1.10	
Lightweight aggregate gypsum concrete, wet fill	Expanded perlite aggregate concrete with gypsum binder, cast in place	40.0 dry	0.87	C317
Gypsum, wet fill	Gypsum with wood chips, cast-in-place	50.0 dry	0.67	C317

* Usually applied as topping over stepped styrene board insulation, but usable as a fill of tapering or uniform thickness.

problem stems from the fact that urethanes, and then the isocyanurates which have largely supplanted urethanes, were observed to lose much of their initial insulating value in service. The problem grew into a disagreement among manufacturers, their associations, and mechanical engineering designers over what aged values of these types of insulation would permit supportable engineered design for thermal performance.

Aged R-values apply to plastic foam insulations only. Aged values, used in energy design, are mandated by Federal Trade Commission Rule 16 CFR 460 which requires that the published insulating value for each product be based on long-term conditions of service on roof. Fresh R-values (as measured in freshly manufactured board) are not acceptable for roof insulation design under any government's energy conservation rules.

An early set of aged insulation performance figures was released by the Roofing Insulation Council and the Thermal Insulation Manufacturers Institute as RIC/TIMA Technical Bulletin 281-1 and also as Polyisocyanurate Insulation Manufacturers Association (PIMA) Technical Bulletin 101. These Conditioned R-value (*aged value*) figures were based on tests made six months following a conditioning procedure described in the RIC/TIMA technical bulletin. However, engineers generally did not agree that the figures represented the true value of the insulation after several years of service.

Six individual insulation manufacturers then came up with testing procedures that resulted in a Design Stabilized R-value (*fully aged value*). The isocyanurate producers' proprietary testing was based on R-value reduction after 5 years in service.

The ASHRAE Manual currently lists the Design Stabilized R-value as the recommended figure for use by engineers in energy calculations and gives the figure of R = 5.56 as the design value for thermal resistance of 1.0 lb/ft³ isocyanurate (and urethane) at 75°F

TABLE 7-14
ROOF INSULATION BOARDS

Roughly in order of thermal efficiency

Type	Description	Density lb/ft³	R-value/in. @ 75°F*	ASTM designation
HCFC foamed plastic, faced	Phenolic—resin foamed, expanded, and molded into rigid boards	2.7	8.33	C1126
HCFC foamed plastic, faced	Polyisocyanurate—resin foamed, expanded, and molded into rigid boards	2.0	5.66	C591 unfaced C1013 faced
HCFC foamed plastic, often faced	Polyurethane—resin foamed, expanded, and molded into rigid boards (not marketed widely)	2.0	Ages to a lower figure than polyisocyanurate	C591 unfaced C1013 faced
HCFC foamed plastic, often faced	Extruded polystyrene—resin expanded in extrusion process to form high density rigid boards	2.4	5.00	C578, similar to Type VII†
HCFC foamed plastic, often faced	Extruded polystyrene—resin expanded in extrusion process to form medium density rigid boards	1.8	5.00	C578, Type IX†
Fibrous basalt, faced	Molten basalt, spun into fibers and formed with binder into rigid boards	7.0	4.20	C726
Pentane foamed plastic, unfaced	Expanded polystyrene—beads expanded in mold to form high density rigid boards	2.0	4.17	C578, Type VI/VII†
Fibrous slag, faced	Molten slag, spun into fibers and formed with binder into rigid boards (not marketed widely)	3.2 approx. unfaced	4.17	C726
Fibrous glass, faced	Molten glass, spun into fibers and formed with binder into rigid boards	3.0 approx. unfaced	4.20 to 3.90	C726
Pentane foamed plastic, unfaced	Expanded polystyrene—beads expanded in mold to form low-density rigid boards	1.0	3.85	C578, similar to Type I/VIII†
Foamed glass, faced	Molten glass, foamed to form rigid boards of cellular glass	8.5	2.86	C552
Perlite beads and wood fiber	Perlite beads and wood fibers formed with binder into boards	9.0	2.78	C728
Fibrous cellulose, low density	Cane or wood fiber, felted and compressed with binder into boards	12.0	2.78	C208
Fibrous cellulose, high density	Cane or wood fiber, felted and compressed with binder into boards	18.0	2.60	C208

* R-values are not uniform:
- For similar products by different producers.
- For slightly different densities in one producer's line not detailed in this generic table.
- For slightly different densities standard in the line of this or that producer and not detailed in this generic table.
- For successive inches of material thickness: for example, by empirical testing a 4-in.-thick board or fill may not be exactly four times as efficient as a 1 in. board or fill. This is especially true of products with skins or facings. To obtain precise design information consult producer literature.

† The types that are listed in ASTM C578 follow no order:

Type	Type I	Type II	Type III	Type IV	Type V	Type VI
Density, pcf	0.90	1.35	not made	1.60	3.00	1.80

Type	Type VII	Type VIII	Type IX	Type X	Type XI	
Density, pcf	2.20	1.15	1.80	1.35	0.70	

192

(22°C). This Design Stabilized R-value is more conservative and realistic than the Conditioned R-value.

Since the industry as a whole has been unable to agree on upgrading the 6-month test to a 5-year test, each producer continues to publish the results of its own 5-year testing according to a procedure that is said to be uniform among the six producers.

Currently, all isocyanurate producers make a product with R = 5.56. Some make insulation with higher or lower R-values as well.

Blowing Agents

All cellular roof deck insulations use a gas other than air to fill the cells and reduce transfer of heat. These blowing agents are released to the atmosphere in small but significant quantities during manufacture and in service on the roof. Chlorofluorocarbons (CFC), which had been used for blowing isocyanurates, urethanes, extruded styrenes, and phenolics, were banned by international agreement in 1987 to slow the worldwide release of CFCs into the atmosphere. This ban proceeds in phases until the year 2015, permitting the industry to develop substitutes and to test them for effect on human health, on initial and aged R-values, as well as on the ozone layer. The ban is thus properly termed a stepped changeover.

In the first step of the changeover, which was completed in 1995, CFC-11 was replaced with a less damaging hydrochlorofluorocarbon, HCFC-141b in polyisocyanurate and polyurethane insulation. HCFC-141b was found to be no health hazard after extensive testing. It did reduce the initial R-value of board insulation by about 5 percent, but this may improve with reformulation and retesting. An alternative solution: the R-value shortfall from using 141b can be balanced by increasing the density of the iso board.

Also in the first step of the changeover, CFC-12 was replaced by HCFC-142b in extruded polystyrene (XPS) insulation. Testing revealed that there was virtually no change in R-value.

Expanded polystyrene insulation (EPS) was little affected—it is blown with pentane, a simple hydrocarbon, C_5H_{12}. More than 90 percent of the pentane that escapes in manufacture can be captured, which keeps it from adding to local smog conditions. Pentane has no effect on the upper atmosphere's ozone layer.

Phenolic insulation also changed over to HCFC-141b from CFC-11. Tests on one brand of phenolic board showed an R-value/in. reduction from 9.4 to 8.5, or almost 10 percent.

Both HCFC-141b and HCFC-142b are not full solutions to the problem of ozone depletion—they are a tenth as damaging as CFCs, still a significant figure. As the second step in complying with the Montreal Protocol these substitutes must in turn be changed over to yet-to-be-developed or yet-to-be-tested blowing agents by 2003 and 2015, respectively.

Board Insulation Types

Table 7-14 describes the comparative composition, weight, performance, and applicable standards for each board-type roofing insulation. Additional information on several types follows.

Phenolic

Phenolic insulation has a high R-value but is more permeable to air and water vapor than other foam insulations. Residue of a sulfonic acid catalyst used in foaming the phenolic resin can be leached out of the foam by action of water condensing within the insulation. This leachate can then flow downward to attack the structural substrate unless a permanent acid-resistant barrier is present. Acid attack on steel decks is frequent in buildings with phenolic insulation.

In addition to the recommendation for adequately protecting steel deck in Chapter 5, designers should consider placing a sturdy, permanent vapor barrier made of acid-resisting material under phenolic foam. Such a vapor barrier will slow the migration of water vapor into the foam from below and also reduce the tendency of some roof membranes on phenolic-insulated roofs to billow due to the pressure of conditioned air in the building pushing air through deck, foam, and joints in the insulation. Caution is advised: any acid will accumulate over the years atop the protective course and may in time find its way to the steel decks and concrete.

Isocyanurate

Further refinement of R-value measurements and the R-value recommended by ASHRAE for energy calculations will occur as industry agreement on aged testing evolves, as the HCFC-141b blowing agent is made more efficient, as a replacement for HCFC-141b is introduced, and as the densities of some or all boards is increased.

In 1993 it was reported that 43 percent of the roofing board used in the United States was isocyanurate. Isocyanurate had so supplanted urethane that no figure was cited for the latter.

Expanded Polystyrene

Reports of serious shrinkage in EPS board insulation in the 1960s caused the adoption of this material to slow. However, reexamination of the circumstances reduced this concern. EPS covered with wood fiber sheets, perlite board or other suitable separation from hot bitumen is now used with little chance of either damage from hot mopping or dimensional change in service.

EPS was the third most commonly used roofing board in 1993, with 10 percent of the United States total.

Foamed Glass

Glass has such structural strength that it is the only board insulation commonly placed under parking deck traffic slabs. In spite of its strength, its edges can crumble easily under construction traffic; it should be protected until roofed in.

Perlite

Perlite board can also be used as a separation course between foamed plastic insulations and hot bitumen, and as a transitional recover board when placing new roofing over old.

Perlite board, in thicknesses over ½ in. (13 mm) must test to a maximum of 1.5 percent water absorption, by volume, following ASTM C728. By comparison, wood fiberboard and mineral fiberboard are permitted 10 percent.

One-half in. (13 mm) perlite board is manufactured differently from board ¾ in. (20 mm) and thicker. One-half in. board should never be encapsulated in bitumen as it may cause blistering of one bitumen surface. Mechanical fastening, then applying roofing, is better.

Perlite was the second most commonly used roof insulation board in 1993, with 21 percent of the United States total.

Wood Fiber

In addition to its use as insulation, wood fiberboard is widely used as a separation course between foamed plastic insulations and hot bitumen. Fiberboard is also used as a recover board in reroofing.

Composites

Many composites of the insulations listed in Table 7-14 are produced. These usually mate a high R-value material such as iso or styrene with a hard, strong, heat-resistant or nailable material such as perlite board, wood fiber board, or flakeboard.

Tapered Board Insulations

All lightweight cellular board insulations (styrene, iso, glass fiber*) can be cut in the shop to various shapes and tapers and shipped to the worksite for assembly as a neat-fitting roofing base that slopes to drains and overflows. Only a wood fiber or perlite board need be added to the heat-sensitive plastic insulations to make the assembly ready to receive hot-mopped roofing courses. See Figure 7-4.

More roof drains, evenly spaced, make such a system work well. The roof layout must be done early in design. Bays must be reasonably equal in size to avoid odd ridge conditions between bays.

Cellular Board with Lightweight Concrete

Stepped cellular board insulation covered with a fill of lightweight concrete is often used to obtain roof slope to drains and overflows. The cost of such an assembly is competitive with that of tapered insulation.

Cellular concrete and concrete with vermiculite or perlite aggregate are the common fill materials. They

* Not foamed.

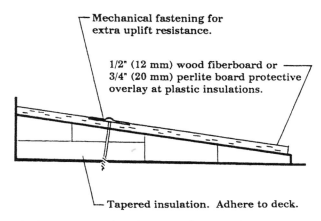

FIGURE 7-4 Tapered insulation. Applications of roofing that do not involve heat will not need protective overlay. Some insulations will not require an overlay for hot bitumen, depending on the nature of the insulation and its facing.

weigh about 28 to 36 lb/ft^3 and have an R-value of about 1.0/in., which is less than one-fourth the value for an EPS board stepped base. The lightweight concrete is placed to a thickness of at least 2 in., at a uniform slope, making its average thickness 2.5 in. for a base with typical 1 in. steps. See Figure 7-5. Clearly, to reach overall R-values of 15 or 20 in the insulation, the EPS (or other insulation board) provides most of the resistance to heat transfer.

The fills are wet and must be vented. Fortunately, cellular concretes, having no aggregate to retain water, cure or dry fast and can be dried in quickly. The concrete makes a surface ready to receive the base

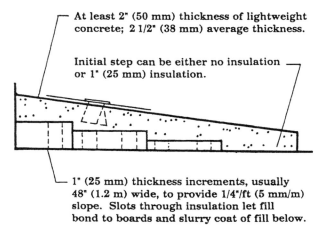

FIGURE 7-5 Stepped insulation with lightweight concrete. In addition to execution with the cellular plastic board insulations implied here, sloped assemblies can be made without lightweight concrete by using poured gypsum or hot asphalt-bound perlite.

sheet of the roofing, which is usually attached by expanding metal fasteners in the lightweight fill.

This composite assembly is located in Division 3 of MasterFormat. However, it is sometimes specified in Division 7 as part of a broadscope roof assembly section.

Resisting Wind Uplift

In high-wind locations, and in moderate-wind velocity locations where parapets and other perimeter conditions create areas of extreme negative pressure (uplift), provisions must be made with all insulation systems to provide mechanical fastenings to the structural deck.

With a sturdy base sheet or a protection board overlay, plate-head screw fasteners can be run through base sheet or board overlay, the full thickness of the insulation, and into the structural substrate. Where nothing substantial overlays the insulation, the size and spacing of the fasteners and their plates must be carefully calculated to provide hold-down force without crushing the insulation.

LOW-SLOPE ROOFINGS

PRINCIPLES

Low-slope roofings employ the strategy of resisting water entry (waterproofing), rather than water-diverting (shingling) or the strategy of pressure equalizing and draining outward. Although they are generally given a slight incline to divert water to the points of drainage, their distinguishing feature is the presence of a membrane that actually resists the passage of liquid water.

Steep roofings, by contrast, are water-diverting systems such as shingle roofs, tile roofs, thatch, and traditional sheet metal roofing. However, steep roofing systems also include one category that is basically waterproof in itself: the structural standing seam roof.

Water-diverting steep roofings are usually backed up by an underlayment or by a waterproof membrane just in case. Thus these two categories—steep and low-slope—cross over into one another in several important respects. The distinction is useful, however, and is the basic roofing classification principle used by the National Roofing Contractors Association (NRCA) in its publications.

LOW-SLOPE SYSTEMS

Roofing systems are designed to perform several functions such as preventing water entry, reducing heat flow, reducing water vapor flow, and providing comfort to occupants and protection to property. Roofs must have the ability to accommodate movement resulting from temperature, structural factors, and natural forces. Roofs must retain their physical properties through temperature cycles, ultraviolet attack, wind, hail, ice, traffic, burning brands, and some level of both abuse and neglect.

Note that these are not called flat roof systems. It is fundamental roofing doctrine that a roof that does not drain freely is a roof that will develop leaks. A coat of asphalt is water-resistant, but not waterproof. Early claims of modified bitumen and single-ply producers that their roofs could be flat and waterproof were followed by enough failures to cause those producers to require slope. This low slope, ideally ¼ in./ft (20 mm/m), is customary for all built-up modified bitumen and single-ply roofs except certain coal tar pitch designs that are engineered to retain water. In a century that caught the ear of the world with the memorable three word mottoes "Machine for living", "Form follows function", and "Less is more", architect Harry Weese of Chicago came up with the best motto of all: "Flat roofs leak."

Low-slope roofing is part of a system that generally consists of the following elements:

1. Structural support
2. Insulation
3. Vapor control
4. Roofing membrane
5. Base (soft) flashings
6. Protection course
7. Metal counterflashings

There are times when insulation or protection can be omitted, and times when vapor control is not needed.

The sequence of these elements is often altered; sometimes insulation is placed above the membrane, and sometimes the insulating is done below the structure.

Vapor control can take the form of a vapor barrier below the insulation or a venting base sheet or type of insulation that carries trapped vapor to points of release at the roof perimeter. Roof vents within the roofing membrane are now considered ineffective and may cause more problems than they solve.

It is a fundamental rule never to place linear metal flashings in the roof plane, but the soft roofing flashings are often augmented by lead drain flashings, even though many of today's soft sheet materials are adequate to this task. The roof flanges of other sheet metal accessories, such as penetration flashings and condensate line supports, are set atop the membrane and are stripped in.

The protection can take the form of a paint, a reflective coating, a cap sheet with embedded mineral particles, small aggregate set in bitumen, or a ballast of large stones held in place by gravity. Protection is primarily from ultraviolet (UV) radiation, but it can also protect from wind or traffic or hail.

Roof insulation and metal flashings are described in other sections of this chapter.

LOW-SLOPE ROOFING TYPES

By 1970 sealants had replaced oil-and-whiting calks, alkyds had replaced linseed oil, and light curtain walls had replaced much ponderous masonry cladding, but roofing technology remained much as it had been 100 years earlier. Beginning about 1970, simpler membranes began to appear in North America as substitutes for the messy, labor-intensive task of fabricating—high in the air—the multi-layered sandwich we call built-up roofing. The substitutes were not totally new—most had seen service in Europe for several years. Not all proved suitable for North America's extremes of climate, but by 1990 a number of these innovations had earned a place in the market. Table 7-15 lists in detail some of the dozen or more types introduced since 1970 and the surviving formulations on which producers have concentrated their efforts. Figures 7-6 and 7-7 show today's favored roofing types in terms of quantities installed in a recent year.

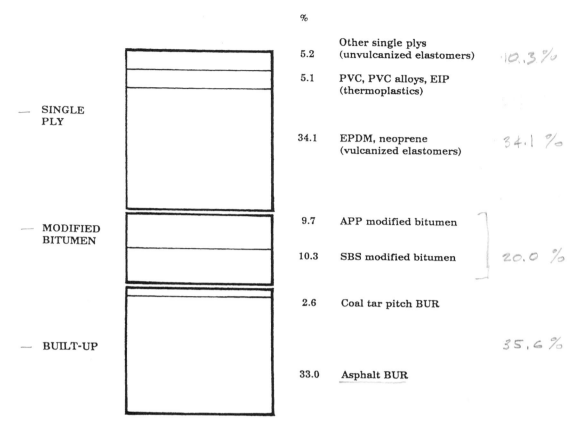

%

5.2	Other single plys (unvulcanized elastomers)
5.1	PVC, PVC alloys, EIP (thermoplastics)
34.1	EPDM, neoprene (vulcanized elastomers)
9.7	APP modified bitumen
10.3	SBS modified bitumen
2.6	Coal tar pitch BUR
33.0	Asphalt BUR

SINGLE PLY

MODIFIED BITUMEN

BUILT-UP

(handwritten annotations: 10.3%, 34.1%, 20.0%, 35.6%)

FIGURE 7-6 Low slope roofing use. A breakdown by percentage of dollar value of the low-slope roofings used in $2.3 billion of commercial new roofing construction in 1994. Figures are adapted by the authors from information in various NRCA publications.

Roof Failures

Almost all components of the seven roof system elements that are listed above are produced following ASTM or other standards. Yet when a roof failure occurs, it is by no means always just a materials failure. Most often it is a failure of the system, in which material may or may not play a major part. The ways in which a low-slope roof can fail seem endless, but high on any list are the following reasons:

- Poor selection of roof system
- Inadequate slope to prevent ponding
- Deflection of deck
- Building movement
- Incompatible materials
- Poor quality of work
- Water vapor damage
- Dimensional instability of insulation

- Material abuse: overheating, burning, creasing, etc.
- Wet materials, especially roll goods
- Blisters, embrittlement, buckling, tearing, shrinkage, or slippage in the membrane itself
- Inadequate adhesion or hold-down of elements
- Differential expansion/contraction of elements
- Inadequate flashing design or execution
- Poor interfacing of soft roofing/flashing and metal flashings
- Disregard for type of traffic or abuse roof will receive
- Trusting that the lowest bidder will do quality work
- Naive dependence on a warranty to keep water out

Engineering for Watertightness

The watertightness of the building, or the lack of it, starts with structural and other engineering decisions.

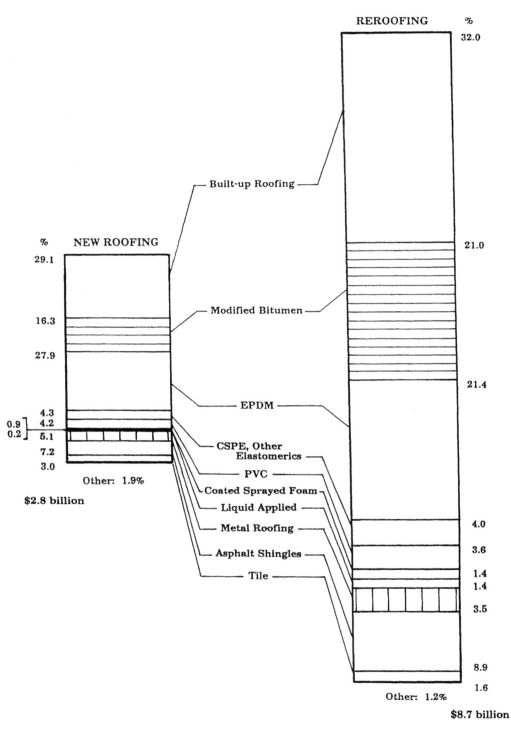

FIGURE 7-7   New roofing and reroofing, low slope and steep types. A breakdown by percentage of dollar value of all the commercial new roofing and reroofing types for 1994. Figures are adapted by the authors from information in various NRCA publications.

TABLE 7-15
MODIFIED BITUMEN AND ELASTOMERIC ROOFINGS

Roofings described in this chapter	Chemical family
Modified Bitumen	
SBS	Bituminous
APP	Bituminous
Elastomeric	
EPDM	Vulcanized elastomer
Chloroprene (Neoprene)	Vulcanized elastomer
Epichlorohydrin*	Vulcanized elastomer
CSPE (Hypalon)	Nonvulcanized elastomer
PIB	Nonvulcanized elastomer
CPE	Nonvulcanized elastomer
NBP (nitrile)	Nonvulcanized elastomer
PVC	Thermoplastic
PVC copolymer alloys	Thermoplastic
EIP (contains PVC)	Thermoplastic

* Primarily used as an overlay to EPDM where certain solvents are present.

Structural engineers should realize that the most efficient structural system may, from a waterproofing standpoint, act like a sieve. Mechanical and electrical engineering strategies must consider long-term effect of external equipment, lines, and penetrations on the building envelope. The architectural designer must check every roof shape and roof texture decision against practical criteria: structural and environmental.

Early attention must be paid during design to:

- Determining where building movement will be relieved by joints
- Locating joints and penetrations so that they can be flashed
- Considering water vapor buildup from concretes, building atmosphere, and likely leak points—and how to vent the vapor
- Limiting deck deflection
- Ensuring adequate slope to all drains, leaders, and overflows
- Selecting insulation weight, thickness, location, sequence, fastening
- Ensuring that treated wood blocking is placed at edges and openings

- Calculating wind uplift in each part of roof
- Jointly analyzing parapets, slopes, and areas of possible water impoundment for both loading and waterproofing consequences
- Putting as little equipment as possible on the roof
- Concentrating and locating mechanical and electrical penetrations so that they pierce the roofing as infrequently as possible
- Committing all design disciplines to making penetrations flashable
- Designing pedestals, condensate drainage, conduit runs, antennae and lightning protection early—not as afterthoughts
- Getting all disciplines to declare war on pitch pans and sleepers
- Predicting wear, damage, and/or vandalism from maintenance personnel, wheeled carts, sunbathers, smokers, added air conditioning units, satellite dishes, and antenna installers
- Devising a recommendation to the facility manager about controlling roof traffic, roof-level alterations, and a roof maintenance program

VAPOR BARRIERS AT ROOFS

See Chapter 1 for a discussion of vapor retarding principles. The primary functions of a vapor barrier in a roofing system are to control the movement of water vapor into the insulation and to reduce the likelihood of vapor blisters in the membrane.

A vapor barrier is a material that has a perm rating of not more than 1.0. The perm rating must often be made lower to prevent the buildup of water vapor over a long period of time. Sometimes what is effectively a vapor stop—a barrier with a zero perm rating—must be employed.

Most roofing producers require that the architect make the decisions as to whether there will be a vapor barrier, and if so, what type. As a guide, producers suggest that vapor retarding be considered in the following circumstances:

- Whenever the average January outside temperature is below 45°F (23°C)
- On buildings with a high relative humidity such as indoor pools, laundries, textile mills, and processing operations that generate moisture

- On roofs where the decks contain appreciable quantities of moisture, such as lightweight concrete and gypsum

In the last case, an alternative strategy of down-venting or lateral venting is often adopted.

For cold storage buildings and other highly insulated or very low temperature installations, a vapor stop of zero perm rating is often justified.

It is just as important not to use a vapor barrier where its use is not needed as it is to use one where it will benefit the design. Sometimes an unneeded vapor barrier can trap moisture and cause problems. There is no solution but to calculate intensity of vapor pressure, ambient conditions, locations of the dew point line, and to consider alternative strategies.

ASTM C755 is a recommended practice for the selection of vapor barriers and outlines the factors to be considered.

BASE FLASHINGS

Each type of roofing must be carried up its bounding walls or parapets, up its curb structures, or must be terminated at a roof edge. Often, the roofing material itself or heavier versions of the roof material type are used to effect this important boundary construction. Sometimes a different material can be used as, for instance, modified bitumen flashing with built-up roofing.

Moisture surveys of roofs that have been in service reveal that most entry of water beneath the roofing is through flashed areas. Attention to flashing details is as important as roof selection.

Roofing producers develop standard details for flashing each roofing assembly, and these in turn exist in generic form in NRCA's *Roofing and Waterproofing Manual.*

Certain basic principles hold with base (soft) flashings.

- Neither roofing nor flashing should bend more than 45°—use a cant.
- Carry roofing to top of cant and up to 2 in. (50 mm) beyond.
- Apply base flashing to a height at least 8 in. (200 mm) above roof level, but not more than 12 in. (300 mm).

- If it is necessary to cover the area above the base flashing with roofing, use an assembly similar to the flashing, but separate from it and lapped at least 3 in. (75 mm).
- Disk-nail or otherwise mechanically fasten the top edge of base flashings, preferably not more than 8 in. (400 mm) on center.
- Cap every base flashing with a sheet metal counterflashing that laps at least 3 in. (75 mm).
- Let moisture escape.
- Keep sheet metal out of roofing and flashing as much as possible (it will be necessary to mate soft roofing with thermally expanding-and-contracting metal at gravel stops).

There are many more rules regarding such essentials as laps, adhesives, runouts over the roof, reglets when used in place of counterflashing, closeness of penetrations, stripping in, and sealing.

BUILT-UP ROOFING

ROOFING BITUMENS

Bitumen is a generic term describing mixtures of solid or near-solid hydrocarbons that melt at temperatures higher than those encountered in service on roofs. In the roofing industry the term refers to coal tar pitch, asphalt, and polymer-modified asphalt.

Overheating any bitumen during the application of built-up or modified bitumen roofing, sloped roof underlayments, or waterproofing results in the loss of fractions (specific hydrocarbons within the bitumen mixture) by evaporation. Inadequate cementing action of the bitumen, brittleness, and shortened service life can result from overheating.

The temperature for application of bitumens should be the Equiviscous Temperature (EVT) ±25°F. The EVT for every batch of bitumen is determined by each producer, who establishes by test the temperature needed to attain a viscosity of 125 centistokes—optimal hot flow rate. This EVT is printed on the label of every bitumen container that is sold. The EVT for ASTM D450, Type I coal tar pitch is usually about 375°F. The EVT for ASTM D312, Type III asphalt is usually about 425°F; Types II and I will be less.

No roofing coal tar pitch of any type should be heated above 400°F. Type III asphalt should not be heated above 500°F.

Coal Tar Pitch

Coal tar pitch is produced by the distillation of crude coal tar, which is in turn derived from the carbonization of bituminous coal in the coking process. A similar pitch is distilled from wood, but is not encountered in roofing. Because of its low softening temperature, coal tar pitch's surface has the ability to self-heal. This same cold flow property dictates that coal tar pitch be used dead level or at slopes generally no greater than ¼ in./ft, and that precautions be taken, such as the use of pitch dams, to limit pitch leakage into the building below. Using organic felts and with the recommendation of the producer, slopes of ½-in./ft can sometimes be designed. The designer must keep in mind however that ply slippage is one of the major problems in coal tar pitch BUR.

Coal tar pitch is very resistant to water absorption and deteriorates little even under prolonged wetting due to chemicals in its makeup that resist fungal and bacterial attack.

Because ASTM D450, Type I *old style* pitch gives off irritating fumes, a *new style pitch* or *nonfuming* Type III coal tar bitumen has been developed that has many of the good properties of Type I, but reduced irritation. With that, it appears there is less resistance to attack by organisms. Attempts have been made to discredit Type I pitch for health and safety reasons. As it stands after 20 or more years of debate, Type I pitch does not violate any federal health standards as long as normal precautions of dress, cleanliness, limiting exposure to sunlight, and limiting contact with fumes are observed by the workers.

Asphalt

Asphalt is one valued by-product in the catalytic cracking of petroleum to obtain a range of products that include gasoline. It can also be collected in the natural state, but it is extremely rare to encounter refined natural asphalt in roofing or waterproofing. Asphalt is slightly more water soluble than coal tar pitch.

The four asphalts recognized by ASTM D312 vary from low-melt-point Type I which is used in low slope situations, to high-melt-point Type IV which is commonly referred to as *extra steep asphalt*. Trade figures show that Type III steep asphalt is the most widely used asphalt—accounting for more than 85 percent of roofing use.

This predominance of Type III is not thought to be in the interest of good roofing practice by many architects and roofing consultants. Type II is the better interply and flood coat material in many designs, but since Type IV is desirable for vertical flashings, the roofer who wishes to bring only one kettle or one tanker to the worksite often selects Type III as an all purpose compromise. Type III has fewer of the light petroleum fractions and is comparatively unyielding in cold weather when stresses in the roof are greatest. It will hold a base flashing on the wall however, and it may be a good choice where rooftop temperatures in service run high. For quality work north of the Sun Belt, it may be better to specify two asphalts, and to select types that give optimal performance. Some specifiers regard Type I asphalt—the asphalt that has its volatile fractions most intact—as the ideal asphalt for long-term service as a flood coat, but its market share is less than 1 percent.

Hot mopped asphalt will be referred to many times, but it should be kept in mind that cold process asphaltic products have been developed for most BUR constructions. Cold process asphalt work is economical and less dirty. In humid parts of the United States less cold process is used, but in the arid climates of the southwest, cold process is functionally equal to counterpart hot mopped roof design.

Polymer-modified asphalt is being used in both BUR and modified bitumen roofing work. Although more expensive, it has superior adhesive qualities and durability.

Pitch and Asphalt Combinations

Coal tar pitch and asphalt are very different in their composition. When permitted to touch one another in molten state, unpredictable reactions may occur, such as hardening of one but softening of the other, or failure of both to adhere. Roofers take care to heat each bitumen in a dedicated kettle.

It is possible however to use asphalt in adhering insulation, and then switch to coal tar pitch for the roofing system. Asphalt can often be used to recover old coal tar pitch roofs. Asphalt base flashings at the perimeter of coal tar pitch roofs are customarily mopped in hot steep or extra steep asphalt. Although coal tar pitch flashing-weight membranes are now available, they are still better mopped in asphalt rather than pitch roofing cement.

It is best to make such pairings of pitch and asphalt products only on the advice of a manufacturer of the roofing products or a professional with wide experience in roofing.

ROOFING FELTS

In a built-up roofing system the felts reinforce the assembly and stabilize the layers of bitumen. They provide the strength needed to span gaps in the substrate, while distributing strain over a greater area.

Roofing felts for multiple ply construction are generally bitumen saturated, not coated, and are generally made with glass or polyester fiber. Coated sheets are sometimes used as base sheets and vapor barriers. As a vapor barrier, a coated sheet should have a perm rating no greater than 0.3. When used as the base ply in a built-up assembly, a coated sheet absorbs some of the stress from insulation gaps and structure cracks, protecting the plies above it.

Table 7-6 shows the various types of felts and their ASTM designations.

Asbestos felts are no longer produced, and glass fiber felts now account for more than 90 percent of all felts used. Polyester felts offer strength and suppleness. Their share of the market is more than 4 percent and rising. Organic felts are still available for specialized uses within roofing systems.

Among glass fiber felts, the ASTM D2178 Types IV and VI are the most widely used in ply construction. Type VI is not required to weigh more than Type IV, but often Type VI is actually produced 15 percent or 20 percent heavier. The real difference shows up in the strength: Type VI felts must have at least 36 percent greater breaking strength lengthwise and transversely than Type IV felts.

PROTECTION COURSES AT BUR

The felts and bitumen in a built-up roof are aged more by ultraviolet (UV) radiation than by any other elemental force, although water brings with it a host of deleterious effects. The longevity of any roofing will be prolonged if an inert or reflective protective course, a sunblock, can be placed over the surface of the membrane.

The protection should be applied as soon as the surface is ready to receive it. Some liquid applied coatings require that the surface cure.

The protection course can also keep roofing and the building cooler, reduce damage from fire, help to hold down the roof in high winds, reduce traffic damage, reduce bitumen flow, and add a decorative quality.

Aggregate Protection

By far the most common protection is by crushed rock or small natural stones set in a hot flood coat of hot roofing bitumen. Aggregate can also be set in cold emulsified asphalt. The aggregate should be a stone that is not deteriorated by acids in the air. It should be reflective or at least light in color, and it should be hard, clean, dry, and free of fines. Sometimes it is necessary to import suitable aggregates hundreds of miles to meet these criteria. Stone aggregate, in as dry a state as possible, is applied to freshly poured bitumen at the rate of about 400 to 450 lb/100 ft^2 (16.9 to 19.0 kg/m^2).

Crushed and graded slag is also used as a roofing aggregate. It is inert, light in weight, light in color, and helps the evaporative drying of roofs after rainfall by wicking moisture up through its porous structure. Only 300 lb/100 ft^2 (12.6 kg/m^2) of dry slag are needed to produce effective coverage.

ASTM D1863 is the threshold standard for crushed rock, stone, and slag roofing aggregates. A fourth type, scoria or porous volcanic rock, is often used in western states because of its similarity to slag in both light weight and capillarity. Scoria's color, which ranges from light gray to deep earth red to charcoal, should be specified for the work at hand.

D1863's Size 67 is a commonly specified gradation for all aggregates, along with Size 6, which permits fewer fines.

Cap Sheets

A heavy, mineral-surfaced felt, called a *cap sheet,* can be mopped over the waterproofing plies as protection. Depending on the climate, a cap sheet offers protection for about 8 to 15 years. In resisting longterm UV attack, a cap sheet performs at a level between aggregate and coatings.

Protection by Coating

Coatings are at best temporary. It does not make sense to design a roof hoping for 20 years of service but to protect it with a material that must be replaced in 5 years or so. Facilities managers often do not understand how critical it is in preserving their roofing investment to institute and follow an inspection, maintenance, and repair plan. With this type of coating, it is important that the facility manager be informed that the roofing coating is a priority maintenance item.

After the top layer of asphalt has weathered some 30 to 45 days, a suspension of fine aluminum flakes in various vehicles can be applied to the roofing to reduce attack from sunlight and absorption of heat into roofing and building. These aluminized coatings should contain at least 3 lb/gal (360 g/l) of aluminum flake. Depending on solar load and air quality, their effective life is 3 to 5 years, at which point they start flaking off, often with discoloration. Failure to recoat the roofing at the critical time can cause irreversible damage to the roofing.

Ballast

Where dead weight is important, as to hold a loose laid membrane or inverted insulation down against wind uplift, large aggregate starting at about 1½ in. (37 mm) size is employed. Ballast rock should not have sharp edges, should be dense, inert, hard, clean, light in color, and should be totally free of fines and small particles.

The amount of rock needed to ballast the membrane or insulation against negative pressures (wind) and float-up (momentary flooding) must be carefully calculated and then checked against the capacity of the building structure.

The shifting of ballast in wind storms can induce dangerous loads on parts of the roof deck. The effects of parapet-caused negative wind pressures in causing ballast shift and any likelihood of the rocks becoming airborne should be considered. In hurricane-prone areas the use of ballast may be prohibited by code.

Ballast is not embedded in a bitumen flood coat or adhered; its dead weight is expected to hold it in place against wind loads short of rare cyclones or hurricanes. Sometimes a blanket of durable, felted plastic fiber is placed between the ballast and the membrane or inverted insulation beneath to reduce the possibility of indentation and to nest the ballast rocks.

PROPERTIES OF BUR SYSTEMS

The individual components of BUR are produced to standards that have been developed by ASTM. Yet roofing failures are rife because these are largely system failures rather than product failures. There are probably more studies available on BUR failures than there are on any other component of a building. The reasons for these failures are attributable to selection, design, quality of work, and worksite conditions. The variables in the on-site manufacture of a BUR are so manifold that only close supervision and inspection will result in an assembly that can be expected to meet its nominal life span while performing satisfactorily. Little wonder that the professional roofing consultant has become a member of many design/ execution teams. Little wonder that there is a host of panaceas and substitutes for BUR.

One characteristic in the design of BUR is the fact that the components are identified and specified, but the assembly that results from these components is not defined by expected performance. The development of system criteria for BUR would help overcome some of the shortcomings in the present product-over-product-over-product method of specifying BUR. A system specification should make reference to overall performance attributes such as tensile strength, thermal expansion, thermal movement, flexural strength, tensile fatigue strength, punching shear strength, impact resistance, water transmission, wind uplift resistance, and fire resistance. A study outlining these performance criteria is contained in National Building Science Series 55, *Preliminary Performance Criteria for Bituminous Membrane Roofing.*

Additional performance criteria for BUR are suggested in the NIST study, but laboratory test procedures had not been formulated at the time the NIST study was published. These procedures include tests for notch tensile strength, moisture effects on strength, creep, ply adhesion, abrasion resistance, tear resistance, pliability, permeability, moisture expansion, weather resistance, and fungus attack resistance.

A review of these performance characteristics is an indication of how earlier building systems were developed and put to use with very little regard for engineering principles and technical scrutiny. Some semblance of science must be introduced into the art of building.

PROBLEMS OF BUR SYSTEMS

Water Cutoffs

Thirty or forty years ago water cutoffs were installed between areas in the insulation to isolate and contain leakage. Because of vapor buildup problems, this practice was discontinued. It is now used only as a temporary device to protect the unfinished edge of the day's work. Current roofing doctrine emphasizes the importance of permitting trapped moisture to migrate laterally to a point of escape.

Hot mopped felt strips should be employed to seal the edges of the work overnight and when rain is imminent. These should be removed before work begins again—not left in place. Cans of removable urethane foam are also marketed to aid the roofer in sealing all edges in the shortest possible time.

Vapor Barriers

Vapor barriers were initially extolled as a virtue. They were then discarded as a cause for failure. Roofing producers today put the onus for the inclusion of a vapor barrier on the architect. Insulation producers often regard them as a necessity.

Vapor barriers are intended to prevent water vapor from entering the insulation and reducing its effec-

tiveness. In addition, water vapor may also find its way up between the joints of insulation pieces to cause ridging and blisters in the roof membrane.

Base Sheets

Special base sheets, roll goods that are different from the roofing plies or other overlying membrane, are often introduced to permit enhanced fastening to the substrate, to block the flow of water vapor, or to conduct water vapor to the perimeter of the roof.

At one time heavily coated (not just saturated) felts were introduced not only as a base for other plies, but also as ply felts. These coated base sheets were found to introduce excessive trapped water into roof construction and resulted in many failures. Base sheets offered by producers today are generally free of such problems.

Most producers have a studded (or granuled, channeled, or waffled) base sheet in their armory of roll goods that can be applied directly over wet insulating fills to vent water vapor to the perimeter or to roofing vents.

All base sheets are asphalt-saturated, and are often also lightly asphalt coated. Most are glass fibered, some are organic (cellulose) fibered. For use with coal tar pitch membrane construction, asphaltic base sheets with a coating designed for pitch compatibility are available.

Roofing Felts

When felts are stored without protection, placed on wet decks, or placed over uncured concrete, they pick up moisture readily. Moisture changes in the felts will cause swelling, and later, shrinkage. For example, when the bottom felt is not coated with bitumen, as at an insulation joint, water vapor enters from below and localized dimensional changes due to moisture absorption result in the ridging of the built-up assembly.

It is equally important to provide complete coatings of bitumen, so that felt never touches felt and to gain good adhesion with no chance of water migrating from layer to layer. No moisture should be permitted to collect between plies for any reason.

Bitumens

Asphalts come from various sources, and it is difficult to ensure uniformity within the specified asphalt grade. The use of tankers large enough to supply entire roof projects has evened out these variations somewhat.

An average of 23 lb/100 ft^2 (1 kg/m^2) is a commonly specified requirement for interply moppings of hot asphalt. NRCA's *Quality Control in the Application of Built-Up Roofing* permits latitude in the actual amount of bitumen applied. If the mopped weight in a small area does not measure more than 25 percent below the specified value, the installation is functionally sound, as long as felt never touches felt.

Some roofers claim that roofs with less than 17 lb/100 ft^2 (0.8 kg/m^2) of interply bitumen function well, as long as the bitumen is evenly applied without starved areas. Undoubtedly some skillfully applied roofs have, on investigation, been measured to have interply bitumen quantities lower than the 25-percent-less-than-specified floor set by NRCA. But to specify anything less than producer's standard and the NRCA tolerance figure is to trust that the low bid will be for the highest quality work. Roofs with interply moppings 25 percent above the specified value can be in danger also—in this case from ply slippage.

A glaze coat is often hastily applied as temporary protection when roofing work must stop for some unforeseen reason. This commonly consists of about 12 lb/100 ft^2 (0.5 kg/m^2) of bitumen. It does not replace any part of the interply bitumen quantity when work resumes.

INSULATED METAL DECKS AND BUR

Factory Mutual System has developed recommendations for metal roof decks over which vapor barriers, insulation, and BUR are placed. FM Loss Prevention Data 1-28 describes acceptable vapor barriers materials and adhesives, and acceptable insulations and methods of fastening. These recommendations govern both Class I and Class II assemblies with respect to wind uplift and fire hazard.

The definition, testing, and qualifying of roofing assemblies for I-60 and I-90 uplift resistance is also covered by the Factory Mutual System.

PROTECTED MEMBRANE ROOFING

A protected membrane roof or inverted roofing is essentially an upside-down roof system where the waterproofing membrane is installed directly on the substrate, with the insulation and ballast applied above the membrane. It is sometimes referred to as IRMA—inverted roof membrane assembly.

This system is simply a rearrangement of the constituent elements of a roofing system to alleviate the problems encountered by BUR when it is exposed to the weather. While we call the system a protected membrane roofing system, it is in reality nothing more than what is normally referred to as membrane waterproofing. See Figure 7-8.

There is no need for a separate vapor barrier, since the membrane acts additionally as a vapor barrier by virtue of its location.

Because of its configuration with the membrane concealed and protected thermally, the waterproofing membrane becomes less vulnerable to a variety of stresses. The stresses which contribute to aging or sudden damage are eliminated. These stresses include heat aging, rapid temperature changes, sunlight, and exposure. Hail, fire, and wind erosion are no longer to be endured with protected membranes. Foot traffic to maintain roof equipment cannot injure the membrane, since it is no longer exposed.

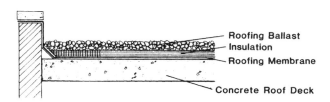

FIGURE 7-8 Inverted insulated protected roof systems.

INSULATION REQUIREMENTS

The introduction of protected membrane roofing could not occur until a suitable insulation which would be impervious to water and which would retain at least 80 percent of its insulating characteristics was developed. With the advent of foamed polystyrene as an insulation material, the protected membrane roof system became viable.

New detailing is required to permit protected membrane roof systems to drain properly. A slope is essential at the membrane surface so that the insulation does not lie submerged in water, thereby affecting its insulating characteristics. Slightly open joints between insulation boards, chamfered bottom edges, and grooved bottoms permit water to flow more easily to drains. By designing for about 15 percent more insulation the effects of wet insulation on thermal transmission is overcome.

MEMBRANE FOR PROTECTED MEMBRANE ROOFING

Initially, with the advent of protected membrane roof systems, the membrane most widely used was the built-up bituminous asphalt roofing membrane. Over the years, as liquid applied waterproofing systems and single-ply sheet systems were developed, they have been utilized as waterproofing membranes for protected membrane roofing. See liquid-applied waterproofing systems and single-ply sheet roofing systems described hereinafter.

THE SINGLE PLY ROOFING SYSTEM

The Single Ply Roofing Institute speaks for both modified bitumen and elastomeric membrane producers.

Since so many *single ply* roofings are of multiple ply construction—especially among the modified

bitumen designs—and since the modified bitumens are installed so differently from the elastomerics, it is easier to discuss these two categories of roofing separately, following CSI's *MasterFormat* which distinguishes modified bitumen, elastomeric, and plastomeric roofings.

There is a tendency in the industry to use single ply to describe the elastomeric roofings and to let modified bitumens, or mod bits, stand alone. Much NRCA literature, in the interest of simple, functional groupings, distinguishes built-up, modified bitumen and single ply.

Since their first appearance in North America during the 1970s, many modified bitumens and elastomerics have been introduced. Some basic chemical formulations have disappeared from use in the ensuing years. Many producers and many brand names have entered and left the market. However, by the late 1980s the more successful products were establishing places in designers' palettes of dependable materials. Table 7-15 shows how a small number of roofing types have gained acceptance, and how the market has stabilized in the 1990s.

This does not mean that the market will not change further, nor that new products will not be offered. This chapter discusses the major players in this major technological shift.

MODIFIED BITUMEN ROOFING

BACKGROUND

In spite of membership by modified bitumen manufacturers in the Single Ply Roofing Institute, single ply is a misnomer for these roofs, which commonly go down over one or more courses of felt, and which often have more than one ply of modified bitumen.

Polymer-modified bitumen roofing assemblies bear many resemblances to built-up roofing assemblies—they can even be described as simplified BURs. They are bituminous at heart, but with fewer plies, less labor-intensive installation, and have been simplified with no protection on top. Because the commonly employed chemical modifiers—SBS, APP, and PAO—alter (and enhance) the behavior of the asphalt, these modified asphalt membranes need less protection from the sun.

Because of its kinship to BUR technology, modified bitumen installation is often undertaken by established BUR roofers. Total retraining of personnel is not necessary. Much in-stock equipment remains in use.

The good effect of the mod bit revolution is this: The shop-level quality control needed to delicately layer three or four plies of felt—with measured quantities of a hot, dirty, bad smelling liquid in hot sun, high in the air, with the wind blowing—is replaced with a less complex, less punishing process. There are fewer rolls to unroll, less hot asphalt (or none) and often no need to spread stone over the sticky surface.

SBS MODIFIED BITUMEN

Asphalt that has been rubberized (*modified*) with styrene butadiene (SBS) for use in roofing dates to the mid-1960s in Europe and was introduced to the United States in the early 1970s. The flexible SBS polymer modified bitumen rolls are usually embedded in a full coat of hot mopped asphalt, although other adhesives and supplementary mechanical fastenings have been used. The SBS is applied as a single or a double ply and is often underlaid by asphalt-glass base sheets which can be mechanically attached if needed. SBS modified bitumen assemblies can be placed on any slope, including use as vertical flashing, if proper fastenings and adhesives are used. Standards that apply to modified bitumen products are shown in Table 7-16.

In almost all SBS installations, sheets with stone or ceramic granules, factory-embedded in the surface, are used to prolong the life of the membrane. Metallic foil-clad sheets are also made. Other protective coatings such as acrylic paints and reflective aluminum coatings can be applied in the field. All SBS membranes are reinforced with glass fiber, polyester fabric, or non-woven polyester—sometimes two layers.

Orientation of the sheet is important. Most SBS membranes are made with reinforcing in the bottom half of the sheet for hot mop or adhesive application. If an uncoated sheet is being used this orientation must not be reversed.

TABLE 7-16
STANDARDS FOR SINGLE PLY ROOFING WORK

Quality standards that can be cited for roofing use.

Common name	SPRI abbrev.	Polymer	ASTM standard
Elastomerics, vulcanized (thermosetting)			
EPDM	EPDM	Ethylene propylene diene monomer	D4637
Neoprene	CR	Polychloroprene	D4637
Epichlorohydrin	ECH	Epichlorohydrin	—
Elastomerics, nonvulcanized (uncured)			
Hypalon*	CSPE	Chlorosulfonated polyethylene	D5019
CPE	CPE	Chlorinated polyethylene	D5019
PIB	PIB/IIR	Isobutylene-isoprene polymers	D5019
Nitrile alloy	NBP	Butadiene-acrylonitrile and PVC	‡
Thermoplastics			
PVC	PVC	Polyvinyl chloride, plasticizers, stabilizers	D4434 D3083†
EIP	EIP	Ethylene Interpolymers and PVC‡	
Copolymer alloys	CPA	PVC alloyed with solid plasticizers, stabilizers and anti-oxidants	‡

* Nonvulcanized as manufactured. Vulcanizes in service.
† For pond, canal, and reservoir lining.
‡ Although the standard does not include them by name, D4434 or D3083 are sometimes used as standards for these products because of similar properties.

As rubberlike materials, SBS modified bitumen and SBR (styrene butadiene rubber) have the ability to accommodate stress from alternations of hot and cold, limited substrate movement, and other punishment. Intensely cold weather induces great stresses in roofing. A BUR assembly, as compared to modified bitumens, is stiff and brittle and is more likely to buckle or tear from internally-induced stresses, even if high-strength Type VI glass fiber felts have been used. Building movement can add its own stress on the membrane. Again, elasticity helps.

APP MODIFIED BITUMEN

Asphalt that has been modified with atactic polypropylene (APP) for use in roofing dates to the early 1960s in Europe and was introduced to the United States in the late 1970s. The stiff APP modified bitumen rolls are most often heated with gangs of propane torch tips and unrolled into place. The liquified undersurface is permitted to bond to the substrate and to the edge of the previous roll. The bead of melted bitumen that forms at the edge is important in sealing each sheet to the one before it. Hot asphalt, adhesives, and supplementary mechanical fastening are used on occasion. APP roofing is applied as a single or a double ply, often over asphalt-glass base sheets which can be mechanically attached if needed. APP modified bitumen assemblies can be placed on any slope. APP can be used as vertical flashing—if proper fastening and adhesives are used.

The rolls can be obtained and left bare, but in some installations stone or ceramic granules are factory-embedded in the top surface of the sheet or factory-laminated metal foils are used. Cold emulsified asphalt with aggregate, acrylic paints or aluminized protective coatings are all suitable for field application. All APP membranes are reinforced with one or two layers of glass fiber, polyester fabric, or nonwoven polyester. The reinforcement must be in the top half of the membrane thickness if the sheets are torch-applied.

Caution must be exercised when working over wood fiber recover board, wood decks, and wood blocking. The torching operation can start fires. Sometimes a smoldering ember can erupt into flame when appliers have left the roof. However, by not having to hoist asphalt and aggregate high in the air, the torched application of bare or adhesive-set cap-sheeted APP modified bitumen assemblies lends itself to roofing tall buildings and other structures where chilled asphalt or asphalt spillage would be unacceptable.

PAO MODIFIED BITUMEN

Asphalt may also be modified with polyalphaolefin (PAO). PAO-modified bitumen roofing may be applied in hot asphalt or cold adhesive, like SBS material, or it may be heat welded in place like APP material. Due to its good weather and ultraviolet resistance, it needs aggregate surfacing no more than SBS or APP roofing. It may be reinforced with a polyester mat or other fibers.

ELASTOMERIC ROOFING

These roofings are what are usually meant by single ply. Often they are put down just that way: one ply thick. CSI MasterFormat does not list the term single ply, using "elastomeric membrane roofing" instead.

Not all single ply roofings are elastomeric. Of the ten dominant single ply materials described in this chapter, eight are elastomeric and two actually produce what is chemically a thermoplastic or plastomeric material. To be exhaustively correct and at the same time colloquial the heading above would have to read "Elastomeric and Plastomeric Single Ply Roofing."

CLASSIFYING SINGLE PLY ROOFING

Truly elastomeric single ply roofing can be further divided into vulcanized and nonvulcanized types. This distinction is useful because it allows elastomeric roofing to be classified according to the method by which it is joined together on a roof. In other words, the kind of mechanic and the kind of equipment that is employed to accomplish the work.

Vulcanized Elastomerics

Vulcanized elastomerics (listed in Table 7-15) or *thermosets* are fully cured when they leave the factory and can be joined (adhesive seamed) only by application of an adhesive or adhesive tape.

Nonvulcanized Elastomerics

Nonvulcanized elastomerics (listed in Table 7-15) are initially uncured, curing over time while in service on the roof. They can be joined to themselves by heating (heat seamed, heat welded) or by application of solvents (solvent seamed, solvent welded). Adhesives, some of which include solvent action, are also used on nonvulcanized elastomers.

Thermoplastics

Thermoplastics (listed in Table 7-15), also called plastomerics, never vulcanize or cross-link their molecules. They are seamed by methods similar to those used for nonvulcanized elastomerics—heat or solvents.

PROPERTIES OF SINGLE PLY ROOFING

In spite of two decades of use, standards making bodies such as ASTM and ANSI, and the roofing industry itself, have not come up with a comprehensive set of standards to govern either products or the execution of single ply roofings. Standards that do apply to elastomeric products are found in Table 7-16.

Architects must make choices largely on the basis of producers' claims and the histories of installations inasmuch as there is only a modicum of standardization. To select a product the following physical properties should be investigated:

Abrasion resistance	Puncture resistance
Elongation	Tear resistance
Fire resistance	Tensile strength
Heat aging	UV resistance
Low-temperature brittleness	Water vapor transmission
Ozone resistance	Weathering resistance

Several of these properties may be investigated using ASTM D3105.

Along with material properties, field application techniques must be analyzed, such as attachment and method of making joints. Does the work require intricate, sophisticated use of welds to be performed by specially trained personnel, or can they be made with commonplace adhesives by ordinary roofers? Some laps can be made with adhesives, others require heat fusion, solvent welding, or tacky tapes.

Application Techniques

At present, in addition to the various types of single-sheet formulations, there are a number of application methods that are utilized and recommended by the single-ply roofing manufacturers. Not all of the single-ply sheets are installed using all of the techniques described below. Manufacturers' products and recommended installation techniques must be investigated and followed in order to avail oneself of the warranties offered. The installation techniques are as follows:

Loose-Laid and Ballasted

This system provides for the application of the sheet membranes laid loosely and with the following vulnerable conditions secured either mechanically or by adhesions: (1) perimeters, (2) roof projections, and (3) expansion joints. The roof is then ballasted with smooth washed river bed stone or with pavers. Stone ballast may not be permitted by code in hurricane areas. See Figure 7-9 for a typical loose-laid system.

Mechanical Attachment

With this system, single ply membranes are secured at intervals to the roof deck system through metal disks or by metal or plastic bars placed at lap joints and secured to the roof deck. See Figure 7-10 for typical mechanically attached systems.

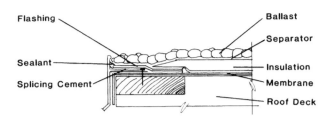

FIGURE 7-9 Loose-laid and ballasted single ply system.

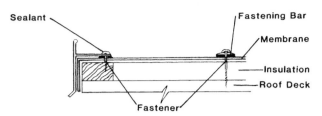

FIGURE 7-10 Mechanically attached single ply roof system.

Bonded or Adhered

In this system the single ply membrane is bonded or adhered partially or fully to the substrate with bitumen or a compatible special adhesive. This system is used where the additional weight of ballast cannot be used and where the geometry of the roof is such that it cannot maintain ballast.

In some situations combinations of these systems are recommended where both mechanical attachment and spot adhesive is used. Various arguments are made relative to the numerous attachment systems. There are those who desire in the loose-laid system to permit uninhibited expansion and contraction of the single ply sheet. There are those who extoll the virtues of complete bonding to detect and correct leaks, since in a bonded system lateral water movement is improbable.

Lap Joints

Joints in single ply roofing are made by heat, fusion, solvent welding, tacky tapes, or by adhesive.

ELASTOMERIC MEMBRANE QUALITIES

EPDM

Ethylene propylene diene monomer (EPDM) is a vulcanized elastomer. Seaming is by direct application of adhesive or by adhesive taping. A sealant bead is often added.

Due to EPDM's good strength and basic dimensional stability, almost all sheets are not reinforced, but there are a few available with polyester reinforcement. EPDM is commonly set in a full bed of adhesive. EPDM is used with insulation boards and ballast in inverted roofing installations; the ballast can be supplemented with mechanical fastening.

EPDM has good UV, ozone, general weathering, acid, alkali, alcohol, and abrasion resistance. It is flexible at low temperatures. However, EPDM is sensitive to both aromatic and aliphatic hydrocarbon solvents and oils. Some EPDMs have shrunk in service. Unless treated, EPDM is readily flammable.

Coatings and aggregate cover are not needed with EPDM, but sometimes white coatings are added to dark EPDM for reflectivity. Some versions of EPDM sheet are light in color and some are made with a white layer bonded to the upper surface to reflect heat and ultraviolet radiation.

CSPE

Chlorosulfonated polyethylene (CSPE, Hypalon) is a nonvulcanized elastomer. Seaming is designed for heat welding, solvent welding, or application of contact adhesive.

CSPE is reinforced with polyester. It is set in a continuous coat of adhesive. CSPE can also be mechanically fastened and held in place by ballast as part of inverted roof construction.

CSPE has good ozone, chemical, and pollutant resistance. The trade name "Hypalon" has almost entered the language as a nonproprietary term. CSPE is basically chlorinated polyethylene containing high molecular weight chlorosulfonyl groups combined with low-density polyethylene.

PVC

Polyvinyl chloride (PVC) is a thermoplastic. Seaming is by solvent welding or hot air welding.

Sheets are reinforced with glass or polyester fiber and are normally left uncoated. Since PVC is not compatible with asphalt or coal tar pitch, mechanical fastening is most often used, or else a full bed of contact adhesive. PVC is used with insulation boards and ballast in inverted roofing installations.

PVC has good fire, bacterial, and pollutant resistance. However, embrittlement and membrane shrinkage due to loss of plasticizer content counterbalances PVC's inherent UV resistance, so long-term flexibility test results are important in selecting a product. Avoid placing PVC and styrene in contact.

Copolymer Alloy

A copolymer alloy is a thermoplastic. Seaming is by hot air or solvent welding.

Sheets are reinforced with polyester fiber and are normally left uncoated. Since these alloys are not compatible with asphalt or coal tar pitch, mechanical fastening or a full bed of contact adhesive is used.

Since they are largely PVC in makeup, copolymer alloys have good fire, UV, bacterial, and pollutant resistance. By adding a plastic alloy rather than liquid plasticizers to the PVC, the tendency toward embrittlement and shrinkage with age is reduced. Copolymer alloys are used with insulation boards and ballast in inverted roofing installations.

PIB

Polyisobutylene is a nonvulcanized elastomer. Seaming is by a factory-applied PIB-based adhesive which, when release paper is removed and the seam walked and rolled in, binds the sheets.

PIB is reinforced with polyester. PIB is compatible with asphalt and may be set in a full hot mopped coat of asphalt or in a full bed of adhesive. PIB is used with insulation boards and ballast in inverted roofing installations. However, PIB is sensitive to petroleum solvents, food oils, and coal tar pitch.

PIB has extremely low water vapor permeability.

Nitrile

Butadiene-acrylonitrile alloys or nitrile butadiene polymers (NBP) are nonvulcanized elastomers. Seaming can be by adhesive or by hot mopped asphalt.

Nitriles are reinforced with polyester. Nitriles are compatible with asphalt and may be set in a full hot mopped coat of asphalt. Or nitrile sheets may be rolled in place with a backing of factory-applied adhesive. Nitriles are used in inverted roofing assemblies.

Nitriles are strong and tear resistant. They are flexible at low temperature and have low water vapor permeability. Nitriles resist most chemicals and solvents except aromatic hydrocarbons, and they are given a protective coating or are surfaced with gravel.

EIP

Ethylene interpolymer (EIP) is a thermoplastic. Seaming is by heat welding, although solvent welding is sometimes employed.

EIPs are reinforced with polyester. EIP is often used in inverted roofing assemblies. It can also be fully bedded in an adhesive.

EIP is fire, oil, chemical, and tear resistant.

Epichlorohydrin

Polyepichlorohydrin is a vulcanized elastomer used mainly as an overlay at EPDM roofs to provide resistance to aromatic and aliphatic hydrocarbon solvents and oils.

The sheets can be set in a full bed of adhesive.

CPE

Chlorinated polyethylene is a nonvulcanized elastomer. Seaming is by solvent welding.

CPE sheets are reinforced with polyester. CPE is compatible with asphalt and may be set in a full hot mopped coat of asphalt. Or CPE may be rolled in place with a backing of factory-applied adhesive. When used in inverted roofing assemblies, CPE can be mechanically fastened as well as ballasted.

CPE is resistant to ozone, many chemicals, hydrocarbons, and airborne pollutants.

Neoprene

Neoprene (chloroprene) is a vulcanized elastomer. Seaming is by contact adhesive.

The sheets are strong, dimensionally stable, and are not reinforced. Neoprene can be used in inverted roofing assemblies. It can also be fully bedded in an adhesive.

Neoprene is resistant to abrasion, oils, and solvents. Coating with weather-resistant Hypalon is recommended for some formulations, and neoprene will accept various reflective coatings.

FACTORY MUTUAL RECOMMENDATION

For single ply roofings, Factory Mutual Engineering Company (FM) recommends certain installation requirements when windstorms, combustibility, and leakage must be considered. These provisions are contained in Loss Prevention Data 1-29.

In Zone 3, which includes areas of the country where the wind velocity pressure is 47 lb/ft^2 or above, FM recommends that paving blocks be used over loose laid assemblies rather than gravel.

LIQUID APPLIED ROOFING

NATURE OF LIQUID APPLIED ROOF COATINGS

These roofing products are usually applied in a heavy coat by squeegee, roller, or spray to form a seamless, self-flashing roof membrane. They are most often applied to a hard, dimensionally stable, low-permeability substrate such as concrete rather than over soft insulations. An exception is the liquid applied coating that is part of a coated foamed roofing system—a softer substrate—which is discussed under Coated Foamed Roofing in this Chapter.

Many small roofs on a building, such as at canopies, porte cocheres, and small structures on roofs, benefit from being roofed by a simple operation that requires little preparation or flashing.

It must be remembered however that the resins used in these coatings are far from indestructible or permanent. They should always be pigmented or coated against UV attack where possible. They must be well drained: water should not pond on them. They should not be subject to foot or wheeled traffic. Liquid applied coatings must be regarded as maintenance items, requiring inspection and recoating on a far shorter cycle than that for conventional roofing.

Since the most frequent use for roofing-quality liquid applied coatings is on traffic surfaces such as balconies, terraces, sundecks, roof activity areas, and the top levels of parking structures, the Traffic Coatings heading in this chapter should be consulted.

SELECTION AND PROPERTIES

ASTM D3468 is the only material standard that applies to this class of products. It is addressed to neoprene and chlorosulfonated polyethylene (CSPE) products only, for waterproofing as well as roofing uses. Neither neoprene nor CSPE is currently a major contender among documented roof coating offerings. Most product literature-supported offerings are urethanes, although other resins also come and go in degree of marketing activity.

The most powerful degrader of roofing coatings is ultraviolet radiation. Ultraviolet radiation may be several times as intense in tropical, desert, and high-altitude locations as at northern latitudes. Air pollutants, occasional traffic, movement or cracks in the substrate, and lack of maintenance are other factors affecting long-term water repellency.

Roof coatings are sold by direct mail advertising as economical quick fixes to harried plant maintenance personnel, and are available at do-it-yourself stores, without benefit of work-specific advice from the manufacturer. This puts a designer or contractor who has a responsibility years after completion of the work at risk if vague label representations are taken as advice. It is best to work with the producer's representative or a contractor or professional who has used the product before, and to have literature with claims of properties and performance in one's files.

Rather than go into the basic properties of the urethanes, polyvinyl chlorides, epoxies, silicones, acrylics, CSPEs, and neoprenes that are marketed from time to time for this purpose, consider some of the factors that rule the success or failure of liquid applied roof coatings. Analyze the representations of the product starting with these considerations:

- *Ultraviolet radiation.* How intense is the UV level at the worksite? How protected is the location? Is the coating pigmented to reduce UV absorption and damage? Can the coating be given a protective coating of white latex, reflective material, or aggregate? Check ozone and Weatherometer tests.

- *Traffic.* Can you be sure there will be no traffic other than an occasional maintenance person? Will anything be rolled or dragged across the roof? Is the roof accessible enough to receive maintenance attention? Check hardness, tear resistance, and penetration tests.

- *Substrate.* Is the substrate monolithic, without joints? If there is a joint, is it flashable? Is the substrate always dry? Is the substrate subject to swelling or cracking or indentation? Will the roofing bridge small cracks, especially after 10 years in service? Check flexibility, elongation, and recovery tests.

- *Adhesion.* Will the product adhere to the substrate, considering the possibility of water vapor, alkali formation, or other bond breakers that may form? Check adhesion tests and peel tests.

- *Chemical resistance.* Will the coating be damaged by the local variety of air pollution? Will oil from machinery drip onto it? Will there be buildups of salts or acids? Check chemical resistance tests.

- *Fire.* Is damage from building fire or from cigarettes a problem? Check fire resistance tests and UL rating.

- *Mode of failure.* No manufacturer's representative likes to talk about this one, but all materials grow old and ultimately fail. Does the coating blister and lift? Erode and blow or wash away? Harden and crack off? Delaminate and blow off? Discolor and require recoating? Beware of materials that never fail.

- *Maintenance, replacement.* How easy is the roofing coating to maintain? Recoat? Repair? Replace?

- *Special warranty.* Over and above the contractor's correction-of-defective work responsibility is there any meaningful special warranty from the coating producer or its applier? Beware of warranties that warrant no more than that the product is correctly labeled, or that material from a defective can will be replaced by another can if you can find the old can two years later when the leak shows up.

Liquid applied roofing coatings are an area of product selection where alertness, asking questions, knowledge of the nature of the work at hand, and the advice of a trusted manufacturing representative are more valuable than identifying chemical content.

COATED FOAMED ROOFING

Coated foamed roofing systems consist of a sprayed foam, which really consists of ingredients foamed-in-place using spray equipment, topped by a liquid applied roofing which follows the installation of the foam almost immediately. About 1 percent of commercial roofing applied each year is of this type (see Figure 7-7).

COMPOSITION

The foams offered for use in this system are two-part urethanes, mixed at the nozzle.

Most coatings are urethane or silicone. CSPE (Hypalon), vinyl, and acrylics are said to have been tried but data on their performance is not readily available.

At least one foam producer has suggested that since urethane forms a good skin there is no need to protect it with a coating as long as UV cannot attack it; gravel placed directly on the foam could protect it from UV attack. Presumably this would be in a location that always has gentle winds and in which there would be no shifting of the gravel.

As part of the agreement to eliminate damaging blowing agents from passing into the atmosphere, the CFC-11 agent formerly used has been replaced with the less damaging HCFC-141b, just as has happened with isocyanurate board insulation. The insulating efficiency of urethane foam of constant density is reduced about 5 percent by the change.

THE FOAM-COATING SYSTEM

A coated foam system is economical both for new roofing and for re-covering old roofs of conventional construction. The system is self-flashing for its *soft flashings,* such as cants, bases, cover plies, and movement joint covers. Only the metal flashings, counterflashings, need be added.

The quality of application is critical to coated foam systems. The work must be done on dry surfaces in conditions of low wind and low humidity. The coating must follow the application of the foam as soon as possible since urethane will deteriorate rapidly in UV radiation. The mechanic who holds the nozzle determines the success or failure of the system. The thickness (therefore evenness and slope) of the foam as well as the thickness and quality of the coating (absence of bubbles, skips, starved areas, inclusion of blown dust or insects) depends on the training and attentiveness of that mechanic.

SYSTEM PERFORMANCE

A paper contributed to the Hurricanes 1992 Conference sponsored by the American Society of Civil Engineers in December 1994 reported that postHurricane Andrew visits to damaged properties showed a heartening rate of survival on the part of coated foam roofs. Generally the roofs held together, stayed in place, and did not admit water. Commonly, the damage observed was that damage inflicted by airborne debris or failure of the supporting deck.

Coated foam roofing's limitations are largely self-evident from the softness of the underlying insulation:

high-traffic, frequent impact areas are not the place to use this system. The surface is not plane; there is an inherent waviness or lumpiness that varies with the wind speed and the way the mechanic wields the foam spray nozzle. This waviness is only partly evened out by the coating. There have been occurrences of birds pecking through the skin material to get at the soft urethane foam below, but this is a rare phenomenon.

SHEET METAL

Information on metals used for ornamental metalwork is contained in Chapter 5, Metals. It includes basic information on aluminum, copper, stainless steel, and steel that may be informative to the reader when reviewing the requirements of these metals for applications to roofing and flashing.

SHEET-METAL FABRICATION TECHNIQUES

Seams and Joints

Metals are joined with seams in a number of ways depending upon the metals and their application. A seam or joint in sheet metal work may be rigid or loose, depending upon its intended function. Rigid seams are developed by: (1) fastening with rivets, screws, or bolts; (2) soldering; or (3) fastening and soldering in combination.

Loose seams and joints are utilized to permit expansion and contraction of sheet metal work. They work in one of two ways, either by sliding or flexing. The loose lock seam is an example of the sliding type. The batten seam is an example of the flexing type.

Watertightness in a seam is best obtained and is more positive with soldering, although modern day sealants such as urethanes, silicones, polysulfides, and butyls are being used successfully for watertight-

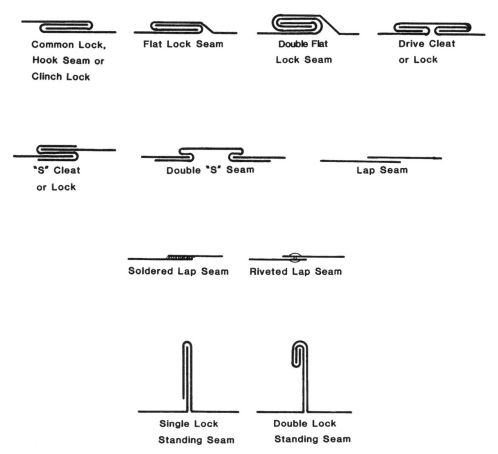

FIGURE 7-11 Typical sheet metal seams.

ness where a loose joint is required. Seams should be oriented properly to shed water. See Figure 7-11 for examples of typical sheet metal seams, locks, and joints.

Soldering

Soldering in sheet metal work is used to join metals using a filler alloy (solder) which melts and flows below 800°F. Since these temperatures are comparatively low, there is no alloying action between the solder and the base metals being joined.

Of all the metals used for sheet metal work only aluminum cannot be soldered successfully. Mechanical joining is recommended for aluminum where strength is required to be transferred and a sealant used in the joint if watertightness is essential.

Cleating

While sheet metal work is attached to a substrate by either fasteners or cleats, cleating is a preferred method because it permits movement of the sheet metal work without buckling. Cleats are usually of the same metal and thickness as the base metal, are usually 2 inches wide by 3 inches long and are generally spaced 12 inches on center. See Figure 7-12 for typical cleat.

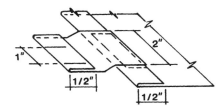

FIGURE 7-12 Typical sheet metal cleat.

FASTENERS FOR SHEET METAL

Since corrosion due to galvanic action can occur if dissimilar metals are used in sheet metal work, the following guidelines are suggested for fastener selection:

Base metal	Fasteners
Aluminum	Stainless steel or aluminum alloy
Copper	Copper or brass
Stainless steel	Stainless steel
Terne	Cadmium plated or galvanized steel fasteners

METAL THICKNESS FOR ROOFING AND FLASHING

When using aluminum, copper, stainless steel, and terne metal for various roofing and flashing applica-

tions, the recommended thickness for each metal and application should be as shown in Table 7-17. In addition, details for execution, as recommended by SMACNA, Sheet Metal and Air Conditioning Contractors' Association, may be found in its publication *Architectural Sheet Metal Manual.*

PHYSICAL PROPERTIES

The tensile strength and coefficient of thermal expansion of the roofing metals are as follows:

Metal	Tensile strength (psi)	Thermal expansion
Aluminum	22,000	.0000129
Copper	36,000	.0000094
Stainless steel	85,000	.0000096
Terne	45,000	.0000065
TCS	80,000	.0000096

TABLE 7-17
SHEET METAL THICKNESS FOR ROOF AND WALL FLASHING

Item	Copper (oz.)	Stainless steel (in.)	Galvanized steel (gage)	Aluminum (in.)	Terne-coated stainless steel (in.)	Terne (gage)
Exposed Flashings						
Cap	16	0.018	26	0.040	0.015	
Through wall	16	0.018	26	0.040	0.015	
Roof projections	16	0.018	26	0.040	0.015	
Roof penetrations	16	0.018	26	0.040	0.015	
Concealed Flashings						
Heads	10	0.010	28		0.015	
Through wall	10	0.010	28		0.015	
Lintels, shelf angles	10	0.010	28		0.015	
Roofing						
Flat seam	16	0.018	26		0.015	28
Standing seam	16	0.018	24	0.040	0.015	28
Batten seam	16	0.018	26	0.032	0.015	28
Copings	16	0.018	24	0.032		
Expansion joints	16	0.018	24	0.040		
Gravel stops	16	0.018	26	0.032	0.015	
Gutters	20, 24	0.018	26	0.040	0.015	
Leaders	16, 20	0.018	26	0.032	0.015	
Reglets	16	0.015	26			
Scuppers	16	0.018	24	0.032		

ALUMINUM

Aluminum is an easily fabricated and silvery appearing metal. It may be left in a mill (natural) finish where it will weather to a uniform gray, or special alloys can be anodized to obtain ranges of gray, bronze, amber, or black. Aluminum may also be prepainted with acrylic, vinyl, fluorocarbon, or alkyd coatings. In addition textured surfaces are available, obtained by rolling or embossing.

Alloys

The alloy and temper of aluminum generally used for sheet metal work is 3000-H14. Where anodizing is required, use specific alloys 1100, alclad 3003, 3004, alclad 3004, 3005, 5005, 5050, and 5052, usually in the H14, H24, and H34 temper.

Advantages

The advantages in using aluminum are as follows:

1. It is a lightweight, corrosion-resistant metal.
2. It will not stain adjoining surfaces.
3. It is ductile, malleable, and easily worked.

Precautions in Use

Since aluminum has a high thermal coefficient of expansion, care must be exercised in detailing to provide for thermal movement. Large flat surfaces should be avoided to prevent waviness. Aluminum sheet metal should not be soldered; instead, mechanical fasteners or welds should be used. Where aluminum is used with other metals or is in contact with concrete or masonry the aluminum should be coated with bituminous paint to act as a dielectric separator.

Sizes

Aluminum is available in widths of 36 and 48 inches and lengths of 96 and 120 inches. It is also available in coil stock. Thickness is expressed in gage or decimals Sheet t, preferably the latter.

Reference Standards

Aluminum may be specified to meet Fed. Spec. QQ-A-250 or ASTM B209.

COPPER

Copper is a ductile, malleable, easily worked metal with a characteristic bright reddish brown color. With exposure to the weather, it changes in color, slowly passing through various brown and green shades. In dry climates the green patina may never occur.

Advantages

Copper is resistant to corrosion by air and moisture. It is easy to work and join in the field. It is not corroded by masonry, concrete, or stucco when flashed or embedded therein.

Precautions in Use

To prevent corrosion or galvanic action it is best not to use copper in direct contact with aluminum, zinc, or steel, unless a dielectric separator is used. Where the wash from copper metalwork would impinge on stone or concrete, use lead-coated copper or detail the metalwork to avoid water runoff to prevent staining.

Sizes

Copper is available in sheets, 36 inches wide by 96 to 120 inches long. Thickness of copper is expressed in ounces per square foot.

Reference Standards

Copper may be specified to meet Fed. Spec. QQ-C-576, ASTM B370 and Copper Development Association alloy 110 or 122.

Lead-Coated Copper

Lead-coated copper is copper that is coated with lead on both sides and has a characteristically gray color. It is used primarily to avoid staining of concrete, stone, and stucco when flashed or embedded therein. The lead coating is applied by dipping or electro-deposition and weighs between 12 to 15 pounds per 100 square feet evenly distributed on both sides. The reference standard for lead-coated copper is ASTM B101, Class A.

STAINLESS STEEL

Stainless steel is a highly durable, maintenance-free, corrosion-resistant metal with a silvery appearance. The 300 series containing chromium, nickel, and manganese are recommended for roofing and flashing applications, using the dead soft, fully annealed types.

Advantages

Stainless steel has excellent corrosion resistance. It is self-cleaning and requires little or no maintenance. It does not stain adjacent surfaces and may be used in conjunction with concrete, masonry, and stone without danger of corrosive attack.

Precautions in Use

Upon completion of soldering operations, surfaces of stainless steel should be cleaned to remove flux and contaminants that may lead to surface corrosion. Long or large flat surfaces should be avoided to reduce waviness.

Sizes

Stainless steel is available in 30-, 36-, and 48-inch wide sheets by 96 and 120 inches long. Thickness is given in gage or decimals.

Reference Standards

Stainless steel may be specified to meet ASTM A167 and ASTM A666.

Alloys and Finishes

The alloys used for roofing are types 301, 302, and 316. Type 316, although expensive, is recommended for highly corrosive areas such as industrial, chemical, and seacoast atmospheres.

Finishes typically used include mill finish 2D and 2B, with No. 4 used for architectural appearance.

TERNE

Terne metal consists of copper bearing steel, coated both sides with a lead-tin alloy. Coating weights are 20 and 40 pounds per 100 square feet.

Advantages

Terne metal is used primarily for sheet metal roofing, most often flat seam, standing seam, and batten seam. When painted and maintained it is durable and has long-term permanence. It is lightweight and has a low coefficient of expansion.

Precautions in Use

Terne metal should be prime painted on both surfaces prior to installation and the exposed side painted soon after installation. It is recommended that cleats be used and that no fasteners be driven through the metal. Terne should not be in contact with aluminum, copper, or acidic materials.

Sizes

Terne metal is available in cut sheet and in rolls of varying widths and lengths, and in thicknesses of 30, 28, and 26 gage.

Reference Standards

Terne may be specified to meet Fed. Spec. QQ-T-201 (roofing terne) and ASTM A308.

Terne-Coated Stainless (TCS)

TCS uses a Type 304 stainless steel sheet with coating on both surfaces of a lead-tin alloy. The material may be exposed to weather to a uniformly dark gray. Because of its core and coating, TCS is highly resistant to corrosion in severe atmospheres.

FIRESTOPPING

FIRE-STOPS, SMOKE SEALS, AND FIRESAFING

Technologically, joint sealers and firestopping materials are related. Firestopping also shares materials and testing technology with many applied fireproofings, especially the intumescent and endothermic types.

Fire-stops

Firestopping today goes far beyond customary earlier efforts, such as placing mortar around pipes. Today's building design must protect penetrating ducts, chutes, cable trays, individual insulated wires, coaxial cables, conduit, bundles of wires, fiber optic cables, water lines, DWV stacks, roof drainage lines, refrigerant lines, condensate lines, clusters of pipes, and conduit banks. They must not only fill the gap but also must expand to tightly protect or replace meltable and flammable materials such as the insulation on electric wires. There is a firestopping assembly for just about every imaginable penetrating entity. There are even steel jacketed, highly intumescent devices that will expand to fully replace the volume of a PVC pipe within a wall should it burn in the course of a fire.

In addition, joints in the building structure, wall tops, as well as joints and gaps in interior wall and floor construction, have to be protected to varying degrees.

Firesafing

Protecting the gap between floor slabs and the inner face of curtain wall construction is considered firesafing and is usually accomplished with different products and assemblies. The space within curtain walls and EIF assemblies must also be firesafed against the vertical travel of flame, drafts, and smoke.

Smoke Seals

A barrier to the passage of smoke is usually accomplished simultaneously with firestopping, but some of the simpler fire-stop assemblies are often used for this. Constructing smoke separating barriers or curtains within ceiling zones is implied by the MasterFormat Firestopping topic. If a special reinforced foil/fabric/paper curtain, fastened against fire draft pressures is needed, it can be specified here.

STOPPING FIRE, GASES, AND WATER

The rules of firestopping start with the need for the fire-stop assembly to have equal fire resistance to the rating of the wall or floor. In addition to meeting the F rating, fire-stops must meet the T (temperature rise) rating where required by Uniform Building Code or its equivalent in other codes. Fire-stops must be able to stay in place under elevated air pressures and ponded or hose-applied water during the course of a fire. The fire resistance of materials designed to act as fire-stops in floor or wall assemblies can be tested in accordance with ASTM E814.

Floor and wall fire-stops should not deteriorate under day-to-day incidental water contact such as floor mopping or condensation. Ideally, it should not be necessary to replace all the firestopping in a portion of a building wet down in the course of extinguishing a fire.

Facilities managers have an interest in having as few types of firestopping material to maintain. Some prefer that in new construction all trades (masonry, gypsum board, plumbing, fire protection, air conditioning, electrical, and communications) use the same line of firestopping products. Likewise, in renovations or additions, the owner may request that only the product line in use be provided. However, one source is not always capable of providing fire-stop assemblies for every condition. It is not unusual for a facilities manager to deal with two or more sources.

Firestopping Products

For penetrations in horizontal construction such as floors, a fire-rated form is often needed, along with a relatively inert filler material. The fire rating may be attained by a nonshrinking putty or an intumescent sealant at the top of the assembly, often at the bottom too. Sometimes one of the components is endothermic (it absorbs heat energy, releasing water vapor in the process). A protective dam is often installed around the perimeter of a fire-stop that may be subject to water damage.

Wall penetrations sometimes need different forms to allow the rest of the assembly to be installed. Again, depending on the size, number, and material of the penetrating line(s), fire resisting foam, fire resisting sealant, fire-resistant putty, intumescent fills, pillows and wraps, endothermic fill, ceramic wool or mineral wool, metallic films, steel liners, and steel plates will be employed to stop fire, heat, smoke, and water.

See Figure 7-13 for an example of firestopping one of the many types of penetration that may occur in a fire-rated partition.

Firesafing Products

Firesafing is often accomplished with fibrous blanket, semirigid, or board materials. It is important that the material not shrink or melt in fire and that it stay in place under intense fire draft conditions. Basalt fiber and mineral fiber materials have higher melting points than glass fiber and can be formulated as dense and dimensionally stable semirigid units. Galvanized

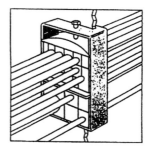

FIGURE 7-13 Firestopping device for multiple cables. An intumescent elastomeric insert module is placed around each cable in the bundle passing through the frame. Steel stay plates separate the rows. A curved compression plate is applied to the last row of insert modules; when made tight, the remaining space is packed. *(Courtesy of Nelson Electric.)*

steel clips can be used to ensure that firesafing will stay in place even under the enormous pressures generated in a large office tower fire.

JOINT SEALERS

With the advent of the aluminum curtain wall in the late 1940s, there arose a need for more sophisticated, elastic, and durable joint sealing materials to glaze large lights of glass and to seal joints between large segments of building elements.

While indeed there was a tremendous development of new elastomeric compounds, gaskets, and preformed tapes, it has taken some time to sort out the various formulations and sealing materials and also the terminology to deal with these developments. The terminology is not yet clearly defined and the term sealants is used somewhat loosely to cover all of these newer joint-sealing products. To put the terminology in perspective, it would be well to define those terms that constitute joint-sealing materials, as well as terms allied with the entire sealing process.

Definitions

Seal.   A material placed in a joint as a barrier to prevent the passage of liquids, solids, or gases; includes sealants, preformed tapes and gaskets.

- *Sealant.*   A bulk compound material that has the adhesive and cohesive properties to form a joint seal. (These are field-molded by applying liquid or mastic material in the joint).

- *Preformed tape.*   A tacky, deformable solid having a preformed shape and designed for use in a joint held in compression.

- *Gasket.*   A preformed deformable device in the form of a continuous shape for use in joints designed to exclude liquid or gas.

Adhesive failure.   A separation of a sealant from a substrate from any cause.

Backup.   A material placed into a joint to control the depth of a sealant.

Backer rod.   A round backup material, compressed in place in a joint to give the optimal shape for a sealant.

Bond breaker.   A release type of material placed in a joint to prevent adhesion of a sealant to a substrate.

Cellular material.   A rubber product containing many cells, either open, closed, or both.

Cohesive failure.   The tearing apart of a sealant internally due to loading where the adhesive characteristics of the sealant exceed the cohesive capabilities.

Compression seal.   A compartmentalized or cellular gasket which is held in a joint by compression.

Elastomer.   A natural or synthetic polymer that is capable of returning to its original dimensions and shape after deformation within a short period of time.

Joint filler.   Strips of nonextruding, resilient, preformed bituminous or nonbituminous material placed in a joint to reduce depth of joint.

Modulus.   In the physical testing of rubber, the ratio of stress to strain, that is, the load in psi of initial cross-sectional area necessary to produce a required elongation; a measure of stiffness.

Open-cell material.   Material having cells not totally enclosed by its walls, thus interconnecting with other cells or with the exterior.

Shape factor.   The relationship of depth to width of a field molded sealant.

Shore "A" durometer hardness.   A term used to identify the relative hardness of rubberlike materials by means of a hardness gage (ASTM C661).

Stress relaxation.   Reduction in stress in a sealant due to creep under strain deformation.

JOINT SEALS

Nearly every exterior joint in a structure must be sealed to exclude the weather and the elements. In addition many interior joints require a seal, primarily to close a discontinuity between varying adjacent materials and occasionally to prevent leakage of air or liquids, depending upon the occupancy or use of the structure.

Some joints are working joints (moving joints) and others may be nonworking joints (no movement or negligible movement). Working joints are introduced to accommodate (1) thermal movement resulting in expansion and contraction and (2) moisture movement caused by swelling and shrinking due to variations in moisture content. Nonworking joints include isolation joints and control or contraction joints. In addition to these joints, there are also exterior joints where metals butt or lap one another that require seals.

The materials encountered that form a part of a joint may include concrete, masonry, metals, glass, ceramics, wood, or plastics. The joint in question may consist of the same material or combinations of the materials listed.

Openings in joints must be sealed to create a barrier against the passage of gases, liquids, or other unwanted substances. For the comfort of occupants, joints are also sealed to reduce noise infiltration and rain infiltration. Structures containing liquids such as swimming pools, tanks, and reservoirs must be sealed to prevent loss of contents through joints.

Building seals in joints must perform their prime function even though they may be subjected to expansion and contraction where butt joints are encountered or to shearing where lap joints are used. All of this must be endured along with moisture changes, temperature changes, exposure to sunlight, ozone, and sometimes corrosive environments of industry.

SEALANT JOINTS

Shape Factor

Elastomeric sealants when installed in a joint will alter their shape as the joint expands and contracts; however, their volume remains constant. The shape factor of the joint (depth to width ratio) has a critical effect on a sealant's capacity to withstand extension and compression. As the cross section of the sealant adjusts to the new size of the opening, internal strains are imposed that are often severe. The strains in the sealant and thus the adhesive and cohesive stresses developed are a critical function of the sealant shape in the joint. Actually the strain is largely determined by the depth to width ratio, and the strain on the extreme fiber is highly significant as shown in Figure 7-14.

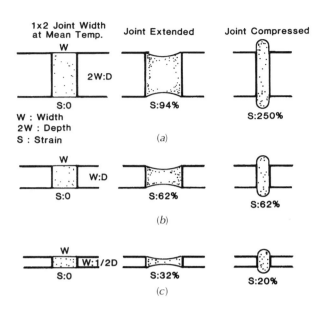

FIGURE 7-14 Joint shape factor and induced strains.

From data developed by R. J. Schutz and reported in "Civil Engineering" ASCE, V32, No. 10, Oct. 1962 under the heading "Shape Factor in Joint Design," Figure 7-14 illustrates the critical importance and economy of using a good shape factor with elastomeric sealants.

Figure 7-14a illustrates the importance of the shape factor. A joint 1 inch wide by 2 inch deep will increase the length of the outer fiber 94 percent when extended ½ inch. Tests have shown that the increase in length of this outer fiber is directly proportional to the increase in strain. By reducing the depth of the joint to 1 inch as shown in Figure 7-14b the strain is reduced to 62 percent. By reducing the depth of the joint to ½ inch as shown on Figure 7-14c, the strain in the outer fiber is reduced to 32 percent. Note also that although the joint width remains constant, the most effective depth from the point of view of strain is one-half the depth providing economy of sealant as well.

Recommended Sealant Joint Dimensions

Utilizing information obtained from the studies on shape factors and good practice from over 40 years of use, the following sealant joint configurations have been adopted by most users:

Minimum size joint; ¼ × ¼ inch

For joints up to ½ inch wide; depth = ¼ inch

For joints from ½ to 1 inch; depth = ½ the width

For joints over 1 inch; depth = ½ inch

Influence of Bond Breakers and Backup Materials

Function of Bond Breaker

Bond breakers which include polyethylene tape, wax paper, and aluminum foil are used in a three-sided joint, generally at the bottom to insure nonadhesion of the sealant to the third side as shown in Figure 7-15a.

Function of Backup Material

Backup materials such as polyethylene foam and urethane open cell foam are used to control the depth of sealant, the shape, and also to support the sealant and prevent sag as shown in Figure 7-15b. The backer rod is the most common backup material. Bond breakers are not required with the backup materials noted herein since adhesion of sealant to backup is minimal. In addition these backup materials have low surface strength and shearing capabilities so that the sealant will not be affected adversely by adhesion to the backup. The backup material is generally oversized and held in place by compression.

Fillers in Sealant Joints

Fillers are used primarily in horizontal work such as walks, roads, and flooring where expansion joints occur to reduce the depth of the joint. Sometimes the filler is used to assist in making the joint and remains there. The filler is usually a preformed wood fiber, corkboard, or cellular neoprene. In addition, since these fillers occur in a pedestrian or vehicular surface they also provide support for the sealant. Bitumen-saturated materials should be avoided since they may affect the sealant used. See Figure 7-16 for sealant joints with fillers.

PROPERTIES OF SEALANTS

There is no one universal sealant that possesses all of the attributes required to satisfy the requirements of all applications. Since sealants were first introduced there has been a shakedown period which allowed assessment of user needs and installation requirements and a refinement of the products initially offered and those that are on the market today.

The properties of sealants might be catalogued to include a variety of requirements. However the properties for a specific joint in a specific area of use may only encompass some of these properties. Fortunately there are a number of sealant formulations that have evolved that can to a large degree satisfy the performance requirements for specific installations.

The properties of sealants that might require investigation for a specific joint problem include the following:

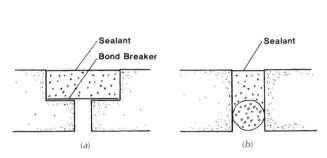

FIGURE 7-15   Function of (a) bond breaker and (b) backer rod.

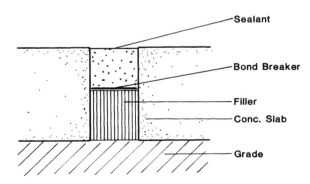

FIGURE 7-16   Fillers in sealant joints.

Physical property	ASTM test
Abrasion resistance	—
Adhesion in peel	C794
Compression set resistance	—
Cyclic tension and compression	C719
Hardness	C661
Modulus of elasticity	—
Movement capability	—
Pot life	—
Resistance to heat aging	C792
Resistance to weathering	C793
Solids content	
Solvent and chemical resistance	
Stain resistance	D2203 and C510
Tear resistance	—
Tensile adhesion	C719
Toxicity	—
Water resistance	—
Water immersion	—

SEALANT JOINT MOVEMENT

Movement Capability

The definition for a sealant (see Definitions herein) includes not only the highly elastomeric polymer compounds but also the old oil base and current resin base caulks. To differentiate among the various types of sealants on the market today, they can be grouped on the basis of their movement capability. This distinction is perhaps the most valid since joint widths and joint spacings can be predetermined and designed and then a suitable sealant selected which has the movement capability together with those other physical properties that are pertinent for the specific joint use. At this time there are three groups of sealants with varying movement capabilities— namely, low, medium, and high.

Low Movement

This group of sealants has a movement capability of up to ±5 percent and includes the oil base and resin base caulks, and some unvulcanized butyl rubber caulks. A movement of ±5 percent however means little or no movement. To begin with, any one of these materials would not be used in a joint wider than about 5/16 inch, and 5 percent movement would

amount to 1/64 inch. That being the case, the joints in which these materials could be used safely are primarily nonworking joints such as around door and window frames, and interior work.

The life expectancy of these materials is from 3 to 5 years for the poorer grades and somewhat longer for the better grades. Used indoors the latex caulks are good for the life of the installation. They are generally one-part products and application is relatively simple. Oil and resin base caulks may be made to meet ASTM C570 standards or Fed. Spec. TT-C-00598C.

Medium Movement

The sealants comprising this group have a movement capability in the range of from ±5 to ±12.5 percent, and include the following polymers: acrylics, butyls, Hypalon, neoprene, and some specialty polyurethanes.

The acrylics (single component sealants) are produced in a number of types (emulsion, solvent, and terpolymer). The emulsion types have a movement capability of about ±7.5 percent but since they are emulsions they are not suited for exterior use. They may be used indoors where they are protected from water. The solvent acrylics are used for narrow joint openings, on the order of 1/8 inch or smaller, particularly for needle glazing and cracks in masonry. The solvent acrylics have movement capabilities up to ±12.5 percent. The acrylic terpolymers have a movement capability of ±12.5 percent, a life expectancy of about 20 years and excellent adhesive characteristics without any need for a primer.

Butyl-based sealants (single component) have a variety of formulations, movement capabilities, and applications. There are butyl-based caulks that have movement capabilities up to ±7.5 percent and are used in nonworking joints and have also been used as acoustical sealants. Other butyl sealants have movement capabilities of up to ±10 percent. There are polyisobutylene butyl sealants that are used in curtain walls for metal to metal concealed joints that remain permanently nondrying and nonskinning. They are also used for bed joints for panels, rails, moldings and other two-piece metal configurations, and for heel beads for glazing.

Hypalon (chlorosulfonated polyethylene) and neoprene (polychloroprene) have movement capability up to ±12½ percent, but have limited applications.

High Movement

This group of sealants, truly the elastomeric type because of their ability to deform and regain their shape rather quickly within wider ranges, are the most widely used in architectural applications. They comprise the polyurethanes, silicones, and polysulfides with movement capabilities between ±12.5 percent to ±25 percent and more. Sealants designed to meet the requirements of ASTM C920 can be expected to perform from between 10 to 20 years or more.

This group of sealants can be used on all types of metal and glass curtain walls, between concrete panels and in masonry joints. Silicones are especially suited for glazing, curtain walls, and exterior insulation and finish (EIF) work. Polysulfides and polyurethanes are useful for horizontal joints for traffic and pedestrian use. Polyurethane has been used successfully for traffic joints up to 12 inches wide provided metal supports are used to support the system. The silicones are primarily one-part sealants, with two-part components used for specialty applications. Polyurethanes are available in one- and two-part components and occasionally in multicomponents.

Joint Design

In the design of working joints, the factors to be considered are their spacing, size, and shape, to accommodate the computed movement. Since the ability of joints to expand and contract varies with the movement capabilities of the sealants discussed herein, the percentage of expansion required will determine the class of sealant to be used—low-, medium-, or high-performance.

It is essential, therefore, to calculate the anticipated expansion and contraction of the joint due to temperature changes. The coefficient of thermal ex-

pansion of the building material containing the joint to be sealed and the summer and winter temperature differential for the region must be known so that the width and spacing of the joint may be determined. Oftentimes, a design may be predicated on a specific panel size, such as a precast concrete panel or an aluminum panel. In such a case, the joint spacing is predetermined and only the joint width based on the temperature range of the material must be calculated.

If it is assumed that a joint will move ¼ inch in width during the contraction–expansion cycle of a high to low temperature range, then the joint width and depth at time of installation should be as noted in Table 7-18, joint width vs. ±¼ inch movement.

To determine the width of a joint, calculate it by using Table 7-19 for coefficients of expansion of building materials. Example: Concrete panels 12.5 feet wide are used in the design of a wall. Find the movement of the joint for a 130-degree temperature range.

Expansion of joint = .0000065 × 130 × 12.5 = 01056 ft, 0.01056 ft × 12 in/ft = 0.126 in. Width of joint based on Table 7-19 will be as shown in Table 7-20.

SEALANT MATERIALS

Sealants are the products of chemistry. Since they were first introduced there have been marked changes in the various formulations and improvement in their physical properties. Chemists needed feedback from users as to user needs and problems of design and installation to improve sealant formulation and technology. To provide detailed information on each of the types of sealants available today and their properties would render this text obsolete tomorrow, since the properties and technology con-

TABLE 7-18
SEALANT FLEXIBILITY AS NEEDED FOR ±¼ INCH MOVEMENT IN STRUCTURE

% Sealant movement capability needed	Mean joint width (inches)	Expanded joint (inches)	Compressed joint (inches)	Sealant joint depth (inches)
12½	2	2¼	1¾	½
25	1	1¼	¾	½
50	½	¾	¼	¼

TABLE 7-19
COEFFICIENT OF THERMAL EXPANSION OF BUILDING MATERIALS

Material	Inches/inch °F
Aluminum	0.0000129
Architectural bronze	0.0000110
Brass	0.0000104
Brick	0.0000033
Concrete	0.0000065
Copper	0.0000094
Float glass	0.0000051
Granite	0.0000047
Limestone	0.0000044
Marble	0.0000056
Stainless steel, 300 Series	0.0000096
Structural steel	0.0000067
Terne	0.0000065
Wood	0.0000029 to 0.0000036

tinue to improve. This type of data is available from manufacturers' product sheets. However, basic information on sealants is given. See Sealant Joint Movement for additional information on sealant materials.

Silicones

Silicones have been on the market since the early 1950s. However because of their original high price they were not utilized to a wide extent until the mid 1970s. They are essentially one-part elastomeric sealants produced by the polymerization of organic siloxanes. Specialty two-component silicones, especially formulated for sealing around pipe penetrations to obtain a fire rating, are also available. Silicones offer excellent primerless adhesion to metal and glass. They have a wide temperature service range and their recovery from deformation is greater than most sealants. They offer superior resistance to UV and are not affected by ozone or oxygen. They offer movement capabilities up to ±50 percent. They are not recommended for use where water immersion is expected. The material for structural silicone sealant used in curtain wall glazing is ASTM C1184.

Polyurethanes

These sealants are elastomeric, produced in the one-component, two-component, and multicomponent parts. They are synthetic polymers produced by the reaction of isocyanates and chain-type polyols. They are used for joints in concrete panels, masonry work, and horizontal surfaces subject to traffic and abrasion. In their pourable grade they are also valuable for topping "pitch pans" where these must be used on roofs. Acoustical sealers, for use in interior steel framed construction, are usually urethanes. They can be manufactured to meet the requirements of ASTM C920 and Fed. Specs. TT-S-230 and TT-S-227. In addition, the polyurethanes have the ability to be combined with other polymers thus permitting the development of specialty formulations providing a wider range of physical properties. Most vertical grades of urethane are paintable.

Acrylics

These are one-component materials whether they are solvent, emulsion, or terpolymer types or whether they are acrylic latex caulks. Acrylics have been on the market since 1959 and are widely used

TABLE 7-20
CONCRETE PANEL JOINT WIDTHS AS NEEDED TO NOT OVERSTRESS SEALANT

Joint movement (inches)	Sealant movement (%)	Mean joint width (inches)	Expanded joint (inches)	Closed joint (inches)
1/8	12.5	1	1 1/8	7/8
1/8	25	1/2	5/8	3/8
1/8	50	1/4	3/8	1/8

NOTE: Since one must take into account the tolerances involved in precasting operations and shrinkage allowances, a mean joint width of 1/2 in. is desirable.

around door and window frames and for interior work. They are paintable soon after initial cure. They have good UV resistance and excellent adhesion properties. Acrylic latex caulks can be manufactured to meet ASTM C834. Acrylics are formed by polymerization of acrylic or methacrylic acid or derivatives of either.

Butyls

These are synthetic rubbers and caulks that are formed by the polymerization of isobutylene and isoprene. Some butyls contain solvents and are therefore subject to shrinkage. They have low permeability to gases and poor resistance to abrasion. As discussed under Sealant Joint Movement, the polyisobutylenes are most useful for concealed metal-to-metal joints in compression. Butyls are not paintable and should not be used where their prolonged tackiness permits them to pick up dirt.

Polysulfides

These are polymer sealants that are obtained by the reaction of sodium polysulfide and organic dichlorides. The two-component formulation was the first successful elastomeric sealant brought into the market in the early 1950s. A one-component sealant was introduced in the 1970s but requires several weeks for a complete cure to take place. Polysulfides have outstanding resistance to light, oxygen, oils, and solvents. When the original lead peroxide catalyst was banned in the United States in the 1970s, urethane use expanded to fill the market demand, the two sealants having many properties in common. Newly developed catalysts have permitted polysulfides to reenter the market.

Polysulfides are good for traffic areas and where abrasion is a problem. They can also be formulated to withstand water immersion for use in swimming pools. However after 30 years of experience it has been found that their use in tropical and semitropical climates is not as successful as are the polyurethanes and silicones. Polysulfides can be manufactured to meet the requirements of ASTM C920 and Fed. Specs. TT-S-230 and TT-S-227.

SEALANT INSTALLATION

Appearance

Above all for exposed architectural applications, joint sealants should provide a good appearance, carefully tooled and weathertight joints, colored properly where required, and with adjacent surfaces unmarred by sealant smears.

Joint Preparation

Open or reduce the joint shape as required to obtain the proper width-to-depth ratio as recommended herein or as recommended by the sealant manufacturer. This may require cutting and sawing to obtain the proper width or filling with backup material to obtain the proper depth. Remove any temporary material or filler used to form the temporary sealant reservoir.

Cleaning

Joint surfaces must be clean and free of defects that would impair or inhibit adhesive bond of sealant. Dust, grease, dirt, and occasionally frost must be removed. When a coating is encountered in a joint on a steel or aluminum surface it must be compatible with the sealant and the bond developed between the sealant and the coating must not be reduced. Consult with both the sealant manufacturer and the coating manufacturer to assure proper results.

Priming

Primers are used to improve joint surfaces to obtain maximum adhesion of sealants. Depending on the surface (i.e., concrete, masonry, steel, aluminum, glass, etc.) and on the specific sealant, solicit explicit instructions from sealant manufacturer for their recommendations.

Backup, Fillers, and Bond Breakers

As noted before, each of these materials performs certain functions within a joint to reduce the joint depth to the optimum and to prevent three-sided adhesion.

Joint fillers in horizontal paving are often installed along with the paving and usually require only reduction in depth. See Figure 7-16. In vertical applications, fillers and backup materials are usually installed oversized so that they are in a slightly compressed mode at all times.

Backup materials and bond breakers are usually installed just prior to application of sealant.

Weather Conditions at Time of Application

Joints are best sealed when the width approximates the mean average temperature. Since adhesive failures are more likely to occur as sealants age and are more brittle in cold weather, the low side of the mean temperature would be preferable for sealant installation as opposed to the high side of the mean temperature.

Other problems associated with temperature at time of installation are (1) shortened working time for two-component materials at elevated temperatures and (2) moisture condensation and frost on the joint substrates at lower temperatures.

Masking

Place masking tape on both sides of the joint cavity to protect adjacent surfaces from sealant smears or smudges. Install prior to priming since some primers may discolor masonry and other porous surfaces.

Applying Sealant

Install sealants as per manufacturers' recommendations, preferably with a caulking gun with a nozzle whose opening may be shaped and sized to mold the required bead of sealant to fill the joint cavity. The bead of sealant should be applied without dragging, tearing, or leaving unfilled areas.

Nonsag sealants for vertical applications should be tooled to force the material into the joint and ensure contact with the joint sides. The tooling also ensures a neat uniform appearance of the sealant.

Pour grade sealants for horizontal applications are best applied by filling the joint just slightly below the surface.

ASTM C1193 is a standard guide for Use of Elastomeric Joint Sealants and provides detailed information on application techniques.

PREFORMED TAPES

Preformed tapes are extruded, continuous ribbonlike shapes, generally rectangular, square, round, or wedgelike sections, sometimes with embedded reinforcement, and are packaged in rolls.

They are generally the products of butyl-based compounds or polybutenes. These tapes are used in permanently tacky, pressure-sensitive applications, which require compressive confinement for effective sealing, generally between metal parts. They are also used in glazing systems in surround joints as a supplementary sealant.

The tapes require no primer and are readily installed, and have good initial adhesion. The built-in-reinforcement or shim is used to control compression.

They must be used under constant compression. Some tapes may stain porous surfaces such as concrete, masonry, or stone. Since they are tacky they generally have a high dirt pick-up when exposed.

Figure 7-17 shows typical uses of preformed tapes in joints other than glazing uses.

Preformed tapes may be referenced to AAMA 806.3, Back Bedding Mastic Type Glazing Tape.

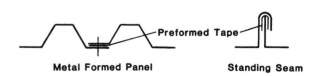

FIGURE 7-17 Preformed tapes in joints.

GASKETS

Other types of joint sealing material are available in foams, open and closed cell materials, and dense, rigid extrusions.

The foams or sponges are usually preformed polyurethane strips that are coated with asphalt, butylene, or some equally satisfactory waterproof material. The coated foams are sometimes used for sealing out moisture or weather. The uncoated *dry* foams are used to seal out dust and air. These gaskets must be used in compression with the degree of compression varying from 50 to 75 percent.

Cellular elastomeric preformed gaskets manufactured to meet ASTM C509 are furnished in a number of shapes, such as rods, for use as compression seals in joints, or in setting of glass and metal panels in frames. They are produced from vinyl chloride polymers, neoprene, butyl rubbers, and polyurethanes.

Dense rigid extrusions of neoprene, EPDM, and PVC are produced in a variety of shapes and are utilized in glass and metal panel frames under compression for watertight joints.

Lockstrip structural gaskets are used primarily for glazing and are discussed in Chapter 8.

9 West 57 Street, New York, NY: structural gasket glazing. Skidmore, Owings & Merrill, Architects. *(Photograph © Wolfgang Hoyt/ESTO.)*

GLASS AND CURTAIN WALLS

GLASS

DEFINITIONS

Discontinued Federal Specification DD-G-451d defined glass as:

. . . an inorganic product of fusion which has cooled to a rigid condition without crystallizing. It is typically hard and brittle and fractures in a conchoidal manner. It may be colorless or tinted and transparent to opaque. Masses or bodies of glass may be made tinted, translucent or opaque by the presence of dissolved, amorphous or crystalline material.

COMPOSITION

Glass is produced from three major ingredients: sand (silica), soda (sodium oxide), and lime (calcium oxide). About 50 other chemical compounds are also used in varying degrees to affect color, viscosity, or durability, or to impart some desired physical property. An average batch contains about 70 percent silica sand, 13 percent lime, 12 percent soda, and small amounts of other materials.

GLASS MANUFACTURING PROCESSES

The batch containing the ingredients is fed into melting tanks or furnaces and melted at about 2800°F, and flows toward the discharge or forming end where the temperature is around 2100°F.

The reference to the manufacturing process is important since with the advent of the float glass manufacturing process and its improvement, there is essentially today only one method—the float glass process—producing flat glass architectural products. Gone are sheet or window glass and plate glass that were produced by two distinct manufacturing processes which have been replaced by the float glass process.

A minor segment of the market produces rolled glass which consists of three types:

    Patterned glass
    Wired glass
    Stained or cathedral glass

FLOAT GLASS

Manufacturing Process

In 1959 Pilkington Brothers, an English company, introduced a new method for the manufacture of glass—the float glass process. In this process, the molten glass at the exit end of the furnace is poured onto a bath of liquid tin on which it floats and spreads to form a wide, flat ribbon of glass that remains untouched until it hardens.

The most striking part of this process is that, unlike the old polished plate glass manufacturing process, it produces glass having parallel surfaces, high optical quality, and fire-finished surface brilliance. It is economical in that the polished plate glass process required an investment in a huge grinding and polishing

operation to obtain smooth surfaces, whereas the float process obtains these results by means of the molten tin bath.

A typical float glass furnace is about 165 feet long, 30 feet wide, and 4 feet deep. The melting tank operates continuously around the clock, 7 days a week, for about 5 to 7 years. After that, it is shut down for inspection and repair.

As the molten glass leaves the furnace and flows onto the molten tin, the speed with which it traverses the molten tin determines the thickness of the glass. Generally, the slower the speed, the thicker the resultant glass product.

The float bath of molten tin is about 150 feet long and wide enough to produce glass that is 160 inches wide.

After the glass leaves the float bath, it enters a lehr (annealing oven) where it is gradually annealed from a temperature of 1200 to 400°F to relieve internal stresses. See Figure 8-1 for a typical float glass manufacturing process.

Float Glass Products

Float glass manufacturing accounts for over 90 percent of the flat glass produced today. The products are clear, heat-absorbing, and tinted glasses.

Clear Glass

Clear glass is colorless and is manufactured to meet ASTM C1036, Type 1, Class 1. It is available in thicknesses for construction purposes ranging from 2.5 mm to 32 mm and from 48 × 84 inches to 120 × 204 inches, depending upon the manufacturer.

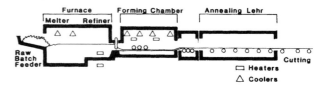

FIGURE 8-1 Advanced float glass process. *(Courtesy PPG Industries.)*

Heat-Absorbing Glass

Heat-absorbing glass is intended for glazing where reduction of solar heat is required and is available in bronze, gray, and blue-green colors. The color density is related to the thickness, whereas the light transmittance is reduced with an increase in thickness. Heat-absorbing glass is manufactured to comply with ASTM C1036, Type 1, Class 2.

Heat-absorbing glass is produced by adding selected metallic oxides in small amounts to the basic glass mixture. Those oxides reduce light transmission, control solar brightness and glare, and absorb solar heat. As the glass becomes warm, it reradiates this heat, with only part of the heat directed indoors. Figure 8-2 illustrates the Lever House, which uses blue-green heat-absorbing glass.

FIGURE 8-2   Lever House, New York, NY: Blue-green tinted glass used in the forerunner of curtain wall systems. Skidmore, Owings & Merrill, Architects.

ROLLED GLASS

Rolled glass is made by pouring molten glass from a furnace and then passing it between the rollers to obtain the required thickness. It then is annealed in a lehr and cut to size. As noted previously, three types of glass are produced under this category of rolled glass: wired, patterned, and stained or cathedral.

Wired Glass

Wired glass is rolled glass in which welded wire netting has been added to the molten material prior to rolling. Wired glass is made with polished faces (polished wired glass) or a pattern (patterned wired glass), following ASTM C1036, Type II, Class 1, Form 1 or 2, respectively.

Formerly widely used for fire-safe glazing and security glazing, the low strength of wired glass, its limited stability at high temperatures, and its danger to persons when broken, have caused designers to compare it with the performance offered by more recently developed fire-rated glasses, tempered glass, and laminated security glasses.

Wired glass is too weak to qualify as a safety glass under the federal rule. It has good hose stream resistance but it begins to fail when fire tests go above the 1640°F (895°C) temperature curve.

Several wired glasses are listed (not labeled) by UL, all of them with square or diamond mesh, not parallel wires. Fused factory labels are not practical on wired glass, since the sheets are cut into small lites in the shop. Any applied labels would have to be numerically controlled by UL or Warkock Hersey Int. (WHI). The authors have no report of any labels being seen—certainly not since the last U.S. producer of wired glass left the field in 1979. Labeling of doors is done under the total opening concept: door, frame, hardware, louver, lite frame, glass. All must be labeled as a unit; for example, a door lite label is meaningful only if that glass is recorded as having been tested with that door.

Patterned Glass

Patterned glass, once also referred to as *figured glass,* is produced by the use of rollers that have a pattern etched on one or both of the roll faces. This imparts a pattern on the glass as it passes through the rolls. A variety of patterns is made with a broad range of obscuration. Patterned glass can be colored, but the choices are limited. Thicknesses range from about 3 mm to slightly more than 4 mm. Patterned glass follows ASTM C1036, Type II, Form 3. Clear is Class 1; tinted is Class 2.

FIRE-RATED GLASS

Not all fire-rated glass is glass. Some of it is a composite of several materials; some of it is transparent ceramic material. Since it is clear and set in glazing frames—themselves made of steel and fire-rated—it is spoken of as glass. Fire-rated glass is expensive; its effect on a construction budget must be analyzed early in design. The position of fire-rated glass under building codes continues to develop as the strong points and weak points of this class of materials is better known, and as earlier dependency on wired glass wanes in the minds of fire safety specialists.

Where the common sizes for wired glass in fire-rated construction were limited to 100 in² (0.065 m²) for Class B protection and 1296 in² (0.836 m²) for Class C protection, the newer fire-rated glass technology opens up the possibility of sizable openings (even sidelites and mezzanine glazing) that were not often considered (or permitted) with wired glass.

Fire-Protective Glasses

Fire-protective glasses such as borosilicates (Pyrex) and clear ceramics provide limited protection for openings in walls with low fire ratings, as permitted or waivered-in by local code officials. These products do not burn or melt, but they do permit considerable temperature rise (radiant heat transfer) across their thickness, to the point that persons close to the *safe* side can be burned. These products generally survive fire hose stream tests well. The European term *G glass* is sometimes used to identify these products. They do not qualify as safety glazing.

The ceramic products are attractive, especially in their fully clear version, being transparent and free of wires. They were introduced to the United States from Japan in 1987. They are usually limited by code to the same lite sizes as wired glass in fire-rated construction, but pieces up to 3 × 8 ft (0.9 × 2.4 m) are available. Laminated versions, which have greater impact resistance, are made in sizes up to 3 × 3 ft (0.9 × 0.9 m). Both a mildly hazy and a premium, fully clear grade are available.

Borosilicate products are fully transparent. Their impact resistance is similar to that of the ceramics.

Another product in this category is a monolithic fire-rated glass which qualifies as safety glass for the most demanding locations, Category II—400 ft·lb impact force (540 N·m) on glass lites greater than 9 ft². It is WHI labeled for 20 and 30 minute protection. In fire doors it can be used as a lite up to approximately 3 × 6.5 ft (0.9 × 2.0 m). In sidelites it can be used in lites up to approximately 3.5 × 8.5 ft (1.1 × 2.3 m). Thicknesses are 6 mm and 12 mm.

Fire- and Heat-Resistive Glasses

An unwired, fire- and heat-resisting glass sandwich, an *F glass,* was introduced to the United States from France in 1983. It consists of two panes of fully tempered safety glass separated by a steel spacer at the perimeter. The resulting cavity is filled with a clear, UV-resistant, nonyellowing gel consisting of water, a polymer, and a sodium salt. Its fire rating increases with the gel thickness. In a fire the gel, in effect, intumesces, i.e., it forms a crusty, heat resisting solid. This sandwich is labeled by UL and WHI for 20, 30, 45, and 90 minutes. The producer will provide its own 2-hour label, supported by test results, for authorities that will accept it. It qualifies as both a Category I and Category II safety glass under CSPC's 16 CFR 1201. The rise in temperature across the glass in a timed furnace test is about 117°F (65°C), which easily qualifies it for a 250°F (140°C) heat rise rating.

As with all glass that will be exposed to fire, the design of the frame is important. The frame and sealants must be compatible with the heat resistive lite material and must be jointly tested for heat rise. The amount of engagement of the lite edge must be ample to accommodate expansion and to withstand pressure.

MANUFACTURING MODIFICATIONS OF GLASS

While there is essentially one major method of manufacturing flat glass, there are a number of glass products that are fabricated from flat glass, including the following:

Heat-treated glass
Chemically strengthened glass
Insulating glass
Laminated glass
Reflective glass
Low-E glass
Transparent mirror glass
Nonvision glass

Heat-treated Glass

Both heat-strengthened and tempered glass are made to meet ASTM C1048 by a process of reheating and rapid air cooling of annealed glass. As a result of heat treating, the outer surfaces of the glass are put in compression, and the central portion or core is in compensating tension.

Two methods are used in heat treating: (1) a vertical pass through the reheat furnace with the glass held by metal tongs producing tong marks and (2) a horizontal pass on rollers. Each manufacturing method will produce a degree of bow and warp, creating some optical distortion. Limits on this bow and warp are established by ASTM C1048.

The heat-treating process is such that it requires all fabrication processes (cutting, drilling, edging, etc.) to be performed prior to heat treating.

Heat treatment results in increased tensile or bending strength and enables such glass to withstand greater uniform loading pressures and solar-induced thermal stresses. As a result, for high-rise structures with varying wind-induced pressure zones, the use of the same thickness heat-treated glass in vision areas allows uniformity of light transmission, color density, and glazing detail.

Most flat glass products can be heat treated; the exceptions are wire glass and rolled glass with deep patterns. Heat treated glass can be ceramic coated for spandrels. It may be tinted to absorb heat and reduce light transmission.

Heat-strengthened glass. The heat treatment increases the resistance of this glass to thermal shock and increases its mechanical strength to two times that of annealed glass. When broken, heat-strengthened glass tends to remain in position in a sash opening, since its break cracks are few in number which limits relative movement. Heat-strengthened glass does not meet the requirements for safety glazing materials.

Tempered glass. The heat treatment increases the mechanical strength to about four to five times that of annealed glass and increases its resistance to thermal stresses. When broken, tempered glass will fracture into many particles, minimizing the chances of injury on personal impact. Tempered glass is available in practically every thickness that is used for flat glass products and meets the requirements of Consumer Products Safety Commission Rule 16 CFR 1201 for safety glazing materials.

Tempered glass is occasionally subject to spontaneous breaking due to inclusions in the glass that expand within the central portion of the pane, causing internal pressure to work against the highly compressed outer surfaces. The pressures generated by these inclusions of nickel sulfide (and sometimes other stones such as quartz, cristobalite, and aluminous minerals) are sufficient to actually explode the glass on occasion—accompanied by a loud report. When the glass merely fractures, the spiderweblike break pattern will often lead the eye to a small, butterfly-shaped point of origin where the inclusion was trapped. The inclusions are so small as to be almost undetectable.

Chemically Strengthened Glass

Glass can be chemically strengthened to a level between that of heat-strengthened and fully tempered glass by placing it in a time- and temperature-controlled bath of molten salts that replaces small sodium ions in the glass with larger ions of potassium. Like tempered glass, it must be cut to size before treating: maximum size 60 × 96 in. (1525 × 2440 mm).

The modulus of rupture (MOR) in glass is expressed in a wide range of empirically-obtained values for each glass type, but approximate average surface compression MOR values for four types of glass are:

Annealed (*plain glass*)	12,000
Heat-strengthened	25,000
Chemically strengthened	33,000
Fully tempered	55,000

Thicknesses of chemically strengthened glass are 4 mm and 5 mm. The glass is used primarily in laminates for security and sloped glazing (skylights). Chemically strengthened glass does not qualify as safety glass if used alone, but as a component of laminated glass it does. One advantage of chemically strengthened glass over the fully tempered product is that it is almost totally free of spontaneous breakage.

Insulating Glass

Insulating glass units are factory-fabricated modules consisting of two panes of glass separated by a metal spacer around the perimeter, with an entrapped, sealed, desiccated air space between. Triple-glazed units utilizing a third pane and a second metal spacer are also available, primarily for use in northern climates where winter temperatures are unusually low. ASTM E774 is a material standard for sealed insulating glass units.

Glass Elements

A wide range of glasses designed for different specific applications are utilized in insulating glass units. In addition to the typical module of clear float glass, special units for heat control, glare control, safety, and acoustical requirements are produced using heat-absorbing, heat-reflecting, tempered, laminated, patterned, and wire glass.

Since the applications can be varied and the types of glass used in the assembly may be of varying types, thicknesses, sizes, and shapes, it is best to consult the manufacturer on specific requirements and recommendations before designing a specific configuration.

Components of Insulating Glass Units

The quality and life of an insulating glass unit depend on a number of factors—primarily, the type of seal, the desiccant, proper design of metal spacers, and correct corner treatment of the spacers.

Sealing systems. Two types of seals are available—a single-seal system and a dual-seal system, as shown in Figure 8-3. The function of the seal is to prevent moisture vapor penetration (see Chapter 1), maintain a structural bond between the two panes of glass, provide adhesion to the metal spacer, and provide long-term resistance to heat, UV, and water. In the single-seal type, or organic seal, polysulfide was the initial seal used, with hot-melt butyls also being used. In the dual-seal system polyisobutylene is the primary seal which provides a superior barrier against MVT. The secondary seal, which is a structural seal as well, may be polysulfide, silicone, or hot-melt butyls. Insulating units utilizing the dual seal may carry a 10-year warranty by the manufacturer.

Desiccant. The desiccant is used to maintain a dry air space between the panes of glass. It is placed within the hollow of the metal spacer which has fine perforations or seams along the inside surface, exposing the desiccant to the entrapped air to maintain its dryness and to prevent condensation. The desiccants used are Silica-Gel and Molecular Sieve, which adsorb both water and solvent vapors from the seal.

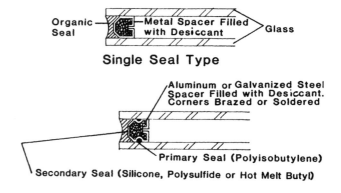

FIGURE 8-3   Sealing systems for insulating glass.

Metal spacers. The metal spacers may be aluminum or galvanized steel, shaped to a rectangular or other configuration to provide the required distance between the glass panes. The corners of the spacers may be joined metallurgically by soldering, brazing, or welding, or they may be mechanically joined by an aluminum, nylon, or plastic key.

Gas filling. Instead of air, the cavity may be filled with argon gas, which will initially increase the efficiency of the insulating unit about 7 percent. Thus, a unit with an air-filled U-value of 0.54 will reduce to $U = 0.50$ with argon. The increase in thermal efficiency is not permanent, however. There will be some diffusion that replaces argon with air over the years, shaving percentage points off the initial saving. Other inert gases such as xenon have also been used.

Testing and Certification

To ensure the quality and performance of insulating glass units, the Insulating Glass Certification Council (IGCC) has a program of testing and certification through specified standards. The testing standards used are outlined in ASTM E774 and ASTM E773 for Sealed Insulating Glass which classifies units into three performance categories: C, CB, or CBA, depending upon the durability of these units in the accelerated testing, with the CBA designation being the highest.

Laminated Glass

Laminated glass consists of a combination of two or more panes of glass with a layer of transparent plastic sandwiched between the panes under heat and pressure to form a single laminated unit having certain characteristics depending upon its intended use.

The plastic used is plasticized polyvinyl butyral, which may be as little as 0.015 inch thick to as much as 0.090 inch or more, as required for a specific use. The vinyl may be colorless for general use or pigmented when used for solar control.

The introduction of the plastic interlayer produces a unit that will prevent sharp fragments from shattering and flying about when it is subjected to a sharp impact and breaks since the glass adheres to the vinyl interlayer. The glass used in its lamination may consist of clear, tinted, tempered, reflective, and wire glass, and the result is an adaptable, high-performance glazing material that is utilized in the following situations:

Safety glazing
Security glazing
Solar control
Sound control

ASTM C1172 is a material standard for laminated glass.

Safety Glazing

The use of laminated safety glass minimizes the risk of injury from glass breakage or accidental impact. It is useful for entrance doors, sliding doors, shower enclosures, skylight, and sloped glazing to name but a few applications.

Hazardous glazing applications are identified by the Consumer Product Safety Commission in its performance standard 16 CFR 1201. Depending upon the degree of safety required, laminated glass components may be annealed or heat treated and the vinyl interlayer may be as little as 0.015 inch thick for Category 1 of Federal Standard 16 CFR 1201, or as much as 0.06 inch thick for overhead glazing.

Security Glazing

Security glazing is used, when properly designed, for three different levels of security as follows:

1. Burglary resistant
2. Institutional security
3. Bullet resistant

Burglary-resistant laminated glass. Combinations have been developed to meet Underwriter's Laboratories Standard UL972, which provides for a number of different levels of security and differing test procedures.

Institutional security laminated glass. Utilizes multiple panes of glass and alternate plies of vinyl interlayer from 0.060 to 0.090 inch thick which are fabricated for such installations as *barless* jails to provide unobstructed vision, detention centers, prisons, and mental health facilities.

Bullet-resistant glass. This glass is manufactured to meet Underwriter's Laboratories Standard UL 752 for a multiple laminated product ranging in thickness from 1³⁄₁₆ to 2 inches and suitable for use against small handguns to high-power rifles.

Solar Control

Laminated glass products utilizing pigmented interlayers of polyvinyl butyral can reduce solar energy transmission, control glare and brightness, and screen out UV, providing both utilitarian and aesthetic qualities.

Sound Control

The use of the plastic interlayer in a laminated glass unit provides a damping characteristic which enhances the acoustic performance of these units, as compared to monolithic glass and insulating glass. Table 8-1 shows typical sound transmission class values (STC) for representative glass thicknesses.

Reflective Glass

Reflective glasses have a transparent, thin metal or metal oxide coating deposited on one surface. These glasses owe their popularity to several factors: aesthetic appeal, solar control resulting in energy savings, and occupant comfort.

TABLE 8-1
ACOUSTICAL VALUES OF GLASS

Thickness	STC value
Monolithic	
3 mm	23
6 mm	28
12 mm	31
25 mm	32
Laminated	
6 mm	34
10 mm	36
12 mm	37
16 mm	38

Since the metallic film acts as a one-way mirror, a person on the exterior has difficulty looking in during the day. However, at night with interior lights on, an occupant cannot see out but anyone on the exterior may see in. The metallic film reflects sunlight and reduces heat gain markedly.

Methods of Coating Deposition

The coatings are applied by three different methods and the deposition method dictates whether the coating may be exposed to the exterior, protected by placing it on the inside of an insulating unit or in a laminate, or exposed on the interior. The methods of coating deposition are:

1. *Wet chemical deposition.* In this process a metallic precipitation is formed on the glass surface by a chemical reaction. Since coatings formed by this process are fragile, these coatings on glass are used in insulating glass and in laminated glass, thereby protecting the coated surface.

2. *Pyrolitic deposition.* A fine spray of metallic oxide coatings is applied to the surface of heated glass (usually tinted), which becomes fused to the glass surface. These glasses may be heat tempered and may be exposed to the weather.

3. *Vacuum deposition.* This process utilizes a vacuum chamber, an inert gas, and electrical energy whereby metallic ions are impinged onto the glass surface, creating thin metallic film. These glasses may be used monolithically or in insulated units.

Glass coated by the wet or vacuum process cannot be heat treated after the deposition process, since those coatings would be destroyed. These coatings may, however, be applied to glass that already has been heat treated. In some instances, the coatings make clear annealed glass so highly heat absorbent that heat treatment (strengthening or tempering) is required to increase resistance to thermal stresses.

Colors and Properties of Reflective Glasses

Metallic or metal oxide coatings may be applied to both clear and tinted glasses. This in turn provides for a variety of colors and reflectances, ranging from blues to blue-greens, greens, silver, gold, bronze, and gray.

The range for transmittance, heat-gain, reflectance, and color when utilizing insulating units of varying combinations becomes so complex that manufacturers should be consulted to obtain the most recent data. In addition, the development of new coatings, processes, and combinations proceeds apace.

To understand and appreciate the various properties of reflective insulating units, one must be cognizant of the glass used and the surface on which the coating is applied. Figure 8-4 shows a typical reflective insulating unit. When reviewing manufacturer's literature or discussing these units with a manufacturer, knowing the configuration of the unit and the numbers assigned to each surface as shown in Figure 8-4 will help the designer in making a selection.

Low-Emissivity Glass

Low-emissivity glass (Low-E glass) is made by the pyrolitic deposition of a thin film of metal on glass, similar to the method used to produce reflective glass. Low-E is fully transparent from inside a building by day, but unlike reflective glass, is transparent when viewed from the outside if the illumination differential is not too great. However, the thin metal film adds considerable energy efficiency to ordinary 2.5-, 3.0-, and 4.0-mm glass, the equivalents of SSA, DSB, and 3/16 in. window glass.

The average summer/winter U-value for Low-E is 0.83, as compared with 1.02 for plain glass in like thickness and clarity. In clear glass, solar transmission is reduced about 13 percent, visible light transmission about 10 percent, and the shading coefficient is in-

creased about 11 percent. Used with gray tinted glass, the most efficient tinting color, the solar and visible light transmissions are reduced 25 and 32 percent, respectively, while the shading value increases 18 percent.

Low-E is also available on commercial glazing products 6 mm and thicker, with comparable improvements in performance. The coating can be used with laminated glass and heat-treated glasses. In insulated glass the outer pane is often heat strengthened if tinted glass has been used to further reduce heat pickup from outside. The Low-E coating is usually put on the #3 surface but can be applied to the #2 surface instead where it will be slightly more efficient in reducing heat transmission to the exterior.

Transparent Mirror Glass

Another specialized use of reflective coatings is in the production of *one way glass,* useful for hidden observation at interior locations in hospitals, prisons, and stores with expensive merchandise. On thin glasses the coating is usually sputter deposited and cannot be further heat treated; on 6 mm glass the coating is pyrolitically deposited.

The reflective surface is oriented to face the area being observed. Illumination levels must be in the ratio of 10:1 between observed and observer areas for the observer not to be seen.

Nonvision Glass

When glass is used in a facade to hide structural members and to continue the visual effect of the vision glass both in color and textural quality, either spandrel glass or opaque-clad glass panels may be utilized.

Spandrel Glass

Spandrel glass is a heat-strengthened, 1/4-inch thick glass with a ceramic frit color fused permanently to the back surface. It may also have insulation that has been factory applied to the back side with an aluminum foil vapor barrier. There is a limitless variety of colors available that will match the vision glass used adjacent to it.

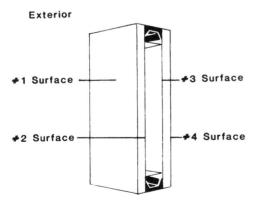

FIGURE 8-4 Configuration of typical reflective glass insulating unit. *(Courtesy PPG Industries.)*

Reflective glass (heat treated) with a factory-applied opacifier to create opaqueness may also be used for spandrel areas for single-glazed situations. Insulating units of reflective glass with a ceramic frit on the inner light may also be employed in spandrel areas.

Opaque-Clad Glass Panels

Glass panels with a ceramic enamel coating fired on the exposed exterior surface are produced to be utilized in a manner similar to spandrel panels. The ceramic enamel coating applied to ¼-inch thick, heat-treated glass is then coated with a protective overspray that permits standard glass-cleaning procedures. The enamel coating is available in a number of standard colors. Factory-applied fiberglass insulation is also available where required, applied to the back of the panel.

GLASS QUALITY STANDARDS

Flat Glass

Flat glass encompasses float products (clear, heat-absorbing, and tinted) and rolled products (patterned or figured and wired). Flat glass is manufactured in accordance with ASTM C1036, which is the current standard for thickness, dimensional tolerance, and other characteristics.

Heat-Treated Glass

Heat-strengthened glass, tempered glass, and ceramic-coated spandrel glass are all governed and manufactured to standards established by ASTM C1048.

Insulating Glass Units

ASTM has established standard test methods that comprise a series of tests for insulating glass units. These standards are as follows:

E774	Sealed Insulating Glass Units
E546	Standard Test Method for Frost Point for Sealed Insulating Glass Units
E576	Standard Test Method for Dew/Frost Point of Sealed Insulating Glass Units in Vertical Position
E774	Seal Durability of Sealed Insulating Glass Units

Mirrors

ASTM C1036 establishes standards for the thickness, dimensional tolerances, and qualities of flat glass used for mirrors. Fed. Spec. DD-M-411 prescribes the standards for mirrors and mirror frames.

Safety Glazing

Federal regulations initiated by the Consumer Product Safety Commission (CPSC) as 16 CFR 1201 in 1977 preempt all model, state, and local codes in the matter of safety glazing. Nearly identical language from 16 CFR 1201 has by now been written into all codes, requiring Category II safety glass in doors, sidelites, glass partitions, and low glazing.

To qualify as safety glass, a material must withstand an impact test designed to simulate a human body walking into a glazed opening. The only materials that have qualified are fully tempered glass, certain laminated glasses, acrylics, and polycarbonates. Wired glass, heat-strengthened glass, and annealed (unstrengthened) glass do not qualify. An exception is made in the case of wired glass where it is used in fire-rated doors. CPSC set a termination date to this acceptance of wired glass in fire doors, assuming that stronger fire-resistive products would be developed. However, the wired glass industry challenged CPSC in court, and the termination date was voided. Now that there are fire-resistive glasses in everyday commerce that meet the bodily impact safety test, it is possible that the anomalous approval of low impact-resistant wired glass will not be permanent.

Category I safety glass requires a lite to withstand a 150 ft · lb (200 N · m) impact force in panels up to 9 ft² in area. It is designed to govern tub and shower enclosure construction and other small, nontraffic area lites. Category II tests are for 400 ft · lb (540 N · m), on lites more than 9 ft² in area.

241

16 CFR 1201 also details just which lites require safety glazing. Designers should consult the code to obtain precise definitions of which doors, sidelites, and partition glass must be safety glazed.

ANSI Z97.1, published by American National Standards Institute, also establishes criteria for the type of glass to be used for safety glazing and the test methods to measure effectiveness.

GLASS THICKNESS AND WIND VELOCITY PRESSURES

The major factor in the determination of glass thickness is wind pressure generated by wind velocity. Because glass is a brittle material with no specific yield point, its strength is highly variable. Tests on identical lights will show failure pressures differing sometimes by as much as 3 to 1. It is therefore necessary to express glass strength on a statistical basis.

Probability of Failure

Architects, engineers, and regulatory authorities must select a safety factor (probability of failure) for glass design that is related to public safety, performance, and economics. By selecting an appropriate safety factor, risks of breakage can be minimized but not eliminated. Table 8-2 shows the relationship of safety factors to the statistical probability of failure when a large number of lights is considered.

Generally, a design factor of 2.5 has been utilized by architects and engineers and also by the major building code authorities. These requirements may be adequate for many structures. However, for tall structures, unusually shaped buildings, and buildings where the surroundings may create unusual wind patterns, it is suggested that wind tunnel tests be run. See Metal Curtain Walls in this chapter.

The designer who feels that a design factor of 2.5 is inadequate may make adjustments based on personal experience by utilizing the following formula:

$$\text{Design load} = \frac{\text{Chosen design factor}}{2.5} \times \text{Actual design load}$$

To determine the strength of other than annealed glass held four sides use the appropriate multiplying

TABLE 8-2
STATISTICAL PROBABILITY OF FAILURE OF ANNEALED GLASS

Safety factor	Probable number of lites* that will break at initial occurrence of design load (of each 1000 loaded)
1	500
2	22
2.5	8
3	4
4	2
5	1

* Rectangular lites adequately supported on four sides in a weathertight rabbet and assuming statistically normal strength distribution, and a coefficient of variation of 25%.

factor shown in Table 8-3. For example, if the allowable uniform load for a lite of 6 mm annealed glass is 30 lb/ft², a lite of 6 mm tempered glass of the same size should be expected to withstand a uniform load of 120 lb/ft² and a similar lite of wire glass a uniform load of 15 lb/ft².

It should be noted, however, that while tempered glass is stronger than the same thickness and size of annealed glass, it has the same rigidity. A thicker lite of tempered glass would be required in the same opening for the higher wind load to limit deflection.

Wind Velocity Pressures

Wind velocity pressures for a given locale are based on measurements of wind speeds developed by the United States Weather Bureau taken over many years at 129 airport locations. Designers may determine

TABLE 8-3
STRENGTH OF OTHER GLASSES COMPARED TO ANNEALED GLASS

Type of glass	Multiplying factor
Tempered glass	4.0
Heat-strengthened glass	2.0
Insulating glass	1.5
Annealed glass	1.0
Laminated glass	0.6
Wired glass	0.5

maximum wind velocities by referring to wind velocity maps, usually employing a 50-year recurrence map as shown in Figure 8-5. The data provided is taken or corrected to an elevation of 33 feet or 10 m.

The relationship between wind velocity and wind pressure is contained in the formula:

$$P = 0.00256\,V^2$$

where   P = wind pressure in lb/ft^2
        V = wind velocity in mi/hr

The formula has a different numerical coefficient when used with SI units.

Wind speed information is collected from a variety of measuring devices. But wind speeds are hard to record, especially during hurricanes. Since Hurricane Andrew, Florida and Louisiana, 1992, frustration from the number of uncalibrated and storm-broken anemometers, nonuniform situating of instruments, nonuniform recording, and variations in

interpretation has caused wind engineers to seek more uniform principles, instrumentation, and procedures. The "fastest mile of wind" measure now cited in ASCE 7-93 was replaced in ASCE 7-95 by an average of wind velocities over a short time period, with a protocol concerning gusts and lulls. The ASCE Basic Wind Speed map, Figure 8-5, will not change for a few years until much new and changed data is collected and evaluated. Meanwhile, it will be the basis of design—the best information developed to date.

Using wind pressure in calculating glass thickness is not a simple matter of reading a velocity-pressure table and sizing glass accordingly. With the near universal use of ASCE 7 for engineering both the main building frame and every component in the building envelope, a more complex calculation must be performed involving eight factors, not just one. It is dangerous to use incomplete answers from obsolete glass thickness-pressure tables. An outline of how the ASCE 7 rule works is found later in this chapter under Metal Curtain Wall, subheading Wind Loads.

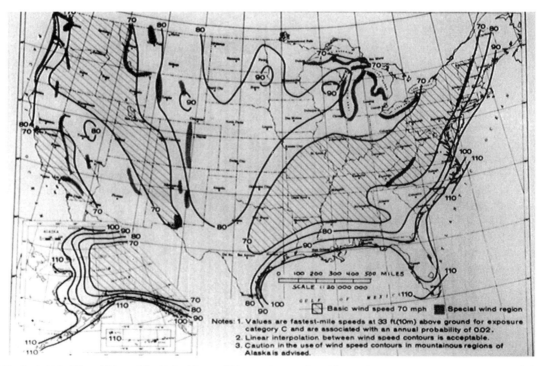

FIGURE 8-5   Basic Wind Speed Map of the United States. This map is reproduced from ASCE 7-93, "Minimum Design Loads for Buildings and Other Structures," with permission from American Society of Civil Engineers. Copyright 1993 ASCE. Copies of this standard may be purchased from ASCE, 345 East 47 Street, New York NY 10017. Basic wind speed for Hawaii is 80 mph and for Puerto Rico, 95 mph. However, ASCE advises that these values be adjusted to account for locally higher wind conditions near mountainous terrain, gorges, and ocean promontories.

Glass Thicknesses

The selection of glass thicknesses for typical rectangular-shaped buildings up to 60 ft in moderate wind speed areas may be determined from charts furnished by the major manufacturers of glass. By determining the wind velocity from the wind speed map (Figure 8-5) and by using the required wind loads of the local building code, the designer may then determine the resultant *wind velocity pressures* and utilize the manufacturers' charts to find the glass thicknesses for the corresponding wind velocities. See Figure 8-6 for a typical wind load chart.

Again, the architect should be cautioned to consult with the structural engineer and with curtain wall consultants whenever unusual shapes or conditions might affect the choice of the proper *design pressure.* Also see Metal Curtain Walls in this chapter for additional guidelines on determining design pressures for structures taller than 60 ft and for structures subject to typhoons and hurricanes.

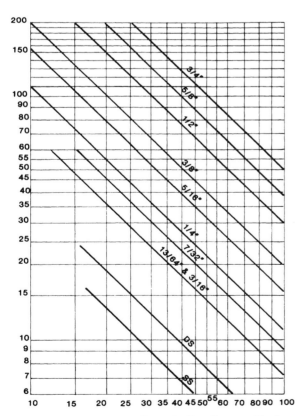

Design Wind Load – Pounds Per Square Foot
Design Factor : 2.5

FIGURE 8-6 Wind load chart.

It should also be noted that the wind load charts of the various manufacturers vary. In addition, the continuing use of large lights of glass all over the world in various climes is adding to the statistical information and is changing standards used before 1993.

GLAZING

Glazing may be defined as the installation or securing of glass in an opening. Glazing materials are the sealants, tapes, and/or gaskets used to provide a weathertight joint between the glass and the surround. Glazing accessories comprise the blocking, shims, spacers, clips, points, and so forth used to position and center the glass in the surround and prevent the glass from touching the frame.

Glazing, glazing design, and glazing systems deal with the installation of glass in openings utilizing varying requirements of the joint materials, joint configurations, and unusual systems and applications.

GLAZING MATERIALS

For architectural applications, glazing materials are used in wet glazing, dry glazing, and combination wet/dry glazing. In addition there are specialized glazing systems utilizing structural gaskets, butt-joint glazing, stopless or structural sealant glazing, suspended glazing, and sloped glazing.

Wet Glazing Materials

Three types of wet glazing materials are available: bulk sealants, preformed tapes, and oil-base and resin-base caulks.

Sealants.   The sealants generally used for wet glazing are the curing type acrylics, polysulfides, silicones, and urethanes where exposed to the atmosphere.

Noncuring, nonskinning polyisobutylene is recommended for heel beads (the material applied at the base of the channel, after setting glass and before installation of removable stop to prevent leakage past the stop). See Chapter 7, Joint Sealing Materials, for specific data on sealants.

Preformed tapes. Butyl- or polybutene-based materials incorporating an integral, continuous shim as discussed in Chapter 7, Joint Sealing Materials.

Caulks. Oil-base and resin-base caulks are not especially effective for glazing medium- to large-size lights. The oils and solvents in these compounds are incompatible with most elastomeric sealants and preformed tapes; they have no place in large scale architectural applications.

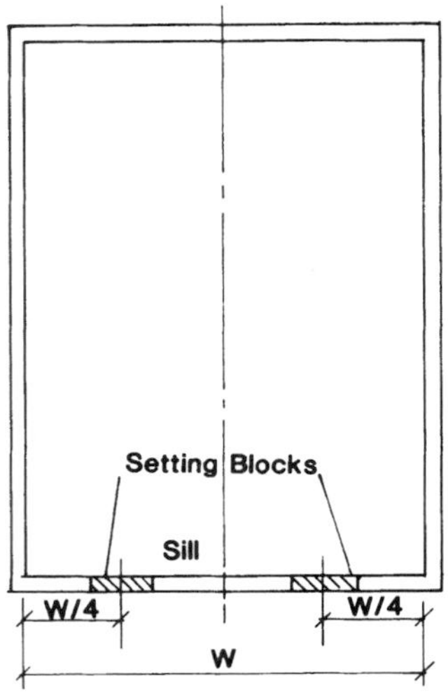

FIGURE 8-7 Setting block location.

Dry Glazing Materials

Dry glazing materials are preformed in a variety of shapes and comprise both soft, closed celled gaskets of PVC, neoprene, EPDM, and butyl; and firm, dense extrusions of neoprene, EPDM, and PVC. See Chapter 7, Joint Sealing Materials for gaskets.

Generally for dry glazing systems, the soft closed cell gasket is used on one side of the glass, and the dense firm gasket is used on the other side to provide the necessary compression. Dense compression seal gaskets are made to meet the requirements of ASTM C864.

and maintain a uniform width of sealant bead. Used primarily with wet glazing they may be omitted where a preformed tape with an integral continuous shim is used.

Spacers are generally 1 to 3 inches long and spaced 18 to 24 inches on center around the perimeter of the light. See Figure 8-8 for typical face and edge clearance and bite. Spacers should be specified to meet ASTM C864.

GLAZING ACCESSORIES

Setting blocks. For glass over 50 united inches (total of one width and one height in inches), two setting blocks are placed at the bottom of the light, spaced at the quarter points of the glass, and used to position the light in the frame. See Figure 8-7 for setting block location. Setting blocks are usually made of neoprene with a Durometer of 80 to 90 and also establish the bite on the glass (see Figure 8-8). Neoprene blocks are manufactured to meet ASTM C864.

Spacers (shims). Small blocks of rubber, or neoprene, of 20 to 40 Durometer are installed on each side of a light to center it in the glazing channel

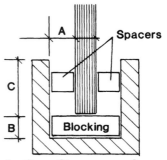

A : Face Clearance – Spacers
B : Edge Clearance – Blocking
C : Bite – Amount of Overlap
    Between Stop and Light

Check with Glass Manufacturer for Recommended Clearances for Various Glass Products and Thicknesses.

FIGURE 8-8 Typical face and edge clearance and bite.

TYPICAL WET AND DRY GLAZING SYSTEMS

In the typical wet glazing system there may often be several different sealants or preformed tapes within the glazing joint. These must be checked for compatibility. In addition, if insulating glass units or laminated glass is used, the sealants used in the insulating unit and the butyl interlayer of the laminated glass must be checked for compatibility with the sealants used in the wet glazing system.

Typical wet and dry glazing systems are illustrated in Figure 8-9. For more detailed information on glaz-

ing refer to the Glazing Manual published by Flat Glass Marketing Association (FGMA).

STRUCTURAL GASKETS

Structural gaskets (often called lock-strip or zipper gaskets) are composed of solid, dense elastomeric material, primarily neoprene, and are manufactured to meet the requirements of ASTM C542. The first major building utilizing structural gaskets was the General Motors Technical Center built in 1952. An example of a project utilizing structural gaskets is shown in Figure 8-10.

Initially an H configuration structural gasket was developed primarily to hold glass or panels in an exterior frame as shown in Figure 8-11. After the gasket

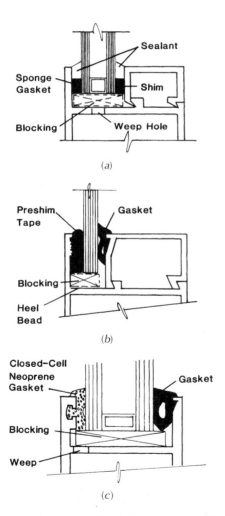

FIGURE 8-9 Typical wet and dry glazing systems. (*a*) Wet glazing, (*b*) Wet/dry glazing, (*c*) Dry glazing.

FIGURE 8-10 9 West 57 Street, New York, NY: structural gasket glazing. Skidmore, Owings & Merrill, Architects. (*Photograph © Wolfgang Hoyt/ESTO.*)

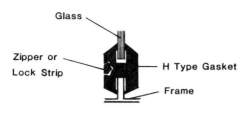

FIGURE 8-11   Typical H type gasket.

FIGURE 8-13   Interlocking gasket.

BUTT-JOINT GLAZING

is installed over the frame, the lock strip or zipper is forced into the groove. As a result, a compressive force is transferred to the lips which induces a pressure to the glass and the frame.

The prime performance characteristics of the structural gasket are to provide weathertightness against water and air infiltration and structural integrity under wind loads.

A later development was the reglet or splined or grooved gasket, which was produced to be used in concrete and now adapted for metal frames, as shown in Figure 8-12. The advantage of the reglet or splined gasket is that roll-out of glass from the gasket is reduced. Consult with manufacturers of structural gaskets to obtain recommendations on allowable wind load for size and thickness of glass.

In addition to the H and reglet gasket there are special interlocking proprietary gaskets that are designed to achieve greater roll-out resistance of the gasket from the frame by mechanically interlocking the gasket with the frame as shown in Figure 8-13.

The use of setting blocks, weep holes, and supplementary wet sealant application should be investigated both with the gasket manufacturer and with the glass manufacturer when structural gaskets are utilized with insulating glass and laminated glass.

Recommended installation procedures of structural gaskets are contained in ASTM C716 and C964.

Where architectural designs require a wide horizontal expanse of glass uninterrupted by vertical mullions, the effect can be achieved by butt glazing. The top and bottom of the glass lights are framed into a two-edge support system with wet or dry glazing systems. However, the vertical open joints between the glass lights are sealed with a silicone sealant in what is termed *butt glazing*.

Inasmuch as the butt-glazed sealant joint is used as a weather seal only, it cannot be considered to be structural. Glass manufacturers have developed wind load charts for two-sided supported glass where the span between the top and bottom frames is expressed in inches and the wind load in lb/ft^2.

Attention must be paid to glass deflections in the absence of vertical supports, and this information should be obtained from glass manufacturers. Likewise, building codes should be checked to ascertain whether this type of detailing is permissible under the code to be used.

Insulating units and laminated glass should not be employed unless the compatibility of the sealants is certified by glass producer and glass installer, since the sealants and the butyral interlayer of the laminated glass are often adversely affected by the silicone sealant.

It is suggested that information concerning recommended joint width be obtained from the glass manufacturer for the varying glass thicknesses, when butt-joint glazing is contemplated.

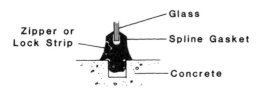

FIGURE 8-12   Typical spline gasket.

EXTERIOR FLUSH GLAZING

Unlike butt-joint glazing, which permits the elimination of vertical framing members but must utilize thicker glass lites since it is only two-sided supported, exterior flush glazing or stopless glazing relies on the adhesive characteristics of the sealant employed to resist negative wind loads in place of metal framing members. Exterior flush glazing utilizes four-sided support for the glass but has the appearance of frameless glazing. It also permits the use of insulating glass units.

In this system the vertical mullions are indoors and, in combination with structural silicone meeting ASTM C1184, provide four-sided support for positive and negative wind loads. Figure 8-14 illustrates monolithic and insulating glass exterior flush glazing details.

If insulating glass or laminated glass is used, the compatibility of sealants should be certified by the glass producer and the installer of the structural silicone or very high bond (VHB) tape.

Interior framing systems have been developed that will support the glass vertically (similar to stone facades) so that the glazing systems will appear to be virtually frameless.

SPECIALIZED GLAZING SYSTEMS

Sloped Glazing

An active area in architectural design continues to be sloped glazing in all its forms. Sloped glazing may include inclined atrium walls, framed skylights, sloped clerestories, greenhouses, and glazed lean-tos. Any overhead glazing that is flat or inclined up to 75° from the horizontal is considered to be sloped glazing, unless it is small enough to qualify as an unframed plastic skylight or some other small opening not considered large enough to allow falling objects, carelessly placed objects, ice buildup, unusual wind loads, or a human body to penetrate. See Figure 8-15 for an example of sloped glazing design.

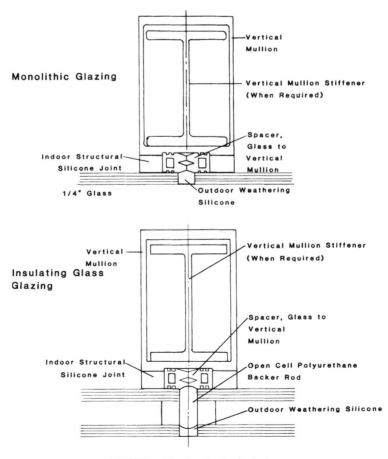

FIGURE 8-14   Exterior flush glazing.

FIGURE 8-15   First Wisconsin Plaza, Madison, WI: typical sloped glazing. Skidmore, Owings & Merrill, Architects.

Overall Design Considerations

The choice and sizing of glazing materials and methods is but one part of a sloped glazing situation. The emphasis is on safety performance, and design choices are generally not set forth or greatly delimited by prevailing codes, although the Uniform Building Code goes more deeply into performance and prescriptive requirements than others. There are no federal regulations as there are with safety glazing for bathrooms and doors. The American Architectural Manufacturers Association (AAMA) guidelines and recommendations, TIR-A7-1983 and AAMA Skylight and Sloped Glazing Series No. 1 remain the most consulted documents in this field, but it is really the architect's responsibility to come up with an overall design that protects roof traffic above from danger and people below from injury.

Strategies that are often considered are:

- Make the opening, bays or interstices small enough that the glazing is not overstressed by foreseeable loads and so that a human body cannot pass through.
- If a strong material that fails suddenly, rather than gradually (such as tempered glass), is to be used, place a protective screen beneath.
- Place guardrails around the skylights to warn persons and block their access.

- Use glazing materials such as laminated glass that fail slowly, either giving a person time to get off or retaining loads up to 300 lb without total failure.
- Do not place sloped glazings where accessible to the public or in areas tempting to intruders.
- Place sloped glazing where ice and snow are not likely to build up.
- Go all out to make watertight under conditions of long service with neglectful maintenance. Use properly sealed, good quality sheet metal flashings rather than rely on sealants alone.
- Where double glazing is to be used, make the top pane impact-resistant and the bottom pane load-retaining. An example would be a tempered or heat-strengthened pane and a laminated glass pane.
- Avoid materials that break to form dangerous fragments. Avoid wired glass which is weak, dangerous when penetrated by a body part, and which may compromise appearance. Avoid plastics which embrittle with age.
- Control fallout and retain glass fragments so that they do not reach the floor.

Glass Breakage

The designer must keep in mind that breaking may result from any of these causes:

- Heavy wind, snow or ice loads
- Impact from hail or wind-borne objects
- Placing of objects on the glass
- Persons walking, sitting, climbing on, or falling against the glass
- Inadequate or improper glazing design
- Thermal stress; damage from shading patterns or material fatigue
- Edge or surface damage to glass due to defective fabrication or handling
- Deterioration in service—as from neglect, weather, or UV

In some instances sloped glazing may be subject to safety glazing requirements. However, sloped glazing involves many more factors than what ordinary horizontal traffic safety to occupants considers. To protect the public and the owner, the responsibility falls on the architect to analyze and design in three dimensions, considering all exterior, interior, and building envelope factors—all to an ordinary level of care.

Suspended Glazing

In this system a glass facade can be suspended from its top edge by hangers. These hangers clamp the top edge, and the building structure carries the entire weight of the glass. In lieu of metal framing members, glass mullions or stiffeners are similarly supported, projecting as fins and secured to the suspended glass by metal patches and sealants. The sill is designed solely to resist positive and negative wind pressures. Pilkington Glass is one of the major producers of a suspended glazing system. See Figure 8-16 for example of suspended glazing.

GLAZING CONSIDERATIONS FOR VARIOUS GLASS PRODUCTS

Insulating Glass

Weep Systems

The glazing system should be designed so that moisture or water does not accumulate and remain in the

FIGURE 8-16 Suspended glass glazing.

glazing rabbet, since exposure to water for prolonged periods may cause failure of the organic edge seal. Figure 8-17 shows typical weep systems for insulating glass glazing systems.

Sealant Compatibility

Wet glazing materials (sealants and preformed tapes) must be compatible with the organic edge seal of the insulating glass unit. Consult both the sealant manufacturer and the insulating glass unit manufacturer for information on compatibility.

Shading Patterns

When heat-absorbing or reflective glasses are used, avoid outdoor shading patterns that create double diagonal shading as shown in Figure 8-18. Also see discussion on tinted and reflective glass glazing considerations reviewed herein.

Laminated Glass

Weep Systems

Laminated glass edges may experience delamination or haziness around the periphery when used in hot, humid conditions over prolonged periods of time. A weep system similar to that recommended for insulating glass in Figure 8-17 should be utilized to ensure a dry environment.

Sealant Compatibility

Sealants and preformed tapes used in conjunction with laminated glass should contain no solvents or oils which would react with the butyral interlayer. Generally, 100 percent solid system polysulfides, silicones, or butyls are suitable and compatible.

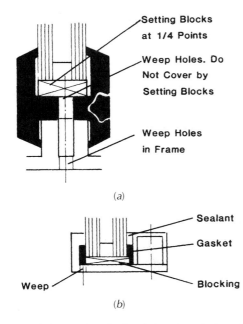

(a)

(b)

FIGURE 8-17 Weep systems for insulating glass glazing. (a) Gasket glazed system, (b) wet glazed system.

Shading Patterns

When heat-absorbing or reflective glasses are used, avoid outdoor shading patterns that create double diagonal shading (see Figure 8-18).

Heat-Absorbing and Reflective Glasses

Edge Characteristics

Heat-absorbing and reflective glasses absorb more solar energy than clear glass. Because of partial shading of portions of the glazing rabbet, the exposed central portion of a light becomes hotter than the shaded edges and will expand faster than the colder shaded edges. This differential expansion results in tension stresses at or near the edges of the light.

To ensure structural reliability, the edges should be free from scratches, vents, nips, and general edge damage. The ability of heat-absorbing and reflective glass to resist solar thermal stress breakage is determined by edge strength which is a function of how the glass is cut.

Clean-cut edges following the recommendations of the glass manufacturer should be used to assure structural reliability. Cuts which produce edge damage may result in thermal stress breakage. Glass ⅜ inch and thicker should be ordered with factory cut edges. For information on acceptable glass edges and borderline or defective edges see PPG Technical Service Report 130, Installation Recommendation for Tinted and Reflective Glass.

To protect clean-cut edges from damage it is essential that the edges not be seamed, ground, polished, or nipped.

Exterior Shading Patterns

Tension stresses in glass edges increase appreciably by partial outdoor shading. Roofs, balconies, overhangs, awnings, framing members, and adjacent structures may introduce shading stress. Horizontal, vertical, and diagonal shading are less severe than double diagonal shading. The most severe shading is a double diagonal shade line with a 70° included angle between shade lines intersecting at the middle of one edge. See Figure 8-18 for outdoor shading patterns.

SURFACE PROTECTION OF GLASS

Water Run-Off and Glass Damage

Glass surfaces will be affected by the runoff of rain water which is absorbed into building materials. As water enters masonry and concrete, it dissolves certain alkaline materials which may be carried down over the face of the glass. In some cases these will either stain or etch the glass.

Staining (and in some cases etching) of the glass is the result of alkalis released from concrete through water that has permeated the concrete and then leached concentrated free alkali onto the surface of the glass.

To minimize or eliminate these effects, concrete frames at window heads should be designed so that they do not splay down and back towards the glass. This particular design invites the maximum possible damage to the glass, since it creates a direct wash down the face of the glass. The introduction of an edge drip and a second drip as another line of defense should be considered (see Figure 8-19).

Weathering Steel

Weathering steels (see Chapter 5) release oxides while aging. If permitted to wash down over glass during construction without periodic washing and allowed to accumulate, the metal oxides will build up a deposit that will adhere tenaciously. This will re-

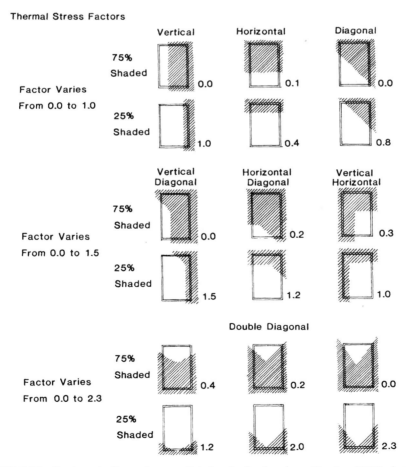

FIGURE 8-18 Outdoor shading patterns on tinted and reflective glass. *(Courtesy PPG Industries.)*

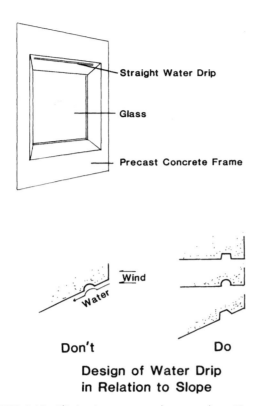

Straight Water Drip

Glass

Precast Concrete Frame

Don't Do

Design of Water Drip in Relation to Slope

FIGURE 8-19 Eliminating water rundown on glass. *(Courtesy of Precast/Prestressed Concrete Institute.)*

quire costly specialized cleaning to remove the residue from the glass surface.

It is recommended that a regular inspection and cleaning program be initiated early during construction to overcome the problem of residue buildup and/or staining.

Identification of Glazed Openings

Identify glazed openings during construction with markers such as tapes, colorful flags, or festoons that are not in contact with the glass but held in position away from the glass and attached to the framing members. Keeping these devices away from the glass prevents them from photographing through the glass when exposed to the sun.

Do not mark or coat glass with an X, floor number, or any other symbol. Such direct marking on the glass may attack the glass, be photographed into the surface, and become incapable of being eradicated.

METAL CURTAIN WALLS

Metal curtain walls are building systems made up of numerous materials described throughout this book— for example, various metals such as aluminum, steel, stainless steel, and copper alloys; glass products; insulations; coating materials; building seals; and other miscellaneous materials. Each of these materials, their properties, and performance are described throughout this book.

When these materials and products are integrated into a composite design, the ultimate metal curtain wall behaves in a specific way. It is the behavior of the wall, which is different from the sum of its parts, that is described in this chapter.

DEFINITIONS

Curtain wall. A nonbearing exterior building wall that carries no superimposed vertical loads.

Metal curtain wall. An exterior curtain wall that consists entirely or principally of metal or a combination of metal, glass, and other surfacing materials supported by or within a metal framework. See Figure 8-2.

Window wall. A type of metal curtain wall installed between floors, typically composed of vertical and horizontal framing members, and containing fixed or operable lights or opaque panels or any combination thereof. See Figure 8-20.

Storefront. A curtain wall typically made up of simple metal *lumber* members that are designed for installations 9 to 12 ft high, incorporating entrance doors. Storefronts usually have simple dry-glazing systems for mounting glass.

FUNCTION OF A CURTAIN WALL

The overall function of a curtain wall (as well as any other wall) is to provide a barrier between indoor and outdoor environments so that the indoor environment can be adjusted and maintained within acceptable limits. The wall serves as the necessary barrier or filter, selectively controlling or impeding the flow inward, outward, or in both directions of those factors which affect the interior environment.

The wall acts as a barrier to wind, rain, particulate matter, insects, and other elements detrimental to the interior environment. The wall also acts as a filter to selectively admit and control light, solar radiation, sound, and air.

FIGURE 8-20 One Liberty Plaza, New York, NY: typical example of a window wall using steel windows and a painted steel facade. Skidmore, Owings & Merrill, Architects. *(Photographer, Bo Parker, New York, NY.)*

FORCES ACTING ON THE WALL

Exterior walls are subject to the ravaging effects of nature which include wind, temperature, rain, and sunlight. In addition the wall must be designed to deal with other factors such as fire and sound. These elements must be considered and acted upon in the design of a curtain wall.

Wind

Wind acting upon a wall produces the forces that determine the structural design of the wall, the requirements of the framing members and panels, and the thickness of glass.

Since winds also contribute to wall movement, joint seals and anchorage are also affected. Both inward and outward pressures are created by winds which in turn cause stress reversal, strains, and deformations that may permit the entry of water at affected joints.

Temperature

Temperature affects walls in two ways:

1. It induces expansion and contraction of the wall materials as a result of thermal movement.
2. It affects the interior as a result of heat movement both inward in summer (heat gain) and outward in winter (heat loss).

Rain

Water has always been one of buildings' most vicious enemies. Water in the form of liquid, vapor, or condensate must be controlled by a curtain wall; otherwise, water may become trapped within the wall and cause serious damage if left undetected long enough. Freezing multiplies the harmful effect of water intrusion.

Sunlight

Sunlight produces two distinct characteristics that must be dealt with: (1) solar radiation and (2) glare and brightness. Solar radiation produces ultraviolet radiation (see Chapter 1), which has a deleterious effect on sealants, gaskets, tapes, and organic coatings unless properly formulated. Glare and brightness must be controlled through the use of tinted or reflected glasses or by interior shading devices.

Fire

Fires produce smoke, heat, and toxic fumes, which are primary causes of death in building fires (see Chapter 1, Fire Safety). Firesafing between the wall and the floor and at pipe and conduit penetrations significantly reduces the effects of fire.

Sound

Sounds are generated externally by any number of sources, e.g., traffic, people, and proximity to airports. Unwanted sound can be controlled and/or decibel levels can be reduced by wall insulation and the use of insulating or laminated glass.

DESIGN CONSIDERATIONS

Structural Serviceability

Since gravity loads for curtain walls are relatively light, structural design for these loadings follow well established procedures and can be dealt with quite readily. The main problem however is to understand the magnitude and nature of wind loads. The determination of *design wind pressures* often may be a complex problem.

Wind Loads

Under the heading Glass Thickness and Wind Velocity Pressures, the conversion of wind velocity to *wind*

pressures was discussed together with the fact that height and terrain play a role and have an influence on wind design pressures.

Since the advent of high-rise curtain wall structures, there has been an interest in and an accumulation of knowledge on the phenomenon of wind and how it behaves. As a result, a new body of information has been developed and the most recent findings have been incorporated in ASCE 7-95 for structural design criteria and ASTM E1300 for minimum thicknesses of annealed glass to withstand a design load.

Wind Velocity Pressures

1. *Terrain.* ASCE 7 describes four exposure categories which influence wind behavior as a result of ground surface irregularities and constructed features. These exposures may be summarized as follows:

> *Exposure A*—Large city centers where 50 percent of the existing buildings exceed 70 feet in height.
>
> *Exposure B*—Urban and suburban areas, wooded areas, areas with numerous closely spaced structures no larger than single family homes.
>
> *Exposure C*—Flat, open country with scattered obstructions less than 30 feet high.
>
> *Exposure D*—Flat, unobstructed coastal areas exposed to winds flowing over large bodies of water.

2. *Height.* Wind velocities increase with height above ground since friction or drag at or near ground level is reduced as the height increases. ASCE 7 provides tables showing factors to use for various heights above grade for the different terrain exposures.

3. *Gust effects.* Wind gusts are usually wind velocities of much shorter duration than the *fastest mile of wind* shown in Figure 8-5 but with significantly greater speeds. Gust factors increase the wind velocity and vary with height and terrain exposure, and are noted in ASCE 7.

4. *Pressure and force effects.* This is a combination of (1) external building shape and orientation, (2) internal pressures resulting from mechanical ventilation and air conditioning, and (3) the stack effect of a high-rise building. Pressure and force coefficients are given in ASCE 7.

Building Shape and Orientation

Wind forces on a building produce varying degrees of pressure on all facades, including negative or suction pressures on the leeward side. Figure 8-21 shows the air flow around a building and how it affects the air stream.

The distribution of pressure depends upon the shape of the building and how it disturbs the air flow. As the air moves over and around the building, the air flow is disturbed, creating varying positive and negative pressures. As a result of wind tunnel tests and field measurements on existing buildings around the world, the importance of negative or suction pressures has attained greater importance than originally conceived. Negative pressures can attain values of up to 8 to 10 times the positive pressures. For a square or rectangular building the areas of maximum negative pressures are generally at the ends and at the top of the building resulting in an inverted U shape, as shown in Figure 8-22.

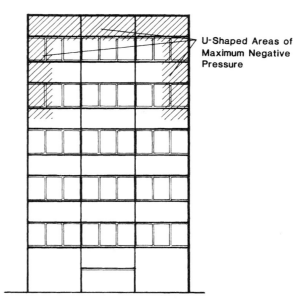

FIGURE 8-22   Areas of maximum negative pressure on a building facade.

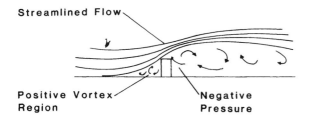

FIGURE 8-21   Wind flow over and around a building.

Converting Wind Speeds to Design Pressures

The *design wind loads* on structures (for purposes of determining their effect on glass and cladding) may be calculated by an analytical procedure or by actual wind tunnel tests. The analytical procedure is set forth in ASCE 7-95 and involves a set of equations for velocity pressures, gust effects, and pressure and force effects.

A wind tunnel test should be conducted to ascertain the design wind pressure on the face of a structure that: (1) has an unusual shape, (2) has peculiar site conditions which would channel the winds in an unusual manner, or (3) is extremely tall.

Converting Wind Speeds to Wind Loads

Engineers base their design on the wind speed map shown in Figure 8-5, which is published in ASCE 7. ASCE 7, Minimum Design Loads for Buildings and Other Structures, by the American Society of Civil Engineers, is adopted in codes either as the 1995 edition or as an earlier edition with different wind speed measuring provisions. This map shows wind speeds no greater than 120 mph for the Atlantic, Gulf of Mexico, and Alaskan coastal areas.

Factory Mutual's Loss Prevention Data 1-28S, dated November 1991, has a similar wind speed map with wind speeds exceeding 130 mph along the Florida and North Carolina coasts, 110 mph along the Gulf coast, and 120 mph for the Alaskan coastline.

Engineers base their designs on basic wind velocity at the site of the building, factored following ASCE 7 procedures to give predicted wind pressures at every part of the structure. Wind velocity is but one of eight ASCE 7 factors by which design pressures are calculated:

- *Basic wind speed.* Wind velocity measured 33 ft (10 m) above the ground.

- *Height aboveground.*

- *Exposure.* Four categories ranging from City Centers (50 percent of buildings over 70 ft), through Suburban/Wooded and Open Country, to Unobstructed Coastal.

- *Mean recurrence (P_a).* Expressed as the probability of a storm of the severity shown on the map actually occurring. Many projects are figured at one storm in 50 years = 0.02 probability each year.

- *Importance factor (I).* A value that is assigned for the degree of hazard to human life and damage to property. *I* modifies P_a. An inland barn may have *I* = 0.95, but an evacuee shelter near the coast will have *I* = 1.11. *I*-factors reflect ASCE 7's Building Categories (assembly, hospital, fire/police, power, communications, refuge, ordinary, and low-priority facilities) and the distance from ocean.

- *Internal pressure.*

- *Gust response factor (G).* From a table in ASCE 7. Different for main structural frame and for envelope components/cladding.

- *Component location.* The basic wind pressure at each part of a building's exterior (roof, eave, back of parapet, windward wall, corner of a windward wall, side wall, corner of a side wall, lee wall, etc.) is multiplied by a coefficient derived from wind tunnel studies to simulate increased or decreased pressures caused by the building's aerodynamic character.

All of these factors, taken together, are what the engineer bases his design on—not just wind velocity. Because of the interaction of all eight of these factors, the pressures calculated from ASCE 7's "120 mph map" will average higher than those calculated from Factory Mutual's "130 mph map".

More important than average values are the higher values that must be dealt with at building corners, overhangs, parapets, and other parts that exhibit inordinately high pressure readings in wind tunnel tests (and inordinately high failure rates in hurricanes). The seemingly low cap of 120 mph on ASCE 7's map conceals a very conservative and chillingly explicit approach to wind-resistant design.

Cladding Components and Main Structural Frame

Also explicit in ASCE 7 is the requirement that each component, and each item of cladding, be designed to withstand the actual pressure at its location on the building. This is in addition to the traditional requirement that the engineer see that the main structural frame is adequate to resist wind loads.

In south Florida, since the 1992 Hurricane Andrew, the *cladding and components* rule has made the building industry analyze, redesign, and gain code approval for each and every window, louver, type of roofing, type of siding, shutter, and door that goes into new construction.

The highest wind pressure that applies to any window or door in the building envelope is the wind pressure that must be applied to all windows or doors: calculate the worst case and specify it throughout.

Upgrading Design for High Winds

As a result of the 1992 hurricane experience in Hawaii, Guam, Florida, and Louisiana, the ASCE convened a conference to review the effects of the major storms. In aggregate, the studies that were presented at these meetings make a series of recommendations to code authorities and structural engineers in high-wind areas. They recommend attention to dozens of needed improvements including, for example:

- Sufficient diaphragm strength in roof construction
- Sufficient lateral support for walls; insufficiency of ceilings as lateral bracing
- Reduction in amount of rooftop-mounted equipment

- Tying-down of rooftop equipment
- Analysis of roof shape, overhangs, and parapets for wind safety
- Strengthening of wood roof truss bracing, especially at gable ends
- Stronger shingles and roof tile and stronger anchoring
- Protection of openings against blowout
- Protection of openings against impact from wind-borne debris
- Strengthening of large door construction
- Redesign of metal roofs and claddings against failure due to metal fatigue and tearing at fasteners
- Improved exterior metal stud procedures, including better stud profiles, more welding, better detailing, protection from rust, and use of stronger fasteners for attaching other work
- Protection of EIF assemblies against water penetration and delamination
- Tying-down of building frames to their foundations and upper floors to floors below
- Higher standards for residential construction (whether expensive single family, tract development, aggregate housing, mobile home), all of which suffered inordinately in the storms of 1992
- Involvement of the design engineer in the execution of the work
- Improvement in the training of code review and building inspection personnel in the public sector
- Improvement in the administration of codes

There has been response to some of these recommendations in jurisdictions where high winds occur. However, structural engineers, architects, and their clients will need to respond to some recommendations without official mandate, in the interest of secure buildings; the will to convert the ASCE conference findings into law has been slow with many public bodies.

Alternative to ASCE 7 Calculation

In spite of the empirical foundations of ASCE 7, structural analysis carried out under its guidance can produce positive or negative loads in some parts of a structure that seem inordinately high—especially in tall structures and structures with unusual configurations. As an alternative permitted by code, structural engineers may recommend wind tunnel analysis of a model. This empirical method sometimes reveals areas where ASCE 7 formula-derived values are indeed higher than those predicted by the wind tunnel test. (Wind tunnel tests, especially where neighboring structures enter the analysis, can also reveal areas of high pressure not predicted by the ASCE 7 process.) Sometimes the cost of the wind tunnel tests are offset by savings in tons of steel, heaviness of cladding, and glass thickness.

For buildings under 60 ft (20 m) in height, the Standard Building Code (SBC) bases its structural requirements not on ASCE 7 but on formulas and factors developed in the 1970s by the Metal Building Manufacturers Association (see Bibliography). Wind loads calculated under this part of SBC are often lower than those that would be required under ASCE 7 analysis.

The Uniform Building Code (UBC) is based on ASCE 7 but simplifies some of the calculations for ease of use by designers.

Pressure Equalization

A significant publication outlining the mechanism by which water penetrates exterior walls was presented by G. K. Garden of the Canadian National Research Council in the Canadian National Digest CBD 40, entitled "Rain Penetration and Its Control". The publication states that "Rain penetration results from a combination of water on a wall, openings to permit its passage and forces to drive or draw it inwards. It can be prevented by eliminating any one of these three conditions." Leakage on a metal curtain wall therefore depends upon three factors: (1) rainwater; (2) openings, or joints; and (3) a driving force such as wind. If any one of these factors is absent, no leakage will occur.

Since the materials comprising a metal and glass curtain wall are nonabsorptive, a substantial film of water can form and flow down the face of such a wall, increasing in thickness or volume as it moves downward. Should all three conditions prevail that induce leakage, considerable leakage could occur at lower levels at imperfect seals, at seals that have degraded with time, or at seals that flex and open with differential movement. One must also recognize from wind patterns shown in Figure 8-21 that the wind flow may occur sideways and upward as well as down the face of the structure and likewise carry rainwater in these directions.

Two methods are in use to prevent water leakage through a wall. One that is in fairly common use in this country is *single-stage weatherproofing*. The other is *two-stage weatherproofing* or *pressure equalization* based on the *rain-screen principle* more widely used in Europe and Canada.

With the single-stage weatherproofing, exterior joints are sealed. However, the designer, recognizing that water may get past these defenses at imperfect seals, degraded seals, or flexing seals, should design flashings and weep holes into the system so that water and condensation may be trapped, collected, and drained outward.

Two-stage weatherproofing or pressure equalization is based upon a treatise entitled "Curtain Walls" published by the Norwegian Research Building Institute in 1962 and authored by Øivind Birkeland in which the rain-screen principle was enunciated. The Canadian Building Digest CBD 40, "Rain Penetration and its Control", published in 1963 expanded on the research of the rain-screen principle.

To counteract the effects of wind-driven rain, the designer must overcome the difference in pressure that exists between the exterior face of a wall and the interior. This can be achieved by pressure equalization. Once this is accomplished, the force that drives the water through the wall is counteracted by a similar and opposite force of equal pressure. To obtain pressure equalization, an air space is provided behind the outer skin or *rain-screen*, keeping the air pressure within this space equal to that on the exterior. To achieve this, air passages must be interconnected and maintained, thus maintaining equal pressures and eliminating pressure differentials which cause the driving effect of water penetration. By permitting exterior joints to be open and not sealed, pressure equalization is achieved. Seals against air leakage occur at joints inside the wall. The masonry cavity wall has long been utilizing this principle. Figure 8-23 illustrates typical walls employing the rain-screen principle.

Thermal Movement

The temperature differences that occur on curtain wall components will vary with geographical location

and may be as high as 200°F and as low as 150°F. When using aluminum as framing members or panels the change in length for a 10-foot-long member may be from ¼ to ⁵⁄₁₆ inch since aluminum has a thermal coefficient of expansion of 0.0000128.

Provision must therefore be made for expansion and contraction of metal parts and for differential movement between adjacent materials with differing coefficients of thermal expansion. Sealant joints too experience expansion and contraction due to the thermal movement of the metal components. Since the temperature of the metals may be as low as 40°F

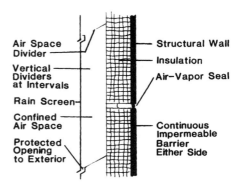

Rain Screen Principle Adapted for Metal Curtain Wall

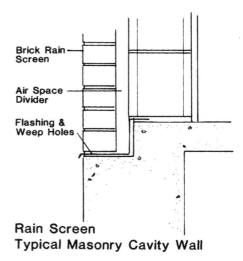

Rain Screen Typical Masonry Cavity Wall

FIGURE 8-23 Rain screen walls. *(Reproduced with permission from American Architectural Manufacturing Association.)*

at the time of sealant installation and the corresponding temperature change as much as 130°F, joint widths must be designed to accommodate the sealant's movement capability.

Thermal Performance

Controlling heat loss in winter and heat gain in summer requires the introduction of several materials into the design of the walls. Insulation materials can be readily incorporated in panels. Heat-absorbing glass, reflective glass, and insulating glass units may be utilized in glass areas to improve thermal performance. The use of thermal breaks in metal framing members too will help eliminate thermal bridges that induce heat flow losses.

Sound Control

In spite of the fact that a massive wall resists sound transmission better than a lightweight wall, the metal curtain wall can be engineered to provide quiet environments through the use of sound insulation and laminated insulating glass units and by special detailing.

Fire Resistance

Firestopping in high-rise construction is an absolute necessity as an ingredient in the overall design of a metal curtain wall. Both the spread of fire and the transmission of smoke and toxic fumes to other parts of the building may occur if some adequate form of firesafing is not properly provided between the floor slab and the wall and firestopping at pipe and conduit penetrations at exterior columns and the floor.

Light Transmission

Controlling the interior environment by the selective choice of glass to reduce glare, brightness, and the ef-

fect of solar radiation is a necessary consideration in the design requirements of a metal curtain wall. Heat-absorbing glass, tinted glass, reflective glass, and insulating units, as well as laminated glass consisting of combinations of the foregoing units, can be selected to control the degree of glare, brightness, and solar heat gain through vision areas.

CURTAIN WALL PERFORMANCE

To overcome or minimize the forces acting on the curtain wall and to provide for the design considerations discussed previously, it is essential that the designs, details, and specifications include the performance requirements noted herein and in the AAMA "Metal Curtain Wall, Window, Storefront and Entrance Guide Specifications Manual."

Resistance to Wind Loads

Design the structure to withstand inward and outward wind loads. Wind load design pressures will vary with geographical location, surrounding terrain, building height, and building shape. At building corners and on the lee side, negative (outward) pressures may exceed positive (inward) pressures. Model testing in boundary layer wind tunnels should be considered for tall buildings, buildings of usual shape, or tall buildings surrounded by other buildings.

Deflections

Deflections of framing members should not exceed $1/175$ of the clear span, except that when a plastered surface is involved the deflection should not exceed $1/360$.

Testing

Testing for resistance to wind loads is performed utilizing ASTM E330, "Structural Performance of Exterior Curtain Walls and Doors by Uniform Static Air Pressure Difference." The test should be conducted at 1.5 times the design pressure to ensure an adequate factor of safety.

Resistance to Water Penetration

Water penetration is usually defined as the appearance of uncontrolled water other than condensation on the indoor face of the curtain wall.

Designs to control water penetration may utilize either single-stage or two-stage weatherproofing as described previously. Designs incorporating the rainscreen principle providing for pressure equalization, if successfully detailed, offer the best assurance against water penetration.

Testing

Two test procedures are available for determining water penetration.

The most widely used test for water penetration is ASTM E331, "Water Penetration of Exterior Windows, Curtain Walls and Doors by Uniform Static Air Pressure Difference." The air pressure difference under which the test procedure is performed must be selected by the designer. This determination is made on the basis of the geographical location since in some sections of the country high winds may accompany heavy rains, whereas in other sections there may be downpours with little attendant wind speed. Usually 20 percent of the design wind pressure is used, with a minimum of 6.24 lb/ft² and a maximum of 12.0 lb/ft². Water is applied by spray nozzles to the test specimen at a rate of about 5 gal/ft²/h, which is the equivalent of an 8-inch rainfall per hour. See Figure 8-24 for typical static pressure test assembly.

A test method to determine water penetration by dynamic air pressure has been formulated by the American Architectural Manufacturers Association AAMA 501.1-94. In this test method a wind-generating device is utilized, such as an aircraft engine and propeller, capable of producing a pressure on the test specimen of 20 percent of the full inward design load. Water in the amount used in ASTM E331 is sprayed on the specimen. The dynamic test-

FIGURE 8-24 Static test pressure assembly. *(Reproduced with permission from American Architectural Manufacturers Association.)*

ing creates lateral and upward wind and water flow so that surface irregularities that may not cause water to infiltrate under the static test method (ASTM E331) often show up in the dynamic test. The high-frequency flutter and vibration induced by dynamic testing may also point up weaknesses in the wall that the static test does not. This test is also suggested in determining the performance of pressure-equalized curtain wall systems. It is recommended that both procedures be used since each reveals different deficiencies in design and quality of work. See Figure 8-25 for a representative dynamic test procedure.

FIGURE 8-25 Dynamic test in progress. *(Reproduced with permission from American Architectural Manufacturers Association.)*

Resistance to Air Infiltration

While air infiltration is of secondary concern as compared to structural integrity and water leakage, control of air passing through a wall should be limited to a minimum amount to reduce heat loss and condensation. Good seals are important in the design of a metal curtain wall not only to eliminate water penetration but also to reduce air infiltration. Good seals also improve thermal and acoustical performance.

Testing

Most designers will require water penetration tests. A lesser number will specify tests for structural performance. Those failing to seek test results on air infiltration are often in the majority. However, since the cost of preparing a test specimen is the major expense, an air infiltration test, once the specimen is in place, is

negligible and should be included as part of the testing program.

ASTM E283, "Rate of Air Leakage through Exterior Windows, Curtain Walls and Doors," is the standard used to measure air infiltration. A pressure of 1.57 lb/ft^2, equal to about a 25 mph wind, is generally recommended. Where high performance characteristics are expected in the wall or in operable windows, a pressure of 6.24 lb/ft^2 representing a 50 mph wind is utilized.

The permissible amount of air infiltration through the fixed glass areas is usually considered to be 0.06 ft^3/m per operable square foot of area, whereas for operable sash and doors an infiltration rate of 0.25 ft^3/m or less per linear foot of crack perimeter is acceptable.

Airborne Missiles and Wind-Load Cycles

For windows, storefronts, glazed doors, and glazed curtain walls in regions highly likely to suffer windstorms, there must be constructions that are resistant not just to wind but also to penetration by windblown debris. Shutters and other protective devices for these openings must also resist penetration.

The impact test requirements for glazed openings and shutters similar to those that were made part of the South Florida Building Code after 1992's Hurricane Andrew are under consideration or have been adopted by code bodies such as SBCCI and BOCA.

The first part of the SFBC heavy missile impact sequence is applied to glazed panels, doors, or protective devices that will be installed less than 30 feet (10 m) above ground. The test simulates wind-borne limbs, roof tile, street lamps, and pieces of lumber. Each of three samples of the device must withstand two end-on impacts of a wood stud weighing 9 lb (4 kg) at 50 ft/s (15 m/s), one in the center and one at a corner. The test specimens are deemed to comply if they reject the missile without penetration and if no crack larger than 5 inches (125 mm) long and 1/16 (1.6 mm) inch wide forms during the first or the second part of the sequence.

The first part of the light missile impact sequence is applied to glazed panels or protective devices (like shutters) that will be installed more than 30 feet (9 m) above ground. This test simulates small wind-borne projectiles such as roof gravel that caused such damage when it hit curtain walls in Houston during Hurricane Alicia. Clusters of ten 2-g missiles are hurled against the specimen in three areas (center, edge, and corner) at 80 ft/s (26 m/s). The test specimens are deemed to comply if they reject the missiles without penetration or cracks as in the heavy missile impact procedure.

The second part of both the heavy and the light missile impact sequence is the cyclic pressure test. The purpose of this examination is to determine if a specimen will stay in place, intact, under both wind pressure and missile impact for the duration of a storm. To do this, the tester applies carefully programmed full and fractional design pressures to the specimen during 9000 inward-outward cycles, simulating the action of a storm in fatiguing a window, panel, or door.

In practice, producers submitting their products for testing choose high design pressures to simulate the action of wind many stories above ground so that their product, when passed by the SFBC authority, will have almost universal approval for buildings high and low, exposed near the sea and protected inland.

Impact and cycled pressure testing of this type, as adopted by other codes for high-wind areas, varies in the details of procedure, but the principle holds. Designers of sensitive buildings in subhurricane locations may choose to apply these tests to cladding components or to use products already certified to follow these standards.

Thermal Performance

The need for curtain wall designs which conserve energy primarily for those walls to be used in colder climates is increasingly important since many codes are incorporating larger values for thermal resistance.

Thermal tests for curtain walls are relatively expensive but may be warranted to ascertain certain characteristics such as: (1) the effectiveness of thermal breaks to find where condensation will occur—on metal or glass elements, (2) whether the details are satisfactory or require improvement to permit expansion and contraction of the elements, and (3) whether the U-value computations are accurate for a composite wall.

Testing Procedures

A standardized testing procedure has not yet been formulated by ASTM or any other standards-making agency to measure air and water infiltration after cycled temperature changes, nor to observe the development of condensation.

A test method adopted by some independent researchers sets forth the following procedure:

1. Provide equipment which will maintain an interior temperature of 75°F and a RH of 30 percent and also lower and raise the exterior wall temperature.
2. Change the exterior wall temperature as follows:
   a. Lower the exterior temperature to 0°F and maintain this for 15 minutes.
   b. Raise the exterior temperature to 170°F for dark surfaces (130°F for light surfaces) and maintain this for 15 minutes.
3. Repeat the above procedure three times and record evidence of condensation.
4. Conduct air infiltration test (ASTM E283) and water infiltration test (ASTM E331) immediately following the three temperature change cycles. Record water and air leakage.

Sound Transmission

To control the transmission of sound through metal and glass curtain walls where sound reduction is paramount, the designer can incorporate laminated glass, sound isolation blankets, and thermal breaks in metal. Sealing of joints and cracks against water leakage likewise increases sound reduction.

Testing

Sound tests are generally conducted in the frequency range of 125 to 4000 Hz. At airports, heavily traveled highways or other major sources of unwanted sound, the performance of the wall at different frequencies may have to be investigated. STC ratings (sound transmission class) may be tested using procedures as per test method ASTM E90.

Performance of Light-Transmitting Glazed Areas

The designer should review the literature of glass manufacturers to select glass products that will satisfy the following requirements:

Light transmittance, average daylight
Thermal transmittance
Shading coefficient

Fire Resistance

While materials for a metal curtain wall may be selected which are noncombustible, have Class A flame-spread ratings, and have fire resistive ratings of 1, 2, or 3 hours, the vulnerable areas are those between the interior wall surface and the building structure, and at penetrations.

Fire-safing products have been developed in recent years for installation between the curtain wall and the building structure. Silicone products have been formulated for sealing penetrations that prevent the spread of fire and the products of combustion.

Safing is a term used to describe the fire-stop between wall and floor slabs to prevent the spread of fire, smoke, and hot gases.

GLAZED OPENING DESIGN

In most areas on the Basic Wind Speed map (Figure 8-5) the design of windows, storefronts, glazed doors, and glazed curtain walls can use the vast traditional array of frames, glass, and glazing techniques that has built up over recent decades and which are described in the earlier glazing headings of this chapter. However, as a result of disastrous typhoons and hurricanes of recent years, there is under development a new approach to glazed opening design for high-wind loca-

tions. This changed approach follows the stringent strength requirements for cladding and components of the building envelope that are required by ASCE 7.

PRESERVING THE BUILDING ENVELOPE

The development of high-strength glazing follows from one of the salient conclusions reached (or reiterated) in ASCE's "Hurricanes of 1992" conference: When as little as 2 percent of a building's envelope is breached, the pressures induced inside the envelope can double the forces acting outward on the shell of the building. This often results in blowout and major collapse. The following is a paraphrase of conclusions from two of the 88 papers presented before ASCE:

Adopt mandatory protection of the building envelope by requiring that the components of exterior walls such as glazing, doors, and windows be designed to preserve the building against wind pressures and impact loads from wind-borne debris. The loss of windows and doors was the most costly aspect of the storm: in most cases structural damage to the building was minimal, but the building was uninhabitable due to the effects of rainwater and wind, i.e., collapsed ceilings and interior walls.

Protective shutters are, of course, one defense against impact, although they rarely do anything to reduce wind pressure on glass. They may be applied to some openings such as glazed doors, windows and storefronts at ground level, or to these same openings above the ground floor where they are accessible by way of balconies. Only a few of the more expensive shutter types can be slid in place, drawn or rolled down, and buttoned tight from inside a building when a windstorm threatens. For most openings that are high-up, as well as for each panel in all-glass towers, permanent protection is a desirable option.

META-GLAZING TECHNIQUES

To permanently armor windows, storefront lites, and glazed curtain wall panels against wind and missiles, the customary design of glass (and frame) must be abandoned. Only glazing materials with great tensile strength may be considered, and the design principle must be more reminiscent of a suspension bridge than a simple beam of glass. Glass strength tables, as published by glass producers and the code bodies, are only sufficient for moderate wind loads with no consideration of impact loads.

For high-wind and flying debris performance only laminated glass, laminated glass-plastic composites, and plastics such as polycarbonate have passed tests so far. A second principle is that the glazing medium must (most times) be anchored to its frame in such a way that it can involve the frame's strength in resisting loads. Meta-glazing must be designed to function as a drumhead in extreme tension and not as a simple beam. A third principle is that the glazing medium must be gripped strongly enough not to pop out.

Meta-glazing starts with existing clear sheet polycarbonate sandwich and clear polyvinyl butyral (PVB) laminated glass technology. Recently developed, strong polyethylene terephthalate (PET) clear films enhances the ability for laminates to act as drumhead structures in their stiff frames if anchored so as not to pop out. An example of a protected PET film added to a PVB fracture-resisting layer, laminated to the #2 surface of a window or curtain wall lite is shown in Figure 8-26. Glass-polycarbonate sandwiches, when restrained from pop-out, have also been tested and maintained lite integrity after imposition of hurricane-level air pressure, heavy and light missile impact, followed by additional cycles of pressure.

Meta-glazing requires deep glazing bites. Structural silicone glazing beads or very high bond (VHB) glazing tapes, generally on both sides of the glazing medium, are needed. This concept is illustrated in Figure 8-27. Until many test results have accumulated so that tentative strength tables can be compiled, performance for each opening configuration will have to be predicted by empirical testing of full-size mock-ups.

GLAZING FOR HIGH-WIND CONDITIONS

The new deep-rabbet aluminum extrusions, PET-reinforced laminates, and polycarbonate-glass sand-

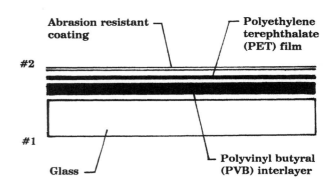

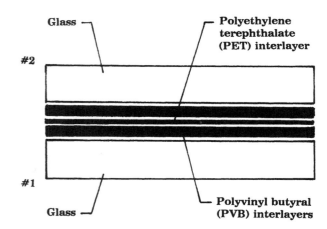

FIGURE 8-26 Laminates for meta-glazing. Two glass laminates that are strong in tension, each forming a drumhead when securely anchored to its frame. The sandwich construction holds glass fragments in place during cycles of positive and negative wind pressure, even when glass has been shattered. Polycarbonate/glass laminates, with the glass usually at the #1 face, are also used. Each diagram above is exploded for clarity.

wiches are still under development so that standard details and specifications have not been published. Most designs must undergo testing—there are few products that have code approval for a wide range of sizes or loads. Meta-glazing is far more expensive than monolithic glass—or even laminated glass in conventional wet- or dry-glazed rabbets. But meta-glazing is currently competitive with the cost of heavy wind-resistant glass covered with permanent shutters.

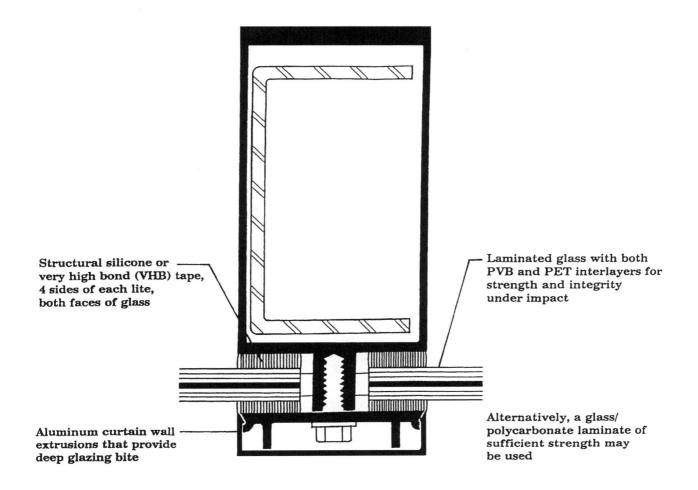

Structural silicone or very high bond (VHB) tape, 4 sides of each lite, both faces of glass

Laminated glass with both PVB and PET interlayers for strength and integrity under impact

Aluminum curtain wall extrusions that provide deep glazing bite

Alternatively, a glass/ polycarbonate laminate of sufficient strength may be used

FIGURE 8-27   One meta-glazing concept. The glass, instead of depending on bending strength, is structurally integrated with the frame to promote drumhead action, i.e., performing as a trampoline under wind and impact forces.

There are intangible factors to be taken into consideration with meta-glazing: There is no need for ladders and no rush to protect dozens (or hundreds) of lites before a storm. In fact no warning of typhoon, hurricane, cyclone, or even gale winds is needed. There are also no shutter storage problems and no aesthetic problems of permanent storm shutter mounting at the exterior. There is full visibility to the outside during and after a storm. And meta-glazing can be used in circular-head windows and other opening shapes that would look awkward with shutter boxes and tracks.

U.S. Steel—One Liberty Plaza, New York, NY: rustic terrazzo paving. Skidmore, Owings & Merrill, Architects. *(Photographer, Ezra Stoller © ESTO.)*

FINISHES

PORTLAND
CEMENT PLASTER

CEMENT PLASTER
OR STUCCO

All basic references except one refer to *cement plaster* or *portland cement plaster* as the common term for this type of material, whether it is used outside or inside. Outside, cement plaster can be used over concrete, block, brick, insulation board (as part of an EIF assembly), metal lath, paper-backed stucco lath, or cement board. It is not recommended that cement plaster be placed directly over wood or gypsum sheathing—unless, in the case of plywood, the surface is first stripped with dimpled metal lath and expansion allowed for at every joint in the plywood. Inside, the substrate possibilities for cement plaster are the same.

Terminology

Three standard works use the term *portland cement plaster* to the almost total exclusion of *stucco*. Each standard, however, starts off by defining the difference between cement plaster and stucco:

Portland Cement Association

> Portland cement stucco and portland cement plaster are the same material. The term "stucco" is widely used to describe the cement plaster used for coating exterior surfaces of buildings. [Portland Cement Plaster (Stucco) Manual, 1980.]

American Concrete Institute

> The terms "stucco" and "portland cement plaster" are often used interchangeably. In this report, "stucco" means plaster applied to exterior surfaces, and "portland cement plaster" means plaster applied to interior or exterior surfaces. [Guide to Portland Cement Plastering, 90-M9, 1993.]

ASTM

> Stucco: Portland cement plaster used on exposed exterior locations. [Specification for Application of Portland Cement Plaster, C926.]

However, PCA adds shortly after its definition: "In some localities 'stucco' is used to refer only to a factory-prepared finish coat mixture." BNi Building News, which publishes excellent color plates of cement plaster textures, sticks with "plaster", explaining that "The term 'stucco' describes a factory-prepared, integrally colored finish which . . . has come to be used to describe all colored portland cement finishes." However, *Walls & Ceilings Magazine,* an authoritative publication in this field, uses *stucco* most of the time to describe the finish. This book will stick with *cement plaster*—as do PCA, ACI, and ASTM throughout their literature. PCA, ACI, and ASTM bring in stucco only to explain the word, which they then do not use again.

TEXTURES

The texture of the finish coat in cement plaster work may range from a simple smooth troweled finish to a deeply indented one. A simple "smooth trowel" and a "smooth finish" are listed as the minimal textured finishes in the finishes lists published in ASTM C926 Annex A26 and ACI 90-M9 Chapter 12, but each publication goes on to describe seven and eight other finishes which are moderately or highly textured.

No cement plaster finish is untextured. Both ASTM and ACI describe the subtle textures that smooth and float finishes have. Clearly, for interior work in bathrooms or on kitchen ceilings that are to be painted, the smoothest attainable texture is desirable. A float finish, according to ASTM, is also known as a *sand finish*. ACI's only reference to float finish is in "sand float texture."

The problem arises: how should one describe the desired finish in the contract documents? To specify "textured finish" begs the question. The designer should try to put in words the type and degree of texture that is wanted and ideally should add a reference to a commonly available photographic illustration. ASTM publishes no such plates. ACI publishes only 11, and only to give an idea of its 12 major categories of finish. The sample wall at the worksite is the only sure standard, but that does not guide the bidder or the preparer of the sample wall.

Table 9-1 tries to make some order of the multitude of other terms that are used to identify textures more pronounced than float. These distinctive patterns give cement plaster its warmth and visual interest and hide the unavoidable imperfections in this age-old material.

Texture Sample

The best standard by which to describe cement plaster texture is the last of a series of panels that is prepared on the worksite and approved by the architect as standard for the work. The sample panels should be specified to be at least 54 ft^2 (5 m^2) in size, to incorporate typical accessories and any reveals or bandings, and to be placed facing the sun, with sufficient clear viewing space in front.

The texture in cement plaster is rarely viewed more closely than 50 ft (15 m), unless a walk carries people to the building. The relief can barely be discerned once the distance is 100 ft (930 m) for fine textures and 500 ft (150 m) for the most coarse. It is imperative that the sample panel be viewed and approved with the architect standing at least 50 ft away. Many a disappointment has resulted from approving a texture that was pronounced at 10 ft but which was found later to disappear at 50 ft.

TABLE 9-1
CEMENT PLASTER TEXTURES

Graded approximately from smooth, through rough texture, to deep relief

ASTM C926 (no illustrations given)	ACI 524R (90-M9)	Walls & Ceilings Magazine "Stucco Textures Guide"	BNi Building News "Plaster Textures"
3.1 Smooth trowel	3.12 Smooth finish	—	—
3.2 Float	3.1 Sand float	Float	Fine Sand Float Medium Sand Float Heavy Sand Float
3.7 Brush finish	—	Broomed	—
3.8 Miscellaneous: swept	3.8 Sacked or brushed (California mission)	Sacked Adobe	—
—	3.3 Scraped textures	—	Scraped
3.6 Spray textured*	3.2 Dash textures	Light Dash Medium Dash Heavy Dash	Light Dash Medium Dash Heavy Dash Tunnel Dash
—	3.6 Brocade* or knockdown dash	Brocade Knockdown Dash	Glacier Knockdown Dash
3.4 Rough textured* such as rough cast, wet dash, and Scottish harl	—	Heavy Lace Frieze Heavy Trowel Swirl	Light Lace Heavy Lace Monterey Frieze Deep Relief Web Rock 'n Roll
3.3 Trowel Textured* such as Spanish fan, English cottage, and Trowel sweep	3.4 Skip trowel or modified Spanish textured 3.11 English texture 3.7 Trowel sweep	Light Lace Spanish† English† Arizona Crowfoot Moonbeam	— Spanish† California English† Trowel Sweep Arizona Briar
3.8 Miscellaneous: raked	3.9 Combed, marked off, carved	Combed Synthetic marble	Combed
3.8 Miscellaneous: scored*	3.10 Simulated stone, brick, or wood	Travertine Terrazzo Synthetic Rock Simulated Stone Classique Brick Stucco Timbers	Travertine Brick Simulated Timber
3.8 Miscellaneous: Punched with pointed or blunt instrument	—	—	Imagination
3.5 Exposed aggregate (Marblecrete)*	3.5 Marblecrete	Marblecrete	—
3.9 Scraffitto (2 coats, 2 colors)*	—	—	—

* Usually requires two applications of material in finish coat.
† Published plates differ significantly in their illustration of like-named textures.

Describing Texture

For estimating purposes it is necessary to give estimators some idea of what texture is intended by the architect, however. As can be seen from Table 9-1, the texture classes defined by ASTM and ACI are general classes and give reasonably precise descriptions in only a few cases. On the other hand, there is a wealth of lingo in the plastering and advertising trade that is meaningless if it is not rendered concrete. What is a bidder (or a buyer) to understand by "briar" or "tunnel dash" or "California" or "glacier"?

The best attempts to publish an extensive (30 or more) collection of color plates showing the light and shadow of cement plaster textures are the two following inexpensive brochures of 8 and 16 pages, respectively:

"Walls & Ceilings Stucco Texture Guide," 1993, by Walls & Ceiling Magazine, LMRector Corp., 8602 N. 40 St., Tampa FL 33604, (813) 980-3982 and (408) 649-3466 (Monterey CA office).

"Plaster Textures," by BNi Building News, 3055 Overland Ave., Los Angeles CA 90034, (310) 202-7775.

One of these color plate standards can be referenced in the specifications as a clear indication of what the design intent is. It is good to have a copy on hand for viewing by interested bidders, although plasterers are usually quite familiar with the standard plates already. *Plaster Textures* is particularly helpful in that each plate carries an inch scale to inform the eye.

GYPSUM BOARD

DESIGNING FOR OVERALL FINISH QUALITY

These organizations have joined to recommend a specification GA-214-90 that defines quality levels of gypsum board finish:

- Association of the Wall & Ceiling Industries—International
- Painting and Decorating Contractors of America
- Gypsum Association
- Ceilings & Interior Systems Construction Association

The sponsors of the standard, in addition to defining six levels of finish quality, call attention to the fact that careless lighting practices and uncontrolled admission of light from the outside can lower the visual quality of any gypsum board finish by emphasizing natural irregularities. They offer guidelines for controlling natural sidelighting from windows next to partitions, for limiting use of surface mounted and wall-wash lighting fixtures, and for introducing decorative fabrics for walls to soften irregularities thus exaggerated. Other recommended strategies are the employment of draperies and blinds and the use of matte and textured paints, rather than gloss and semigloss.

Finish Levels

Of the six levels of quality, Level 4 can be seen to be the level that will ordinarily be sought for good quality commercial, institutional, and residential construction. With Level 5, the most expensive, the entire wall is skim coated with joint compound or thincoat plaster to give the utmost in smoothness.

Level 0. No taping, finishing, or accessories required.

> *Level 0 is suitable for temporary construction or until final level of finish can be determined.*

Level 1. Joints and interior angles with tape embedded in joint compound. Surface free of excess joint compound. Tool marks and ridges acceptable.

> *Level 1 is suitable for attics, ceiling plenums, and service areas not normally seen by public.*

Level 2. Joints and interior angles with tape embedded in joint compound. A separate coat of joint compound over joints, angles, fastener heads, and accessories. Surface free of excess joint compound. Tool marks and ridges acceptable.

Level 2 is suitable for garages, warehouses, or other areas where surface appearance is not of primary concern. Use where water-resistant gypsum backing board is used as substitute for tile.

Level 3. Joints and interior angles with tape embedded in joint compound. Two separate coats of joint compound over joints, angles, fastener heads, and accessories. Joint compound smooth and free of tool marks and ridges.

Level 3 is suitable for appearance areas which are to receive heavy- or medium-texture finishes before final painting, or where heavy-grade wallcoverings are to be applied as final finish. This level of finish is not recommended where smooth painted surfaces or light- to medium-weight wallcoverings are specified. Note: Painters should coat prepared surface with a primer/sealer before applying final finishes.

Level 4. Joints and interior angles with tape embedded in joint compound. Three separate coats of joint compound over joints, angles, fastener heads, and accessories. Joint compound smooth and free of tool marks and ridges.

This level should be specified where light textures or wallcoverings are to be applied, or where economy is the concern. Gloss and semigloss paints and enamels are not recommended over Level 4. Carefully evaluate weight, backing, texture, and sheen of wallcoverings. Note: Painters should coat prepared surface with a primer/sealer before applying final finishes.

Level 5. Joints and interior angles with tape embedded in joint compound. Three separate coats of joint compound over joints, angles, fastener heads, and accessories. A thin skim coat of joint compound, or other product made for this purpose, shall be applied to the entire surface. Joint compound smooth and free of tool marks and ridges. *Note:* Painters should coat prepared surface with a primer/sealer before applying final finishes.

Level 5 is recommended where gloss and semigloss paints and enamels are going to be used or where severe lighting conditions occur. This highest quality finish provides the most uniform surface. It minimizes the possibility of joint photographing and of fasteners showing through the work.

FLOORING MATERIALS

TYPES

The types of flooring materials are endless and continue to proliferate with the help of chemistry. Flooring materials may be categorized on the basis of the following types, which contain subtypes related to them as follows:

Carpet. Acrylic, nylon, polyester, polypropylene (olefin), and wool.
Cementitious. Monolithic concrete, concrete toppings, concrete tile, special shake-on (emery, quartzite, iron filings).
Clay products. Brick, ceramic tile, quarry tile. See Chapters 2 and 4 for brick.
Resilient. Vinyl composition tile, cork, rubber, and vinyl tile.
Seamless. Acrylic, epoxy, neoprene, polyester, polyurethane, polyvinylchloride.
Stone. Granite, marble, slate, travertine, sandstone, bluestone. See Chapters 2 and 4.
Terrazzo. Marble chips, granite chips in a cementitious or acrylic matrix.
Wood. Hardwood strip, hardwood block (parquet), plastic-impregnated wood.

SELECTION

The selection of flooring is an important item as far as initial building costs and maintenance costs are concerned for the following reasons:

1. The cleaning and upkeep of flooring is a major item in the maintenance budget.
2. The major area of wear in a building is the floor.
3. It contributes to comfort, safety, and appearance.

There is no universal flooring material that will serve as a floor under all conditions of use. Although there are countless types of flooring, each with certain properties, the conditions of use under which the floor is expected to perform varies with the occupancy and the internal environment.

If one reviews the flooring requirements of just one type of building, a hospital, the requirements—including occupancy, use, and service conditions—would warrant a wide variety of flooring materials to meet the needs of each space: carpeting or stone flooring in lobbys; special seamless flooring in laboratories and animal rooms; resilient flooring or carpet in corridors; concrete in storage areas; carpet, terrazzo, or resilient flooring in patient areas; ceramic tile in toilets, showers, and hydrotherapy areas; and wood flooring in physical therapy areas.

On what basis, then, does one make a judgment on the selection of a flooring material? By utilizing the performance characteristics outlined in Chapter 1, the essential properties of flooring material may be examined on a more rational basis and an evaluation made by a more realistic analysis.

PERFORMANCE CHARACTERISTICS

Structural Serviceability

Indentation

Of all nonfabric flooring only resilient flooring will yield and indent under the weight of furniture. Vinyl and rubber will have good recovery but vinyl composition tile may have residual indentation.

To measure indentation there are several test methods available as follows:

ASTM	F142
Fed. Spec.	SS-T-312B
Fed. Spec.	L-F-475
MIL Spec.	D3134

Fire Safety

Flame Spread

The flame-spread index for floors is generally covered by the local building code for the specific area of use.

Measurement of flame spread typically required by building code is ASTM E84. Other test methods include ASTM E662, E648, E162, and MIL Spec D3134.

Smoke Development

Smoke development (or smoke density) is a requirement usually included in local building codes and is tested under ASTM E162 and E662.

Toxicity

The products of combustion, as noted in Chapter 1, may produce toxic fumes, especially among the plastic materials used in seamless or resilient flooring. Toxicity is measured by a test method cited in Chapter 1.

Habitability

Acoustic Properties

Sound transmission and sound absorption qualities are best obtained by the use of carpet, cork, and rubber flooring materials and by the use of poured or board-type underlayments. Structure-borne sounds within a space are best controlled by the use of carpet and padding.

Impact noise ratings (INR) for floor assemblies may be determined by methods described in FHA Bulletin No. 750.

Sound Transmission Class (STC) for floor assemblies measured by ASTM E90 may also be utilized to ascertain airborne sound transmission losses for floor–ceiling assemblies.

Water Permeability

Cementitious, clay products, stone, and terrazzo flooring materials are for the most part unaffected by dampness and may be used on slabs on grade or below grade. However, wood and resilient type flooring products require vapor barriers, waterproofing, or mastic-type adhesives to be utilized in the details in order to overcome the effects of dampness. Manufacturers' literature must be reviewed for these latter products to ascertain the precautions necessary for proper installation under these conditions of use.

Seamless flooring and carpeting too must be protected from moisture migration when it is contemplated that they will be installed on concrete on grade or below grade. Adhesives or backing materials used in the installation of these products should be alkali-resistant; otherwise, vapor barriers or waterproofing must be installed to prevent water vapor transmission.

Hygiene

Sanitation

Flooring materials that are monolithic (without seams), impervious, easily cleaned, and nonabsorbent are usually the most sanitary. Generally these include terrazzo, some seamless flooring materials, and sheet vinyl. Where the joints can be waterproofed, ceramic tile and stone offer comparable degrees of sanitation.

Comfort

This characteristic is evidenced by the resiliency and shock-absorbing qualities that produce sure footedness and evenness. Comfort is obtained in the use of carpet, rubber, cork, and cushioned vinyl. Wood, vinyl, and seamless are satisfactory. However, stone, clay products, and terrazzo, while attractive and useful for walking, are not suitable for occupancies where standing is required.

Safety

Slip-resistive characteristics, especially where interior surfaces may be wetted accidentally or may be slightly exposed to the weather, may be measured by test methods described in Chapter 1, under Hygiene, Comfort, and Safety.

Slipping may be defined as a sudden loss of pedestrian equilibrium following an unexpected, uncontrollable slide of the foot. A slip, as it affects a person walking, is caused mainly by insufficient friction between the foot and the floor. "Foot," in this context, is normally considered to be the heel of a walker's (not a runner's or a shuffler's or a slider's or a pivoter's) shoe. Most slips originate in the moment that the back of the heel impacts the floor. There are many unquantifiable human factors that affect how a person slips, but ASTM, UL, GSA, Chemical Specialties Manufacturers Association, and the Federal Trade Commission

agree that the most important measurement of the slip resistivity of a flooring material is its coefficient of friction when tested with weight-bearing dry or wet heel materials.

Slip-resistivity of uncoated floor products (materials to which no polish such as a wax or dressing has been added) and of coated floor products, is largely determined by the wet or dry state of the floor and by whether the heel is leather or rubber. It is then measured by the resulting coefficient of friction at their area of contact. The weight of the walker seems to have little effect on test results. Assuming that the floor is level and clean, and that the rate of walking is not greater than about 3 mph (1.3 m/s), a coefficient of friction between heel and floor that is greater than 0.50 is considered a slip-resistive situation. This situation is not one in which a slip will not occur, but one in which the probability of a slip is very low—just how low no study to date has revealed.

There are not a lot of data with which to measure slip-resistivity of flooring materials. One series of tests done by Hillyard Chemical Company in 1947 showed the following coefficients of friction, dry, with leather heel material, and fully cured proprietary coatings:

	Coefficient of friction		
Flooring	Uncoated	Waxed	Sealed
Quarry tile	0.30	0.50–0.52	0.50–0.63
Linoleum	0.50	0.60–0.70	0.67–0.70
Rubber tile	0.60	0.59–0.77	0.65–0.74

Near the top of the scale, stair treads with embedded abrasive have tested to a coefficient of friction of 0.90.

A value of not less than 0.50 meets the requirements for Rule 5 of the Federal Trade Commission's Trade Practice Rules for the Floor Wax and Polish Industry issued in 1953 regarding the use of the terms *slip retardant, slip resistant* and similar terms.

Ceramic tile surfaces in shower, bath, and toilet areas may incorporate nonslip carborundum or aluminum oxide to render the surfaces nonslip.

The performance characteristic known as conductivity is specified for use where explosive dust and gases are encountered and is measured by NFPA 56A, ASTM F150, and C483. Sheet vinyl, some seamless flooring, and ceramic tile are produced to meet the specified requirement of an electrical resistance not greater than 500,000 ohms nor less than 25,000 ohms.

Durability

Resistance to Wear

This performance requirement is measured in terms of abrasion resistance, scratch resistance, scrubbing, and scuffing. Chapter 1 specifically cites examples of this requirement for resistance of flooring materials to wear under the heading Durability. It also provides test methods for abrasion resistance for various types of flooring materials. To that listing one can also include the following abrasion and scratch resistance test methods:

Fed. Test Method 141a, Method 6192
ASTM C501
Fed. Spec. L-T-345

Flooring most resistant to wear from foot traffic includes stone, clay products, cementitious materials, and terrazzo. Less durable but certainly acceptable for foot traffic would be wood and seamless flooring, whereas the remaining categories of flooring are fairly satisfactory.

Dimensional Stability

This characteristic of expansion and contraction due to thermal and moisture changes is well understood in the older flooring materials since a history of their performance is documented. However, the shrinkage characteristics of flooring products which are the result of chemical formulations are less well known. When vinyl asbestos and vinyl tile were first introduced in the late 1940s, these products suffered from shrinkage due to solvent evaporation and other manufacturing defects that would leave ¼ inch joints between adjacent tiles at the end of one or two years. Some of the newer seamless floors which are primarily the products of chemistry must also be examined warily, since all of the problems associated with maintaining a dimensionally stable product may not have been worked out by the producer.

Compatibility

Some flooring materials are chosen specifically for use in special areas that may be subjected to the spillage of acids and alkalies, grease and oil, animal wastes, chemicals, or foodstuffs. Obviously the idea should be to select a flooring product for this specific service that will withstand each attack.

In selecting such a flooring material it is essential to acquaint producers with the intended use of the space and the possible spillage problems that might occur, and to obtain test data that indicates compatibility or noncompatibility. A test method to measure chemical attack is contained in ASTM D543.

CEMENTITIOUS FLOORING

CONCRETE

Hardened surfaces on concrete floors may be obtained as part of the structural slab, as an applied chemical or shake-on aggregate, as an integral topping, or as one of several bonded topping types.

If a low water-cement ratio concrete, cast with a low slump, is troweled hard and moist-cured, a hard surface with little likelihood of dusting or easy chipping or gouging will result. Sometimes hardeners are called for in contract documents where properly executed bare concrete work would give adequate performance.

The addition of microsilica to the concrete mix and depressing the water-cement ratio by the use of high range water reducing agents (HRWRs, *superplasticizers*) can easily triple or quadruple the strength of the concrete slab, with attendant increase in hardness. This cannot be done on a room-by-room basis: the entire slab must be designed this way.

Applied Hardening Agents

Commonly used hardeners for industrial level traffic are the fluosilicates, which are applied after the concrete has cured for a period of time. They primarily reduce dusting and wear but should not be expected to protect the concrete against steel wheels, impact spalling, or acids.

Special heavy-duty floors can be produced through the use of shake-on materials such as emery, silica-quartz aggregates, and iron aggregates. For the most part these are proprietary products that are designed to harden floors for special purpose use. Manufacturers of these proprietary shake-on materials should be consulted about their products.

Integral Topping

Another technique in producing industrial-grade floors that can attain compressive strengths of the order of $f_c' = 10,000$ lb/in^2 is a proprietary vacuum process that incorporates very hard stone aggregates in the wearing surface. The base slab is cast an inch or so below its ultimate level, and the topping is made virtually monolithic with the base, undergoing an excellent moist cure while free water is removed by vacuum as part of the operation.

Bonded Toppings

So far, all of the descriptions for upgrading of concrete to industrial strength and durability involve materials and methods that are best specified as part of the concrete work, not as a separately applied finish involving mechanics other than concrete finishers.

A separate wearing surface may also be placed on the base or structural slab using a bonded topping, after the slab has set and cured. These separately applied products are often designed to enhance appearance. They can be used to obtain exposed aggregate finishes and heavy-duty wearing surfaces since these finishes can be controlled more readily. This method will be more cost-effective than attempting to obtain the same results in a monolithic slab.

TILE

There is a growing tendency in the design, manufacturing, and construction fields to limit the use of the word "tile" to hard units that would commonly be used on roofs, floors, and walls. CSI's MasterFormat still contains anomalous headings such as "metal roof tiles," "plastic roof tiles," "resilient tile flooring," and "carpet tile," but the drift of language is toward limiting "tile" to the familiar ceramic products and nonceramic products that imitate them in appearance, physical properties, size, and installation method.

CERAMIC TILE

Ceramic tile is one of the oldest building materials, dating back over 5000 years. It is both functional and decorative. Since it is generally impervious and smooth, it is used widely in wet areas, where sanitation is important and easy maintenance is required.

Manufacture

Two processes are used in the production of tile:

1. *Dust pressed process.* The clays are finely ground and mixed with a minimum of water. The mixture is then put in filter presses where the excess water is pressed out. The resulting mixture is placed in steel dies and then fired in kilns.

2. *Plastic process.* The clays are combined with water and mixed until a plastic consistency is reached. They are then pressed by hand or machine in dies or molds and subsequently fired in kilns.

Tile Bodies and Finishes

Tile bodies may be classified on the basis of the density which is also a measure of the amount of water they will absorb. This also determines the extent of vitrification. Four classifications exist as follows:

1. *Impervious.* Tile with water absorption of 0.5 percent or less. These are the hardest tiles and most readily cleaned.

2. *Vitreous.* Tile with water absorption of more than 0.5 percent, but not more than 3 percent. The body density is such that dirt can easily be removed.

3. *Semivitreous.* Tile with water absorption of more than 3 percent but not more than 7 percent.

4. *Nonvitreous.* Tile with water absorption of more than 7 percent. Wall tile is an example of non-vitreous tile.

The ANSI and ASTM standards that govern ceramic tile are found in Table 9-2.

Unglazed tile is a homogeneous composition that may include clay, flint, silica, and kaolin. The color and texture of the tile body depends on the proportions of these ingredients.

Flashing, or a partial glazing usually dark in color, can be applied to the surface of the tile body before initial firing, or under a new process, the flashing minerals can be marbled into the tile body so that the flashing is integral and never wears off as the tile body wears down. Flashing is used mainly with paver units to simulate the natural surface discoloration that occurred when tiles were stacked in beehive kilns for firing.

Glazed tile is finished by fusing ceramic materials to the surface. Traditionally the glaze has been applied to the already vitrified tile body and fired a second time to bond the glaze. A newer single-firing process is also in use, monocottura, in which the body and the glaze are fired together—once. Mono-pressatura describes a variety of monocottura manufacture in which the body and the glaze are pressed together intimately before single firing. The monocottura/monopressatura method produces tile that meets ASTM A137.1 but which are also documented under European Norms (EN) and German Industrial Norms (DIN) for testing such as:

EN 98	Dimensional and appearance properties
EN 99	Water absorption
EN 100	Breaking strength
EN 101/102	Scratch resistance
EN 103	Thermal expansion
EN 104	Thermal shock resistance
EN 106	Chemical resistance
DIN 51094	UV stability

A wide variety of colors is used, whatever the glazing process. Pavers and quarry tile are sometimes given a clear salt glaze. Most tile are glazed in plain opaque colors, some mottled, some stippled, others polychrome, and still others with applied designs. The glazes may vary from a highly reflective bright glaze to a matte glaze which has very little sheen. There may also be intermediate glazes having semilustrous or satin finishes.

Special glazes are used for areas subject to abrasion or wear. Hard glazes are produced by firing at higher temperatures when the tile is to be used on floors, countertops, or kitchens. For decorative wall tile, a soft glaze is sufficient.

Ceramic Mosaic Tile

Ceramic mosaic tile is formed by either the dust-pressed or plastic method. It is usually ¼ to ⅜ inch thick and has a face area of less than 6 square inches. It may be unglazed or glazed. Ceramic mosaic tiles may either be porcelain tiles or natural clay tiles. Porcelain tiles are generally made by the dust-pressed process with a composition that is dense, impervious, fine grained and smooth, with sharply formed faces. Natural clay tile is made by either the dust-pressed or plastic method from clays that produce a dense body having a distinctive, slightly textured appearance.

Unglazed ceramic mosaic tiles generally can be used for floors and walls on both the interior and the exterior. Glazed tiles may be used for both interior and exterior walls and judiciously on interior floors in dry areas not subject to wetting or heavy traffic.

Nonslip tile is produced by the addition of an abrasive admixture such as silicon carbide, or by its use in the surface, or by grooves or patterns in the surface.

Mosaic tiles are usually mounted in the factory on paper, face down, in sizes of 1 × 2 feet or 2 × 2 feet to facilitate installation. The units are spaced to permit grouting between tiles.

Paver Tile

Paver tiles are glazed and unglazed porcelain or natural clay formed by the dust-pressed method and are similar to ceramic mosaic tile in composition and physical properties. However, the major difference occurs in face size and thickness. Pavers have a face area of 6 square inches or more and a thickness of ⅜ to ½ inch. They are generally used for interior and exterior heavy-duty floors.

To provide slip-resistive properties, paver tile may have textured surfaces, raised patterns, or, like some quarry tile, may incorporate silicon carbide aggregate distributed lightly but evenly over the surface before firing.

Quarry Tile

Quarry tiles are generally unglazed and made from clay or shale by the plastic extrusion process. They are usually 6 square inches or more in size and from ½ to ¾ inch thick. Quarry tile is suitable for both exterior and interior use and will take moderate to heavy traffic.

TABLE 9-2
STANDARDS FOR TILE WORK

American National Standards Institute (ANSI)

INSTALLATION SPECIFICATIONS

A108.1-1985	Glazed Wall Tile, Ceramic Mosaic Tile, Quarry Tile and Paver Tile Installed with Portland Cement Mortar
A108.4-1985	Ceramic Tile Installed with Organic Adhesives or Water-Cleanable Tile Setting Epoxy Adhesive
A108.5-1985	Ceramic Tile Installed with Dry-Set Portland Cement Mortar or Latex-Portland Cement Mortar
A108.6-1985	Ceramic Tile Installed with Chemical-Resistant, Water-Cleanable Tile-Setting and Grouting Epoxy
A108.7-1985	Electrically Conductive Ceramic Tile Installed with Conductive Dry-Set Portland Cement Mortar
A108.8-1985	Ceramic Tile Installed with Chemical-Resistant Furan Mortar and Grout
A108.9-1985	Ceramic Tile Installed with Modified Epoxy Emulsion Mortar/Grout
A108.10-1985	Installation of Grout in Tilework
A108.11-1990	Interior Installation of Cementitious Backer Units

MATERIAL SPECIFICATIONS

A118.1-1985	Dry-Set Portland Cement Mortar
A118.2-1985	Conductive Dry-Set Portland Cement Mortar
A118.3-1985	Chemical-Resistant, Water-Cleanable, Tile-Setting and Grouting Epoxy and Water-Cleanable Tile-Setting Epoxy Adhesive
A118.4-1985	Latex-Portland Cement Mortar
A118.5-1985	Chemical-Resistant Furan Mortar and Grout
A118.6-1985	Ceramic Tile Grouts
A118.8-1985	Modified Epoxy Emulsion Mortar/Grout
A118.9-1990	Test Methods and Specifications for Cementitious Backer Units
A136.1-1985	Organic Adhesives for Installation of Ceramic Tile
A137.1-1988	Ceramic Tile

American Society for Testing and Materials (ASTM)

TEST PROCEDURES

C373	Water Absorption
C484	Thermal Shock Resistance of Glazed Tile
C485	Measuring Warpage of Tile
C499	Facial Dimensions and Thickness of Tile
C501	Resistance to Wear
C502	Wedging of Tile
C609	Measuring Color Differences Between Tile
C648	Breaking Strength of Tile
C650	Resistance of Tile to Chemical Substances

Quarry tile may be glazed, but this application restricts its use for exterior floor and heavy-duty flooring. Check for slip resistance.

Glazed Wall Tile

Glazed wall tile is made using a nonvitreous body and is dry pressed from soft clay. Color is achieved by adding a glaze and firing or baking to the desired finish as noted under Tile Bodies and Finishes.

Since the typical nonvitreous body permits moisture absorption, it is not intended for exterior use, as freezing will crack the tile body. Where glazed wall tile is required for exterior use, a vitreous body and glaze should be utilized in areas subjected to freezing temperatures.

Conductive Flooring

Ceramic mosaic tile is usually employed to produce conductive flooring. Finely divided carbon is added to the clay mixture to aid in the prevention of static electrical discharge where such a discharge might cause an explosion as in laboratories or in manufacturing facilities where explosive dust or gases may be present.

AGGLOMERATE TILE

Not fired, and therefore not ceramic or vitreous by nature, agglomerate tile are handled, installed, and used like ceramic tile. Agglomerate tile are 90 to 95 percent finely and uniformly graded granite, silica, or marble, with the full remainder of the tile body being a polyester, acrylic, epoxy, or other resin binder. The tile are dense, hard, strong, water resistant, and generally emulate the properties of ceramic products. Their advantage is their granular appearance, which extends the palette of the designer in the direction of a nubby, natural look.

It is hard to compare agglomerate tile test results with those of ceramic tile because agglomerate tile producers perform some tests on their products under ASTM C97 which is designed for natural building stone. Very low absorptions are published as the

ASTM C97 results, figures such as 0.26, 0.05 and 0.02 percent being examples. Ceramic tile are tested under ASTM C373 and are deemed impervious and therefore most frost resistant if they absorb less than 0.50 percent water by weight. The correlation between ASTM C97 and C373 figures is not readily available, if known at all.

OTHER NONCERAMIC TILE

Today's simple, durable methods of installing tile have caused a number of familiar materials to appear in tile sizes, often marketed by ceramic tile producers in order to present a full line of floor, counter, pool, and wall coverings. These products are designed and sized so that Tile Council of America methods of installation can be employed.

Natural Stone Tile

Marble and granite are made in thicknesses as little as $\frac{3}{8}$ in. (9 mm), and slate in $\frac{1}{4}$ in. (6 mm) thickness for thin-set application in customary ceramic tile face sizes. Marble fragments, reconstituted with polyester resins, form a $\frac{3}{8}$-in. agglomerate tile with the look reminiscent of natural marble, but far more water-resistant.

Terrazzo and Cement Tile

These familiar materials, the latter with very fine, very durable aggregates at the surface, are made in sizes similar to paver and quarry tile sizes. Although not as resistant to wetting as ceramics, these tile wear well and add new textures and colors to the designer's kit of visual effects.

TILE INSTALLATION

Tile for floors and walls can be set by two methods: (1) the older, conventional method (thick bed or mud-set) using portland cement mortar and (2) the thin bed or thin-set method utilizing a variety of different setting materials.

The conventional full mortar bed method is particularly useful where slopes in floors are required and the mortar bed can generally achieve the slope more economically than adjusting the structural system.

The thin-set method was developed to reduce installation costs and resist certain chemical environments with specialized setting materials. Another advantage of the thin-set bed method is that the tiles do not require soaking in water to enhance adhesion to the setting bed.

The *Handbook for Ceramic Tile Installation,* published by the Tile Council of America, provides details and covers most installation methods and conditions. It is a useful tool and can serve as a basis for developing specific details of a project with recommended specifications.

Mortar Setting Beds

Portland cement mortar setting beds are nominally ¾ to 1¼ inches thick for floors and ⅜ to ¾ inch thick on walls. Scratch coats may first be applied to walls to smooth and fill the substrate.

The installation of all types of tile (glazed wall tile, floor tile, ceramic mosaic, paver, and quarry tile) in a conventional portland cement mortar bed is governed by ANSI A108-1. Nonceramic tile (natural stone, terrazzo, cement, and agglomerate tile) should not be set directly on mortar—only thin-set.

Thin-Set Methods

Organic Adhesive

Organic adhesives are suitable for setting tile on vertical surfaces on most substrates and on horizontal surfaces not subject to immersion. Application of these materials is by a notched trowel to a thickness of about ¹⁄₁₆ inch.

Organic adhesives are manufactured to meet ANSI A136.1: Type I for prolonged water resistance and Type II for intermittent water resistance. Installation of tile in organic adhesive is governed by ANSI A108.4.

Dry-Set Mortar

Dry-set mortar is a mixture of portland cement with sand and additives which impart water retentivity. This material is used as a bond coat for setting tile and is available either factory sanded or unsanded.

Dry-set mortar may be applied to a variety of substrates but is not intended for truing or leveling these substrates. It may be applied in one layer as thin as ³⁄₃₂ inch. It may also be used for exterior applications.

The material for dry-set mortar conforms to ANSI A118.1; the installation of tile with this method may be performed following ANSI A108.5.

Latex–Portland Cement Mortar

This material is a mixture of portland cement, sand, and a special latex additive and is used as a bond coat in setting tile. It is used in a manner and in situations similar to dry-set mortar; however, it is less rigid than straight portland cement mortar.

Where water is anticipated after installation, as in swimming pools, gang showers, or hydrotherapy areas, it is recommended that the installation be thoroughly dry before exposure to this water. Since the latex additive varies with the manufacturer it is recommended that the manufacturer be consulted as to its proposed use and their directions followed as to the drying out period.

The latex–portland cement materials should conform to ANSI A118.4, and the installation of tile should conform to ANSI A108.5.

Epoxy Mortar

The epoxy material is essentially a 100 percent solids package using two or more parts that must be mixed immediately before use. Epoxy setting is best employed where chemical resistance, high bond strength, and high impact resistance are anticipated. Proper substrates are required: epoxy should not be applied over gypsum board.

Epoxy materials should conform to ANSI A118.3, and the installation should comply with ANSI A108.6.

Furan Mortar

This material is a proprietary mixture consisting of a furan resin and hardener. It is intended for use where chemical resistance is the paramount need. Furan is generally used on concrete, steel plate, and plywood substrates. Furan mortar sets very rapidly and is of value where this property is essential.

Since the material is proprietary and not covered by other tilework standards, its application should be governed by directions issued by the manufacturer. Tiles are generally prewaxed to prevent furan from adhering to the tile faces.

Conductive Dry-Set Mortar

This material is a water retentive, presanded, moderately electrically conductive portland cement mortar utilized in the setting of conductive tile. Its manufacture should conform to ANSI A118.2.

The application of conductive tile in conductive dry set mortar is governed by ANSI A108.7. Nonconductive grout is used for grouting conductive tile.

GROUTS FOR TILEWORK

Initially, grouting materials for joints in tilework were either neat portland cement for wall tile or sanded portland cement for floor tile. With the advent of thin-set installation methods and for special applications, specialized grout materials have been developed.

Commercial Sand–Portland Cement Grout

Essentially a mixture of portland cement and other ingredients that will produce a water-resistant, dense, uniformly colored material. This grout is usually white for wall tile, although it may be colored. Floor grouts are usually gray or colored, not white. Damp curing of grout is required.

Sand–Portland Cement Grout

This mixture is essentially the conventional older portland cement–sand grout with the amount of sand

added dependent upon the joint width. The grout is used for both floor and wall tile and must be damp cured. It is not acid-resisting.

Dry-Set Grout

This is a mixture having essentially the same characteristics of dry-set mortar. While damp curing is not essential, it may be desirable under very dry conditions or where strength is required.

Latex–Portland Cement Grout

Any one of previous three grouts may be modified by the use of a latex additive. The addition of the latex additive helps cure the grout, making it more resilient and less absorptive. It is available in acid-resisting formulations.

Silicone Rubber Grout

This is a single-part grout that has excellent adhesive properties without use of primer. It cures rapidly and is resistant to hot cooking oils, steam, humidity, and prolonged high and low temperatures. Silicone grout should not be used on food preparation surfaces unless it meets FDA Regulation 21, CFE 177.2600.

Epoxy Grout

These grouts are essentially the same materials as those used for epoxy mortars which comply with ANSI A118.3. They provide chemical resistance, high bond strength, and impact resistance. Joint width should be greater than $\frac{1}{4}$ in. (6 mm), and tile body should not be thicker than $\frac{1}{2}$ in. (13 mm).

Furan Grout

Furan grout is the same as the furan mortar materials and offers the same properties. After the grout is applied, it cures within minutes, and the tile surfaces may be open to traffic immediately. Prewaxed tile surfaces are necessary to prevent staining by the furan.

EXPANSION JOINTS

Exterior

For exterior applications, expansion joints are recommended at not more than 16 feet on centers in both directions for horizontal and vertical surfaces, over all construction and expansion joints in the substrate, and where the substrate surface materials change. See Figure 9-1 for details.

Interior

For interior applications, expansion joints are recommended over construction or expansion joints and where the substrate materials change. For large floor areas of quarry and paver tile, expansion joints should be provided at about 24 to 36 feet on centers. See Figure 9-1 for details.

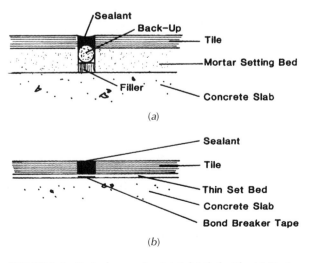

FIGURE 9-1 Typical expansion joint details for tile. (*a*) Mortar setting bed, (*b*) thinset tile.

RESILIENT FLOORING

Resilient floor covering materials comprise both sheet and tile forms and include cork tile, rubber tile and rubber sheet, vinyl composition tile, and vinyl tile and vinyl sheet.

Resilient floorings are used primarily indoors. They provide underfoot comfort. The foambacked vinyls offer a high degree of resiliency.

Selection of a resilient flooring material is generally based on economics, aesthetics, and the substrate and functional qualities desired. Standards governing resilient flooring are found in Table 9-3.

VINYL COMPOSITION FLOORING

Vinyl composition tile (formerly vinyl asbestos tile) is a composition of vinyl resins, plasticizers, color pigments, and mineral fillers, formed under heat and pressure.

Vinyl composition tile is a highly versatile resilient flooring with a high resistance to abrasion, requiring little maintenance. It may be used on below-grade substrates.

RUBBER FLOORING

Rubber tile and sheet are composed of natural or reclaimed rubber, or a combination of these with reinforcing fibers, pigments, and fillers. Rubber flooring provides underfoot comfort and good resistance to indentation.

Rubber flooring may be softened by petroleum derivatives and may require buffing and waxing to retain a high gloss. Also, rubber flooring should not be installed in wet areas, areas with intense sunlight, kitchens, rubber-tired car showrooms, areas with steel-wheeled traffic, nor outside of buildings except in very sheltered locations.

TABLE 9-3
STANDARDS FOR RESILIENT FLOORING

American Society for Testing and Materials (ASTM)

PRODUCT STANDARDS

F1066	Vinyl composition floor tile
F1306	Sheet vinyl
F1344	Rubber tile
D4078	Water emulsion floor finish

TEST PROCEDURES

D2047	Slip resistivity
F137	Flexibility
F142	Indentation
F150	Electrical resistance (conductive floors)
F373	Depth of embossing
F386	Thickness (flat floor coverings)
F387	Thickness (foam-backed floor coverings)
F510	Abrasion resistance
F540	Squareness of tile floor coverings
F924	Puncture resistance (cushioned floor coverings)
F925	Chemical resistance
F970	Static load limit (vinyl sheet floor coverings)
F1037	Appearance (after foot traffic)
F1205	Impact resistance
F1304	Deflection in rigid floor coverings

Federal Specifications (FS)

PRODUCT STANDARDS

SS-T-312B	Resilient Floor Tile
	Type II Rubber
	Type III Vinyl
L-F-475A	Vinyl Sheet
L-F-001641	Vinyl Sheet

Rubber flooring is also made in large metric tile and large metric sheet sizes that have a studded or raised pattern. These are often set in epoxy for long wear in high traffic public areas. The studs can be round or square and are available with stud profiles from 0.4 to 1.1 mm high. Body thicknesses (without studs) run from 2.6 to 4.8 mm (approximately $\frac{7}{64}$ to $\frac{3}{16}$ inch).

CORK FLOORING

Cork tile consists of compressed, granulated cork bonded with a suitable thermosetting resinous binder.

It is made unfaced or faced with a transparent vinyl layer. It is most comfortable, quiet and can be used in areas of light traffic.

VINYL FLOORING

Vinyl Tile

Homogeneous vinyl tile is a blended composition of thermoplastic PVC binders, fillers, and pigments. The colorless PVC resin permits a wide range of colors. Homogeneous vinyl is a wear-resistant material having good recovery from indentation and is resistant to oil, grease, and alkalies.

Sheet Vinyl

This flooring material consists of a vinyl wearing surface compounded as described above for vinyl tile and with a backing material that may consist of felts, films, foam vinyl, or other type of backing. The face material provides the wearing qualities inherent in homogeneous vinyl, and the backing provides the underfoot comfort.

CONDUCTIVE RESILIENT FLOORING

Conductive resilient flooring is primarily a homogeneous vinyl with conductive carbon that is heat and pressure fused and sealed into the flooring material. A conductive epoxy adhesive is utilized with the installation to provide lateral tile-to-tile conductivity. Conductive resilient flooring installations are tested as per ASTM F140, Test for Electrical Resistance of Conductive Resilient Flooring.

RESILIENT BASE

Protective resilient base strips in several heights are made for room perimeters, for use with resilient tile and other hard floorings (coved, projecting bottom edge), and for use with carpet and stair flights (straight or flush bottom edge).

Vinyl is in common use, but rubber is also widely used because of its ability to conform to sharp corners and irregularities.

Roughened backs and special adhesives reduce the likelihood of detachment in service. Where there are many pilasters and corners, preformed external and internal corner pieces may be called for.

INSTALLATION

Adhesives for resilient floor coverings and bases are constantly being developed and refined for the various substrates to which they bond. If the application is for wet areas, below-grade areas, or unusual applications, it is wise to consult with the manufacturer of the flooring material concerning application.

Materials that are available include water-base emulsions, cut-back adhesives (solutions of asphalt in hydrocarbon solvents), resinous waterproof adhesives, latex adhesives, and epoxy adhesives.

Adhesives must not out-gas more than 5 mg/m^2/h total volatile organic compounds (VOC) after 24 hours in place.

SEAMLESS FLOORING

Seamless floors are proprietary products of chemistry that utilize such resins as acrylics, epoxies, neoprenes, polyesters, polyurethanes, and polyvinyl chlorides as the synthetic resin binder together with stone chips, plastic chips, ceramic-coated granules, or graded aggregates to produce a floor covering that is unified, unjointed, monolithic, and field applied. The flooring materials can be decorative as well as functional. By formulating specific requirements, flooring can be produced to resist chemical and industrial environments, heavy traffic, high temperature conditions, and corrosive environments.

Since seamless floors cover a wide variety of polymeric resins and aggregates, the choice of floorings is legion. In addition, there are no standards that can be used as a guide or gage to measure competing products. The user is therefore cautioned to exercise prudence in the evaluation and selection of these products. Occasionally one will find competitors using different resins and offering the same glowing advertisements for their products for similar applications. A more rational assessment can be undertaken by utilizing the evaluation method outlined in Chapter 1 and Performance Characteristic described in this chapter.

Often multicourse construction is used, consisting of a glass fabric reinforced waterproofing course, over which a heavy service layer of the primary resin, pigments, and fillers is troweled. A dressing of clear urethane can then be elected for application over the base courses. Usually the life of this dressing under normal traffic, cleaner, and UV attack cannot match the life of the base courses; it must be clearly identified in the specifications as an item requiring periodic replacement by the manager of the facility.

Depending upon the specific product and the manufacturer, seamless flooring is usually applied by brush, roller, squeegee, or trowel from as little as ¹⁄₁₆ to 1 inch thick. As noted previously, by adjusting the formulation various physical characteristics can be built into the product. Some are sparkproof, some are used where sanitation in a food plant is essential, some are designed for industrial floors, and some are used simply where a sturdy flooring material or good appearance is desired.

Chemical-resistant seamless floors utilizing epoxy resins, polyester resins, or any resin capable of forming a chemical resistance surfacing material may be evaluated for conformance to the requirements of ASTM C722.

TERRAZZO

Terrazzo is defined by the National Terrazzo and Mosaic Association (NTMA) as: "A composition material, poured in place or precast, which is used for floor and wall treatment. It consists of marble chips, seeded or unseeded, with a binder or matrix that is cementitious, noncementitious, or a combination of both. The terrazzo is poured, cured, and then ground and polished, or otherwise finished."

As noted in the definition, terrazzo may be used for floors and walls. It may also be used for wainscots, treads, bases, shower receptors, and other items. It is an aesthetic, functional material with an extremely durable surface available in a wide variety of color combinations, depending on the species of aggregate used in the mix.

CEMENTITIOUS TERRAZZO

Cementitious terrazzo generally consists of a cementitious underbed and a topping with divider strips. However, there are variations of the above where a sand cushion is used below the underbed and also where the topping may be bonded directly to the concrete substrate. Figure 9-2 illustrates several variations of cementitious terrazzo designs.

Sand Cushion Terrazzo

Sand cushion terrazzo (see Figure 9-2a) provides the best protection against cracking and transferring of building movement to the terrazzo by means of a sand cushion and an isolation membrane that divorces the system from the structural concrete base.

Bonded Terrazzo

Bonded terrazzo (see Figure 9-2b) consists of a terrazzo topping installed over a cement underbed which is placed directly over a concrete slab. The underbeds are typically ¾ to 1½ inches thick.

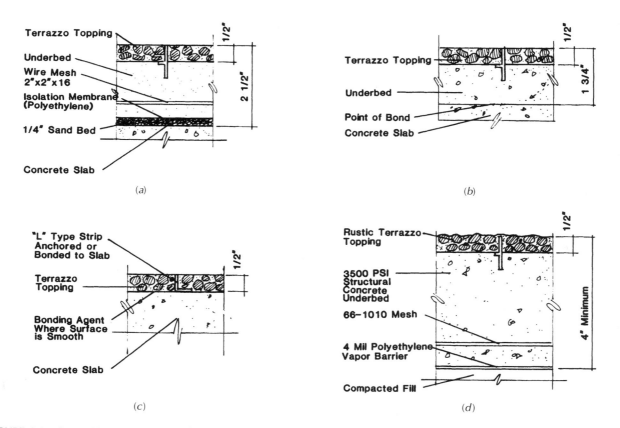

FIGURE 9-2 Cementitious terrazzo installations. *(Courtesy of National Terrazzo & Mosaic Association.)* (a) Sand cushion terrazzo, (b) bonded to concrete, (c) monolithic terrazzo, (d) structural terrazzo.

Monolithic Terrazzo

Monolithic terrazzo (see Figure 9-2c) is the least expensive of the cementitious terrazzo systems and is used principally for large installations where the concrete slab is placed by others to a controlled height and finish.

Structural Rustic Terrazzo

Structural rustic terrazzo (see Figure 9-2d) is intended for exterior use. In this system, the terrazzo contractor installs the structural concrete slab over a prepared base in addition to the terrazzo topping. The rustic terrazzo finish is described under Finishing Terrazzo. See Figure 2-3 for an exterior structural terrazzo installation.

CEMENTITIOUS TERRAZZO TOPPINGS

Marble Chips

Marble chips are available in a wide variety of colors and sizes. The type of marble to be used should be governed by its hardness or abrasion resistance. ASTM C241 measures the abrasion resistance of marble, and none should be used with a value below H_a 10. For exterior terrazzo, the abrasion resistance should be H_a 50 minimum. In addition no marble should be used that has a 24-hour absorption rate in excess of 0.75 percent for interior terrazzo and 0.25 percent for exterior terrazzo, since it may result in an unsightly appearance. Marble chip sizes are graded in accordance with standards adopted by the NTMA as shown in Table 9-4.

Portland Cement

To better control the ultimate topping matrix color it is best to confine the use of portland cement to white

TABLE 9-4
MARBLE CHIP SIZES FOR TERRAZZO

Number	Passes screen (inches)	Retained on screen (inches)
0	1/8	1/16
1	1/4	1/8
2	3/8	1/4
3	1/2	3/8
4	5/8	1/2
5	3/4	5/8
6	7/8	3/4
7	1	7/8
8	1 1/8	1

portland cement. Gray portland cement is not color controlled, and variations in color may result. White portland cement should meet the requirements of ASTM C150.

Colorants

Use alkali-resistant, nonfading color pigments.

Topping Mix

The topping mix is typically one bag of portland cement, 200 pounds of marble chips, colorant as required to produce the desired color, and 5 gallons of water.

TERRAZZO UNDERBEDS

Terrazzo underbeds are mixtures of gray portland cement and sand in the ratio of 1:4½ plus sufficient water to provide workability at as low a slump as possible.

STRUCTURAL TERRAZZO UNDERBEDS

Structural terrazzo underbeds consist of a mixture of gray portland cement, pea or crushed gravel less than ⅜ inch diameter, sand, and water to produce a mixture with a slump less than 3 inches and a strength of 3500 lb/in².

DIVIDER STRIPS FOR CEMENTITIOUS TERRAZZO

Divider strips may be a white alloy of zinc, brass, stainless steel, or plastic. Thicknesses range from ⅛ to ¼ inch or more, and depths from ¾ to 1½ inches.

Expansion or control strips are sandwich-type dividers with a filler of neoprene or a removable filler to allow for installation of a bulk sealant compound.

Divider strips are utilized to control and localize any shrinkage or flexure cracks. They are also used to permit changes in the terrazzo mix design. Expansion-type dividers are used over expansion joints in the substrate and where greater movement is anticipated. Divider strips also serve as leveling guides.

FINISHING TERRAZZO

Ground and Polished Surface

Rough grinding. Grind with 24 or finer grit stones; then follow with 80 or finer grit stones.

Grouting. Upon completion of rough grinding, apply a grout consisting of the portland cement and colorant used in the topping mix. Allow the grout to cure.

Fine grinding. Grind the surface with 80 or finer grit stones until all grout is removed. The finished surface should show a minimum of 75 to 80 percent marble chips.

Rustic Terrazzo Finish

Granite or quartz chips may be substituted for marble chips for exterior rustic terrazzo. To finish, expose the aggregate by means of a pressure hose, absorbent rolling, or use of a retarder so that approximately ¹⁄₁₆ inch of the cement matrix is removed.

SEAMLESS TERRAZZO SYSTEMS

In seamless terrazzo systems, two alternative matrix materials are used. In an *acrylic* system, the latex is used to modify the portland cement so that the topping varies between ¼ and ½ inch. In the *resinous* matrix system, epoxy or polyester resins are used which may result in toppings that are ⅛ to ¼ inch thick. Consult the NTMA guide specifications for placing, finishing, and testing seamless terrazzo flooring.

Special divider strips for these thin-bed terrazzo toppings are available. These are used to simulate the appearance of standard cementitious terrazzo, not to control cracking.

Also review requirements set forth in this chapter for seamless type floors to evaluate thin-set resin matrix terrazzo floor systems.

WOOD FLOORING

Finished wood floors used for architectural applications are generally the hardwoods that are selected for color, grain, and texture. Hardwoods that have dense, hard surfaces will withstand heavy wear and abrasion. These include oak, sugar maple, birch, beech, pecan, and teak.

TYPES

Wood flooring for architectural applications is available in several forms as follows:

Strip flooring. Long, narrow strips, with tongued and grooved edge along the sides (T&G) and on the ends (end matched).

Plank flooring. Similar in every respect to strip floor except that it consists of wide boards.

Parquet flooring (thin block flooring). An assemblage of solid wood strips in small panel forms that varies in thickness from 5/16 to 3/4 inch and in face size from 6 × 6 inches to 18 × 18 inches and produces a mosaic effect in varying patterns. Sometimes, the patterns are the result of integrating varying species of wood.

Solid Block Flooring

Wood floors for heavy-duty industrial and commercial applications are made in solid block form, from 2 to 4 inches thick, 3 to 4 inches wide, and 6 to 8 inches long. The species of wood used are yellow pine and oak, edge grained. The flooring is treated against decay, vermin, and moisture with either creosote oil or CCA preservative treatment.

Wood floors for use in certain architectural applications such as museums, lobbies, libraries, and airports are made in solid wood block form that is assembled into a strip or parquet pattern. The wood block uses douglas fir, hemlock, or pine, 1 to 2½ inches thick and 3 to 5 inches wide with an edge grain and is preservative treated.

Irradiated Wood Flooring

Specially treated wood flooring is obtained by forcing an acrylic resin into the cell structure of the wood using a vacuum/pressure cycle and then subjecting the units to gamma ray irradiation. The resultant composite is claimed to have an abrasion resistance and hardness superior to that of untreated wood. This flooring is available in strip, plank, tile, and parquet, in a variety of wood species.

GRADES

Grading for hardwood strip flooring is controlled by two associations, National Oak Flooring Manufacturers' Association (NOFMA) and Maple Flooring Manufacturers' Association (MFMA). NOFMA grades oak, beech, birch, maple, and pecan flooring. MFMA grades maple, beech, and birch flooring. The grading rules of both associations also govern sizes and lengths.

Unfinished oak is graded Clear (Plain or Quarter Sawn), Select & Better, Select, No. 1 Common, and No. 2 Common.

Beech, birch, and maple are graded First Grade, Second & Better Grade, Second Grade, Third & Better Grade, and Third Grade.

Pecan flooring is graded First Grade Red, First Grade White, First Grade, Second Grade Red, Second Grade, and Third Grade.

Prefinished oak flooring is graded Prime, Standard & Better, Standard Grade, Tavern & Better Grade, and Tavern Grade.

INSTALLATION

Parquet flooring (thin-block) and block flooring are laid in asphaltic mastic on concrete. Strip and plank flooring are laid in a variety of ways as described herein.

Installation of Strip and Plank Flooring on Concrete

For slabs on grade place a vapor stop below slab if grade is ever damp. For slabs above grade place a vapor barrier (6 mil polyethylene) on the slab with ends and edges lapped 4 inches. A wood nailing base using either plywood or sleepers is then placed over the vapor barrier and the flooring blind nailed to the nailing base as shown in Figure 9-3. Free movement of air must be provided for by allowing at least a 1-inch space around the entire perimeter. When plywood is used as a nailing base there should also be a ¼ to ½ inch space between the plywood panels.

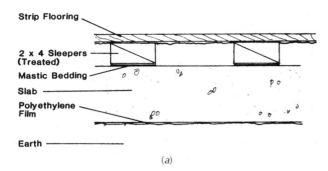

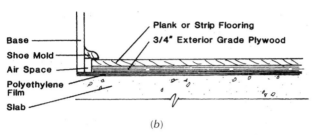

FIGURE 9-3 Installation of plank or strip flooring over concrete slabs. (a) Strip flooring over sleepers, (b) strip flooring over plywood base.

Special Attachment and Installation Systems

For gymnasium floors, sports floors of all types, and large expanses of wood strip floors, special proprietary steel channel and clip systems and resilient neoprene pad systems are available utilizing a multitude of installation techniques.

Nailing

Strip and plank floors installed over plywood on wood sleepers must be securely and adequately blind nailed to provide a rigid installation and to prevent squeaks.

Precautions

Wood floors should be installed only after all the wet trades (masonry, plaster, tile, terrazzo) have com-

pleted their work and after the concrete slabs on which they are to be placed are dry. While the work of these wet trades is being performed, the wood flooring to be used should not be stored within the building.

CARPET

DEFINITION

Carpet. A general designation for fabric used as a floor covering of woven, knitted, or needle-tufted yarns.

FIBERS AND YARNS

Fiber

Fiber is any substance, natural or synthetic, used in thread or yarn form for processing as a textile. Pile fibers commonly used in carpet include:

Acrylic and acrylic/modacrylic blends

Nylon

Olefin (polypropylene)

Polyester

Wool

Yarn

Yarn is defined as a continuous strand for tufting, weaving, or knitting:

Continuous filament yarn. Yarn formed into a continuous strand from two or more continuous filaments.

Spun yarn.   Yarn formed from staple by spinning or twisting into a single continuous strand or yarn.

FIBERS, APPEARANCE, AND WEAR LIFE

Acrylic.   Good wearing ability; low moisture absorbency leads to good soil resistance. Excellent resilience; easy to clean, good color retention; low static build-up.

Nylon.   Exceptional abrasion resistance and color and texture retention. Tends to show soil more readily.

Olefin (polypropylene).   Not attacked by mildew. Highly resistant to soiling and staining. Lacks resilience and luxurious feel underfoot. Used for indoor-outdoor carpeting. Check flammability.

Polyester.   Excellent mildew and abrasion resistance. Good color retention.

Wool.   Good wearing qualities, excellent texture retention and resiliency.

MANUFACTURING TECHNIQUES

There are several different types of carpet construction, the more important being woven, tufted, needlebonded, knitted, and loomed.

Woven carpet is produced by three basic machine techniques—namely, on Velvet, Wilton, and Axminster looms. The looms generally interweave the pile yarns and the backing yarn in one operation. These carpets are the most dimensionally stable and have good wearing qualities.

Tufted carpet today represents about 90 percent of all carpet manufactured. The carpet is produced by needles rather than by a weaving process. A row of needles, the width of the carpet, is used to stitch the yarn into backing. The yarn is held there by a latex coating.

Needlebonded carpet is a technique used with polypropylene for the production of indoor-outdoor carpeting.

FACTORS AFFECTING CARPET QUALITY

To compare the relative quality of carpet regardless of the manner of manufacture, one need only compare (1) face weight, (2) pile height, and (3) density factors, everything else being equal. In general, the deeper, denser, and heavier the pile, the better the carpet.

Face weight.   Weight of face yarn in one square yard expressed in ounces.

Pile height.   Depth of pile between backing and top of pile, expressed in decimals of an inch. In woven carpet, pile height is given as wire size also in decimals of an inch.

Density factor (tufted carpet).   This aspect is defined in terms of gage and stitches per inch. Gage represents the distance between rows of tufts across the width of the carpet: $1/8$ inch gage means the vertical rows of yarn across the width are $1/8$ inch apart. The narrower the gage, the denser the yarn. Stitches per inch indicate the number of horizontal rows of tufts per one inch of length. The more stitches per inch, the denser the carpet.

Density factors (woven carpet).   This aspect is defined in terms of pitch and rows per inch. Pitch is the same as gage for tufted carpet except that it is traditionally measured in a 27-inch width of finished goods. For example, if pitch is specified as 216, there are 216 rows of yarn in every 27 inches of width or the tufts are $1/8$ inch apart. Rows per inch for woven carpet is the same as stitches per inch in tufted carpet.

CARPET CUSHION

Carpet cushion is defined as any material placed under carpet to provide softness when it is walked on. Other terms used in place of cushion include padding, underlayment, and lining. Carpet cushion under carpet offers several advantages as follows:

1. Adds additional acoustical value
2. Adds additional thermal insulation
3. Provides additional comfort
4. Adds to the life of the carpet

Carpets are available both with and without attached cushions. Cushion-backed carpets are much more difficult to seam, since they cannot be stretched to meet installation conditions.

Types of Cushions

Several types of carpet cushion are available, including:

Felt.   Composed of natural hair, fiber, or a combination of both.
Foam and sponge rubber.   Composed of synthetic rubber, latex, or urethane foams.
Proprietary types.   Including polyester pneumatic cellular fiber and resinated synthetic fiber.

Sizes and Weights

Cushion material comes in a variety of sizes and weights. Felt cushion is available in widths up to 12 feet and in weights from 32 to 86 ounces per square yard. Sponge rubber is available in widths up to 12 feet and in weights from 41 to 120 ounces per square yard.

UNITIZED BACKING

Carpet is available with a heavy fiber cushion adhesively attached to the backing plys, and known as unitized backing.

PERFORMANCE CHARACTERISTICS

Safety, Health

Architects must ascertain which flame spread test method will be accepted for carpet. ASTM E84 is still required by many codes. The radiant panel flooring flammability test, ASTM E648, is favored as a measure of flame spread. Another test is the Methanamine Tablet Test DOC FF1-70. Since there is little correlation between these test methods, check the local building code.

Total VOC emission of newly installed carpet should not exceed 0.1 mg/m^2/h after 72 hours in place.

Static Control

Static electricity is generated by friction when one walks across a carpet. The variables include humidity, shoe soles, and generic fiber types. Static can be controlled by raising the humidity above 40 percent or by the use of built-in static inhibitors such as special fibers to reduce the amount of static accumulation.

Test Methods

Producers monitor carpet for styrene and VOC emissions following Carpet and Rug Institute tests. Other tests are listed in Table 9-5.

TABLE 9-5
TEST PROCEDURES FOR CARPET

American Association of Textile Chemists and Colorists (AATCC)	
COLORFASTNESS	
Crocking*	8
Light	16-E
Water	107
Ozone	129
SOILING	
Visual rating	121
Service soiling	122
Accelerated soiling	123

American Society of Testing and Materials (ASTM)	
TEST PROCEDURES	
Moth and larvae resistance	D116
Shrinkage	D138
Pile yarn construction	D418
Tuft bind	D1335
Abrasion	D1175
Flammability	D2859
Critical radiant flux	E648

Federal Specifications (FS)	
TEST PROCEDURES	
Mildew resistance	CCC-T-191B

* Crocking: Loss of color due to rubbing off as a result of improper dye penetration.

CARPET INSTALLATION

Two methods of installation are used:

Glue-down. Using no cushion or an attached cushion, carpet is adhered directly over a dry substrate. Adhesive should out-gas less than 3 mg/m²/h total VOCs after 24 hours.

Tackless or stretched. Carpet stripping consisting of water-resistant plywood with angular pins protruding from the top is nailed or glued around the room perimeter. Carpet cushion is then placed within the confines of the carpet stripping. The carpet is then placed over the cushion and stripping by kicking or power stretching the carpet over the stripping.

Shop drawings should be required to show seam locations and pattern direction.

PAINTS AND COATINGS

The chemistry of paints and coatings is rather complex and is outside the needs of the individual responsible for selecting a paint or coating system for covering a specific surface in an architectural application. The architect's interests are better served by acquiring a knowledge of the generic properties of paint products and their optimal use in a particular environment on a specific substrate. Starting with this performance information is far more valuable to the architect or specifier than a knowledge of the chemistry of paints and coatings.

PERFORMANCE

A paint is usually selected to perform satisfactorily in several of the following ways: protection, appearance, sanitation and cleanliness, illumination and visibility, safety and psychological impact, fire resistance, and serviceability.

Protection

Protection of the surface is afforded by a paint or coating system against moisture, chemical and industrial fumes, sunlight, abrasion, dust and dirt, and temperature variations.

Appearance

Color, texture, and luster are properties that an architect can use in selecting a paint or coating system to enhance the appearance of specific surfaces and to create comfortable living and working areas.

Sanitation and Health

Specific paint and coating formulations may be selected to provide tilelike surfaces in areas of food preparation, food processing, shower and hydrotherapy areas, and similar spaces. In addition to being lead free, latex paints should be free of fungicides containing mercury compounds.

Illumination and Visibility

To brighten rooms and increase visibility, white and light-tinted paints are used to enhance these characteristics. In addition the degree of gloss used has an effect on the amount of reflected light and on the diffusion and distribution of light.

Safety and Psychological Impact

Colors are useful in (1) the degree of safety that can be improved around operating machinery, (2) identifying piping and ductwork, (3) identifying hazardous areas, (4) traffic control, (5) providing for the well-being of patients in hospitals by careful choice of colors for specific responses, and (6) providing eye relief in areas where severe visual tasks are undertaken.

Fire Resistance

Selection of specific formulations with fire-resistive and fire-retardant properties is beneficial for application on specific substrates in certain areas requiring these properties.

Serviceability

The paint must be cleanable without change of luster, must resist mildew and yellowing, and must be easily recoated. Other practical, functional aspects can be added for each project type and location.

PAINT MATERIALS AND THEIR PROPERTIES

There is no one universal paint material that can be applied to cover all substrates under all conditions of use. Paint formulations therefore are compromises by which manufacturers incorporate certain ingredients having specific properties to serve certain intended purposes over a period of time.

What Is Paint?

A paint or coating in a general sense is any liquid material, which when spread in a thin layer, solidifies into a film that obscures the surfaces on which it is applied, and provides a protective and decorative coating.

Paint Composition

Pigmented paints or coatings are made up of two basic components—a pigment and a vehicle. The vehicle, which is the liquid component, generally consists of two primary materials: one nonvolatile (the binder) and the other volatile (the solvent).

BINDERS

The binder or nonvolatile material forms the film. Its name comes from the fact that it binds and holds the pigment to the surface. The volatile part (a solvent or water) dissolves or emulsifies the film-forming binder material and is used to adjust the viscosity of the mixture to make it easy to apply.

In addition to these primary materials, the vehicle will contain other materials whose function varies according to the nature of the binder and the volatile component. Dryers, for instance, are heavy metal compounds that catalyze the resin vehicles in oil based paints and enamels. Emulsifiers are necessary adjuncts to the water in emulsion paints. Emulsion paints are also formulated to include antifreeze and fungicidal substances as needed for the conditions of use.

The different properties of paints and coatings stem primarily from the differing characteristics of the binders. The basic description of a paint comes from the type of binder it contains. We speak of latex paints or oil paints—broad categories of binders—and to this we often add the name of the resin: vinyl, acrylic, alkyd, and so forth.

Flat, semigloss, and enamel paints describe the relation between the binder and the vehicle. Enamel vehicles almost totally encapsulate the pigment particles in binder, giving a smooth, glossy appearance. Flat paints tend to let pigment particles show, producing a matte finish. Flat paints do not protect the pigment particles from UV and pollution attack the way an enamel does. When flat paints are cleaned, the particles at the surface tend to be scrubbed off, leaving the cured vehicle film behind, and visibly *shining up* the paint.

The Basic Binders

The workhorses of paint for architectural decoration and protection are based on the two classes of binders described below. Except for a few surfaces with out-of-the-ordinary performance requirements, varieties of these two paint types can be used to protect and beautify every part of a building—inside and out.

Water Reducible Paints

As their technology advances, these paints take over a larger portion of the paint market with each passing year. The rise of volatile organic compound (VOC) restrictions requires reduction in the quantities of hydrocarbon solvents that are present in alkyd and other oil paints. Water reducible paints not only include the widely used latex paints, which dry by evaporation of water, but also the water reducible chemical cross-linking paints which simultaneously dry and chemically cure.

Formerly styrene-butadiene and polyvinyl acetate latexes were the most widely used water reducibles. Their advantages were their substrate alkalinity-resistance, ease of thinning, low odor, quick drying, and simplified cleanup. Acrylic-based, vinyl-based, and vinyl acrylic-based water reducibles have taken over many of the more demanding painting tasks such as exterior coatings, metal coatings, deck coatings, and enamel-like coatings. There are also acrylic-epoxy and polyester-epoxy water base paints. With some water reducible resin components, mixing must be done and the *digestion time* observed before they may be applied.

Alkyd Paints

Alkyd binders are oil-modified phthalate resins which cure by exposure to oxygen in the air. They are widely used because of their versatility and moderate cost, many being based on soybean oils. Alkyd, alkyd-acrylic, and alkyd-oil paints are used both indoors and outdoors in various degrees of luster including flat, semigloss, gloss, and high gloss. They can be applied directly to gypsum wallboard, woodwork, old paint, and fully cured masonry or plaster without a prime coat. They make excellent enamels over exterior metal. For masonry and other cementitious materials that have not fully cured, a primer (usually water based) must be used.

Special Purpose Binders

The following binders produce a variety of paints for specialized uses, e.g., at problem surfaces. Examples of problem surfaces are ones that are hot, easily corrodible, or subject to traffic or abuse.

Epoxy

Two types of epoxy are available—an epoxy ester and a two-component epoxy resin utilizing a polyamide or a polyamine hardener. The epoxy ester is similar to an alkyd and can be used indoors and outdoors. The epoxy ester is somewhat more resistant to chemical attack and fumes than alkyds. The two-component epoxy is an expensive paint formulation intended for heavy-duty service in chemical and industrial environments. The cured film has outstanding hardness, adhesion, and abrasion resistance and is also used as a tilelike glaze coating over concrete and masonry.

Epoxy Coal-Tar

Epoxy coal-tar is a two-component epoxy modified by the introduction of coal tar, intended for wet or submerged areas and for protection against splash and spillage of a wide variety of chemicals. It is limited in colors because of the coal-tar.

Inorganic

Inorganic binders consist of silicates of sodium, potassium, lithium and ethyl, and are used with *zinc-rich* anticorrosive paints for use on metal surfaces. They are extremely resistant to wet, humid, and marine environments.

Oil

Linseed oil was one of the chief binders in exterior house paints and is still used for certain primers for exterior structural steel. Oil paints have good wetting properties and are used as primers for structural steel since surface preparation is less demanding. Although they are not particularly hard or resistant to abrasion, chemicals, or industrial fumes, they are durable in normal environments. Alkyds have almost universally replaced linseed oil.

Oleoresinous

Oleoresinous binders have been processed by combining drying oils and hard resins by a cooking process. The resin increases the hardness and chemical resistance as compared to a straight oil paint. Depending on the resin used, there may be increased gloss, faster drying, improved adhesion, and greater durability.

Phenolic

Phenolic binders are among the first truly synthetic resins. They may be used as clear finishes or pigmented in a range of colors. Phenolic paints are used as topcoats on metal for humid environments and as primers for freshwater immersion.

Rubber-Base

Chlorinated-rubber-base binders are solvent thinned and are not to be confused with the latex types, which are water thinned. Chlorinated rubber is a product of chlorine and polyisoprene. It has outstanding resistance to water and common corrosive chemicals and possesses a high degree of impermeability to water vapor. It is highly resistant to strong acids and alkalis. It is used for areas where excessive moisture exists, such as swimming pool areas, hydrotherapy areas, wash and shower rooms, commercial kitchens, and laundry rooms.

Silicone Alkyds

A silicone alkyd binder is a combination of silicone and alkyd resins. It has excellent color and gloss retention and is very suitable for exterior architectural steel surfaces. It is also resistant to high temperatures and is used on metal chimneys.

Urethane

Three types of urethane finishes are available. *Single-component types* are available in two formulations— one an *oil-modified urethane* which has been modified with drying oils and alkyds, and the other a *moisture-curing urethane* which cures by solvent evaporation and reaction with moisture in the air. The *two-component system* has outstanding abrasion and chemical resistance, hardness, flexibility, and good exterior gloss and color retention. The oil-modified urethane is similar to the phenolic varnishes, has better initial color and color retention, and can be used as an exterior spar varnish or tough interior floor finish. The moisture-curing urethane has excellent flexibility and chemical and water resistance.

Vinyls

Vinyls are copolymers of vinyl chloride and vinyl acetate. They are low in solids and multiple coats are required. They have good weathering qualities and can be used on exterior metal.

Binder Comparisons

Paint formulations based on current chemical technology are so ever changing that the specifier and user are urged to compare products of competing manufacturers carefully and to stay abreast of these developments since there is a constant upgrading of products and development of new binders and resins. For a comparison of binders with reference to specific substrates and environment see Table 9-6. Also see Table 9-7 for performance characteristics.

PIGMENTS

The other main component of opaque paints and coatings beside the binder is the pigment component. The pigment is basically made up of lightfast minerals, colors, and, occasionally, bodying or texturing materials. Transparent coatings are binders without pigment.

Since the opaqueness of a paint is one of its prime attributes, both hiding the substrate and blocking ultraviolet radiation, paint quality can often be measured by its titanium dioxide (TiO_2) content. Rutile titanium dioxide has one of the highest indexes of refraction of any mineral, natural or synthetic—short of finely ground diamond dust. Basically, titanium turns the sun's rays around or loses them within the paint film. This same refractive power gives titanium dioxide its excellent hiding power, based on the same physical principle.

In addition to titanium dioxide, one will often find "titanium-calcium" listed on paint labels. This is an impure form of titanium dioxide, with good refractive power, but not as good as the pure mineral. Calcium carbonate and silica, also found in some quantity on most paint labels, provide little hiding power and are present largely to give texture, or body, or as extenders.

Strictly speaking the true pigments are the colorants. Formerly these were minerals or man-made

TABLE 9-6
PAINT BINDER SUITABILITY

	Water reducible*	Alkyd	Oil	Vinyl	Phenolic	Urethane	Chlorinated rubber	Epoxy
Substrate								
Cured concrete, plaster	EX	G	NR	VG	NR	G	VG	VG
Metal	F	VG	VG	EX	VG	G	G	VG
Wood	G	G	G	NR	G	G	NR	G
Gypsum board	EX	G	G	G	NR	F	NR	NR
Environment								
Severe industrial	G	F	NR	EX	G	VG	G	EX
Marine	F	F	NR	EX	G	EX	EX	EX
Rural	VG	VG	G	EX	G	VG	G	EX

EX—excellent. VG—very good. G—good. F—fair. NR—not recommended.
* Water reducible paints incorporate many binders (see text). The correct binder will perform as rated here.

inorganic materials that did not fade and which had distinctive colors, such as chrome yellow or the red oxide of iron. Today the paint chemist has a large number of man-made pigments to work with. These pigments are inorganic or organic and have been tested in use over the years. Many color pigments fade little and add somewhat to the hiding power of the paint. Toxic pigments such as the oxides of lead are prohibited from use today except in microscopic amounts.

SPECIAL PURPOSE PAINTS AND COATINGS

For certain specific requirements, there are special paints and coatings that have been formulated to cope with these problems as follows: abrasion-resistant, fire-protective, heat-resistant, mildew-resistant, and slip-resistant.

TABLE 9-7
IMPORTANT PROPERTIES OF PAINT BINDERS

Property	Water reducible*	Alkyd	Oil	Vinyl	Phenolic	Urethane	Chlorinated rubber	Epoxy
Adhesion	G	VG	VG	F	G	VG	G	EX
Flexibility	G	G	EX	EX	G	EX	G	EX
Hardness	G	G	F	G	VG	EX	VG	EX
Resistance to								
Abrasion	G	G	P	VG	EX	EX	G	EX
Acid	G	F	P	EX	VG	EX	EX	G
Alkali	VG	F	P	EX	G	EX	EX	EX
Detergent	G	F	F	EX	VG	EX	EX	EX
Heat	G	G	F	P	G	G	VG	G
Strong solvents	G	P	P	F	G	EX	P	EX
Water	F	F	F	EX	EX	EX	EX	G

EX—excellent. VG—very good. G—good. F—fair. NR—not recommended.
* Water reducible paints incorporate many binders (see text). The correct binder resin will perform as rated here.

Abrasion-Resistance

To resist abrasion for traffic areas and to withstand repeated washings and scrubbings as in institutional use (e.g., hospitals, schools, food-processing), there are several paints that are especially designed and formulated for this purpose. Those include epoxy coatings, polyurethane coatings, and polyester-epoxy coatings.

Fire-Protective

Two aspects of fire protection should be understood—one dealing with fire retardancy, the other with fire resistance.

Fire-Retardant Paints

Fire-retardant paints are used to inhibit the spread of fire on combustible surfaces such as wood. Typically they are used to obtain a Class A flamespread of between 0-25 as per ASTM E84. Interior type paints having this capability should be specified to meet Fed. Spec. TT-P-26. Exterior paints should be specified to meet Military Specification MIL-C-46081.

Fire-Resistant Paints

Fire-resistant paints are those which are used to obtain UL rated protection of steel framing of 1 or 2 hours based on ASTM E119 fire test. The coatings which provide this protection are either intumescent mastics or subliming mastics.

Heat Resistance

Where heated surfaces such as high-pressure steam, metal chimneys, or equipment are to be painted, heat-resistive paints meeting Fed. Spec. TT-P-28 or TT-E-496 may be utilized.

Mildew Resistance

Where mildew may be a problem, paints containing zinc oxide may be used, or a mildewcide may be added to the paint. Mildew resistance may be tested in accordance with Federal Test Standard No. 141, Method 6271.1.

Slip Resistance

Slip resistance is produced by incorporating an abrasive grit into the paint formulation, or abrasive may be added to the paint in the can before application or broadcast onto the freshly painted surface.

PAINTING

SURFACE PREPARATION

The importance of proper surface preparation to the durability and longevity of a coating system cannot be overemphasized. Without this preparation the most costly paint material applied in the most professional manner will not live up to expectations. Thorough cleaning of the surface, and pretreatment where needed, will enhance adhesion of the coating and, in the case of metals, provide a barrier against corrosion.

Methods of surface preparation may vary from a light cleaning or brushing to a heavy sandblasting for removal of dirt, grit, or scale, and the use of solvent washes to remove oils or grease.

Steel Surfaces

Solvent Cleaning

A very effective method to remove oil, grease, waxes, and other solvent-soluble materials from steel is to employ a system described in Steel Structures Painting Council, SSPC SP1. Solvent cleaning precedes mechanical treatment.

Mechanical Treatment

Three methods may be employed to remove rust, mill scale, dirt, and dirt incrustations. The degree to which these will be removed depends upon the specific treatment selected as follows:

Hand cleaning. Wire brushes and scrapers are used to remove loose rust and loose scale. This process will not remove heavy or tightly bound rust and mill scale. It is used where mild, noncorrosive atmospheres will be encountered and a linseed oil wetting type of primer will be used. The process can be specified to meet SSPC-SP2.

Power tool cleaning. This method is obviously much faster than hand tool cleaning and is accomplished with power wire brushes, power sanders, power grinders, or by a combination of these tools. It may remove small amounts of tightly adhering contaminants which hand tools may not remove. This process can be specified to meet SSPC-SP3.

Blast cleaning. Several methods utilizing blast cleaning are available in which sand, synthetic grit, or other abrasive materials are utilized to remove rust, scale, and other contaminants. The degree to which these materials are removed are contained in Steel Structures Painting Council specifications identified with the method.

1. *White metal blast—SSPC-SP5.* This is the ultimate, most expensive, and effective method. It removes all rust, mill scale, and all other contaminants, leaving a completely clean uniform surface with an ideally roughened textured surface for maximum paint adhesion and durability under the most severe conditions. This method is warranted only for the most demanding service in corrosive environments. The paint coating system should be a zinc-rich system, an epoxy system, or a high-build vinyl system, depending on the exposure.

2. *Near-white metal blast—SSPC-SP10.* In this method a small specified amount of streaking and shadowing will appear across the general surface area. It is less expensive than a white blast and is generally used for exposed architectural steel utilizing coating systems of zinc-rich primers, and either silicone alkyd or high-build vinyl finishes, depending on the environment.

3. *Commercial blast—SSPC-SP6.* This method will remove loose rust and scale resulting in a satisfactory surface that is generally adequate for all but the most vigorous types of service exposure. The coating system to be selected should suit the environment except the most rigorous and corrosive.

4. *Brush-off blast—SSPC-SP7.* This method of blast cleaning is intended to remove only loose rust scale leaving only tightly adhering, intact mill scale and rust. This degree of surface preparation is comparable or superior to hand or power tool cleaning and should be used only for mild exposures with linseed oil primers having good wetting ability.

Galvanized Steel

Adhesion of paint systems to new galvanized steel is especially difficult. The paint peels or flakes off often after a short period of exposure. Oil and grease should be removed by solvent cleaning. Factory-applied stabilizer (antirust) coatings are not always removed by solvents and must be chemically treated or brush blasted. A pretreatment wash primer (MIL-C-15328) should then be applied to develop good adhesion for a zinc-dust primer, Fed. Spec. TT-P-641. Wash primers are thin coats containing polyvinyl butyral resin, phosphoric acid, and a rust-inhibitive pigment.

Aluminum

When aluminum is to be painted, it is best prepared by solvent cleaning and the application of a wash primer as described above for galvanized steel surfaces.

Wood

Wood surfaces should be clean, free of cracks and splinters, and have a moisture content below 15 percent for exterior wood and 9 percent for interior wood. Cracks and nail holes should be filled with putty or plastic wood. Puttied areas should then be sanded smooth. Knots, pitch streaks, or visible sap spots should be treated with Formula WP-578 Knot Sealer developed by the Western Pine Association.

Concrete and Masonry

Surfaces should be clean, free of dust, dirt, oil, grease, efflorescence, chalk, and loose material. Aging of the surfaces permits them to dry out and neutralizes the alkalinity.

Surfaces are cleaned by bristle brushing or hosing down with water. Scraping, wire brushing, or sand-blasting may be employed on concrete where necessary. Efflorescence may be removed from concrete by wire brushing or sand blasting. Large cracks, holes, and other blemishes should be repaired by patching with cementitious mixtures. Open textured masonry may be filled with a sand cement grout coat if a smooth surface is desired.

Concrete surfaces that have a glazed finish resulting from smooth nonabsorbent forms should be soaked with water, then etched with 5 percent hydrochloric acid (HCl, muriatic acid), or a proprietary buffered acid solution. Rinse thoroughly.

Cement and Gypsum Plaster

Cracks, holes, indentations, and similar defects should be repaired with a spackling compound or patching plaster, and then sanded smooth. New plaster should be aged a minimum of 2 weeks before application of latex paints. If oil or oleoresinous paints are used, new plaster should age at least 2 to 3 months before paint application.

Gypsum Board

Minor cracks and holes should be repaired with finishing compound and then sanded when dry. Surfaces should then be wiped free of dust, preferably with a damp sponge.

PAINT SELECTION

Having acquired this knowledge of overall paint performance needed for specific situations, the designer must then select brands and formulations that can be trusted to perform. These products are already chemically formulated, and the specifier need only select them for the task at hand.

Reference Standards

Notice that in choosing paints and coatings, the use of reference standards is largely irrelevant. There are few standards for coatings that do more than define the very lowest level of quality. This stems from the fact that for 50 years or more advances have been made in paint and coating technology at such a rate, and the secrecy engendered by competition among new chemistries and new formulations has been so great, that attempting to get industry agreement has been impossible. There are a few federal standards for paints, but they are largely frozen in the technology of 20 or more years ago when they were last updated to place a floor under quality for government work. Except for a few test procedures, ASTM is not active in setting standards for paint formulations.

Product Description

Thus, a specifier's directions for painting include few if any standards and few if any listings of ingredients. The closest a specifier gets to this is to require that latexes be mildew-resistant, that oil paints be nonyellowing, that they be free of lead and mercury, and, sometimes, that they be odorless.

It is futile to list a desired label analysis for each paint. Not only would it be a monumental task to obtain comparable analyses from a multitude of producers, but the analyses would not reveal the qualities that often distinguish a good paint from a poor one: lightfastness of color pigments, fineness of grind, quality of resin, balance of ingredients, and selection of emulsifier or dryer to form the best film in a reasonable time.

Products

The paint selection process, after a knowledge of what is needed has been acquired, becomes one of knowing producers of paints, their product line, and their record of performance. For this reason, the detailed paint and coating schedule, with its brand names, is the best assurance that the right product, embodying up-to-date technology, is being specified for each surface.

FURTHER SELECTION CRITERIA

Type of Exposure

Questions concerning exposure can be related to whether it is an interior or exterior environment and the conditions of that environment as follows:

Interior	*Exterior*
Chemical	Dry
Dry	Industrial
Industrial	Marine
Dirty	Rural
Traffic	Temperature extremes
Damp	Urban
	Wet

Surfaces and Substrates

Surfaces to be painted in the same space may or may not require the same type of paint based on a number of factors. Ceilings require paints with good reflectivity for optimum illumination. Walls require a paint that will not run or sag on a vertical surface when applied, and one which will permit repeated washings for maintenance purposes. Floors require a paint that will withstand abrasion and will dry quickly so that the space may be utilized without much downtime.

Substrates such as drywall, plaster, concrete, concrete block, wood, and metal must be reviewed for their special needs and their special environments. Some woods require special primers or sealers to prevent resins in knots from bleeding through the paint. Plaster and concrete may be excessively alkaline when new and may require pretreatment before application of oil paints. Concrete floors may have a glaze which requires etching to insure paint adhesion. Some metals, such as aluminum and galvanized steel, may require wash primers to etch the surface to insure adhesion of coating systems.

By reviewing Tables 9-6 and 9-7 together with manufacturers' literature, the user and specifier will be in a better position to make evaluations and selections.

METRIC IN THIS BOOK

INTERNATIONAL STANDARD

Metric units of measurement which are included in *Architectural Materials for Construction* follow ASTM E380 conventions for the Système international d'unités—abbreviated SI—the rationalized version of metric. By international treaty, this is the system that all nations will ultimately adopt. Pre-SI metric is still in use in parts of many European, Asian, and Latin American economies, although most of these countries are in the process of converting to the SI version of metric.

In 1866 Congress made it "lawful throughout the United States of America to employ the weights and measures of the metric system in all contracts, dealings or court proceedings." This was well before the 1875 multinational Treaty of the Meter which set up well-defined standards for length and mass and which also set up permanent machinery to recommend and adopt further refinements. Although the United States was one of the 17 signers of the treaty, American industry did not move itself to seriously engage in changing to metric until well after World War II. However, in 1893, all U.S. Customary units (the inch-pound-second system) were redefined in terms of basic metric units. It was not until 1975 that Congress passed the Metric Conversion Act which called for a coordinated national program for conversion to SI in the United States.

SI standards were adopted internationally in 1960. A series of modifications were worked out and universally agreed upon by 1979. Thus the United States, Canada, and Australia—late entrants in the metric field—are adopting the most systematic version of metric, without passing through a transitional "old metric" stage.

SI METRIC

SI metric expressions in this book conform to ASTM E380-91a, Practice for Use of the International System of Units (SI), the Modernized Metric System, which is the standard for metrication in the United States.

SI units and their equivalents in the U.S. Customary system are grouped in this book's conversion tables in the three categories used by ASTM E380:

Base units:
Mass   Length   Time

"Units in use with SI":
Temperature   Frequency

Compound units:
Area   Volume   Density
Force   Pressure
Mass/area   Force/length   Velocity

Units for angular measure, energy, power, heat, sound, electricity, illumination, and radioactivity have not been included in these tables as they do not apply to this book's subject matter.

FOR YOUR CONVENIENCE

Some equivalencies among U.S. Customary units are included at the end of each table. Comparison and conversion can be difficult unless the relation between gallons and cubic feet, or acres and square feet, is at hand for reference.

Because units of force and pressure are the hardest to grasp when one begins to perform SI calculations for architecture and engineering, a discussion titled Mass, Force, and Pressure follows the conversion tables.

THE STRUCTURE OF SI TERMINOLOGY

A further note on differences between "old metric" and "SI metric": ASTM E380 3.2.2 states: ". . . prefixes should be preferably chosen so that the numerical value lies between 0.1 and 1000. . . . It is recommended that prefixes representing powers of 1000 be used."

Thus, the United States/Canadian construction industries have standardized on millimeters, meters, and kilometers as units of length because each is separated by a factor of 1000. This reduces human error in confusing units.

Under SI metric, grams and kilograms are standard units of mass. Square millimeters and square meters are standard, as are cubic millimeters and cubic meters. All these series of units differ by powers of 1000.

Since mm^3 and m^3 differ by a factor of 1 000 000 000, the liter, a "special name . . . for use in SI" is permitted by ASTM E380 as a convenient intermediate unit. 1.0 l is 1 000 000 mm^3. 1000 l = 1.0 m^3.

Almost never are centi-, deci-, deka-, or hecto-prefixed units resorted to when using SI. Centimeters are still encountered in designs and products originating in continental Europe and other countries that early standardized on "old metric."

In SI metric, instead of using a comma to separate digits into groups of three, international practice calls for separating each group of three, counting from the decimal point toward the left and toward the right, using a small space to separate the groups. In numbers of four digits the space is not necessary, except for uniformity in tables.

In English-speaking countries the SI decimal marker is a point on the line—a period. For numbers less than one, a zero is placed before the decimal marker. Multiplication is expressed by a raised dot, set off with a small space to each side.

CONVERSION TABLES—METRIC TO CUSTOMARY AND CUSTOMARY TO METRIC

Metric units, symbols, and values are given in their SI version. ASTM E380 uses "metre", rather than "meter." Since SI units are never spelled out (except in discussions such as ASTM E380 and this appendix), the variance in spelling is of no importance.

E380 3.5.1 and 3.5.4 list the rules for the writing of symbols and numbers in SI.

Each U.S. Customary unit symbol is given as it appears in ASTM E380 and as it is printed in publications of ASTM, ASCE, ACI, and other professional and technical societies in the United States: without an "s" in the plural, and without a period at the end (except where the symbol spells an English word—as in the symbol "in."

In this book, exponents are shown as superscripts—m^3, for cubic meter.

For purposes of converting large dimensions from one system of measurement to another, many more decimal places are listed below than are needed to merely compare units or to convert small dimensions. Round off as appropriate to the purpose. See Note 1.

BASE SI UNITS AND THEIR MULTIPLES
with some equivalents among U.S. Customary units

MASS Base unit: gram

1 gram (g)	=	0.035 oz	1 ounce (oz)	=	28.35 g
	=	15.432 grains	1 pound (lb)	=	453.6 g
1 kilogram (kg)	=	2.20 lb		=	0.45 kg
1 metric ton*	=	1.1 (U.S.) ton	1 (U.S.) ton	=	0.907 metric ton
			1 ton	=	2000 lb
			1 lb	=	16 oz
			1 oz	=	437.5 grains

LENGTH Base unit: meter

1 millimeter (mm)	=	0.03937 in.	1 inch (in.)	=	25.40 mm
1 meter (m)	=	39.37 in. exact	1 foot (ft)	=	304.8 mm
	=	3.28084 ft			
	=	1.0936 yd	1 yard (yd)	=	0.9144 m
1 kilometer (km)	=	3280 ft			
	=	0.6214 mi	1 mile (mi)	=	1.609 km
			1 mi	=	5280 ft
			1 yd	=	3 ft
			1 ft	=	12 in.

TIME Base unit: second
Identical in SI and U.S. Customary systems

1 day (d)	=	24 hours
1 hour (h)	=	60 minutes
1 minute (m)	=	60 seconds
1 second (s)	=	1 000 milliseconds (ms)
	=	1 000 000 nanoseconds (ns)

(Continued)

CONVERSION TABLES—METRIC TO CUSTOMARY AND CUSTOMARY TO METRIC (*Continued*)

UNITS IN USE WITH SI

TEMPERATURE   Base unit: kelvin
1 kelvin (K)   =   1 degree Celsius (°C)   1 degree Fahrenheit (°F)   =   1.8 degree Celsius

To convert Fahrenheit to Celsius:
  $t°C = (t°F - 32)/1.8$ (See Note 2.)

FREQUENCY   Base unit: hertz
                  Applies to periodic phenomena
1 hertz (Hz)   =   1 per second (1/s)   1 cycle = 1 Hz
1 kilohertz (kHz)   =   1 000 Hz
1 megahertz (MHz)   =   1 000 000 Hz

COMPOUND SI UNITS
using SI (including hectare and liter) and U.S. Customary symbols, with some equivalents among U.S. Customary units

AREA

1 mm²	=	0.001 55 in²	1 in²	=	645.160 000 mm²
1 m²	=	10.763 9 ft²	1 ft²	=	0.092 903 04 m²
		1 hectare (ha) = 10 000 m² (Note 3)			
1 hectare	=	1 076 390 ft²			
	=	2.471 044 acre	1 acre	=	0.404 687 hectare
			1 acre	=	43 560 ft²
			1 yd²	=	9 ft²
			1 ft²	=	144 in²

VOLUME

1 mm³	=	0.000 061 in³	1 in³	=	16 387.064 mm²
				=	0.016 387 l
		1 liter (l) = 1 000 000 mm³ or 0.001 m³ (Note 4)			
1 l	=	61.025 in³			
	=	0.264 184 gallon (gal)	1 gal	=	3.785 412 l
	=	0.035 315 ft³	1 ft³	=	28.316 579 l
1 m³	=	35.313 35 ft³	1 ft³	=	0.028 316 854 m³
	=	1.308 yd³			
	=	26.418 gal	1 ft³	=	28.315 854 l
			1 ft³	=	7.480 555 gal
				=	1 732 in³
			1 gal	=	231 in³
				=	0.133 685 ft³

DENSITY

1 g/mm³	=	36.127 17 lb/in³	1 lb/in³	=	0.027 68 g/mm³
	=	578.035 oz/in³	1 oz/in³	=	0.001 73 g/mm³
1 kg/m³	=	0.062 428 lb/ft³	1 lb/ft³	=	16.018 46 kg/m³
	=	1.685 556 lb/yd³	1 lb/yd³	=	0.593 276 kg/m³

FORCE

1 newton (N)	=	0.224 809 lbf	1 pound-force (lbf) =		4.448 222 N

PRESSURE

1 pascal (Pa)	=	0.000 145 lbf/in² (psi)	1 lbf/in² (psi)	=	6 894.757 Pa
1 kilopascal (kPa)	=	0.145 lbf/in²		=	6.894 757 kPa
1 megapascal (MPa)	=	145 lbf/in²		=	0.006 895 MPa

(*Continued*)

CONVERSION TABLES—METRIC TO CUSTOMARY AND CUSTOMARY TO METRIC (*Continued*)

MASS PER UNIT AREA

1 kg/m²	=	0.204 816 lb/ft²	1 lb/ft²	=	4.882 428 kg/m²
			1 kip/ft²	=	4 882.428 kg/m²
			1 kip	=	1 000 lb

FORCE PER UNIT LENGTH

1 N/m	=	0.068 521 lbf/ft	1 lbf/ft	=	14.593 900 N/m
			1 kipf/ft	=	14 593.900 N/m

VELOCITY

1 meter/second (m/s)	=	3.280 84 foot/second (ft/s, fps)	1 mile/hour	=	0.447 045 m/s
1 kilometer/hour (km/h)	=	0.621 37 mile/hour (mi/h, mph)		=	1.609 344 km/h exact
			1 mile/hour	=	88 ft/m
				=	1.466 7 ft/s
			1 foot/second	=	0.681 8 mi/h

* Non-SI unit, but defined in multiples of SI units in ASTM E380.

NOTE 1: Rounding Off. Rules are found in ASTM E380 4.

NOTE 2: Temperature. The base SI unit of temperature is the kelvin (K), which requires no degree mark. The identical unit *degree Celsius* (°C) is, by long tradition, widely used for expressing temperature and temperature intervals. Since the multiplier in converting °C to °F involves a repeating decimal—0.55555 . . . —the operation is usually accomplished by multiplying °C by 5/9. See ASTM E380 3.4.2.

NOTE 3: Area. Large areas of land or water can be expressed in square hectometers (hm²) or square kilometers (km²), but the use of the *hectare* as an alternative name for hm² is frequently encountered. See ASTM E380 3.3.3.1.

NOTE 4: Volume. The widely used name *liter* has been approved for the cubic decimeter when measuring liquids and gases. No prefix other than milli- is used with it. See ASTM E380 3.3.2.3.

MASS, FORCE, AND PRESSURE

MASS AND FORCE IN SI

Mass is the quantity of matter and is expressed in grams (g) or gram-multiples. Mass is constant no matter where measured: 1 kg is the same in Death Valley, atop Everest, in an orbiting satellite, or on the Moon.

Weight is mass under the influence of gravity. Weight varies according to altitude and other factors. For most construction purposes, weight-force can be assumed to be mass times an acceleration of 9.807 m/s/s or m/s². The acceleration due to gravity for stationary terrestrial objects will not vary more than

0.5 percent from this figure. Weight, or the preferred term "force of gravity," is measured in newtons (N).

$$N = kg \cdot g$$

Where g = acceleration due to gravity.

U.S. Customary units have, of late, distinguished between pounds (lb) for mass and pounds-force (lbf) for weight, as can be seen in all ASTM standards updated since the 1980s. For simple, rough structural calculations, it is safe to let lb = lbf and to let customary safety factors absorb the error, which will be less than 0.5 percent.

Observe however that newtons compute to numerical values that are significantly different from numerical values of mass expressed in kilograms.

$$N \cdot 9.80665 = kg$$

In sensible terms, 1 N exerts a force on your desktop approximately equal to that exerted by an apple that sells five-to-the-pound at the grocery.

We use newtons to signify force of gravity (*weight*) in expressing floor loads, beam loads, and beam reactions. However, when describing the mass-carrying capability of a floor or a bridge, force of gravity is often (and conveniently) expressed in the more familiar kg/m^2. In such a situation, N describes downward force, or "loading," while kg/m^2 is describing load-carrying capacity.

FORCE AND PRESSURE IN SI

Pressure is force per unit area and can be expressed in SI as newtons per square meter. However, we customarily distinguish pressure from force by employing a distinct unit, the pascal (Pa), which rhymes with the word *rascal.*

$$Pa = N/m^2$$

Until one has some appreciation of the sensible magnitude of SI units, it is difficult to choose units, to calculate with "feel," or to check calculations. Spread over a square meter, the pressure exerted by newton is a very small unit. 1 N is approximately equal to the pressure exerted by a sheet of paper on your desktop.

Because this is so small, we tend to use multiples of a pascal such as the kilopascal (kPa) or the megapascal (MPa) to express pressures or stresses commonly encountered in architectural and engineering design. 1 kPa can be visualized as a couple of reams of copy paper exerting pressure on an area the size of one sheet. 1 MPa is of the order of having 2000 packages of paper—a column about 330 feet high—exerting pressure in the same area.

MPa and kPa are used to express stress in all its forms, including shear, compressive, and flexural stress. Tensile strength, the strength grade of structural materials, modulus of elasticity, as well as high pressures in liquids and gases, are usually expressed in MPa units. Pressures of smaller magnitude, such as many expressions of soil-bearing strength, bearing pressures, and lower pressures in liquids and gases are often expressed in the smaller kPa units. When the pressure is very small, as in some vacuums and air duct pressure differentials, the still smaller Pa is often resorted to as the most convenient unit.

Although forces per unit area expressed in N/mm^2 are numerically the same as stresses expressed in MPa, expressing stresses as MPa is preferred.

The distinction between SI mass, SI force of gravity, and SI pressure or stress (force per unit area) is observed in the text of *Architectural Materials for Construction.*

BIBLIOGRAPHY

CHAPTER 1—PERFORMANCE CONSIDERATIONS

Canadian Building Digests, National Research Council of Canada, Ottawa, Canada.

Durability of Building Materials and Components, ASTM STP 691.

Testing Building Constructions and the Performance Concept. Robert F. Legget, Division of Building Research Paper No. 701, Oct. 1976 National Research Council of Canada, Ottawa, Canada.

CHAPTER 2—SITEWORK

Asphalt Pavement Construction, ASTM STP 724.

Borates Offer Effective Protection with Less Hazard to the Environment. A. B. Curtis and L. H. Williams, Utilization Report R8-UR6, USDA Forest Service, Southern Region, 1990.

Concrete Floors on Ground, Portland Cement Association.

Finishing Concrete Slabs, Exposed Aggregate, Patterns & Colors. Portland Cement Association, 1979.

Technical Notes on Brick Construction, Brick Institute of America.

TEK Bulletins, National Concrete Masonry Association.

CHAPTER 3—ARCHITECTURAL CONCRETE

Architectural Precast Concrete. Precast Concrete Institute, 1973.

Bushhammering of Concrete Surfaces. Portland Cement Association, 1972.

Canadian Building Digests Nos. 15, 56, 93, 103, 116, 136 and 203, National Research Council, Ottawa, Canada.

Cementitious Bonding Agents, Noel P. Mailvaganam and Stacey Nunes, The Construction Specifier, December 1993, pp 110–119.

Color, Form & Texture in Architectural Precast Concrete. Precast Concrete Institute, Chicago.

Color & Texture in Architectural Concrete. Portland Cement Association, 1980.

Concrete Floors on Ground, 2nd Edition, Portland Cement Association.

Fabrication, Handling and Erection of Precast Concrete Wall Panels. ACI Journal, April 1970.

Finishes to In-Site Concrete. J. Gilchrist Wilson, Exposed Concrete Finishes, Vol. 1, John Wiley & Sons, New York, 1979.

Finishes to Precast Concrete. J. Gilchrist Wilson, Exposed Concrete Finishes, Vol. 2. John Wiley & Sons, New York, 1964.

Finishing Concrete Slabs, Exposed Aggregate, Patterns & Colors. Portland Cement Association, 1979.

Guide to Cast-in-Place Architectural Concrete Practice ACI Journal, July 1974.

Jobsite Precast Concrete Panels—Textures, Patterns & Designs. Portland Cement Association, 1975.

Petrography Applied to Concrete and Concrete Aggregates, ASTM STP 1061.

Plywood for Concrete Forming. American Plywood Association, 1971.

Site Cast Architectural Concrete. Concrete Construction, November 1972, Construction Publications Inc., Elmhurst, IL.

Specifications for Structural Concrete for Buildings, ACI 301-84(89), 1989.

Surface Defects in Concrete, ACI SDC.D094, 1994.

Tilt-Up Concrete Walls. Portland Cement Association, 1970.

CHAPTER 4—MASONRY

Brick

Brick & Tile Engineering. Harry Plummer, Brick Institute of America, 1962.

Canadian Building Digests Nos. 2, 6, 21, 169 and 185. National Research Council, Ottawa, Canada.

Cleaning Stone and Masonry, ASTM STP 935.

Details from Brick in Architecture. Brick Institute of America, 1978.

Masonry: Materials, Properties and Performance, ASTM STP 778, 992, and 1180.

Technical Notes on Brick Construction, Brick Institute of America.

Concrete Block

Concrete Masonry Handbook. Portland Cement Association, 1976.

Specifications for Masonry Structures, ACI 530.1/ASCE 6-92/TMS 602-92, 1992.

TEK Bulletins. National Concrete Masonry Association, Herndon, VA.

Stone

Indiana Limestone Handbook. Indiana Limestone Institute of America, Inc.

Marble Design Manual II. Marble Institute of America. Farmington, MI.

New Stone Technology, Design and Construction for Exterior Wall Systems, ASTM STP 996.

Stone Catalog. Building Stone Institute, New York.

CHAPTER 5—METALS

Aluminum

A Guide to Aluminum Extrusions. The Aluminum Association, 1979.

Aluminum Standards and Data. The Aluminum Association, 1982.

Designation System for Aluminum Finishes. The Aluminum Association, 1976.

Copper, Brass, and Bronze

Copper Brass Bronze Design Handbook. Copper Development Association, New York, NY.

Stainless Steel

Stainless Steel: Concepts in Design and Fabrication. American Iron & Steel Institute.

Steel

Fire Safe Structural Steel: A Design Guide. American Iron & Steel Institute.

General

Metal Finishes Manual. National Association of Architectural Metal Manufacturers.

CHAPTER 6—ARCHITECTURAL WOODWORK

Architectural Woodwork Quality Standards. Architectural Woodwork Institute.

Architectural Woodwork Interiors—Wall & Ceiling Treatment. Architectural Woodwork Institute.

Building Code Flame Spread Classifications. Architectural Woodwork Institute.

Factory Finishing of Architectural Woodwork. Architectural Woodwork Institute.

Fine Hardwoods. American Walnut Association.

Fine Hardwoods Selectorama. American Walnut Association.

Fine Hardwood Veneers for Architectural Interiors. American Walnut Association.

Guide to Wood Species. Architectural Woodwork Institute.

High Pressure Laminates as an Architectural Woodwork Material. Architectural Woodwork Institute.

Manual of Millwork, Woodwork Institute of California.

Small Homes Council. University of Illinois D7. 2 Plywood.

Wood, Colors & Kinds. U.S. Forest Products Laboratory, Agricultural Handbook No. 101, 1956.

Wood Handbook, U.S. Forest Products Laboratory.

CHAPTER 7—THERMAL AND MOISTURE PROTECTION

Water Repellents

Clear Consequences. Clayford T. Grimm, Construction Specifier, May 1993.

Selecting Clear Water Repellents. Edward McGettigan, Construction Specifier, June 1994.

Thermal Insulation

An Assessment of Thermal Insulation Materials & Systems for Building Applications, U.S. Department of Energy, BNL-50862, June 1978.

Canadian Building Digests Nos. 16, 36, 52, 70, 102, 167, and 178. National Research Council of Canada, Ottawa, Canada.

Commercial & Industrial Insulation Standards. Midwest Insulation Contractors Association.

Project Pinpoint Analysis, Ten-Year Performance Experience of Commercial Roofing 1983–1992, William C. Cullen, NRCA, 1994.

Roofing and Waterproofing Manual, 1995 Edition. National Roofing Contractors Association (NRCA).

Roofing Materials Guide, 1995 Edition. NRCA.

Exterior Insulation and Finish

Getting the Best from EIFS. Robert Thomas Jr., Construction Specifier, February 1995.

Low-Slope Roofing

Annual Market Survey, 1994–1995. National Roofing Contractors Association (NRCA).

Canadian Building Digests No. 24, 67, 68, 73, 74, 95, 99, 150, 176, 179, 181, 211, and 235.

Manual of Built-Up Roof Systems, C. W. Griffin, McGraw-Hill, New York.

Project Pinpoint Analysis, Ten-Year Performance Experience of Commercial Roofing 1983–1992, William C. Cullen, NRCA, 1994.

Roofing and Waterproofing Manual, 1994 Edition. NRCA.

Roofing Materials Guide, 1994 Edition. NRCA.

Single Ply Roofing Technology, ASTM STP 790, June 1981.

Sheet Metal

Aluminum Sheet Metal Work in Building Construction. Aluminum Association, September 1971.

Architectural Sheet Metal Manual. Sheet Metal & Air Conditioning Contractors National Association (SMACNA), 1993.

Architectural Sheet Metal. SMACNA, April 1976.

Contemporary Copper. Copper Development Association.

Roofing and Waterproofing Manual, 1994 Edition, National Roofing Contractors Association.

Stainless Steel: Suggested Practices for Roofing, Flashing. American Iron & Steel Institute, November 1972.

Joint Sealing Materials

Building Deck Waterproofing, ASTM STP 1084.

Building Sealants, ASTM STP 1069.

Canadian Building Digests Nos. 19, 96, 97, 155, and 158. National Research Council of Canada, Ottawa, Canada.

Construction Sealants and Adhesives. Julian R. Panek and John R. Cook, John Wiley & Sons Inc., New York, 1992.

Exterior Wall Systems, Glass and Concrete, ASTM STP 1034.

Guide to Joint Sealants for Concrete Structures. ACI Committee 504R, 1977.

CHAPTER 8—GLASS AND CURTAIN WALLS

Glass

Canadian Building Digests Nos. 55, 60, 101 and 132. National Research Council, Ottawa, Canada.

Glazing Manual 1980. Flat Glass Marketing Association, Topeka, KS.

Installation Recommendation, Tinted & Reflective Glass. TSR 130, PPG Industries, Pittsburgh, PA.

Installation Recommendations for Twindow (Insulating Glass). TSR 230, PPG Industries, Pittsburgh, PA.

Sloped Glazing Guidelines AAMA TIR-A7-83, American Architectural Manufacturing Association, Chicago, IL.

Curtain Walls

Aluminum Curtain Walls Series, 1-12, American Architectural Manufacturers Association (AAMA), Chicago, IL.

Canadian Building Digests Nos. 28, 34, 39, 40, and 48, National Research Council, Ottawa, Canada.

Design Wind Loads for Aluminum Curtain Walls. TIR-A2-1975, AAMA.

Low Rise Building Systems Manual, with 1986/90 Supplement, Metal Building Manufacturers Association.

Metal Curtain Wall, Window, Store Front & Entrance Guide Specifications Manual, AAMA, 1976.

Methods of Tests for Exterior Walls. 501–94, AAMA.

Minimum Design Loads for Buildings and Other Structures, ASCE 7-95.

Science and Technology of Glazing Systems, ASTM STP 1054.

CHAPTER 9—FINISHES

Cement Plaster

Guide to Portland Cement Plastering, Technical Paper 90-M6, ACI Materials Journal, American Concrete Institute, February 1993.

Plaster Textures, BNi Building News, Los Angeles, CA.

Portland Cement Plaster (Stucco) Manual, Portland Cement Association, 1980.

Stucco Textures Guide, Walls & Ceilings Magazine, LMRector Corp, 1993, Tampa, FL.

Gypsum Board

Levels of Gypsum Board Finish, Gypsum Association.

Carpeting

Carpet Specifiers Handbook 1974, The Carpet & Rug Institute, Dalton, GA.

Contract Carpeting. Lila Shoshkes, Watson-Guptil Publications 1974, New York, NY.

Ceramic Tile

Canadian Building Digest No. 206, National Research Council, Ottawa, Canada.

Ceramic Tile Manual, 1982, Ceramic Tile Institute, Los Angeles.

Handbook for Ceramic Tile Installation, Tile Council of America, Princeton, NJ.

Concrete Floors

Canadian Building Digest No. 22, National Research Council, Ottawa, Canada.

Finishing Concrete Slabs, Exposed Aggregate, Patterns & Colors, Portland Cement Association.

Guide for Concrete Floor & Slab Construction, ACI Committee 302, 1980, American Concrete Institute.

Terrazzo

Terrazzo Technical Data, The National Terazzo & Mosaic Association, Des Plaines, IL.

Paints and Coatings

Canadian Building Digests Nos. 76, 78, 79, 90, 91, 98 and 131. National Research Council, Ottawa, Canada.

Organic Coatings, 1968, A. G. Roberts NBS BSS 7, National Institute of Standards and Technology.

Paints & Protective Coatings, Depts. of the Army, Navy and Air Force, 1969. U.S. Government Printing Office.

Steel Structures Painting Manual, Vol. 1 Good Painting Practices; Vol. 2, Systems & Specifications, Steel Structures Painting Council, Pittsburgh, PA.

INDEX

ABOUT THE AUTHORS

Harold J. Rosen is a leading consultant in the field of construction specifications. As an expert in building materials he developed a course at the University of Wisconsin, "A Systematic Approach to Building Materials Evaluation and Selection." This system, described in this book, enables the reader to make rational decisions in evaluating and selecting materials.

Tom Heineman is a consultant with North American Design Consulting Inc. in Miami, Florida, where he specializes in construction administration, quality control, and specifications for architects, engineers, and governments. He frequently writes about construction specifications for *The Construction Specifier* and lectures on the topic at the University of Wisconsin, Madison.